DATE DUE

Bloom's Modern Critical Views

African American Poets: Wheatley-Tolson
Edward Albee
American and Canadian Women Poets, 1930–present
American Women Poets, 1650–1950
Maya Angelou
Asian-American Writers
Margaret Atwood
Jane Austen
James Baldwin
Honoré de Balzac
Samuel Beckett
Saul Bellow
The Bible
William Blake
Jorge Luis Borges
Ray Bradbury
The Brontës
Gwendolyn Brooks
Elizabeth Barrett Browning
Robert Browning
Italo Calvino
Albert Camus
Lewis Carroll
Willa Cather
Cervantes
Geoffrey Chaucer
Anton Chekhov
Kate Chopin
Agatha Christie
Samuel Taylor Coleridge
Joseph Conrad
Contemporary Poets
Stephen Crane
Dante
Daniel Defoe
Don DeLillo
Charles Dickens
Emily Dickinson
John Donne and the 17th-Century Poets
Fyodor Dostoevsky
W.E.B. DuBois
George Eliot
T. S. Eliot
Ralph Ellison
Ralph Waldo Emerson
William Faulkner
F. Scott Fitzgerald
Sigmund Freud
Robert Frost
Johann Wolfgang von Goethe
George Gordon, Lord Byron
Graham Greene
Thomas Hardy
Nathaniel Hawthorne
Ernest Hemingway
Hispanic-American Writers
Homer
Langston Hughes
Zora Neale Hurston
Aldous Huxley
Henrik Ibsen
John Irving
Henry James
James Joyce
Franz Kafka
John Keats
Jamaica Kincaid
Stephen King
Rudyard Kipling
Milan Kundera
D. H. Lawrence
Ursula K. Le Guin
Sinclair Lewis
Bernard Malamud
Christopher Marlowe
Gabriel García Márquez
Cormac McCarthy
Carson McCullers
Herman Melville
Arthur Miller
John Milton
Molière
Toni Morrison
Native-American Writers
Joyce Carol Oates
Flannery O'Connor
Eugene O'Neill
George Orwell
Octavio Paz
Sylvia Plath
Edgar Allan Poe
Katherine Anne Porter
J. D. Salinger
Jean-Paul Sartre
William Shakespeare: Histories and Poems
William Shakespeare: Romances
William Shakespeare: The Comedies
William Shakespeare: The Tragedies
George Bernard Shaw
Mary Wollstonecraft Shelley
Percy Bysshe Shelley
Alexander Solzhenitsyn
Sophocles
John Steinbeck
Tom Stoppard
Jonathan Swift
Amy Tan

Bloom's Modern Critical Views

Alfred, Lord Tennyson
Henry David Thoreau
J. R. R. Tolkien
Leo Tolstoy
Mark Twain
John Updike
Kurt Vonnegut
Alice Walker
Robert Penn Warren
Eudora Welty
Edith Wharton
Walt Whitman
Oscar Wilde
Tennessee Williams
Thomas Wolfe
Tom Wolfe
Virginia Woolf
William Wordsworth
Richard Wright
William Butler Yeats

Modern Critical Views

GABRIEL GARCÍA MÁRQUEZ

Edited and with an introduction by

Harold Bloom
Sterling Professor of the Humanities
Yale University

CHELSEA HOUSE PUBLISHERS
New York ◇ Philadelphia

The Chelsea House World Wide Web site address is
http://www.chelseahouse.com

Printed in the United States of America

10 9

Contents

Editor's Note

This book gathers together a representative selection of the best criticism available in English on the fiction of Gabriel García Márquez. The critical essays are reprinted here in the chronological order of their original publication. I am very grateful to Cesar Salgado who, with the assistance of Frank Menchaca, made the editing of this book his personal and creative obsession.

My introduction acknowledges the astonishing richness of *One Hundred Years of Solitude,* while intimating that there are certain aesthetic limits to the novel's achievement. The chronological sequence of criticism necessarily begins with the novelist Mario Vargas Llosa's somewhat biographical appreciation of García Márquez's development.

Floyd Merrell reads *One Hundred Years of Solitude* as a scientific chronicle, while William Plummer and Harley D. Oberhelman explore the influence of Faulkner upon García Márquez. Coming between them, Lois Parkinson Zamora examines problems of temporality in *One Hundred Years of Solitude* and *The Autumn of the Patriarch.* John Gerlach applies the structuralist critic Todorov to García Márquez's use of "the endless resources of fantasy."

The anthropologist Mauss is employed by Eduardo González as an aid to reading García Márquez. The best interpretation to date of *One Hundred Years of Solitude* is offered by Roberto González Echevarría, who emphasizes the influence of Borges.

Colombian politics is invoked as a crucial context by Regina Janes, and necessarily figures also in the account of *The Autumn of the Patriarch* by Raymond Williams. The cultural context of Afro-American literature centers the essay of Vera M. Kutzinski, while Humberto E. Robles compares the travel writings of Antonio Pigafetta to the "magic realism" of García Márquez.

Deconstruction is found prefigured in García Márquez by Patricia Tobin, after which Isabel Alvarez-Borland offers an exegesis of *Chronicle of a Death Foretold*. The influence of Carpentier upon García Márquez is traced by Morton P. Levitt, after which Michael Palencia-Roth celebrates García Márquez as the Columbus of a new world of fictional consciousness.

An admirable analysis of the relation of writing to ritual in *Chronicle of a Death Foretold* by Carlos J. Alonso is followed by this volume's concluding essay, in which Anibal González discusses the theme of translation in *One Hundred Years of Solitude*.

Introduction

Macondo, according to Carlos Fuentes, "begins to proliferate with the richness of a Columbian Yoknapatawpha." Faulkner, crossed by Kafka, is at the literary origins of Gabriel García Márquez. So pervasive is the Faulknerian influence that at times one hears Joyce and Conrad, Faulkner's masters, echoed in García Márquez, yet almost always as mediated by Faulkner. *The Autumn of the Patriarch* may be too pervaded by Faulkner, but *One Hundred Years of Solitude* absorbs Faulkner, as it does all other influences, into a phantasmagoria so powerful and self-consistent that the reader never questions the authority of García Márquez. Perhaps, as Reinold Arenas suggested, Faulkner is replaced by Carpentier and Kafka by Borges in *One Hundred Years of Solitude,* so that the imagination of García Márquez domesticates itself within its own language. Macondo, visionary realm, is an Indian and Hispanic act of consciousness, very remote from Oxford, Mississippi, and from the Jewish cemetery in Prague. In his subsequent work, García Márquez went back to Faulkner and Kafka, but then *One Hundred Years of Solitude* is a miracle and could happen only once, if only because it is less a novel than it is a Scripture, the Bible of Macondo. Melquíades the Magus, who writes in Sanskrit, may be more a mask for Borges than for the author himself, and yet the Gypsy storyteller also connects García Márquez to the archaic Hebrew storyteller, the Yahwist, at once the greatest of realists and the greatest of fantasists but above all the only true rival of Homer and Tolstoy as a storyteller.

My primary impression, in the act of rereading *One Hundred Years of Solitude,* is a kind of aesthetic battle fatigue, since every page is rammed full of life beyond the capacity of any single reader to absorb. Whether the impacted quality of this novel's texture is finally a virtue I am not sure, since sometimes I feel like a man invited to dinner who has been served nothing but an enormous platter of Turkish Delight. Yet it is all story, where everything conceivable and inconceivable is happening at once, from creation to apocalypse, birth to death. Roberto González Echevarría has gone so far as to surmise that in some sense it is the reader who must die at the end of this story, and perhaps it is the sheer richness of the text that serves to destroy us. Joyce half-seriously envisioned an ideal reader cursed with insomnia who would spend her life in unpacking *Finnegans Wake*. The reader need not translate *One Hundred Years of Solitude,* a novel that deserves its popularity as it has no surface difficulties whatsoever. And yet, a new dimension is added to reading by the book. Its ideal reader has to be like its most memorable personage, the sublimely outrageous Colonel Aureliano Buendía, who "had wept in his mother's womb and had been born with his eyes open." There are no wasted sentences, no mere transitions, in this novel, and so you must notice everything at the moment that you read it. It will all cohere, at least as myth and metaphor if not always as literary meaning.

In the presence of an extraordinary actuality, consciousness takes the place of imagination. That Emersonian maxim is Wallace Stevens's and is worthy of the visionary of *Notes toward a Supreme Fiction* and *An Ordinary Evening in New Haven.* Macondo is a supreme fiction, and there are no ordinary evenings within its boundaries. Satire, even parody, most fantasy—these are now scarcely possible in the United States. How can you satirize Ronald Reagan or Jerry Falwell? Pynchon's *The Crying of Lot 49* ceases to seem fantasy whenever I visit Southern California, and a ride on the New York City subway tends to reduce all literary realism to an idealizing projection. Some aspects of Latin American existence transcend even the inventions of García Márquez. I am informed, on good authority, that the older of the Duvalier dictators of Haiti, the illustrious Papa Doc, commanded that all black dogs in his nation be destroyed when he came to believe that a principal enemy had transformed himself into a black dog. Much that is fantastic in *One Hundred Years of Solitude* would be fantastic anywhere, but much that seems unlikely to a North American critic may well be a representation of reality.

Emir Monegal emphasized that García Márquez's masterwork was unique among Latin American novels, being radically different from the diverse achievements of Julio Cortázar, Carlos Fuentes, Lezama Lima, Mario Vargas Llosa, Miguel Angel Asturias, Manuel Puig, Guillermo Cabrera Infante and so many more. The affinities to Borges and to Carpentier were noted by Monegal as by Arenas, but Monegal's dialectical point seemed to be that García Márquez was representative only by joining all his colleagues in not being representative. Yet it is now true that, for most North American readers, *One Hundred Years of Solitude* comes first to mind when they think of the Hispanic novel in America. Alejo Carpentier's *Explosion in a Cathedral* may be an even stronger book, but only Borges has dominated the North American literary imagination as García Márquez has with this grand fantasy. The paperback translation I have just reread is in its thirtieth printing, and the novel's popularity seems certain to be permanent. It is inevitable that we are fated to identify *One Hundred Years of Solitude* with an entire culture, almost as though it were a new *Don Quixote,* which it most definitely is not. Comparisons to Balzac and even to Faulkner are also not very fair to García Márquez. The titanic inventiveness of Balzac dwarfs the later visionary, and nothing even in Macondo is as much a negative Sublime as the fearsome quest of the Bundrens in *As I Lay Dying. One Hundred Years of Solitude* is more of the stature of Nabokov's *Pale Fire* and Pynchon's *Gravity's Rainbow,* latecomers' fantasies, strong inheritors of waning traditions.

Whatever its limitations may or may not be, García Márquez's major narrative now enjoys canonical status as well as a representative function. Its cultural status is likely to be enhanced by the end of this century, and it would be foolish to quarrel with so large a phenomenon. I wish to address myself only to the question of how seriously, as readers, we need to receive the book's scriptural aspect. The novel's third sentence is: "The world was so recent that many things lacked names, and in order to indicate them it was necessary to point," and the third sentence from the end is the long and beautiful:

> Macondo was already a fearful whirlwind of dust and rubble being spun about by the wrath of the biblical hurricane when Aureliano skipped eleven pages so as not to lose time with facts he knew only too well, and he began to decipher the instant that he was living, deciphering it as he lived it, prophesying himself in the act of deciphering the last page of the parchment, as if he were looking into a speaking mirror.

The time span between this Genesis and this Apocalypse is six generations, so that José Arcadio Buendía, the line's founder, is the grandfather of the last Aureliano's grandfather. The grandfather of Dante's grandfather, the crusader Cassaguida, tells his descendant Dante that the poet perceives the truth because he gazes into that mirror in which the great and small of this life, before they think, behold their thought. Aureliano, at the end, reads the Sanskrit parchment of the gypsy, Borges-like Magus, and looks into a speaking mirror, beholding his thought before he thinks it. But does he, like Dante, behold the truth? Was Florence, like Macondo, a city of mirrors (or mirages), in contrast to the realities of the Inferno, the Purgatorio, the Paradiso? Is *One Hundred Years of Solitude* only a speaking mirror? Or does it contain, somehow within it, an Inferno, a Purgatorio, a Paradiso?

Only the experience and disciplined reflections of a great many more strong readers will serve to answer those questions with any conclusiveness. The final eminence of *One Hundred Years of Solitude* for now remains undecided. What is clear to the book's contemporaries is that García Márquez has given contemporary culture, in North America and Europe, as much as in Latin America, one of its double handful of necessary narratives, without which we will understand neither one another nor our own selves.

MARIO VARGAS LLOSA

García Márquez: From Aracataca to Macondo

In about the middle of 1967, the novel *One Hundred Years of Solitude* was published in Buenos Aires, provoking a literary earthquake throughout Latin America. The critics recognized the book as a masterpiece of the art of fiction and the public endorsed this opinion, systematically exhausting new editions, which, at one point, appeared at the astounding rate of one a week. Overnight, García Márquez became almost as famous as a great soccer player or an eminent singer of boleros. The first translations have received an equally enthusiastic response. But the reasons behind the popularity of a book are hard to detect and often extraliterary, and what is especially remarkable in the case of *One Hundred Years of Solitude* is that its thundering fame should be due to virtues which can only be defined as artistic.

What then are the virtues of this book whose existence contradicts the gloomy assertions that the novel is an exhausted genre in the process of extinction? I wish to single out three. First, the fact that this is a "total" novel, in the tradition of those insanely ambitious creations which aspire to compete with reality on an equal basis, confronting it with an image and qualitatively matching it in vitality, vastness and complexity. In the second place, something that we could call its "plural" nature; that is, its capacity for being at one time things which were thought to be opposites: traditional and modern; regional and universal; imaginary and realistic. Yet perhaps the most mysterious of its virtues is the third: its unlimited accessibility; that is, its power to be within anyone's reach, with distinct

From *Review* no. 70 (1971).

but abundant rewards for everyone: for the intelligent reader and for the imbecile; for those with a complex mind and for those with a simple one; for the refined who relish prose, contemplate structure and decode the symbols of a story, and for the impatient, who only respond to a crude anecdote. The literary genius of our time is usually hermetical, minoritarian and oppressive; *One Hundred Years of Solitude* is one of the rare instances among major, contemporary literary works that can be read, understood, and enjoyed by all.

The author of this narrative achievement, Gabriel García Márquez, was born in 1928 in a tiny Colombian town of the coastal region overlooking the Caribbean. The town's name is rather like a tongue twister: Aracataca. Founded around the end of the last century, between Barranquilla and Santa Marta, by people who apparently fled the civil wars which decimated Colombia, Aracataca had its golden era between 1915 and 1918, when the banana craze reached its acme, scattering plantations in the region and attracting many people who needed jobs.

United Fruit, an unfortunate famous North American company, established itself in that area and started with a single crop to exploit the land. Many fortunes grew under the shade of banana trees, and popular imagination would later maintain that in those days of prosperity "whores danced the *cumbia* in the nude before magnates who, for them, would use one hundred peso bills instead of candles, to light the candelabra." That was also an era of violent social conflicts: the government repressed a strike of farm workers with the use of machine guns which cut down the lives of hundreds; the bodies were thrown into the sea. At the end of World War I, the banana fever ended, and for Aracataca it was the beginning of an economic collapse, the exodus of its inhabitants, the slow and suffocating death of tropical villages. The town was assaulted by outlaws, decimated by epidemics, ravaged by deluges. At the time when García Márquez was born, however, all that had almost stopped: paradise and hell belonged to the past, and present reality consisted of a limbo made up of poverty, heat and routine. Yet that extinct reality remained alive in the memory and imagination of the people and it was their best weapon against the desolation and emptiness of their present reality. In want of anything better, Aracataca—like so many Latin American towns—lived on remembrances, myths, solitude and nostalgia. García Márquez's entire literary work is built with this material which fed him throughout childhood. When he was born, Aracataca lived off memories; his stories will take life from his memories of Aracataca.

In the neighborhood of the town there was a banana plantation, which, as a child, García Márquez explored many times. It was called Macondo. This will be the name with which he will later baptize the imaginary land where almost all his stories take place, and the "history" of which he will tell, from beginning to end, in *One Hundred Years of Solitude.*

García Márquez was not raised by his parents, but by his grandparents, who were, according to him, his most solid literary influences. They lived in a huge and awesome house, filled with spirits, they were both superstitious and credulous. From the lips of his grandmother, García Márquez heard the legends, fables and prestigious lies with which the popular imagination of Aracataca evoked the ancient splendor of the area, and sometimes he saw his grandmother chatting naturally with ghosts who came to visit her. The elderly woman was an implacable storyteller: she used to tiptoe into her grandson's room at night and wake him to tell stories. Last year, a journalist asked García Márquez about the origin of the fluid, transparent, vital style of his stories, and he answered: "It's my grandmother's." In a certain manner, his grandmother is also the prototype of a whole series of female characters from Macondo: those women who happily converse with dead people, like Ursula Buendía; or like Fernanda del Carpio de Buendía, who correspond with invisible doctors.

But still more decisive than his grandmother, was the influence exerted on García Márquez by his grandfather, whom García Márquez describes as "the most important figure in my life." The old man had participated in the civil wars, and it was from the memories of that veteran that the grandson relived the most explosive episodes of Colombian violence, as well as the frustration felt by these warriors in their old age, when they discovered that they had fought for nothing and that no one even bothered to remember them anymore. The grandfather had a devil who haunted him: he had once killed a man. He would take his grandson to the circus and, quite suddenly, he would stop in the street and exclaim: "Oh! You don't know how much a dead body weighs." In *One Hundred Years of Solitude,* the founding of Macondo will, to a certain extent, be the result of a similar remorse. The first José Arcadio Buendía, founder of the clan whose story intermingles with that of Macondo, kills a man, Prudencio Aguilar, the bloody corpse of the victim harasses him with visions until José Arcadio decides to abandon the heights of Riohacha, crosses the mountain range with twenty-one companions and finds Macondo. The grandfather of García Márquez used to sing: "Mambrú has gone to war / how painful / how painful / how sad." Years later, García Márquez would discover that this song was a Castilianized version of a

French song ("Marlborough s'en va-t-enguerre") and that "Mambrú" was in reality "Marlborough." Since the only wars his grandfather had known were the Colombian civil wars, García Márquez decided that a Duke of Marlborough had been a protagonist in the Colombian violence. Hence the phantasmagoric warrior who in five of García Márquez's books presents himself at the military camp of Colonel Aureliano Buendía, disguised in tiger furs, claws and teeth, turns out to be the Duke of Marlborough. The figure of the grandfather is another of the constant male models in the work of García Márquez: he appears in the first novel *La hojarasca* (*The Leafstorm*) in the person of the ancient Colonel who defies the wrath of Macondo when be buries the French doctor; he is the hero of García Márquez's second novel *No One Writes to the Colonel,* and appears doubly in *One Hundred Years of Solitude*, magnified in the mythical personality of Colonel Aureliano Buendía, and in that of his friend and companion, Colonel Gerineldo Márques (this time with his own surname).

García Márquez's grandfather died when the writer was eight. "Since then nothing interesting has happened to me," the author asserts. Two books he read through the years contaminated the material he gathered from his grandparents: *The Thousand and One Nights* and *Gargantua and Pantagruel.* Traces of both will appear later in Macondo, not so much in the story, as in the style in which it was written: from the first episodical richness and proliferation as a narrative rule, and from the second, the vocation for excess and exaggeration. All the sources of *One Hundred Years of Solitude* seem already assembled in the mind of García Márquez when he abandoned Aracataca in 1940 to study in a school run by Jesuits in Bogotá. However, many things would have to take place before he could definitely exorcise the devils of his childhood in one great verbal construction.

He claims that since he was eight years old nothing interesting has happened to him, but in reality, many things have. Like almost every Latin American writer, García Márquez undertook the intense study of law; at the end of his secondary education, and also, like most, he soon renounced it. He traded law for journalism. He was a journalist and a writer of editorials for *El Espectador*, a Bogotá paper, in whose literary page his first stories appeared in 1946. In 1950 he lived in Barranquilla, and there, in the café "Colombia," he used to meet Ramón Vinyes, a Catalonian bookseller, as well as three other friends, Alfonso Fuenmayor, Germán Vargas and Alvaro Cepeda, the latter of whom would become a novelist. These people, including Gabriel García Márquez himself, will appear transfigured in the last years of Macondo, when Aureliano Buendía, the hermetist, discovers the prodigious bookstore of the encyclopedical Catalonian scholar, collector of incunabula and seller of Sanskrit manuscripts. In this bookstore Aureliano initiates his friendship with Alvaro, Germán, Alfonso and Gabriel, from whom he learns the art of revelry and with whom he visits the Babilonic, zoological brothel, which, at the age of one hundred and forty-five, Pilar Ternera rules. With these friends Aureliano discovers that literature "is the best toy for making fun of people."

In 1954, *El Espectador* sent García Márquez to Italy to cover the death of Pius XII which was believed to be imminent. But the pontiff died years later, and in the meantime, García Márquez arranged to remain in Europe and from there he sent articles to Bogotá. For a while, he studied at the "Centro Sperimentale Cinematográfico" in Rome and later that year he traveled through Eastern European countries. In 1955, while he froze in the cold weather of Eastern Europe, his Colombian friends discovered inside a drawer of his desk in his office in Bogotá, the manuscript of a novel he had finished just before leaving Colombia but which, due to an exaggerated sense of self-criticism, he had decided not to publish. His friends, *manu militare*, took the manuscript to the printer and so, in 1955, *La hojarasca* appeared. To write a novel is always an attempt at restitution and exorcism; an enterprise by which a man in conflict with reality tries simultaneously to recover from death certain key personal experiences which have remained in his memory and to free himself from those memories which have become tormenting obsessions of "devils." García Márquez's entire work up to the present has been a diligent effort to project into a novel this world, at once real and fantastic, the one which nourished his childhood. The first phase of this enterprise is *La hojarasca* where he describes a period in the history of Macondo between 1903 (the year in which the Colombian civil wars theoretically ceased) and 1928 (the year in which he was born).

In his first novel, Macondo is described in a purely subjective way through the alternate monologues of three characters: a boy of eleven, his mother Isabel, and his grandfather, a gentlemanly and lame old Colonel, appearing before the dead body of a mysterious doctor who hanged himself the night before and whom the people have sworn to leave unburied because they hated him. An odor of putrefaction, a physical, historical and moral decay overwhelms this narrative. Through the story of this anonymous doctor, whom the monologues slowly reveal, appear fragments of the history of Macondo. Who is this doctor? His past, his tragedy are unknown to us. We only know that he arrived in Macondo twenty-five years earlier; that he seemed to be a military man, and that he read French newspapers, which led the people to call him "the Frenchman." He brought with him a letter of recommendation from a certain Colonel Aureliano Buendía, General Governor of the Provinces of the Atlantic Coast. This letter so greatly impresses the Colonel, that he gives him lodging in his own house where the Frenchman will remain for seven years. For a while, he practices medicine, but soon, the banana company falls like a nightmare upon Macondo, dragging with it *La hojarasca* (*The Leafstorm* or human ruins of other settlements) and exploiting the town, making it dizzy with an illusion of prosperity, other doctors settle down in the area and the Frenchman loses patients. But instead of becoming disturbed, in an act of tranquil haughtiness, he abandons his profession and cloisters himself. He first lives closeted up in the Colonel's house but then later he moves to the dwelling across the street, taking with him as his mistress Meme, a maid the Colonel's family has raised. One night—by now the banana company has squeezed Macondo dry and departed, leaving in its wake apparent prosperity and the human refuse which is its monument—Macondo is filled with wounded men brought into the city from a neighborhood battlefield. There are not enough doctors to tend them. The people remember that the cloistered Frenchman is also a doctor and take the wounded to the door of his house, but the foreigner refuses to help. "I have already forgotten all that" he exclaims without deigning to open the door. From that time, the people have sworn revenge. They try to poison him, and the doctor lives in terror, not daring to drink local water for fear that it might poison him. For many years he lives closed up in his cave, by now abandoned by Meme, since she could not stand his determination to destroy himself. Only for one night did he leave his refuge and that was to heal the Colonel when the doctors gave up hope for the old man. In retribution, he asked the Colonel "to throw some earth over his body so the vultures would not eat him" after his death. That is the promise the Colonel has come to fulfill at the beginning of the novel, thus defying the feelings of the people of Macondo, who wish to leave the suicide unburied.

But in this first novel Macondo is still a subjective country, a metaphor of evil. Its reality, the material of fact is that García Márquez had read Faulkner around that time ("When I read Faulkner I discovered I wanted to become a writer," he will later confess), and Macondo bears the metaphysical dew of Yoknapatawpha County. However, the style he chose for the narration is not gratuitous: These intimacies of the three characters presented directly to the reader's experience have as their mission a revelation of Macondo, an exposition of its soul. The characteristic notes of

Macondo are, in this instance, frustration, resentment, solitude, wickedness. The voluntary and somewhat incomprehensible seclusion of the doctor symbolizes the seclusion Macondo lives in—a town out of contact with the rest of the world, condemned to fall apart, to rot slowly in broad daylight, just as the people of Macondo would like to see the body of the unsociable foreigner rot. The voluntary frustration of the doctor personifies the frustrating lives of all those in Macondo who appear in the novel: of Isabel, the frustrated wife (her husband Martín has abandoned her years before and it is suspected that he only married her out of self-interest: that is, to acquire certain powers and credit from the Colonel); of Meme, who thought that by going to live with the doctor she would escape her condition of a *guajira*, but who, instead, when on the first Sunday she shows up for Mass dressed up as a lady, discovered that she had won the hatred of the entire town, which would not forgive her affront to social conventions; of the Colonel himself who, though appearing to be the only upright man and the only one capable of a noble act, is in his own life a victim of the ardent immobility and the prostration of Macondo. What the inhabitants of Macondo hate in the doctor is both the reflection of their own frustration which the foreigner brings them, and his ruin which tragically synthesizes the conditions of total meanness in which Macondo agonizes.

In this first novel, Macondo, like Yoknapatawpha County and Onetti's imaginary port of Santa María, appears as a mental territory, a projection of the guilty conscience of man. On the other hand, the beings inhabiting it and the events which take place there belong to that level of reality which we can call objective or concrete (even though the description of that reality is subjective): everything happens on a rational and probable level. Nevertheless, there already appears here a series of elements which indicate that the unusual also has gained ready acceptance in Macondo. The daughter of the barber is haunted by a male "ghost," which is futilely exorcised by the "Dog," the local parish priest who arrived in Macondo the same day the French doctor did, but who is opposite. Religion is contaminated by madness: the "Dog" delivers sermons which consist of his reading weather forecasts from the Bristol Almanac, rather than teachings from the Gospels. The French doctor practices an unusual diet: he only eats herbs, "those with which asses feed themselves." These are the first traces of the beautiful face of Macondo which will only appear in all its richness in *One Hundred Years of Solitude*.

In the meantime, García Márquez was stranded in Paris, jobless and penniless, because the dictator Rojas Pinilla had shut down the daily news-

Espectador, which was the author's only source of income. in a small hotel on the rue Cujas in the Latin Quarter where he on credit, he rewrote eleven times a short and masterful work: *No* *e Writes to the Colonel*. He worked day and night in a real fury, and one day his typewriter broke down so he had to take it to a repairman. The latter, scratching his head, exclaimed with pity: "Elle est fatiguée, monsieur!" He finished the novel in January 1957, shortly before returning to Latin America, yet he was still unsatisfied: that was not the Macondo he carried in his head. That is probably why, when the book appeared, the location of the novel is only referred to as "the town"; and that is also why Macondo is mentioned in it as a different place. In reality, *No One Writes to the Colonel*, though not the total picture of this imaginary world which obsessed García Márquez, is a revelation which enlarges and enriches what we already knew about it through *La hojarasca*. That world has descended in this book from its psychological clouds to geography and history. That soul now has a body—the Colonel has endowed it with blood, muscles and bones: a landscape, habits, customs and a tradition in which some of the most recurring themes in Latin American regionalism are unexpectedly found but employed in a new sense: not as values, but rather as nonvalues; not as pretexts to exalt local color, but as symbols of frustration. The famous gamecock which, pompous and ruffled passes through the worst Latin American literature like a folkloric apotheosis, metaphorically crosses the pages which describe the moral agony of the Colonel who expects the impossible pension and embodies the provincial sordidness and daily horror of the town. Like the Colonel in *La hojarasca*, like the grandfather of García Márquez, the hero of this novel is a survivor of the civil wars and contemplates a bitter political frustration. For the last fifteen years he has been expecting the government to answer his petition for recognition of services rendered by granting him his pension. Each Friday, he stations himself on the dock to meet the mail boat which will never bring him a letter. He lives with an asthmatic wife, who maintains objectively: "We are rotting alive." Their son Agustín dies nine months before in the cockpit, pierced by gunshots for distributing secret information, and the Colonel inherited from him the gamecock on which he now places all his hope. He hopes to make him compete with a champion cock from a neighboring town. But until the moment of the battle, the cock must be fed, and the Colonel and his wife have no food even for themselves. The people of *La hojarasca* suffered ills which were psychological and moral; the devils which torment these people are physical: violence, the destructive downpours, political oppression, and above all, hunger.

Hunger, from which García Márquez suffered in his little hotel room on the rue Cujas while he wrote the book (he claims, in all seriousness, that he boiled chicken bones after chewing them, then placed them on the windowsill and used them over half a dozen times for soup), and the memories of which infected his imaginary world, is perhaps the town's most stinging nightmare. The book opens up with an image of poverty—the Colonel prepares himself coffee by scraping the remains out of a can so that the resulting drink is an infusion of coffee with tin oxide—and concludes with one much worse. The Colonel has decided not to sell the rooster, as his wife suggests, even though there are still forty-five days to go before the fight. "And in the meantime what shall we eat?" she asks. The Colonel answers: "Shit." The entire new face of this world—its corrupt materialism, its abject carnality—is condensed in that ferocious expression which closes the narrative. Also here, as in *La hojarasca*, there is a slovenly parish priest. His name is Father Angel, he has established a code of film censorship based on bell tolls. Twelve tolls means "bad for everyone," and it has been one full year since any film exhibited at the only theater in town has escaped Father Angel's prohibition. But the unusual element is now minimal and is overwhelmed by scrutiny of the most everyday and naturalistic levels of reality: the suspicion and fear inspired by the enactment of martial law, the recent political repression of which only Don Sabas was able to escape—Don Sabas the Colonel's comrade who now is the rich person of the town; the atmosphere of sloth, of boredom and of tedium which the constant rains of October exacerbate. Even the delineation of the characters is naturalistic: the mayor's cheeks swollen by the pain in his molar teeth; Don Sabas's diabetes; the digestive disorders provoked in the Colonel by October; his wife's asthma. The prose in *La hojarasca* has undergone a real process of refinement and technique has been radically simplified. The Faulknerian traces have disappeared. "I have fought them by reading Hemingway," says García Márquez in jest. The style is one of maniacal economy and transparency; the construction of perfect simplicity; the adjustment between the material and the form of the story total. To anyone who might have read in 1957 the then recently finished manuscript (which García Márquez buried, tied with a colored ribbon, in the bottom of a suitcase) the author's decision not to publish it, because he considered the book a failure, would have sounded inconceivable. This novel, *per se,* is a totally successful work. Only later, with the appearance of *One Hundred Years of Solitude*, was it possible to realize that, as a description of Macondo, this excellent narrative could still be surpassed.

In 1957, García Márquez returned stealthily to Colombia to marry a beautiful woman with Egyptian features who had been waiting for him in Barranquilla for four years. Those who wish to know her have only to read *One Hundred Years of Solitude*. She appears in it, with her own name of Mercedes, as a reserved and silent pharmacist "with a thin neck and sleepy eyes," who, to top it off, is engaged to a certain Gabriel. From Colombia he moved to Venezuela, where he lived for a couple of years working for magazines and newspapers, in a Caracas shaken by terrorist attempts: the bullets and bombs with which Pérez Jiménez tortured the people throughout his dictatorship. During these years, García Márquez wrote most of the stories which would make up his third book, *Los funerales de la Mamá Grande*, and which would only be published in 1962. These stories follow the stylistic line of *The Colonel:* a precise, spare language, worked over, stripped of all artifices and without a shade of excessive rhetoric; a lineal structure, freed from complications; short and efficient dialogues. Only the narrative from which the title of the book is taken differentiates itself clearly from the rest by a tone of cunning farce and the rambling cry in which it is written, by the rich and inflated language used. But, though they extend the form of the previous book, these stories offer an image of Macondo in which a new dimension of that world appears, one only vaguely insinuated before: the magic dimension. Macondo is now not only a territory oppressed by evil, mosquitos, the heat, hunger, political violence and inertia: but also a stage for inexplicable and wonderful successes: to a widow who languishes bitterly on a rainy day, "with a white sheet and a comb on her lap and crushing lice with her thumbs," appears the ghost of Mamá Grande, a woman who has been dead for years. Instead of getting frightened the widow asks her "When will I die?" "When your arm starts to hurt you," Mamá Grande answers mysteriously and disappears; there is a strange plague of birds who burst into the houses breaking through the screens on the windows, and dying in the dwellings: the priest is no less original than those of the previous books: his name is Father Antonio Isabel del Santísimo Sacramento del Altar Castañeda y Montero, and, at the age of 94, he has seen the devil on three occasions, and, as if that were not enough, one day he finds the Wandering Jew walking along the streets of Macondo; the funeral of Mamá Grande brings to Macondo figures from the four cardinal points and, among them, the Pope and the President of the Republic, and also a few dead people. Many of the stories in the book are like fragments, chapters of a vaster text, and, in spite of their clean execution, they leave the reader with a certain unsatisfied appetite. That is because these narratives were actually written as episodes of a novel, that novel about Macondo, tried for the third time by García Márquez and for the third time abandoned, in some ways, in the middle.

It was the year 1960 and García Márquez had returned to Bogotá to open there the *Prensa Latina*, an agency founded by Cuba in the year of the revolution. In 1960 this agency sent him to New York as its correspondent, and he remained in this city for a few months until he resigned one day. He then undertook a Homeric trip through the Deep South "in homage to Faulkner and carrying that author's books under his arms." But as a sign of protest, he did not remain in the South, because, one day, after many of abstinence, he succeeded in borrowing some money and in the best restaurant of New Orleans, ordered *filet mignon,* which they brought "crowned with a peach in syrup." He continued to travel by land, and when he reached Mexico "the sound of the Spanish language and hot food" encouraged him to stay. He spent eight years in the Mexican capital writing subtitles for movies. There, his friends recovered the manuscript of *No One Writes to the Colonel* which by now was becoming moth-eaten in that suitcase and published it in 1961; the following year they arranged to have the stories of *Los funerales de la Mamá Grande* printed. Finally they forced him to enter in a literary contest in Bogotá the manuscript of a new novel written in Mexico, but first they advised him to change the original title, *Este pueblo de mierda* for a less bold one—*La mala hora*. The novel won the contest and was published in 1962. García Márquez had changed the original title; the owners of the press in Madrid, where the sponsors of the competition chose to publish the book, changed the entire text, gave it to an editor who cut all Americanisms and made the inhabitants of Macondo speak in the language of the *Diccionario de la Academia Española*. García Márquez rejected the edition and in the new edition of *La mala hora* placed the following note: "In 1962, when *La mala hora* was first published, a copy-editor gave himself permission to change certain terms and to stiffen the style in the name of the purity of language. On this occasion, the author in his turn has given himself permission to restore the idiomatic inaccuracies and stylistic barbarisms, in the name of his sovereign and arbitrary will." Some time ago a journalist asked García Márquez why he wrote, and the writer replied: "So that my friends will like me." The journalist doubtless thought that it was a good joke, but the truth is that without the obstinacy of his friends, García Márquez would perhaps still today be an unknown writer.

La mala hora does not amplify the view of Macondo as presented in his previous books; rather, it assembles in one novel the different data concerning the imaginary world which was dispersed in the stories and in his two novels. The most immediate effect of the story is one of a detailed and almost entomological realism, but this implacably objective surface hides a fact, which still remains unexplained, perhaps unexplainable. This fact is the appearance of pasquinades stuck on the doors of houses, in which the gossip and slander of the people are described. These lampoons do not invent anything: they repeat what people say in secret, the murmurs, calumnies or forbidden truths which travel in a whisper. Who places the lampoons on the doors? Everyone and no one. The effect is cataclysmic: this collective unfaithfulness revives rivalries, old hatreds, and sows mistrust and enmity. The secret filth of Macondo stands exposed in broad daylight. In a series of static pictures through which pass, one by one, sordid, unusual or picturesque characters, *La mala hora* presents a collective view of the human fauna of Macondo, a social X-ray of their ills.

This novel displeased García Márquez even more than the other; his disappointment resulted in a literary silence which lasted for a few years. He thought that perhaps he would never be able to write the novel of which he dreamed; he decided, in all probability, to forget about Macondo. And suddenly, one day in 1965, the miracle occurred, that is to say, the reward for so many years of faithfulness to what we could call his obsessions. He was traveling by car from Acapulco to Mexico City—he tells us—and suddenly, he "saw" the novel on which mentally he had been working since he was a boy. "I had it so completely formed," he says, "that right there I could have dictated the first chapter word by word to a typist." He immediately closed himself in his office with large supplies of paper and cigarettes and announced to Mercedes that he was going to remain there for about six months and asked her not to disturb him for any reason, least of all with domestic problems. In fact, he stayed walled in that part of his house for a year and six months. When he left that room, euphoric, intoxicated with nicotine and on the verge of a physical breakdown, he had a manuscript of one thousand and three hundred pages (and a household debt of ten thousand dollars). In the wastepaper basket there were some five thousand pages. A few months later *One Hundred Years of Solitude* was published.

One Hundred Years of Solitude extends and magnifies the world erected by his previous books, but also signifies a rupture, a qualitative change within that dry, rough, asphyxiating reality which Macondo was until then. That world, in spite of its coherence and its vitality, suffered a limitation which retrospectively *One Hundred Years of Solitude* revealed: its modesty. Everything in it was struggling to develop and to grow: men, things, dreams suggested more than showed, because a verbal straitjacket restrained their movements and cut them off the moment they were about to come out of themselves. The critics used to praise the austerity of García Márquez's prose, his power of synthesis, the parsimony of his stories. All that was true and revealed an original writer who had domesticated his devils and ruled them at his whim. What provoked García Márquez, on that already distant evening, between Acapulco and Mexico City, to open the cages of those devils and let himself be dragged by them into one of the most daring creative adventures of our times? We will probably never know. But we know, on the other hand, and this is what is most important, that thanks to whatever it was, the tight and claustral town of Macondo changed into a universe, a Broceliande of wonders.

In *One Hundred Years of Solitude* we witness a prodigious enrichment. The mathematic, contained and functional prose became a style with volcanic breath, capable of communicating movement and grace to the most audacious creatures of imagination. Fantasy has broken its chains and gallops wild and feverish, permitting itself all excesses, until it has outlined in space and time the life cycle of Macondo, through its most conspicuous inhabitants: the family of the Buendías. The novel does not leave out any of the levels of reality in which the history of Macondo is recorded: it includes the individual and the collective, the legendary and the historical, the daily and the mythical. Restoring a tradition of writing that seemed dead—that of the medieval novels of knighthood—García Márquez rediscovers that the novelist is God, that the limits of literature are those of reality—that it has no limits and that all excesses are permissible to the creator if he has the sufficient verbal power of persuasion to justify them, and that the hero can die and come back to life many times if it is necessary for the perfect realization of the story. In Macondo, as in the enchanted territories where Amadís and Tirant rode, the boundaries separating reality from unreality have gone to pieces. Everything can happen here: excess is a rule, beauty enriches life and it is as truthful as war and hunger: there are flying carpets that take the children of Macondo on rides over the roofs of the town; a plague of insomnia and loss of memory; a gypsy who dies and returns to life "because he is unable to bear loneliness"; a priest who levitates after drinking a cup of chocolate and a woman who rises to heaven body and soul, escorted by linen sheets; a man who drifts through life with a halo of yellow butterflies, and a hero, inspired by the knightly crusaders, who promotes thirty-two wars and loses them all. In a chapter of *The Death of Artemio Cruz,* a novel by Carlos Fuentes, a character, Colonel Lorenzo Gavilán, gets lost. García

Márquez rescues him and settles him in Macondo, where Gavilán will die swept by grapeshot in the historical episode of the massacre of the strikers. With the same ease, he gives hospitality in Macondo to Víctor Hugues, a character in a novel by Alejo Carpentier, and to Rocamadour, a character of Julio Cortázar. But this dexterity could suggest the idea that *One Hundred Years of Solitude* is something like an agreeable and brilliant game. In reality, it is quite the opposite. It is not about a castle in the air, but about an imaginary construction that has its roots deeply anchored in Latin American reality, a reality which is reflected through transfigurations and mirages. The landscapes of Macondo contain all the natural elements of Latin America: its snows, its mountain ranges, its deserts, its cataclysms. Its dramas also appear refracted in the political and social life of Macondo: the story of the banana company and of its president, the haughty Mr. Brown, who travels in a train of glass and velvet, synthesizes the drama of colonial exploitation of Latin America and the tragedies it engenders. Not everything is magic or erotic feast in Macondo: a clamour of hostilities between the powerful and the miserable resounds from behind these blazes of fire and sometimes explodes in orgies of blood. And along the gorges, as in the wilderness of the mountain ranges of Macondo, there are, furthermore, those armies which tear each other to pieces while searching endlessly for each other: a ferocious war which decimates men and frustrates the destiny of the country, as it has occurred and still occurs in many places in Latin America. But this is not only an exclusively Latin American reality: it is a spiral of concentric circles, the first of which would be a family with characters more or less extravagant, the second the tiny town of Aracataca with its myths and problems, the third Colombia, the fourth Latin America and the last one, humanity.

In the chronicle of Macondo, living on their own account, and at the same time valid as symbols, beings, problems, and myths pass by, symbols which the readers of any country and language can identify and interpret as their own, because they are universal and express the condition of humanity. But that universality has been attained by starting from a more concrete reality, deepening it and recreating it from a perspective which is not local, but rather human.

As any novel erected in the image and semblance of reality, *One Hundred Years of Solitude* admits of different readings, because it consists of several levels. The most immediate is that of adventure. The story of the Buendías starts with a crime and ends a century later with the birth of a monster: a child with the tail of a pig. Between both facts the most absurd adventures, the most unusual characters, the most daring phantasies proliferate in an incessant sizzling. But this line of prodigious beings, who want to portray God, who study demonology, who take delight in "creating only to destroy," who engage in improbable wars, or shut themselves up as biblical hermits, are something more than creatures of a pure game of the imagination: they are a testimony to and a metaphor of human experience in its most ample meaning. In the lives of the Buendías (of this tribe where the name of men is always Arcadio or Aureliano and the name of women Ursula or Amaranta) are described and mingled actions and dreams, what men do and what they wanted to do, what is within reach of their bodies and what only their fantasy and insane dreams allowed them to perform. But in the waking reversals and adventures of the Buendías, their nightmares and torments also reproduce themselves: solitude, which is a hereditary infirmity of the Buendías, alienation which prevents them from communicating (and frustrates them in all their undertakings), inability to adapt to a world they do not understand and to a society in which everything seems possible, except happiness. With the strictest weapons of fiction, *One Hundred Years of Solitude* offers a vast narrative representation of the human reality of our time. Due to the determination, obstinacy and patience of this writer, the anecdotes, fables and lies of a tiny Colombian town lost between marshes and mountains have served in this manner, through reincarnations and changes, as key pieces for the construction of a story in which the men of today find the reflection of their own true selves.

FLOYD MERRELL

José Arcadio Buendía's Scientific Paradigms: Man in Search of Himself

The stuff of the world may be called physical or mental or both or neither as we please; in fact the words serve no purpose.
—BERTRAND RUSSELL

Gabriel García Márquez's *Cien años de soledad* (*One Hundred Years of Solitude*) presents a multidimensional microcosm. The novel can be construed as symbolic of Colombia (the socio-political level), Latin America (the mythico-cultural level), Christianity (the mystico-religious level), the world (the historical/archetypal levels), or the universe (the cyclical/entropic levels). In light of this observation, our analysis will focus on certain elements of García Márquez's novel which are analogous, on broad historical/archetypal levels, to Western man's struggle to explicate and comprehend nature. Our procedure entails the construction of a system of parallels between the "scientific paradigms" postulated and implemented by José Arcadio Buendía, founder and patriarch of Macondo, and the structural history of scientific philosophy in the Western World.

One of the first great scientific movements arose among the Ionian philosophers, a branch of the Asiatic Greeks, from six hundred to four hundred years B.C. They attempted to present ideas as bare facts devoid of all subjectivity. In so doing they removed the gods from nature and repudiated magic and mysticism. However, having established commercial relations with the Mesopotamian cultures, they were inevitably subjected to certain "exotic" ideas from the East.

From *Latin American Literary Review,* no. 4 (Spring–Summer 1974).

In *Cien años de soledad*, José Arcadio Buendía's attitude *vis-à-vis* the exotic gypsies who visit Macondo is favorably analogous to that of the Ionians when introduced to Eastern thought. The gypsies' inventions, revealing a mystico-religious substratum, are the product of a knowledge as an end in itself. On the other hand, José Arcadio desires knowledge solely as a means to an end. Thus the gypsies, whose non-utilitarian, "animistic" conception of nature implies a ritual-oriented play element predominating over seriousness, represent the polar opposite to José Arcadio, who seeks practical ends through the methodical exploitation of a nature of which he considers himself no integral part. One world-view connotes cyclicality, an eternal recurrence where chaos is periodically ordered and where there is a continuous tendency toward conjunction between man and nature. In contrast, a rectilinearity is implied by the opposing world-view where disjunction is engendered, where time can not be regained, and where a reordering of the universe is denied.

Therefore, José Arcadio, whose imagination went far beyond miracles and magic, believes that he can find a practical application for the "useless" inventions in spite of the fact that Melquíades, spokesman for the gypsy tribe, warns him that his attempts will lead to naught.

When the gypsies return to Macondo and introduce the astrolabe, the compass, the telescope, and the magnifying glass (all Arabic contributions to the Western World from the tenth to the twelfth centuries), José Arcadio significantly plays the role of innovator rather than creator: he once again searches for a practical use for these inventions. Thus, from the very beginning a polarity between the utilitarian and the non-utilitarian world-view is apparent in García Márquez's novel. In addition, as illustrated through the Ionian philosophers (historically) and José Arcadio (symbolically), Western man, with his developing view of reality, optimistically begins his ascent into time toward an objective comprehension and a systematic utilization of nature.

Melquíades later returns to Macondo introducing the fabled seven metals corresponding to the seven planets, documents describing the possible construction of the philosopher's stone, and formulas for the alchemical transmutation of lead into gold. This event is analogous historically to the revival of astrology and alchemy in the Western World, primarily through contact with the East, during the eleventh and twelfth centuries. José Arcadio's interest still remains discreetly with the practical aspects of these inventions. He immediately conducts an experiment to produce gold but his mixture is burned to a crisp.

At the same time, José Arcadio recognizes the superiority of the gypsies' (Arabic) technology over the stagnant knowledge of the people of Macondo (Western World): "En el mundo están ocurriendo cosas increíbles, . . . mientras nosotros seguimos viviendo como burros (Incredible things are happening in the world, . . . while we keep on living like donkeys)." Melquíades, the "foreigner," is exercizing a predominant influence on José Arcadio, the "westerner"; and the latter is undergoing an intellectual transformation as a result of this contact. Historically, it may be safely posited that, in a similar manner, traditional European learning changed radically after the Arabs entered Spain. Kurt Seligman observes how:

> endowed with an insatiable curiosity concerning foreign learning, guided by a truly Oriental imagination, and filled with the energy of a people who had extended their boundaries from the Indies to the Pyrenees, the Arabs in their writings show a dynamism which contrasts sharply with the passive wisdom of the West.
>
> (*Magic, Supernaturalism, and Religion*)

José Arcadio is temporarily overwhelmed by the gypsies' new inventions. However, contrary to his utilitarian spirit, they are intuited ideations, constructed to satisfy lucid curiosity and invariably tinged with mystical qualities. Perpetually oriented toward the future, confident that the projected ends will be ultimately achieved through the eclectical formulation and utilization of practical means, he nevertheless attempts to transform each of these inventions. The futility of each of his projects leads only to renewed obstinacy rather than discouragement or admission of defeat.

To José Arcadio's surprise, when the "foreigners" arrive once again they appear even more exotic than before: "Eran gitanos nuevos . . . ejemplares hermosos de piel aceitunada y manos inteligentes, cuyos bailes y músicas sembraron en las calles un pánico de alborotada alegría (They were new gypsies . . . handsome specimens with oily skins and intelligent hands, whose dances and music sowed a panic of uproarious joy through the streets)."

Historically, the philosophical and ideological separation of the East and the West is epitomized by the arrival of the new gypsies. Melquíades, the divulger of ideas, is no longer with them. The new inventions they introduce appear relatively frivolous, mere gadgetry, with the sole exception of a block of ice. Overcome with curiosity, José Arcadio puts his hand on the ice, "y la mantuvo puesta por varios minutos, mientras el corazón se le hinchaba de temor y de júbilo al contacto del misterio (and held it there for several minutes as his heart filled with fear and jubilation at the contact with mystery)."

José Arcadio's experience with the ice is both inspiring and confounding since it opens him up to his inherent conflict between the "ideal" and the "real." After having witnessed the mysterious ice, he "idealistically" envisions Macondo as a city constructed entirely of ice. This is an isomorphism of his *a priori* conception (intuited image) of a utopian city whose houses have mirrored walls and simultaneously a city where man is perpetually confronted with a reality which is the mirror-image of himself, a reality he himself has created. And as this reality "out there" coexists with him it becomes eternally inseparable from him; a dualism from which he cannot escape. At the same time he feels compelled to pursue his quest for a comprehension of perceptual reality (empirical knowledge) and consequently resumes his observations in the laboratory.

This dualism parallels historically the coming of the Renaissance and the Copernican revolution when the ideality of *Utopia* existed side by side with the quasimathematized model of the universe, or when lofty visions of the future of mankind fomented by the discovery of a *New World* were juxtaposed with the birth of a precise experimental method and the rejection of secondary (sensory) qualities in favor of the exclusive use of primary (quantitative) qualities in all attempts to comprehend natural phenomena.

The separation of the East and the West is also becoming absolute since the gypsies, whose explication of nature exalts mystery over reason, atemporality over historicity, no longer attract the attention of José Arcadio. The rift becomes more distinct after their subsequent visit since these new gypsies, unlike Melquíades's tribe, soon give evidence that they are no longer "heralds of progress but purveyors of amusement." Unlike José Arcadio, most of the people of Macondo remain intrigued by the new frivolous inventions. When they dig up their last pieces of gold to pay for a ride on the flying carpet, José Arcadio contemptuously declares: "Déjenlos que sueñan. . . . Nosotros volaremos mejor que ellos con recursos más científicos que ese miserable sobre-camas (Let them dream. . . . We'll do better flying than they are doing, and with more scientific resources than a miserable bedspread)." Just as Eastern science did not "develop" rapidly enough for the Western World, so José Arcadio is no longer interested in the gypsies' "useless toys." Only through a systematic study of nature can true knowledge, and ultimately the practical application of that knowledge, be acquired.

Eventually, however, the inevitable consequences of José Arcadio's position *vis-à-vis* nature become evident. His son, who falls in love with a gypsy girl, abandons Macondo and Ursula leaves in search of his whereabouts. José Arcadio seems to have lost a part of himself when his wife leaves but rather than despair, he soon resumes work in his laboratory. However, nature now begins to behave in a mysterious fashion:

> Una cazuela de agua colocada en la mesa de trabajo hirvió sin fuego durante media hora hasta evaporarse por completo. José Arcadio Buendía y su hijo observaban aquellos fenómenos . . . interpretándolos como anuncios de la materia. Un día la canastilla de Amaranta empezó a moverse con un impulso propio y dio una vuelta completa en el cuarto, ante la consternación de Aureliano, que se apresuró a detenerla. Pero su padre no se alteró.
>
> (A pan of water on the worktable boiled without any fire under it for a half hour until it completely evaporated. José Arcadio Buendía and his son observed those phenomena . . . interpreting them as predictions of the material. One day Amaranta's basket began to move by itself and made a complete turn about the room, to the consternation of Aureliano who hurried to stop it. But his father did not get upset.)

In the light of these rare occurrences José Arcadio nonchalantly states: "Si no temes a Dios, témele a los metales (If you don't fear God, fear him through the metals)." Here may be observed various aspects of José Arcadio's conception of reality which are analogous to seventeenth-century scientific thought. First, Ursula's absence symbolically indicates that José Arcadio's science has been "separated from humanity" just as during the seventeenth century the conception of the universe as a vast perpetual-motion apparatus and man as a machine marked a further stage in the separation of the sciences and the humanities. Second, God the creator and mover of this clockwork universe gradually begins to fade away and the "metals," or nature, begin to replace him; that is, divine law is being replaced by physical law and God is being substituted by human reason as the instrument for understanding life. Third, this period in history best represents the stage where the dominance of a materialistic, inductive science and the industrialization of Western societies is indicative of a transformation of man's ambient to conform to the accepted mechanical model of man and the universe. Correspondingly, José Arcadio is separated from "humanity," he no longer fears God in the traditional sense, and his world vision has become materialistic.

When Ursula finally returns to Macondo she is followed by a multitude of immigrants. But this time the newcomers are not gypsies:

> Eran hombres y mujeres como ellos. . . . Traían mulas cargadas de cosas de comer, carretas de bueyes con muebles y utensilios domésticos. . . . Ursula no había alcanzado a los gitanos, pero encontró la ruta que su marido no pudo descubrir en su frustrada búsqueda de los grandes inventos.
>
> (They were men and women like them. . . . They had mules loaded down with things to eat, oxcarts with furniture and domestic utensils. . . . Ursula had not caught up with the gypsies, but she had found the route that her husband had been unable to discover in his frustrated search for the great inventions.)

The town is consequently transformed. There is renewed activity; new stores, shops, and homes go up, public works are inaugurated, a permanent trade route is established between Macondo and the outside world. José Arcadio is so fascinated by this activity he loses interest in his idealistic speculations and in his experiments in the laboratory. He soon imposes a state of "order and progress" in the village and it begins to prosper as in the first days after its establishment. The *acacias* (acacias, or locusts) which were planted along the streets during the early days are replaced by almond trees. And Ursula significantly contributes to the industry of the town with her production of candied fish and little roosters.

It was, as José Arcadio realized when Ursula returned, exactly what he had been unconsciously longing for. He believed that man, or humanity, had once again arrived in Macondo. This period in *Cien años de soledad* is historically reminiscent of the Enlightenment. The mechanization of man proceeds when the birds in the cages are turned out and replaced by clocks, and consequently the town is now dominated by a new demon: time. The acacias, or "thorny" trees, having been replaced by almond trees, man now optimistically proclaims his ability to transcend the biblical fall from Paradise, overcome his drab existence where suffering is inevitable, and commence to construct his utopian world. The rise of capitalism is depicted by Aureliano's fabrication of golden fish for sale and by Ursula's peddling of her wares. Aureliano also replaces his father in the laboratory and the nature of the experiments simultaneously to gain lucre. As a final note, having previously lost his fear of God, José Arcadio now feels that he can exercize dominion over the "metals," or nature.

Thus, José Arcadio's retirement is accompanied by the institutionalization of the materialistic paradigmatic model of nature he established. It has now become a standard norm governing all activities, just as the materialistic view of nature became the norm in the Western World.

Very shortly two plagues attack the town: insomnia and loss of memory. Insomnia because Macondo, not unlike the eighteenth and nineteenth century Western World, having realized success with its postulated materialistic conception of nature, considers itself wide awake, or enlightened concerning the ultimate realities of the universe. Loss of memory because the people of Macondo forget that the mechanistic view they have adopted, was, in the beginning, only a hypostatized model rather than an invariable truth. It is also significant that during the plagues Melquíades returns from the dead to introduce the daguerrotype, an optical instrument the Arabs contributed to the Western World.

With his daguerreotype José Arcadio endeavors to prove scientifically the existence (or inexistence) of God. However, when his experiments result in failure, rather than modify his established scientific paradigm, he continues blindly to accept it on faith, convinced of his *a priori* postulate that God does not exist, and proceeds to conduct his life accordingly. It is, of course, difficult to make reality fit into a preconceived mold. The neatness of the hypostatized paradigm is marred by an incorrigible reality and a dichotomy between theory and practice inevitably ensues. This dichotomy has been prevalent in history. For example, Rousseau, postulating the innate goodness of man, could appear as the apostle of liberty (theory) and at the same time advocate a coercive collectivism (practice). And utilitarianism could embody a doctrine of laissez faire but inevitably lead to a system of parental government.

Analogous to the thought of the Western World edified upon the foundation of rationalism, José Arcadio's paradigm—knowledge on the basis of *a priori* postulation—is not entirely valid. Nevertheless, he doggedly retains faith in this paradigm even though nature refuses to conform. José Arcadio's science (the mechanical principle) becomes predominant and Melquíades slowly wanes away while his conception of knowledge (the vitalist principle) becomes nil. Simultaneously, the dualism inherent in José Arcadio's epistemological method becomes apparent: an undying faith in his scientific paradigm—in spite of its apparent shortcomings—as the ultimate road to total comprehension is opposed by an existence which forces him into certain patterns of action notwithstanding his desires to the contrary.

José Arcadio's final crisis parallels the fate of the classical mechanistic model of the universe at the beginning of the present century. The first indication of this impending crisis occurs when he realizes that all forms of evolution and chronological succession had existed only in the mind:

> "¿Qué día es hoy?" Aureliano le contestó que era martes. "Eso mismo pensaba yo", dijo José Arcadio Buendía. "Pero de pronto me he dado cuenta de que sigue siendo lunes, como ayer. . . ." Al día siguiente, miércoles, José Arcadio Buendía volvió al taller. "Esto es un desastre—dijo—mira el aire, oye el zumbido del sol, igual que ayer y antier. También hoy es lunes."
>
> ("What day is today?" Aureliano told him that it was Tuesday. "I was thinking the same thing," José Arcadio Buendía said, "but suddenly I realized that it's still Monday, like yesterday. . . ." On the next day, Wednesday, José Arcadio Buendía went back to the workshop. "This is a disaster," he said. "Look at the air, listen to the buzzing of the sun, the same as yesterday and the day before. Today is Monday too.")

José Arcadio's thought, implying reversibility, periodicity, and stasis, is a mirror image of the ultimate extension of classical physics. Inherent within the Newtonian corpuscular-kinetic theory of matter where it is meaningful to speak of a definite state of the universe at a particular instant, and where the universe is made up of a finite number of distinct, unvarying atomic entities, time becomes in essence reversible (the eternal return). Consequently the image of a definite number of identical cycles succeeding each other *ad infinitum* implies the negation of real novelty or change: stasis. Therefore, buried within the foundation of the materialistic philosophy is a denial of a thoroughgoing evolutionary philosophy.

Significantly, cyclicality, or periodicity, which has become the basis for the mechanistic explanation of matter, fascinated José Arcadio just prior to his death. He considered his greatest invention a small figurine he connected to a clock pendulum:

> El juguete salió sin interrupción al compás de su propia música durante tres días. Aquel hallazgo lo excitó mucho más que cualquiera de sus empresas descabelladas. No volvió a comer. No volvió a dormir. . . . Pasaba las noches dando vueltas en el cuarto. Pensando en voz alta, buscando la manera de aplicar los principios del péndulo a las carretas de bueyes, a las rejas del arado, a todo lo que fuera útil puesto en movimiento.
>
> (The toy danced uninterruptedly to the rhythm of her own

> music for three days. That discovery excited him much more than any of his other harebrained undertakings. He stopped eating. He stopped sleeping. . . . He would spend the nights walking around the room thinking aloud, searching for a way to apply the principles of the pendulum to oxcarts, to harrows, to everything that was useful when put into motion.)

Obsessed with his mechanistic view of reality, he attempts to periodize all movement. However, he finally realizes that his concept of cyclicality, although producing the illusion of dynamism, is in reality sterile, repetitive motion where novelty is impossible. He soon hypothesizes that: "¡La máquina del tiempo se ha descompuesto. . . . Pasó seis horas examinando las cosas, tratando de encontrar una diferencia con el aspecto que tuvieron el día anterior, pendiente de descubrir en ellas algún cambio que revelara el transcurso del tiempo (The time machine has broken. . . . He spent six hours examining things, trying to find a difference from their appearance on the previous day in the hope of discovering in them some change that would reveal the passage of time)."

Unable to come to grips with this new realization, his only recourse is violence. He smashes his alchemical apparatus, his daguerreotype, and his silver workshop. Ten men are required to throw him down, fourteen to tie him up, and twenty to drag him to the chestnut tree where he remains until his death.

In his state of apparent dementia, José Arcadio can not cope with present reality and insists on returning physically to the past, to the "beginning of time." This is evidenced by his ability to effectively communicate with only one person: Prudencio Aguilar. He and Prudencio had fought a duel in the "beginning," before the creation of Macondo (the world). After José Arcadio succeeded in slaying his adversary he found it necessary to take Ursula and flee into the "wilderness" where he created Macondo, his dream city. Now, after his psychic abolition of time, he can communicate at will with Prudencio, that is, he can regress to the mythical beginning.

José Arcadio, not unlike modern man, is on the one hand attempting to satisfy his desire for the eternal return to the beginning in order to counteract the "terror of history." On the other hand, there exists the paradox of the mechanical view of the universe which, rather than tracing a linear historical trajectory, reveals on the contrary the image of a vast machine governed by timeless cycles. Time loses meaning, yet man ages irreversibly within this great timeless machine. All attempts to seek timelessness through the abolition of "time's arrow" become, for José Arcadio and for man, futile.

Shortly before his death, José Arcadio, when alone, found consolation in his dream of the infinite rooms:

> Soñaba que se levantaba de la cama, abría la puerta y pasaba a otro cuarto igual. . . . De ese cuarto pasaba a otro exactamente igual, cuya puerta abría para pasar a otro exactamente igual, y luego a otro exactamente igual, hasta el infinito. Le gustaba irse de cuarto en cuarto, como en una galería de espejos paralelos, hasta que Prudencio Aguilar le tocaba el hombro. Entonces regresaba de cuarto en cuarto, despertando hacia atrás, recorriendo el camino inverso, y encontraba a Prudencio Aguilar en el cuarto de la realidad. Pero una noche . . . Prudencio Aguilar le tocó el hombro en un cuarto de intermedio, y él se quedó allí para siempre, creyendo que era el cuarto real.
>
> (He dreamed that he was getting out of bed, opening the door and going into an identical room. . . . From that room he would go into another that was just the same, the door of which would open into another that was just the same, the door of which would open into another one just the same, and then into another exactly alike, and so on to infinity. He liked to go from room to room. As in a gallery of parallel mirrors, until Prudencio Aguilar would touch him on the shoulder. Then he would go back from room to room, walking in reverse, going back over his trail, and he would find Prudencio Aguilar in the room of reality. But one night . . . Prudencio Aguilar touched his shoulder in an intermediate room and he stayed there forever, thinking that it was the real room.)

José Arcadio's illusions during the final days of his life are indicative of a cosmological vision pushed to its extreme form in face of new circumstances which will inevitably destroy it. Historically, this is analogous to the first decades of the twentieth century when the classical conception of the universe was challenged by a new model. José Arcadio's *anguish* before a static universe of timeless corpuscles where there is no novelty and where all is rigidly determined is converted into a *desire* for a return to the origin, to a communion with himself in the *illud tempus*. At the same time the rooms through which he could freely pass represent an alteration of his traditional mode of reasoning to conform to new evidence.

Similar modification of a traditional scientific paradigm may be observed in the twentieth century when the quantum theory gave rise to speculations concerning the possibility of spacio-temporal intervals, or "pulses" (the *hodon* and the *chronon*), which render both space and time finitely divisible (microscopically and quantitatively), but, for practical purposes still infinitely divisible (macroscopically and psychically, or qualitatively). Given this atomistic view, not only may a certain variation of the corpuscular-kinetic theory of infinitely divisible time and space be maintained but the idea of temporal reversibility may also be implied.

José Arcadio's "infinite rooms" might indicate these spaciotemporal intervals, his passage through the rooms temporal reversibility, the sameness of the rooms a static corpuscular-kinetic conception of matter, and the "room of reality" that state in the idyllic beginning with Prudencio Aguilar. José Arcadio is not bound by finitude inasmuch as he can, at will, return to the origin (the eternal return) but once he mistakenly assumes he is in the "room of reality" when actually in another of the infinite number of rooms, he instantaneously tastes death (becomes finite). It is also significant that as he returns to the origin he traverses the rooms "waking in reverse"; that is, an awakened state comes in simultaneity with the return to the primordial origin while a linear projection into the infinite future is merely a dream.

José Arcadio's impulse to modify his traditional paradigm in view of new circumstances which contradict it also represents a universal human trait. He is attempting to ascertain and delineate—in a confusing, vastly changed world of relativity, finitude, and indeterminacies—a new road to the absolute where the eternal need for security is satisfied albeit at the expense of the eternal desire for novelty.

Soon after José Arcadio dies, when the carpenter is measuring him for a coffin; "vieron a través de la ventana que estaba cayendo una llovizna de minúsculas flores amarillas. Cayeron toda la noche sobre el pueblo en una tormenta silenciosa (through the window they saw a light rain of tiny yellow flowers falling. They fell on the town all through the night in a silent storm)."

The flowers, indicative of the brevity of life, are significantly yellow since this color represents the "farseeing sun, which appears bringing light out of darkness only to disappear again into darkness." Thus, José Arcadio's struggle for total comprehension of reality, symbolic of Western man and his materialistic conception of nature, was in a way futile while at the same time potentially beneficial. Man's course in history was forever altered and in the end he was opened up to himself once and for all, forced to realize that rather than standing above nature as a neutral observer he is a participant with nature and both comprise one organic whole.

In conclusion, it appears plausible that certain elements in *Cien años de soledad* may be projected out and amplified to give universal implications. If, as the psychologist Jean Piaget maintains [in *Psychology and Epistemology*], an individual's stages of psychogenetic development are isomorphic to the various stages in the history of scientific thought, it may be safely posited that the transmutations in José Arcadio's conception of reality may be analogous to the development of scientific thought in the Western World.

WILLIAM PLUMMER

The Faulkner Relation

> *The writer's only responsibility is to his art. He will be completely ruthless if he's a good one. . . . If a writer has to rob his mother, he will not hesitate; the "Ode on a Grecian Urn" is worth any number of old ladies.*
>
> —WILLIAM FAULKNER, *Paris Review* interview with Jean Stein

Naturally, wanting to know more about the author after having had the top of my head blown off by *One Hundred Years of Solitude*, I looked around for interviews with Gabriel García Márquez. I learned that García Márquez is not keen on formal audiences with his admirers, in part because of a fear of becoming conscious where he should be unconscious, in greater part because he has yet to recover from the trauma of being the Latin American phenom of 1967. Prior to that date he had published four books in fifteen years to the lamentable tune of some five thousand copies sold. Suddenly, thanks to the chronicle of the Buendía family, García Márquez had an instant celebrity, comparable in its whirlwind intensity to Erica Jong's, as well as that rare popular-critical success on the order of Joseph Heller's with *Catch-22*. At one point new editions were spewing forth at the incredible rate of one a week.

The few interviews with García Márquez available in English offer a number of departures. But especially striking are the remarks about Faulkner, who might well be touted, by a thorough-going Bloomian, as the featured player in the Colombian writer's "family romance." *Influence* is, to say the least, a loaded word, and I don't want to tote Harold Bloom's cabalistic baggage. But the "relation" between García Márquez and

---

From *Fiction International* nos. 6/7 (1976). © 1976 by *Fiction International*, Joe David Bellamy, publisher.

Faulkner is unavoidable. Actually, *relation* is a better word for my purposes, for it enables not merely a discussion of influence, but a consideration of the two writer's shared stance before some third entity: say, the novel itself. Treating the Faulkner relation, however sketchily, is useful to getting at García Márquez's development, up to and including the new novel, *The Autumn of the Patriarch.*

In a 1968 interview, in Barcelona, García Márquez told Armando Duran, "The truth is that I had already published my first novel, *La hojarasca* (*Leafstorm*), when I started reading Faulkner by pure chance." To Duran's subsequent comment, "It seems as though Faulkner's influence bothers you," he replied:

> Of course it's not that it bothers me. I should rather take it as a compliment, since Faulkner is one of the great novelists of all times. What happens is that I do not understand very well the way in which the reviewers determine influences. In reality, a writer who knows what he is doing tries not to be like anyone else and works more on eluding than on imitating his favorite author.

Yet, writing a year later, Mario Vargas Llosa, a friend and fellow novelist, says that García Márquez "confessed" to him: "When I read Faulkner I discovered I wanted to become a writer."

In the summer of 1971, the furor over *One Hundred Years of Solitude* having abated, a more collected García Márquez advised Rita Guibert, again on the subject of influence:

> That's to say I would have written what I did anyhow without Borges and [Alejo] Carpentier, but not without Faulkner. And I also believe that after a certain moment—by searching for my own language and refining my work—I have taken a course aimed at eliminating Faulkner's influence, which is much in evidence in *Leafstorm* but not in *One Hundred Years.*

There will be more to say about *One Hundred Years* in a moment, but, first, a look at *Leafstorm*, and the bothersome Faulkner relation.

The *Leafstorm* (1955) turns on the promise made by the old Colonel to provide a decent burial for a mysterious doctor, who is hated by the townspeople and has just hanged himself. The immediate, present-tense conflict is between the Colonel and the town, which prefers that the doctor rot above ground. Little by little we learn that the doctor—called "the Frenchman," for reading French newspapers—came to Macondo twenty-five years ago; that the Colonel took him in; that the doctor practiced for a time, until the banana company possessed the town, bringing with it "the leaf storm" (the rubbish of the twentieth century) and its own doctors; that when the Frenchman's patients deserted him for the banana company's doctors, he closed up shop and closed himself off from the town. The crucial event: years later, the banana company and its personnel having left Macondo, taking prosperity with them, the townspeople turn to the reclusive doctor to treat the wounded of a local skirmish. The Frenchman refuses, saying he has lost his skills. From that night the town relentlessly seeks revenge. The enigmatic doctor practices just once more: he heals the old Colonel, who, in turn, promises to throw dirt on his grave to fend off the vultures.

The story is, basically, García Márquez's, and actually partakes of the history of his own Aracataca, which was subject to a leaf storm induced by the infamous United Fruit Company at the time of World War I. Yet the means of rendering, of giving fictional shape, smack unmistakably of Faulkner.

García Márquez told Rita Guibert that *Leafstorm* was his favorite book:

> It's the most spontaneous, the one I wrote with most difficulty and with fewer technical resources. . . . It seems to me a rather awkward, vulnerable book, but completely spontaneous . . . I know exactly how *Leafstorm* went straight from my guts onto the paper.

The first thing one notices about *Leafstorm* is the way the spontaneous spill is channeled. The narrative mode is lifted, quite without embarrassment, from *The Sound and the Fury* (and *As I Lay Dying*). Just as in *The Sound and the Fury* we are never made privy to Caddy's thoughts, although hers are the crucial actions in the novel, so in *Leafstorm* we are denied access to the doctor's consciousness. We are limited to the mental life of the old Colonel, his daughter, and the daughter's son, whose thoughts and emotions are precipitated by the doctor. We are introduced to the story proper through the boy's point of view, and we know right away that we've been here before. The boy is seeing his first corpse, but he does not *see* so much as *sense:* "The vapor that rises up from Mama's head, warm and smelling like a cupboard." It's his function to render the preparation of the corpse graphic, tactile, to fix the atmosphere of the event, which, in turn, is meant to resonate as a symbol for the post-leaf storm state of the town, and, probably, for (Latin American) civilization itself. "The heat won't let you breathe in the closed room. You can hear the sun buzzing in the streets, but that's all." *Personification* ("The heat"): Faulkner's economical means of conveying the unadorned, primitivistic, therefore reliable, nature of Benjy. And *Synesthesia* ("sun buzzing"): Faulkner's device to render Benjy's emotional turmoil, whose very inarticulateness is poetical and, of course, true, because undissembling. The boy's function is a modest version of Benjy's: both introduce us to a decadent, claustrophobic world, which finds its expression in death.

And sex, of course. "The front door and the back," Faulkner called sex and death in *Soldiers' Pay.* The mother is the Quentin of *Leafstorm*, with a lot of Rosa Coldfield thrown in. Like Quentin she suffers from an acute sensitivity to the passing of time: *"It's still Wednesday in Macondo."* Like Rosa she is rigorous in her puritanic morality, and is resentful and frustrated. She has been married to Martin, a brash young adventurer, whose "design" recalls Thomas Sutpen's; she, too, has been deserted. The mother's self-hatred and sexual frustration find a locus in the Frenchman (Faulkner's Frenchman of "Frenchman's Bend"?), whom she vilifies for "his way of looking at women with his lustful, greedy dog eyes." That the doctor is a surrogate for Martin is made all but explicit by her thought that "no place would be more appropriate for [Martin] than the small locked room" vacated by the Frenchman.

The old Colonel retains the moral code of the Sartorises, especially the ante-bellum passion for honor: he takes on the whole town to fulfill his promise to the dead man and, in the process, puts his daughter and grandson through hell. Yet the Colonel is not as obsessive as the most passionate Sartoris, and he often sounds remarkably like Faulkner himself at the University of Virginia or West Point, trotting out the old verities—the Colonel's variant being "pity, amazement and sorrow." Just as the boy's function is to immerse the reader in the immediate corruption of the scene, and the mother's is to confuse sex and death, the Colonel's job is to offer historical perspective and to bring out the Frenchman by trying to understand him, although the Colonel is severely limited by a much too conventional mind. He is alternately the Sartoris, Faulkner, and Dilsey of the piece.

All this is by way of suggesting how *Leafstorm* went straight from García Márquez's guts onto paper. Perhaps even more transparent than the conscription of Faulkner's characters and narrative method is the appropriation of his overall strategy: the strategy of delay, of withholding information from the reader, a technique Faulkner himself doubtless stole from the likes of Raymond Chandler. What's more, now and again one hears actual Faulknerian cadences:

> Someone must have brought the news to the main road, but it occurred to no one to ask what the priest was doing in that hut. They must have thought that he was related to the woman in some way, just as she must have abandoned the hut because she thought the priest had orders to occupy it, or that it was church property, or simply out of fear that they would ask her why she had lived for more than two years in a hut that didn't belong to her without paying rent or without any one's permission. Nor did it occur to the delegation to ask for any explanation, neither then nor any time after, because the priest wouldn't accept any speeches.

We hear Faulkner, getting his usual rhetorical mileage less from what actually transpired than from what did not and, still more, from *what must have:* all related in serial negatives, and in subordinate clauses that don't qualify and clarify so much as multiply and opacify.

There are at least three problems evident in *Leafstorm* that must be met before García Márquez will be capable of *One Hundred Years of Solitude*. First and easiest: García Márquez is not an experimentalist; the novel does not present itself to him as a formal challenge, as it does, in part, to Faulkner. "What is form," William Gass asks in *On Being Blue,* "but a bumbershoot held up against the absence of all cloud." García Márquez is not temperamentally suited to the Quixotic tilt with established forms; no bumbershoots for bumbershoots' sake, for him. He simply hasn't the patience to do justice to the scheme of alternating limited points of view that he adopts from Faulkner. With the latter, we feel that through Benjy, Quentin, and Jason we get a full picture of Caddy; actually we don't care whether we do or not, because the emotional life of the three and the formal experiments with interior monologue are engrossing enough. Indeed, the extreme formal predicaments Faulkner gets into seem to give him juice, push him into occasions for rhetoric. In *Leafstorm* García Márquez's handling of the mechanics (switching back and forth in time, cross-referring among the monologues) is "awkward," at best, and he has so little investment in these three Faulknerian characters that not only can he scarcely bring us to care about them; he is incapable of endowing them with distinct voices. We find ourselves longing for entry to the doctor's consciousness, which is so assiduously avoided in this first novel.

Which brings me to my second and allied point: García Márquez is not a *modern*, but a *post-modern*. He is not interested in being "difficult," formally difficult, the way Joyce, Eliot and Faulkner were. It might even be said that the major impediment to García Márquez's progress to *One Hundred Years of Solitude* is modernism itself: I refer not only to modernism's insistence on difficulty as the measure of artistic integrity and achievement, but, above all, to its reactionism. The Latin American critics refer to the tandem limitations of "realism" and "subjectivism" in García Márquez's early work. But what they are pointing to, without saying as much, is the Colombian writer's inability to respond creatively to his own age. His early fiction recalls Joyce's *Dubliners* or Faulkner's *Soldiers' Pay:* reactionary works, concerned to *get* the paralysis (an explicit theme in each) of the modern era. The theme of paralysis, "the leaf storm," while it energized Joyce, acted virtually by contagion to stultify the imaginations of Faulkner and García Márquez.

My third point. To write *One Hundred Years of Solitude*, García Márquez does not need to "elude" Faulkner, as his apparent misreading of the latter assumes. Rather he needs to replicate Faulkner's model, the paradigm D. H. Lawrence located in "The Leatherstocking Tales" and called the American myth. García Márquez must regress, in Lawrence's words, "from old age to golden youth," from feeling jaded and cynical to being open and capable of wonder. I say replicate Faulkner, because Faulkner the failed poet slumming in the novel with *Soldiers' Pay* and *Mosquitoes* needed to slough his world-weary *fin de siècle* and post–*Waste Land* attitudes before he could write the first version of "The Spotted Horses" story (chapter four in *The Hamlet*), his first Yoknapatawpha venture and itself a parable about the confrontation of innocence and the modern, Snopesist age. "The Spotted Horses" story, written in 1927, is the transitional work between *Soldiers' Pay* and *Mosquitoes*, the apprentice fiction, and the *The Sound and the Fury*. It is a wondrous, high energy depiction of grown men casting aside all propriety, all concern about worldly profit, expending their last cents to purchase phantasmal particolored nags that they know they will never be able to catch and break and, what's more, that they know belong to Flem Snopes, Faulkner's archetypal modern con man. The horses, meretricious as Gatsby's green light, are the stuff of wonder in the dissolute, duplicitous modern world; they are wonderful not for any intrinsic value, but when perceived from the standpoint of innocence. And innocence, the assumption of it almost by force of will, is requisite to the fiction of both Faulkner and García Márquez.

II

To do just the opposite is also a form of imitation, and the definition of imitation ought by rights to include both.

—G. C. LICHTENBERG

In the ten years between *Leafstorm* and the writing of *One Hundred Years of Solitude*, García Márquez wrote numerous short stories and the novella, *No One Writes to the Colonel,* as well as another, untranslated novel, *La mala hora* (The Bad Hour). In these works the prose is overhauled, stripped of extravagance, made merely efficient. The Faulkner relation is stood on its head: García Márquez "jestingly" tells Vargas Llosa, on the subject of Faulknerian rhythms: "I have fought them off by reading Hemingway." Nevertheless, in 1960, sponsored by the Cuban agency, Prensa Latina, he makes a pilgrimage through the American South.

García Márquez had the bad luck to be born too late. By the time he arrived in 1928, as Vargas Llosa tells it, Aracataca's "paradise and hell belonged to the past, and present reality consisted of a limbo made up of poverty, heat and routine." Not exactly inspiring. Indeed, the original title of *La mala hora* was "Este pueblo de mierda" (This Shitty Town), a charmless index to his feelings about his geographical and temporal situation. Clearly, it was necessary for García Márquez to "invent" another world, an environment hospitable to his imagination and rhetoric: "A World Elsewhere," Richard Poirier would call it.

"The world was so recent that many things lacked names, and in order to indicate them it was necessary to point." So begins *One Hundred Years*. It would be all but impossible for me to summarize the novel: suffice to say that it is a family chronicle, not in the mold of *The Forsyte Saga* but of *Absalom, Absalom!*; that it begins with the escape from civilization to "the territory ahead," where José Arcadio Buendía and a select band establish their own community, where José Arcadio and Ursula Buendía plant a family tree that bears a seemingly endless harvest of José Arcadios, Aurelianos, Remedios and Amarantas.

García Márquez is engrossed by the same spectacle as Faulkner: that of innocence confronting the inscrutable artifacts and attitudes of the contemporary world, and of the innocent's always awesome, often farcical attempt to make sense of them. In Faulkner, Thomas Sutpen comes down from the mountains, knocks at the front door of the mansion, and, abruptly, has to sort out the meaning of being sent around to the servant's entrance; or Joe Christmas steals a taste of toothpaste and, unaccountably, is rewarded for his *crime*. Faulkner is energized, provoked to acrobatic prose, by the bafflement of his protagonists and their groping efforts toward making sense, toward drawing a moral from what has happened to them. While Faulkner's hero generally ends up "outraged" by the collision of innocence with the world of experience, the *One Hundred Years* counterpart is invariably awestruck. When afforded a look at an "enormous, transparent block with infinite internal needles in which the light of the sunset was broken up into colored stars," José Arcadio Buendía declares it the largest diamond in the world. When advised by the gypsy owners, "No, it's ice," José Arcadio Buendía pays five reales to touch it, "as his heart filled with fear and jubilation at the contact with mystery." "This is the greatest invention of our times," he exclaims.

José Arcadio Buendía sees his first daguerreotype and is moved to the project of photographing God; he perceives the invention of false teeth as Ponce de Leon did the fountain of youth; independently, from pure astronomical speculation, he makes the prodigious discovery that the earth is round! José Arcadio Buendía, innocence itself, typifies García Márquez's regression to "golden youth." Plenitude and heterogeneity, the world perceived from the perspective of childhood, are the new notes. To wit: José Arcadio Buendía and Ursula marry in spite of the oracle that their union will result in a monster with a pig's tail. Ursula determines that she will remain chaste rather than defy the prophecy; she fashions a chastity belt from sailcloth and iron. During the day José Arcadio Buendía sublimates with his fighting cocks, but:

> At night they would wrestle for several hours in an anguished violence that seemed to be a substitute for the act of love until popular intuition got whiff of something irregular and the rumor spread that Ursula was still a virgin a year after her marriage because her husband was impotent. José Arcadio Buendía was the last one to hear the rumor.

The husband is always the last to know. No fairy tale or romance element, no cliché, no device of melodrama or overdone psychoanalytic idea is beneath García Márquez, who is suddenly a connoisseur of twentieth-century dreck; someone Barthelme might tip his hat to.

Above all, *One Hundred Years of Solitude* is fun. It is not "difficult," but wholly accessible; it is told in a seamless anecdotal style that García Márquez credits to his grandmother, who was the source of much of the novel's fantastic-historical material. It is an utterly preposterous novel, written less to "elude" Faulkner, finally, than to counter the tedious anti-imperialist and "committed" fiction of such Latin American heavies as Miguel Asturias, the Guatemalan Nobel laureate. Much of the fun is in its literary reflexiveness and allusiveness. Early in the novel José Arcadio wraps a red cloth around his head and goes off with the gypsies, as the novel's protagonists have been wont from Fielding to Lawrence. So, too, *One Hundred Years* would hardly merit the designation, novel, without the timely and time-honored novelistic revelation that José Arcadio and Rebeca, apparent brother and sister, are not related at all, and thus can safely, legally, consummate their passion. At one point the Wandering Jew himself passes through Macondo, causing "a heat wave so intense that birds broke through window screens to come to die in the bedrooms." Colonel Aureliano Buendía is elaborately and archly invested with a ubiquity that seems meant to recall Moby Dick (and Marlon Brando's Zapata?), while Remedios the Beauty, otherworldly in her bovine voluptuousness, is clearly Faulkner's Eula abducted from *The Hamlet.*

In a novel so hospitable to the full range of the author's imagination, it is not surprising that refugees from other fictional worlds are welcomed. Colonel Lorenzo Gavilán disappears from view in Carlos Fuentes's *The Death of Artemio Cruz,* but surfaces in Macondo; Victor Hughes and Rocamadour, characters from novels by Alejo Carpentier and Julio Cortázar, also find a home in *One Hundred Years*. The novel is, as well, in a small way, a *roman à clef:* just one example, Aureliano Buendía discovers the bookstore of the Catalonian scholar and starts a friendship with Alvaro, Germán, Alfonso, and Gabriel—Gabriel being García Márquez, of course, and the other three, close friends from Barranquilla, Colombia. What's more, there are numerous private allusions: each date corresponds to some friend's birthday, one character wants to give his children the names of García Márquez's kids.

García Márquez's energizing recognition—and one made by Faulkner before him—is that everything is permitted the novelist, who is under the sole obligation to be interesting. Nothing is sacrosanct, least of all our deepest fears and desires, which lend themselves wonderfully to grotesque, comic depiction. There are many instances, but one will have to stand for all: the "premature adolescent" Aureliano José's passion for his mature maiden aunt, Amaranta. Long in the habit of inviting Aureliano José under her mosquito netting to lie with her in an increasingly less innocent way, Amaranta discovers one day that "the kissing games with a child" have grown into "an autumnal passion." She tries to end it. Aureliano goes off to the wars, but deserts, only to return as "a barracks animal" to engage in the war of the sexes.

> He had fled from her in an attempt to wipe out her memory, not only through distance but by means of a muddled fury that his companions at arms took to be boldness, but the more her image wallowed in the dunghill of the war, the more the war resembled Amaranta.

This is Leslie Fiedler's turf and familiar ground to Faulkner: the relentless contention between the male and female principles; the discombobulated male making a mockery of his revered celibate concepts of bravery and honor, the abstract masculine ideals of war, then deserting to at once conquer and submit to the Great Mother (the aunt being, of course, a surrogate for mom), the dunghill and the primal swim.

García Márquez images deep fears and desires in *One Hundred Years of Solitude*, but the contours are comic; for this is not finally a gothic novel for all its cheapjack gothic machinery. The oedipal goings-on are treasured by García Márquez as a source of rhetorical capital, rather than as profound insights into the human condition. It is the rhetoric occasioned by the Freudian idea that he is after.

> "Can a person marry his own aunt?" he asked, startled.
>
> "He not only can do that," a soldier answered him, "but we're fighting this war against the priests so that a person can marry his own mother."

There *is*, however, something "serious" going on in *One Hundred Years of Solitude*, a book within the book. True, what one probably remembers most after a first reading is the wonder-filled treatment of folk magic, the lovely license taken with fantasy and reality. The people of Macondo are so innocent, so close to elemental truth, that they are clairvoyant; a population of Jeane Dixons and Uri Gellers. In perhaps the most memorable incident, a priest, rebuffed in his efforts to tithe, convinces the infidels by a latter-day equivalent of walking on water: he ascends six inches from the ground by drinking a mug of apparently transubstantiated chocolate. In another instance, Pietro Crespi, a rejected suitor of Amaranta, throws the entire town into an "angelic stupor" by giving sweet vent to his anguish on his zither.

These incidents are handled brightly, though often with the sentimentalism the Colombian author revels in. The Pietro Crespi episode, however, points to a subject that is treated elsewhere with notable seriousness: the theme of solitude. When García Márquez writes about Colonel Aureliano Buendía, the tone sobers; the awe continues, actually intensifies, but the playfulness largely subsides. The details and consequences of power retained, virtually exuded by a figure of the stature of José Martí or Che Guevara, a living legend—the spectacle of omnipotent solitude requires of García Márquez a voice no less rhetorical, no less energized, but less whimsical, a voice resonant with irony-free "significance." It is not so much Colonel Aureliano Buendía's sentencing of his oldest friends to death by firing squad that chills us. Rather it is the Colonel's decision that no human being, not even his mother Ursula, can come within ten feet of him. Still more chilling is his finding in the chalk circle, which his aides draw around him wherever he stops, the perfect emblem for his solitude, his complete solipsism and absolute power.

What commands García Márquez's imagination only in part in *One Hundred Years of Solitude*, and what will attain total hegemony over his comic resources in *The Autumn of the Patriarch,* rings clear in this passage, which turns on another assassination.

> "It's quite simple, colonel," [an aide] proposed. "He has to be killed."
>
> Colonel Aureliano Buendía was not alarmed by the coldness of the proposition but by the way in which, by a fraction of a second, it had anticipated his own thought.
>
> "Don't expect me to give an order like that," he said.
>
> He did not give it, as a matter of fact. But two weeks later General Teofilo Vargas was cut to bits by machetes in ambush and Colonel Aureliano Buendía assumed the main command . . . . The intoxication of power began to break apart under waves of discomfort. Searching for a cure against the chill, he had the young officer who had proposed the murder of General Teofilo Vargas shot. His orders were being carried out even before they were given, even before he thought of them, and they always went much beyond what he would have dared have them do.

III

> *I'm no longer interested in writing comic novels. . . . I'm wary now of the "safety" inherent in the comic form. . . . From now on I want to come still closer to terror.*
>
> —JOHN HAWKES, *TriQuarterly* 30

It is possible to think of the descent from Faulkner as two-tined. One might, of course, point to the arch mythopoetizing of "The Bear" as an important patrimony for Faulkner's literary progeny. But Faulkner here was too deeply indebted to Joyce and Frazer to be considered a "first cause." A more obvious debt of his sons is the comic-grotesque legacy, whose main bequest is *The Hamlet;* the most obvious beneficiaries are the John Hawkes of *Second Skin* and, especially, Stanley Elkin. Yet the greatest windfall for the tribe of Faulkner has been the surreal and nightmarish inferiority of *Light in August* (to be distinguished from the more controlled and artful Nighttown section of *Ulysses*). Interestingly, the most distinguished members of the tribe, Hawkes and Jerzy Kosinski, qualify by psychic affinity rather than influence. With *The Autumn of the Patriarch*, García Márquez again parallels Faulkner's pattern: his movement is from reactionism to comedy to comic nightmare.

At first glance *The Autumn of the Patriarch* appears to be an "experimental novel." There are no paragraphs and the sentences are interminable, but they are not, strictly, Faulknerian sentences.

They are without grammatical or rhetorical difficulty, and although the language is often passionate, we seldom sense, as with Faulkner, that the full volume of a lake is being drained through a three-inch pipe. The same seamless anecdotal style prevails, but the old sign posts have been removed. *Autumn* appears to be strained through a French sieve: it is not consciously antistory, anticharacter, etc.; but there is no proper story, only a situation; there is only one "real" character (abetted by numerous foils), and he is more a locus of ideas than an integrated being. *The Autumn of the Patriarch* is a narrow, intense act of the imagination—what Albert Guerard calls an "anti-realist" novel; it mingles two parts fantasy and one part reality, returning a hybrid of grotesque comedy and horror; it is concerned exclusively with the machinations of mind and their conversion into a rhetoric of psychoanalytical ideas.

The novel is divided into six sections, each of forty to fifty pages, each beginning with pretty much the same situation: the dictator's body has been found in his sprawling, decrepit palace by unidentified revolutionaries who enter with care, for the death of the dictator, who may be 250 years old when he dies for good, has been declared prematurely many times before. The revolutionaries traipse through rooms notable for the incongruous mix of the old and the new, the real and the fantastic, the seemingly meaningful and the curiously trite.

Among the camellias and butterflies we saw the berlin from

> stirring days, the wagon from the time of the plague, the coach from the year of the comet, the hearse from the progress of order, the sleep-walking limousine of the first century of peace . . . we went up to the main floor along a bare stone stairway where the opera-house carpeting had been torn by the hoofs of cows, and from the first vestibule on down to the private bedrooms we saw the ruined offices and protocol salons through which the brazen cows wandered, eating the velvet curtains and nibbling at the trim on the chairs, we saw heroic portraits of saints and soldiers thrown to the floor among the broken furniture and fresh cow flops, we saw a dining room that had been eaten up by the cows, the music room profaned by the cows' breakage, the domino tables destroyed and the felt on the billiard tables cropped by the cows, abandoned in a corner we saw the wind machine, the one which counterfeited any phenomenon from the four points of the compass so that the people in the house could bear up under their nostalgia for the sea that had gone away.

A waking dream scape, the dream-work painting its own emphases, insisting on the cows, who are obviously out of place, are displaced, the censoring furies of reality avenging the flight into a fantasy of stirring days, comets, and wind machines.

From the initial meditation on the dictator's body, each section moves fluidly back and forth in time, at last settles on the dictator's "relationship" (too normalized a word) with one or two characters, whether it be mother, wife, lover, or friend. The mechanics of the chapters are virtually identical, so I will select just one for extended description and discussion, the first one.

The first section treats the relationship with Patricio Aragonés, the dictator's "perfect double," who had been found "without anyone's searching for him" (crucial language to García Márquez's intentions in *Autumn*), going from one Indian village to another, doing "a prosperous business of impostoring." Patricio Aragonés has the dictator's features, "the hand of a sensitive bride"; Patricio Aragonés's feet are tamped flat to match the dictator's feet of a sleepwalker, his nuts are pierced with a shoemaker's awl to duplicate the dictator's herniated testicles, he is made to drink turpentine to wash away the memory of reading and writing. Patricio Aragonés becomes "the most essential man to the seat of power"; he performs all the public ceremonies, takes care of the armed forces (instills paranoia among the branches). And now, with the presence of Patricio Aragonés, the dictator is able "to relax his concern with self-preservation," to drive out among his people and be loved, to become increasingly more decadent, to wallow "in the great slough of felicity," to tiptoe "like an evil thought in pursuit of the tame mulatto girls," to catch one alone and "make rooster love to her behind the office doors."

The pertinent analytical tool is Freud's *Interpretation of Dreams,* for clearly García Márquez is working the idea of wish-fulfillment. Patricio Aragonés springs onto the scene, "without anyone's searching for him," to gratify the absolute power of the dictator, who needs to divide in two, since his libidinal self will no longer toe the psychic line. The world of *Autumn of the Patriarch* is still further regressed than that of *One Hundred Years*, from innocence to infancy, where complete egoism is rampant, where the mechanism of sublimation is ineffectual. A form of Manichaeism reigns, not the forces of light versus those of the dark, but desire versus fear. The dictator's lusts assuaged, suddenly he perceives a series of omens and, of course, he is the only one to spot them, since everyone else in the novel is a figment and function of his egoistic solitude. He clings to Patricio Aragonés, but "his fierce struggle to exist twice was feeding the contrary suspicion that he was existing less and less." Patricio Aragonés must go. He does, fatally wounded by a poisoned dart, no more ordered by the dictator than the cutting up of General Teofilo Vargas by Colonel Aureliano Buendía.

The disposal of his double, in turn, provides the dictator with the opportunity to gratify yet another infant wish: to see the effect of his death on the rest of the world. The broad range of responses is affectingly conveyed by García Márquez's rhetoric, but before long the greatest fear of all is evinced: the rhythms of daily life return, business as usual. The world exists without him. The dictator returns in all his glory; much as the Duke in *Measure for Measure*, he deals out rewards and punishments, then proclaims a general amnesty and decides, à la Ben Franklin, "that the trouble with this country is that the people have too much time to think on their hands." In his most overdetermined symbolic stroke, the dictator establishes a free school in each province to teach *sweeping,*

> where the pupils fantasized by the presidential stimulus went on to sweep the streets after having swept their houses and then the nearby highways and roads so that piles of trash were carried back and forth from one province to another without anyone's knowing what to do with it in official processions with

> the national flag and large banners saying God Save The All Pure who watches over the cleanliness of the nation.

One wonders where García Márquez will go from *The Autumn of the Patriarch*. Every word of the novel, he told Rita Guibert, was written under great strain, as he felt the weight of the success of *One Hundred Years of Solitude*. He has said that he wants to start writing short stories again. One wonders whether he will, like Hawkes, completely extirpate playfulness from his writing. Let's hope that the pressure of being a public figure does not dry up his creative juice, make him into a mouthpiece for uncongenial ideas, reduce him to self-caricature: like the later Faulkner.

LOIS PARKINSON ZAMORA

The Myth of Apocalypse and Human Temporality in García Márquez's Cien años de soledad *and* El otoño del patriarca

For all our days are passed away in Thy wrath: we spend our years as a tale that is told.

—Psalm 90:9

The novels of Gabriel García Márquez are extended considerations of temporal reality, of the beginnings and ends of human beings and humanity. García Márquez's perspective is mythical and eschatological: he looks forward in time to create fictions of a future—a future that embodies the potential of past and present. Time is neither aimless nor endless: it is successive and purposeful, moving toward a meaningful end. It is this end that makes time finite and comprehensible, giving significance and shape to our temporal existence. Time unpunctuated by endings is intolerable: we need fictions of succession and ending to humanize time and deliver us, as Frank Kermode says [in *The Sense of an Ending*], "from the long meaningless attrition of time." The history of Macondo, presented whole by García Márquez in *Cien años de soledad* (1967), is a monumental fiction of succession and ending, a fiction of temporal fulfillment. Origin and ending are harmonized, temporal coherence is imposed by the comprehensive apocalyptic perspective of Melquíades's narrative. In *El otoño del patriarca* (1975), the apocalypse is political. Moral and social degeneration becomes a function of the political travesties of the general in the novel, his dictatorship an image of the last loosing of Satan, his prolonged

From *Symposium* 32, no. 1 (Spring 1978).

domination suggestive of the reign of the Beast which in Revelations signals the end of time. Gregory Rabassa has written: "The broadest tale of a people, and therefore of an individual, is more often than not elegaic or apocalyptic. Beowulf's funeral pyre is also sensed to be that of all the Geats." García Márquez's fictive world becomes our world, its inhabitants ourselves, as we attempt to understand our present time in terms of our past and our future.

The temporal structures of *Cien años de soledad* and *El otoño del patriarca* differ markedly from García Márquez's earlier short fiction. *El coronel no tiene quien le escriba* (1961) and *La mala hora* (1966) are structured chronologically, reflecting the journalistic training of their author in their tone of sober neutrality as well as their sequential narration; in *La hojarasca* (1955), the present is punctuated with characters' memories of the past, but the temporal organization of the narrative is nevertheless strictly chronological. It is in two short stories in the collection *Los funerales de la Mamá Grande* (1962) that García Márquez seems to free himself from the rigid realism of clock time by employing the temporal structure of the myth of apocalypse. "Un día después del sábado" and "Los funerales de la Mamá Grande" are stories about the end of time, about individual death and the death of the world: both assume that time is linear and limited, but both suggest in a highly comic mode the divagations and detours, the loops and turns that will be taken by human beings along the way toward the end of time.

In "Un día después del sábado," the approaching apocalypse is signaled not by horses with lions' heads breathing fire or by beasts with seven heads and ten horns rising out of the sea but by a quantity of dead birds. Father Antonio Isabel del Santísimo Sacramento del Altar, the ninety-four-year-old priest of Macondo, interprets the pre-apocalyptic portent, but compared to the fervent traditional apocalyptists, he is comically confused and lacking in conviction. Padre Antonio Isabel locates the agent of the catastrophe not in a horrific Antichrist embodying evil but in a peasant boy—in Macondo, briefly, because he has missed his train. The muddled priest labels the boy "El Judío Errante" but the label is of course ludicrous, as the townspeople and the reader know: the priest's preposterous "revelation" reduces the proportions of apocalyptic anxiety with laughter. "Los funerales de la Mamá Grande" parodies the hyperbole of the apocalyptists' descriptions of the end of the world with its own fantastically exaggerated account of the end of Big Mama, which is, in effect, the end of the world of Macondo. In fact, Big Mama and the world of Macondo are coterminous, but it has never occurred to anyone that she—or the town—might be mortal. Big Mama's possessions are limitless, including such abstract items as the rights of man, the meat problem, the purity of the language, and the high cost of living. Of course Big Mama is herself an abstraction, a caricature that comically distorts traditional apocalyptic concerns: her funeral is a comic saturnalia rather than a *dies irae*. By using the apocalypse, that mythic version of human and cosmic history, García Márquez can suggest the reality of chronological progression and yet imbue that reality with poetic dimensions and fantastical visions. It is his use of this myth in *Cien años de soledad* and *El otoño del patriarca* that I wish to examine.

Cien años de soledad is a novel about the finite duration of man's individual and collective existence. In one hundred years, the history of the Buendía family and of their town is chronicled from beginning to end. Like Revelation, *Cien años de soledad* sums up the Bible, projecting its patterns of creation, empire, decadence, renovation, catastrophe onto history. Like St. John of Patmos, García Márquez's narrator, Melquíades, stands outside time, recounting the past, present and future of Macondo from an atemporal point beyond the future: like St. John, Melquíades responds to the command, "Write the things which thou has seen, the things which are, and the things which shall be hereafter" (Rev. 1:19). Melquíades, "un fugitivo de cuantas plagas y catástrofes habían flagelado al género humano" whom death follows everywhere, "husmeándole los pantalones, pero sin decidirse a darle el zarpazo final," transcends time and his own mortality in order to record the mortal condition of the Buendías and their world. He constantly relates past events to subsequent events in a retrospective future tense, because the events for which the characters must wait are already known to him: for Melquíades, the future is past. He also relates past events to an even more remote past, revealing the lifespan of Macondo and its inhabitants with sweeping totality. Thus, in a room of the Buendía house where it is always March and always Monday, Melquíades unifies past, present and future in the timeless realm of his narrative art, concentrating "un siglo de episodios cotidianos de modo que todos coexistieran en un instante."

The temporal structure of *Cien años de soledad,* like apocalypse, is basically rectilinear rather than cyclical. Of course, human temporal reality is never merely flat or linear: García Márquez manages to convey in words the vagaries of our temporal condition, the unpredictable whimsy of time which makes moments seem endless and ages like moments, which makes Macondo's history seem to double back upon itself and describe circles in time. Several critics have commented on the cyclical movement inherent in Macondo's structure. Julio Ortega, Ricardo Gullón, and G. D. Carillo emphasize the repetition of the Buendía's names and personalities, the recurring events and activities from one generation to another, the seemingly endless series of futile civil wars that involve one character after another; Carmen Aruau describes Macondo as cyclical in the Spenglerian sense that the town participates in birth, growth, maturity, decline, death, and rebirth. This is certainly so during the course of Macondo's one-hundred-year history, but those one hundred years do come to an end, a rebirth ultimately fails to occur. García Márquez concludes his novel on this very point: "las estirpes condenadas a cien años de soledad no tenían una segunda oportunidad sobre la tierra." Thus, the endless generational cycles of the Buendías and the recurring sequences of events are in fact finite and reach their end: "la historia de la familia era un engranaje de repeticiones irreparables, una rueda giratoria que hubiera seguido dando vueltas hasta la eternidad, de no haber sido por el desgaste progresivo e irremediable del eje." José Arcadio Buendía's city of mirrors, with its seemingly infinite self-reflections, proves itself in fact an unrepeatable mirage: "estaba previsto que la cuidad de los espejos (o los espejismos) sería arrasada por el viento y desterrada de la memoria de los hombres": the end of the Buendía line is anticipated from its beginning.

Eschatological pressure is inherent in the temporal organization of the narrative: the phrase "muchos años después" begins the novel and is repeated frequently. As the narrative progresses, "muchos años después" becomes "algunos años después," "pocos años después," then "pocos meses después": the end of the history of Macondo approaches relentlessly. The decline of Macondo, which begins with the banana boom, is filled with reminders that the "huracán de la compañía bananera" is an anticipation of the "viento profético que años después había de borrar a Macondo de la faz de la tierra." "Los acontecimientos que habían de darle el golpe mortal"—the oppression of the banana company, the strike and massacre of the banana company workers, the ensuing flood—are explicit omens of the inevitable moment when Macondo will become "un pavoroso remolino de polvo y escombros centrifugado por la cólera del huracán biblico." The cataclysm occurs at the moment the last surviving Buendía, whose name is significantly Aureliano *Babilonia,* completes the deciphering of Melquíades's coded history of his family. He understands that the family's history has been fulfilled, that the child with a pig's tail, long predicted, has arrived. The end of the apocalyptic manuscript and the end of time coincide: in a luminous moment of eschatological insight, Aureliano Babilonia is able to see his history whole: "El primero de la estirpe está amarrado en un árbol y al último se lo están comiendo las hormigas."

Just as the whole history of Macondo is revealed, so the whole history of the characters is revealed, their beginnings constantly related to their ends by Melquíades, from his point of view beyond the end. Colonel Aureliano Buendía's long career is summarized before its exposition in the fiction: long before his death is described, Melquíades tells us that all that is left of his illustrious life is a street that bears his name, and indeed, "según declaró pocos años antes de morir de viejo, ni siquiera eso esperaba." Meme, one of the ill-fated Buendías, experiences a tragic love affair as a young girl. Melquíades quickly recapitulates the rest of her life in terms of her tragic love for Mauricio Babilonia; she enters a convent, thinking about her lover, "y seguiría pensando en él todos los días de su vida, hasta la remota madrugada de otoño en que muriera de vejez, con sus nombres cambiados y sin haber dicho nunca una palabra, en un tenebroso hospital de Cracovia." Meme's individual span is related to the collective span when Melquíades comments, as she leaves Macondo, "el tren pasó por la llanura de amapolas donde estaba todavía el costillar carbonizado del galeón español, y salió luego al mismo aire diáfano y al mismo mar espumoso y sucio donde casi un siglo antes fracasaron las ilusiones de José Arcadio Buendía."

All the characters in *Cien años de soledad* feel the pressures of time from two directions: past and future, memories and premonitions burden the present and separate the characters from one another. Unlike many twentieth-century novels, in which the hero, in existential fashion, leaves his past behind in order to remake himself according to his own design, García Márquez's characters are inextricably bound to their past. In *Studies in Human Time* Georges Poulet discusses "romantic nostalgia," which seems to describe the situation of the inhabitants of Macondo very accurately: "It is as if duration had been broken in the middle and man felt his life torn from him, ahead and behind. The romantic effort to form itself a being out of presentiment and memory ends in the experience of a double tearing of the self." The characters in *Cien años de soledad* constantly search on both sides of the moment for an escape from their solitude.

Memories are very important to the Buendías, for they offer the illusory possibility of transcending the momentary, or as Poulet puts it, the possibility of participating in duration. It is thus poignantly ironic that, throughout the novel, memories are associated not with duration but with death. The characters' most vivid memories are recounted as they realize that they are about to die: the novel begins with Colonel Aureliano Buendía's first memory as he awaits death before the firing squad. The memories of Arcadio, Aureliano Segundo, Meme also irrupt as they face death. José Arcadio Segundo sees a man shot, which "no era sólo su recuerdo más antiguo, sino el único de su niñez." Memories are a special source of isolation for José Arcadio Segundo, for he remembers with painful clarity the slaughter of the workers by the forces of the banana company, a fact everyone else has been induced by those forces to forget. Aureliano Babilonia covers the corpse of the last Buendía, born with a pig's tail, and then wanders "sin rumbo por el pueblo desierto, buscando un desfiladero de regreso al pasado" as he awaits the hurricane. The characters' memories, as they are facing death, only serve to heighten their realization that the past is irretrievable and incommunicable. The wise Catalan bookstore owner speaks for most of the Buendías when insisting that "el pasado era mentira, que la memoria no tenía caminos de regreso, que toda primavera antigua era irrecuperable, y que el amor más desatinado y tenaz era de todos modos una verdad efímera." Memory accentuates, rather than mitigates, each Buendía's isolation in the time capsule of his own history.

Premonition, like memory, leads the characters to the inevitable fact of death. Amaranta has a premonition of her own end; she sees death, a woman dressed in blue with long hair and an antiquated look: "La muerte no le dijo cuándo se iba a morir ni si su hora estaba señalada . . . sino que le ordenó empezar a tejer su propia mortaja el próximo seis de abril." Amaranta devises ways to prolong her task and thus prolong her life, but her resignation to the truth of her presentiment of death is absolute: "era tan honda la conformidad con su destino que ni siquiera la inquietó la certidumbre de que estaban cerradas todas las posibilidades de rectificación." As she painstakingly stitches her shroud, she understands why Colonel Aureliano spent his last years making little gold fishes, melting them down, and making them again. She understands that the vicious circle of little gold fishes, like the intricate embroidery of her shroud, reduces the world to a surface and protects the inner self from suffering. She sails at dusk, carrying letters to the dead.

Úrsula, the matriarch of the Buendías, also knows with certainty when she will die. After the banana company massacre, it rains for four years, eleven months and two days: She is waiting until the rain stops to die. Úrsula, in the clairvoyance of her decrepitude, perceives a progressive breakdown in time itself, realizing that a sentence has been passed upon her by time: "Pensaba que antes, cuando Dios no hacía con los meses y los años las mismas trampas que hacían los turcos al medir una yarda de percal, las cosas eran diferentes." She knows that "el mundo se va acabando poco a poco," that there is nothing in the future to assuage her solitude. It is clear that not only Úrsula but the whole town of Macondo is waiting for the rain to clear in order to die. One of the Buendías observes Macondo's inhabitants, "sentados en las salas con la mirada absorta y los brazos cruzados, sintiendo transcurrir un tiempo entero, un tiempo sin desbravar." From the epoch of the flood, time stretches undifferentiated before Macondo: all that can be anticipated is the end of time.

Memory and premonition have not always reinforced the solitude of the characters' present: in prelapsarian Macondo, the past and the future are scarcely distinguished from the present, for time is unified in innocence. Thus memory and premonition enhance the present, and do indeed allow the earliest Buendías to participate in duration. José Arcadio Buendía founds Macondo in a "paraíso de humedad y silencio, anterior al pecado original" where the men in his expedition "se sintieron abrumados por sus recuerdos más antiguos." The most intriguing of the gypsies' inventions for José Arcadio are "el aparato para olvidar los malos recuerdos, y el emplasto para perder el tiempo": indeed, suggests the narrator, José Arcadio must have wanted to invent a memory machine in order to remember all of the wonderful things the gypsies brought to Macondo. The young and innocent town even survives the plague of forgetfulness, preserving its memories by labelling everything and describing its use. José Arcadio's premonitions are not about death but, on the contrary, about the existence of the Buendías *"per omnia secula seculorum."* In the paradise of early Macondo, "el tiempo puso las cosas en su puesto": José Arcadio is a prophet who guides his people to the promised land which, like Israel, represents the fulfillment of history.

Not long after the founding of Macondo, José Arcadio's prophetic vision is replaced by the apocalyptic vision of his heirs. This shift from prophetic to apocalyptic eschatology occurred during the course of Hebrew history as well. With the growth of the great empires of Persia, Greece, Rome, and with the consequent political powerlessness of the Hebrew people, the contradiction between prophetic ideals and the actual experience of the nation became more and more apparent. The prophets' vision of their history as moving toward the establishment of a community based on a special relationship with Yahweh seemed less and less likely in view of their contemporary historical situation. The apocalyptists began to replace the prophets, insisting on a radical change or break in history, when the present age would end and only the righteous would survive the eschatological revolution.

Similarly, early in Macondo's history, José Arcadio's prophetic eschatology can justifiably envision a luminous city with great glass houses, a dazzling new community separated physically and morally from the old world of temporal decay. After all, he has left the old world behind, arriving full of insight into the possibilities of moral freedom in a new world. Certainly he conforms to Earl Rovit's description of the "seminal image" of American literature, "man against the sky, the lone figure in an infinite cosmos, trying either to come to terms with the cosmos or force the cosmos to come to terms with him." For a brief moment, Macondo remains balanced between the terms of the cosmos and those of José Arcadio, but inevitably death, war, pestilence, and the banana company intrude upon his Arcadia. It is the breakdown of the patriarch's perpetual motion machine that heralds the shift from prophetic to apocalyptic eschatology: with the failure of his perpetual motion machine, José Arcadio is forced to recognize that time is discontinuous, that Macondo is no longer a timeless paradise. With this realization, an old man with white hair appears to José Arcadio. He is Prudencio Aguilar, whom José Arcadio has killed years before, and who signals the advent of death in Macondo. Prudencio's appearance initiates Macondo's apocalyptic progress, just as the appearance of a man whose "hairs were white like wool" initiates the apocalyptic vision of St. John. It is José Arcadio's realization about time that drives him crazy: he begins by imposing names confidently on his inchoate new world, and ends up babbling in medieval Latin. He is tied to a chestnut tree and there he remains, insensible to the apocalyptic decline and destruction of the city he prophesied would endure forever.

If *Cien años de soledad* is about the history of the Buendías and Macondo, it is also about the deciphering of the manuscript recording and preserving that history, and about the equivocations inherent in recording temporal reality in words. Melquíades's words chronicle Macondo's annihilation and yet insure its permanence. It is with words that he transmutes the temporal world of its history into a timeless artifact—the novel itself—which survives the biblical hurricane intact. Melquíades "concentró un siglo de episodios cotidianos, de modo que todos coexistieran en un instante," the timeless instant of his verbal artifice; and yet, his artifice is composed of verbs in the past, present and future tenses, of events filtered through the veil of time passed or time to come. And just as we have recognized that memory deceives and betrays the Buendías and their search for temporal continuity, so we must also recognize that memory assures their survival. Melquíades's manuscript is a response to his need to remember, to deny time's annihilation, to relate beginning to end with words. He returns to Macondo after dying on the dunes of Singapore because he cannot stand the cruel and irrevocable forgetfulness of death.

Faithful to life, he stays in Macondo, first operating a daguerreotype laboratory—where he fastens the whole Buendía family "en una edad eterna sobre una lámina de metal tornasol"—then installing himself in his timeless room to remember and record one hundred years of solitude. As Aureliano Babilonia understands that the end of the parchments and the end of Macondo will coincide, he mistakenly assumes Macondo will be "desterrada de la memoria de los hombres." In the agony of his own impermanence, he fails to recognize the enduring nature of Melquíades's art. And, of course, even Melquíades is annihilated in the end, an arbitrary creation of Gabriel García Márquez like the other characters, as much a fiction of the novelist-artificer as the Buendías. The novel's apocalyptic ending is the choice of the novelist, as fictional as its beginning or any part of its one-hundred-year history. Nevertheless, the arbitrary invention of García Márquez, like the paradigms of apocalypse, is elaborated in order to elucidate the origins and endings of the individual and his culture. If in our time, with our lengthening scale of history, the end has become an individual predicament and we find it unlikely that our individual and collective endings will coincide, as they do for the Buendías and Macondo, we nevertheless gain understanding of our human condition, with its inevitable end, from the apocalyptic fiction of Melquíades and Gabriel García Márquez. The temporal structure of their art imposes form upon our formless reality and gives meaning to our present by placing it in the context of an end.

El otoño del patriarca presents the chaotic and violent ambience of a pre-apocalyptic world, a world without moral discrimination or human decency, a world denied temporal coherence by the tyranny of force. The Latin American country in which the novel is set is suffocating under the prodigiously evil domination of an aging dictator, a political Antichrist; the arid wasteland that he creates with his brutality corresponds to the world of the pre-apocalyptic stage called the transition. The period of transition does not properly belong to either the end or to the age preceding it, but is an interregnum having its mythological origin in the three and one-half year reign of the beast described in Revelation. St. John describes the beast: he is "like unto a leopard, and his feet were as the feet of a bear, and his mouth as the mouth of a lion" (Rev. 13:2). He is specifically a political scourge: commentators agree that he is meant to represent the pagan state, in particular the Roman Empire, with its seven heads representing the seven Roman emperors who had been given divine honors and were thus guilty of blasphemy. The mood of the transition period is that of the most grotesque nightmare: disorder and dislocation of man's personal and social relationships, utter confusion of truth and falsehood, reality and appearance, and abject fear of the future are its features. The general of García Márquez's novel and his benighted reign of terror epitomize the pre-apocalyptic period of Satan's last loosing.

The chaos of the general's realm is everywhere apparent. Each of the six chapters begins with a description of the "fabulous disarray" of the palace after the general's death, related by a collective narrative voice, that of the people who have survived the general and have timorously entered the "rubble pits of the vast lair of power." The disorder and neglect of the government house are rendered from many points of view. An American ambassador, in his "memorias prohibidas," describes the "muladar de papeles rotos y cagadas de animales y restos de comidas de perros dormidos en los corredores," and "la sala de audiencias donde las gallinas picoteaban los trigales ilusorios de los gobelinos y una vaca desgarraba para comérselo el lienzo del retrato de un arzobispo." The disorder and decay of the general's physical realm suggest its moral decay: even the general's own comments are punctuated with the phrase, "What a mess!" The spiritual desolation of the realm is suggested by its physical sterility: the general tries to grow a garden but it is eaten by the hogs and turns into a "dungheap of pestilential slime." St. John describes the poisoning of the waters, the drying up of the sea during the period of transition in Revelation. The general here actually sells the sea to the Americans to pay off the national debt. Nautical engineers carry it off to Arizona in numbered pieces, and the country is left a flickering inferno, reminiscent of Satan's realm in *Paradise Lost,* "el horizonte instantáneo de relámpagos pálidos del crater de ceniza del mar vendido" visible below the "cuidad dispersa y humeante." And lest we imagine that the contrary of political disorder is order, or that the moral degeneration of the general's world is reversible, García Márquez introduces José Ignacio Sáenz de la Barra. The diabolical political terrorist establishes order in the form of a remarkably efficient organization, the better to torture and murder and plunder. He describes his activities as "peace within order" and "progress within order," and justifies his cruelty by saying, "tuvimos que acudir a este recurso ilícito para preservar del naufragio a la nave del progreso dentro del orden." So complete is the moral disorder of the dictator's world that it subverts and destroys the very conception of order.

The general, monster of iniquity and agent of pre-apocalyptic chaos, is in absolute control of the lives of his subjects, of their physical and moral status; he controls the country's natural resources, its weather, even the time of day. He is often described in terms of divinity (either as God's enemy or as His replacement), and his activities are an ironic parody of Christ's: he is "asediado por una muchedumbre de leprosos, ciegos y paralíticos que suplicaban de sus manos la sal de la salud, y políticos de letras y aduladores impávidos que lo proclamaban corregidor de los terremotos, los eclipses, los años bisiestos y otros errores de Dios." When his boat enters the rural settlements, the people receive him with Easter drums, thinking that the "times of glory" had arrived: "que viva el macho, gritaban, bendito él que viene en nombre de la verdad, gritaban." The general is the Antichrist who orchestrates the last days, and he is utterly ruthless in exercising his authority: with the slightest hint of insubordination—and often without it—he wreaks instant reprisal. He rapes a woman and then has her husband cut into very small pieces because he knows the man would be a mortal enemy, if allowed to live. When a faithful underling is suspected of treason, the general has him roasted, stuffed with pine nuts and aromatic herbs, steeped with spices, garnished with cauliflower and laurel leaves and a sprig of parsley in his mouth, and served to his comrades for dinner.

It is evident that *El otoño del patriarca* is not written in any conventional novelistic mode: with its grotesque extremes, its outlandish images, its exaggerated horrors, it is in fact a caricature of conventional fiction, presenting comic distortions and fantastic perversions of normal novelistic material. The social setting and plot of *Cien años de soledad* is abandoned. Patterns of poetic association, images which project mental realities, fears, dreams, nightmares, and suggestive gestures replace the discursive movement of Melquíades's manuscript. Of course, *Cien años de soledad* is also a poetic novel, but the imagery is used less to project mental realities than to create a novelistic ambience suggestive of man's prodigious capacities for both good *and* evil, love *and* hatred. Now images of decay describe the country's political and moral autumn; images also suggest its seething and repressed violence. The matriarch of the realm, the general's mother, literally rots away; the general's palace is described as having walls that ooze blood. The characters are also described by images. García Márquez uses a series of metonyms to portray the general: the gloved hands, the huge "graveyard" feet, the buzzing ears, the herniated testicle, the sound of the single gold spur. This metonymic description suggests the paranoia of the general (he never stands fully in view of the people), his insidious and stealthy exercise of power, and the elusive nature of evil itself. The general's extended reign is described as "el légamo sin orillas de la plenitud del otoño"; his inability to face temporal reality is suggested by his nagging suspicion "que el barco del universo había llegado a un puerto mientras el dormía." Like the apocalyptists, García Márquez employs fragmentary and distorted images to make his portrayal of evil the more suggestive and terrifying. The beasts, the dragons, Gog and Magog are abstract embodiments of evil; although the general is more specifically portrayed than the beasts of Revelation, he, like they, becomes a universal symbol of human suffering. Like the apocalyptists, García Márquez seems to feel that only through grotesquely exaggerated and fantastical imagery can the political evils of his time be fully apprehended.

As in *Cien años de soledad,* the apocalyptic vision of *El otoño del patriarca* focuses upon the nature of human temporality and upon man's relation to endings. The general is terrified by time's passing and by the approach of his own annihilation. Of course the apocalyptists saw time as the medium for the fulfillment of divine purpose, and temporal progression as necessary for the destruction of their persecutors; the vanquishing of the Antichrist is a temporal phenomenon. Thus, for the general, time can only destroy him; it becomes a personal enemy, the only opposition that has ever threatened his absolute power, the only assassin who will succeed inevitably. Just as the three-and-a-half-year reign of the beast is obliterated in "the great winepress of the wrath of God" (Rev. 14:19), so the general knows that the transitional period of his dark reign will end, that the "las últimas hojas heladas de su otoño" will fall. Nevertheless, for decades and even centuries, the general revises past and present time in a futile attempt to deny time's succession.

The general's control over time in his country is so great that when he asks what time it is, he receives the answer, "las que usted ordene mi general." This is exactly the case, for when the general decides to rearrange time, he does so, and then constant bewilderment follows as the people try to figure out his schedule. In one elaborate temporal maneuver, supposed to assuage the pain of unrequited love, the insomniac general orders the clocks advanced from three to eight in the morning: "son las ocho, carajo, las ocho, dije, orden de Dios." Night and day are reversed at his whim, and cookie-paper stars and silver plated moons are hung in the windows to attest to his power over time.

As the general imagines he can deny the reality of present time, so he attempts to deny the past. He substitutes for the factual reality of history a grotesque fiction of his own making. He revises history to obscure his illegitimate beginnings and outrageous conduct, employing "los artifices de la historia patria" to entangle and destroy "los hilos de la realidad." In order not to assume responsibility for the death of two thousand children, he falls into "el vértigo ilusorio de un precipicio surcado por franjas lívidas de evasión," and simply denies their existence. So inclusive is the fiction in which he lives that he even writes his own graffiti on the walls of his toilet: "que viva el general, que viva, carajo." At the conclusion of the novel the people serve as a kind of chorus, commenting on the general's retreat from the temporal reality of the past: "descubría en el transcurso de sus años incontables que la mentira es más cómoda que la duda, más útil que el amor, más perdurable que la verdad, había llegado sin asombro a la ficción de ignominia de mandar sin poder, de ser exaltado sin gloria y de ser obedicido sin autoridad."

As the general ages, he becomes less and less able to distinguish between temporal reality and his own illusions. Early in his reign, he could manage to "confront the hazards of reality," but as he deludes himself about his omnipotence and immortality he can no longer tolerate the prospect of temporal progression. He surrounds himself with adulators who proclaim him undoer of dawn and commander of time, who give him "una jerarquia mayor que la de la muerte." As he grows increasingly terrified of the future and the end, he begins to insist his sycophants call him "the eternal one," and their shouts of "long live the general" are taken in the most literal sense. Like the Antichrist in Revelation, the general must be twice vanquished. When his double dies and everyone thinks it is the general who has died, in a fierce struggle to exist twice he reappears and kills his cabinet members for the crime of imagining they had survived him. Afterward circulates a macabre joke that "alguien había anunciado al consejo de gobierno que [el general] había muerto y que todos los ministros se miraron asustados y se preguntaron asustados que ahora quién se lo va a decir a él, ja, ja, ja." The general frantically attempts to read the future in cards, coffee grounds, his palm, and basins of water, desperate to know the circumstances of his death. He finds a fortune teller who can tell him, and then strangles her because he wants no one else to know he is mortal. The general never learned what the people always knew about life, that "era ardua y efímera pero que no había otra, general."

The general's attempts to transcend time with lies, with a double who takes the risk of appearing in public for him and dies in his place, and with any number of other maneuvers to satiate his irrepressible passion to endure is cast in ironic light by the very structure of the novel. Each chapter opens with an account of the general's death and the rotting grandeur of the colonial basilica he had turned into a filthy milking barn. On the first page of the novel, his survivors enter the palace, this time with impunity, stirring up the "stagnant time," the "lethargy of centuries" created by the general's fear of the future. The structural irony is reinforced by the general's own sense of the futility of his efforts to forestall the ending. The more he listens to shouts of "long live the general," the more convinced he is that the end is near. It is in a final moment of grudging acceptance of his temporal condition that he becomes a human being rather than a monster: "al cabo de tantos y tantos años de ilusiones estériles había empezado a vislumbrar que no se vive, qué carajo, se sobrevive, se aprende demasiado tarde que hasta las vidas más dilitadas y útiles no alcanzan para nada más que para aprender a vivir." In this moment, the general faces the full extent of his self-deception and understands that he is a victim of his own sect, that he has believed his followers with their "letreros venales de vida eterna al magnífico que es más antiguo que su edad." He understands that his desire to reign "hasta el fin de los tiempos . . . era un vicio sin término cuya saciedad generaba su propio apetito hasta el fin de todos los tiempos mi general." In short, the general understands the temporal reality of his very human condition. But it is, of course, too late: he is indeed time's victim.

The people comment on the general's life and death: like the general, they are misled by their own adulation of the "eternal one." Even when his second death appears to be irrefutable, they cannot believe he in fact is not eternal. They are unable to fathom the meaning of his death, the meaning of the end of the general's seemingly infinite autumn. For the decades, centuries of the general's oppression, they have experienced what Kermode describes as the "intemporal agony" of the modern sense of the period of transition, a sense which "registers the conviction that the end is immanent rather than imminent." The period of transition becomes an age in itself as crisis succeeds crisis. The people have accepted the notion that the stage of transition has become endless, that they live, as Kermode puts it, "in no intelligible relation to the past, and no predictable relation to the future." When they finally bring themselves to believe the period of transition over and time has been punctuated by a meaningful ending, they ecstatically celebrate with "las músicas de liberación y los cohetes de gozo y las campanas de gloria que anunciaron al mundo la buena nueva de que el tiempo incontable de la eternidad había por fin terminado."

With these words the novel ends, less a cataclysmic apocalypse than a millennial one. The emphasis is not on the final upheaval when time shall cease, as in *Cien años de soledad,* but on the prospect for a better future which may succeed the radical break in time caused by the general's death. After all, innocence does survive persecution, as the apocalyptists promised; the people, to their surprise, live to celebrate the annihilation of the Antichrist; time does not cease but moves forward in the hands of the survivors. And having survived, the people understand their temporal condition; they know that life is arduous and ephemeral, and that if time's movement from past to present to future is a human contrivance, it is a contrivance that responds to basic human need and is not to be abused carelessly. Thus the survivors know who they are, unlike the general who "se quedó sin saberlo para siempre." García Márquez, leftist journalist and social activist as well as apocalyptic novelist, gives us cause for hope rather than despair.

The apocalyptic myth has always engrossed our imagination; we seem never to tire of imagining endings to reassure ourselves, to complete our poor human attempt to understand the world's design. It is as Kermode insists: "In the middest, we look for a fullness of time, for beginning, middle and end in concord." In all his fiction, Gabriel García Márquez uses the paradigms of apocalypse to give meaning to our moment in history, to integrate past, present and future into the immediacy of his plot. The vast temporal perspective of the apocalyptic myth suits the scope of García Márquez's fictive vision—like apocalypse, Macondo is, after all, nothing less than a symbolic outline of the history of the world. Like that eternal myth about time which is the apocalypse, García Márquez's fiction transmutes our temporal world into a timeless mythic realm that is at once about history and beyond it.

HARLEY D. OBERHELMAN

The Development of Faulkner's Influence in the Work of García Márquez

After García Márquez returned to Bogotá in 1954 to resume work for *El Espectador,* his journalistic and literary career in the years that follow is well documented. As he moved to Rome in 1955 and later to Paris as a correspondent and sometime student of cinematography, he continued to write fiction, but not without great economic difficulty due to the closing of *El Espectador* by the Rojas Pinilla dictatorship. *El coronel no tiene quien le escriba* came out in 1961, and *La mala hora* appeared the following year. García Márquez, however, refused to accept the 1962 edition of *La mala hora,* published in Madrid, because a Spanish proofreader made numerous changes in an effort to improve the style. Many words also were changed to more "acceptable" terms. The first edition of this novel that the author was willing to accept was done four years later in Mexico. The volume of short stories called *Los funerales de la Mamá Grande* also came out in 1962.

After a journalistic venture to the Iron Curtain countries, where he did a series of ten articles, and a return to Bogotá and Caracas for additional forays into newspaper work, he opened the office of Fidel Castro's Prensa Latina in the Colombian capital, went briefly to Havana, and was sent in 1960 by Prensa Latina to become assistant bureau chief in its New York office. He remained in New York only a few months, resigned from Prensa Latina, and made a trip through the South for the purpose of seeing Faulkner country first hand. Continuing in 1961 with his family on to

---

From *The Presence of Faulkner in the Writings of García Márquez.* Graduate Studies—Texas Tech University, no. 22 (August 1980).

Mexico, García Márquez began writing what was to become Spanish America's best selling novel, *Cien años de soledad* (1967). With its unprecedented success García Márquez and his fiction became the object of an avalanche of critical inspection and interpretation.

Various collections of short stories and newspaper articles followed *Cien años*. These collections contain one volume of more recent short stories, *La increíble y triste historia de la cándida Eréndira y de su abuela desalmada,* and unauthorized editions of much earlier short stories, *Ojos de perro azul* and *El negro que hizo esperar a los ángeles*. These three 1972 volumes were followed in 1973 by *Cuando era feliz e indocumentado,* a fascicle of newspaper articles from his Caracas days, but an ardent public was forced to wait until 1975 before the appearance of his heralded next novel, *El otoño del patriarca,* whose theme and style are in many ways vastly different from his earlier fiction. Critics and readers alike reached conflicting opinions regarding its merit, its method, and its literary value. *Todos los cuentos de Gabriel García Márquez* also appeared in 1975, but the volume, published in Barcelona, is unfortunately neither complete nor inclusive of any previously unpublished short stories. An authorized version of *Ojos de perro azul* was published in Buenos Aires in 1976, and the same year saw the Instituto Colombiano de Cultura issue *Crónicas y reportajes,* a valuable collection of newspaper contributions from the 1954–1955 period. Since 1977, García Márquez has left the field of fiction, at least temporarily, for political journalism. He has written a lengthy account of Cuba's involvement in Angola and granted the Washington *Post* first publication rights in English. Three extracts appeared in the 10–12 January 1977 editions.

Beneath the flow of thirty years of writing fiction, the evidence of Faulkner's presence is apparent in varying degrees. It is most evident in certain early short stories, in *La hojarasca,* to a degree in *Cien años de soledad* and—at least stylistically—in *El otoño del patriarca.* Faithful to the roots of their native soil, both Faulkner and García Márquez are engagés in their dedication to the revelation of the struggle of human beings against social and material decadence, the common lot dealt to all in Yoknapatawpha County and Macondo. Both writers show a hostility to "intellectuals" and to critics and prefer to allow their writings to speak for them. Although both have granted interviews and engaged in public discussions of their works, these remarks are at times misleading and contradictory.

McGrady's 1972 study was the first to point out the Faulknerian techniques used in García Márquez's early short stories. These works are frequently discounted by critics as short stories of minor importance that deal primarily with death and irrational states of mind. McGrady, however, points out definite relationships between such stories as "Nabo, el negro que hizo esperar a los ángeles" (1951) and *The Sound and the Fury.* Both employ multiple points of view and chronologically move from a point in time near the end of the action backward and forward without any discernible temporal pattern. Various stories are carried on simultaneously, and only at the end do all the pieces fit together into a unified tale. Nabo, one of García Márquez's few black protagonists, is in charge of an idiot girl; Versh, and later Luster, have identical roles in relation to the idiot Benjy, the stream-of-consciousness narrator of the first section of *The Sound and the Fury.* Benjy's sense of smell is related to his older sister Caddy, who "smells like trees" as a child but who upsets Benjy as she grows up and begins to use perfume. Nabo has a similar acute sense of smell for the odors of the stable that he tends.

"La otra costilla de la muerte," published in 1948 shortly after García Márquez arrived in Cartagena, gives further evidence of Faulkner's early presence in his fiction. Here García Márquez inserts fragments of past recollections within the framework of interior monologues written in the present tense. Although James Joyce may be ultimately responsible for this approach to writing, Faulkner made almost constant use of the same technique in most of his major works. In the short stories published by García Márquez before 1955, the vague silhouette of Macondo and of its inhabitants begins to take shape. Although Antonio Olier traces the first pages of *La hojarasca* to an obscure corner of the *El Universal* newspaper office where García Márquez worked from 1948 to 1949, McGrady points out four short stories called the La Sierpe series, which appeared in *El Espectador* in 1954 as a preview of Macondo as it was to appear in later fiction. The dates of original publication of all of these early stories have been established, but it must be remembered that many of them were written during earlier years. The central figure of the La Sierpe series is La Marquesita, in many ways the prototype of Mamá Grande and Ursula Buendía, Macondo's greatest matriarchs. Immensely wealthy, La Marquesita de La Sierpe ruled with an iron hand and with the help of the devil over "un país de leyenda dentro de la costa atlántica de Colombia." The costumbristic details of magic spells and ageless despots in the tropical coastal region clearly prefigure *La hojarasca, Los funerales de la Mamá Grande, Cien años de soledad,* and *El otoño del patriarca.* In 1955, with the publication of *La hojarasca,* García Márquez's own Yoknapatawpha County was ready to emerge as a vehicle for some of his most significant statements regarding the human comedy.

With good reason, *La hojarasca* is considered by most critics to be García Márquez's most Faulknerian novel. Written during the years that he spent on the Caribbean coast, it shows the plot pattern and style of the author of *As I Lay Dying.* In its creation of a fictional setting based on the realities of the Aracataca region, one can see the presence of *The Hamlet,* the first novel to be read by the Grupo de Barranquilla. The three long, intercalated monologues recall the narrators of *The Sound and the Fury,* and the moral and economic pillage of Macondo by the North American banana company is reminiscent of the carpetbaggers who invaded Jefferson and Yoknapatawpha County in *The Unvanquished* and *Absalom, Absalom!* The axis around which the memories of the past swirl in *La hojarasca* is the body of a mysterious French doctor whose strange and defiant actions caused great hostility in Macondo. The vicissitudes of burying the body of a prominent or controversial figure were to appear frequently in García Márquez's later fiction, but the archetypal burial sequence in Faulkner is the struggle to overcome the forces of fire and flood in *As I Lay Dying* so that Addie Bundren's family can transport her remains to Jefferson for interment according to her wishes. There is a pervasive feeling of solitude that dominates all of the action of *La hojarasca,* and the title itself suggests the idea of decadence and decay. This mood is frequently present in Faulkner as he describes the disintegration of the South which later generations attempt to expiate. Both Yoknapatawpha County and Macondo bear the scars of prior civil strife, and both contain enigmas that are insoluble.

La hojarasca is developed through a series of twenty-eight monologues by three characters attending a wake for the doctor, an unnamed recluse who appeared in Macondo twenty-five years earlier. The three narrators are Isabel, an abandoned mother; her father, a retired colonel who is highly respected in Macondo; and Isabel's ten-year-old son. The action of the novel is centered on the colonel's determination to carry out a promise made three years earlier to give the doctor a decent burial. There is great opposition on the part of the inhabitants—especially the mayor and the new priest—inasmuch as the doctor had refused to care for the wounded men brought to his door years ago during a local political confrontation. The promise of a decent burial informs the novel in much the same manner that Anse Bundren's promise to his wife that he would take her body to Jefferson to be buried with her kin creates the framework of Faulkner's novel.

As I Lay Dying is made up of the thoughts and feelings of fifteen characters, whereas only three relate their stories and memories in *La hojarasca.* In both novels, the process of physical deterioration is parallel to exterior natural and emotional forces that react against the "decent" burial. Natural disasters confronting the Bundrens are accentuated by Darl, the second son, who feels broken and rejected and suffers mental disintegration following his mother's death. His anguish leads him to attempt to burn the barn where Addie's body is temporarily resting, but Jewel, Addie's illegitimate son, rescues the body. The colonel "rescues" the doctor's body from those in Macondo who still hold revenge in their hearts. The novel closes as the doors of the doctor's house open, and the casket emerges into the afternoon light. The novel ends here, and the reaction of the town's inhabitants is never related. The suggestion that violence may follow is present, and it is violence that dominates the atmosphere of many subsequent short stories and novels published by García Márquez after 1955. This atmosphere is described by José Stevenson in the following fashion: "Vemos la influencia de Faulkner asumida, pero ya en una personalidad estilística, madura que aspira a dominar la forma y a cosechar nuevos derroteros. En esos monólogos lánguidos, parsimoniosos, que brotan del interior de sujetos enraizados en un pueblo donde no sucede nada, donde el tiempo o el progreso se detuvieron, oímos el eco rabioso del naufragio de ciertos valores: el amor, la lealtad, la fidelidad; el miedo y por último, el odio, son sentimientos que parecen prolongarse más allá de la muerte."

The dramatic tension apparent in both works is derived from a social conflict between one's ethical sense of responsibility (the burial promise) and societal pressures to allow emotional reactions to intervene. The end result is what J. G. Cobo Borda calls "condena fatal destinada a heredarse hasta no encontrar alguna forma de absorción." This condemnation of the South and of Macondo continues throughout the fiction of both authors. Regional history is the backdrop for both writers, but after *La hojarasca,* García Márquez gradually places historical events in a mythical perspective. Macondo becomes more ahistorical and offers its creator greater freedom of development. Yoknapatawpha County, on the other hand, remains firmly within an historical (although fictional) context. García Márquez ultimately destroyed Macondo, but death denied Faulkner the opportunity to describe Yoknapatawpha County's doomsday.

Only from the vantage point of his later novels is a retrospective assessment of Faulkner's impact on *La hojarasca* possible. Macondo existed in embryonic form before the appearance of García Márquez's first novel. While still in Barranquilla, he frequently made reference to a work he called "La casa," which was never published with that title. "La casa" was an ambitious attempt that was later to produce *La hojarasca* and ultimately *Cien años de soledad.* García Márquez developed this relationship in dialogue with Mario Vargas Llosa when he stated: "'La Hojarasca' fue el primer libro que yo publiqué cuando vi que no podía escribir 'Cien años de soledad.' Y ahora me doy cuenta que el verdadero antecedente de 'Cien años de soledad' es 'La Hojarasca,' y en el camino está 'El Coronel no tiene quien le escriba,' están los cuentos de 'Los funerales de la Mamá Grande' y está 'La mala hora.'" He continues with the statement that as the Colombian political situation began to deteriorate, his level of political consciousness began to identify him more closely with the national drama.

El coronel no tiene quien le escriba, La mala hora, and certain short stories in *Los funerales de la Mamá Grande* corroborate this statement. Neither of the novels is set in Macondo, but the title story and two others in *Los funerales* do continue the development of Macondo. The novels take place in an unnamed town called "El pueblo" and recall geographical details of the river port of Sucre where García Márquez's parents lived for a time after leaving Aracataca. The creation of a new milieu for these works may correspond to an effort on the part of the novelist to free himself from the Faulknerian tag so often given to *La hojarasca.* Many critics felt that the first novel fell into a Faulknerian trap and that García Márquez failed to demonstrate the profound human vision Faulkner accomplished in the Yoknapatawpha cycle. In any case, the second and third novels are quite different from *La hojarasca* and do not represent a continuation of the chaos and lack of discipline sometimes associated with the Faulknerian influences in the first novel.

Los funerales de la Mamá Grande is a transitional work, yet Agustín Rodríguez Garavito sees in it "la influencia siempre presente de Faulkner . . . [y] el patrón literario de Faulkner." It is not the style or the use of multiple narrators that occasioned this observation, but rather the emergence of reappearing characters, family clans, and recurring episodes that shows a continuing presence of Faulkner's method. Colonel Aureliano Buendía, certainly García Márquez's most fully developed character, is mentioned in many of these novels and short stories, and the Montiel, Asís, and Buendía families emerge to parallel the Sartoris, Compson, and Snopes families of Yoknapatawpha County. Emir Rodríguez Monegal asserts that "A Rose for Emily," translated to Spanish in Cartagena in 1949, is most certainly a model for many of the stories in the Mamá Grande series. There are close parallels between this story and many of the stories in *Los funerales de la Mamá Grande.* Miss Emily Grierson's death and the subsequent discovery in her decaying house of the decomposed body of her lover, Homer Barron, are analogous to "La viuda de Montiel" and "Un día después del sábado," both of which describe widows living in solitude, isolation, and spiritual poverty. Resistance to the will of authority, as demonstrated by Miss Emily's refusal to pay local taxes, recalls the dignity and inner strength of the mother and her daughter who arrive in Macondo to lay flowers on the grave of her son, accused of and subsequently shot for attempted robbery. "La siesta del martes," which relates this event, is one of the best stories in the entire collection. "Un día después del sábado," also set in Macondo, introduces two other motifs—a plague of dying birds, which suggests to the village priest the approach of the apocalypse, and the vision of the Wandering Jew—that recur in *Cien años de soledad.*

These short stories are valuable in that they form links with *La hojarasca* as well as with future novels to be published by García Márquez. The doctor in the first novel, who commits suicide in the same house in which he lived with the Indian servant Meme, and the colonel, who is determined to bury him properly, recall the details of "A Rose for Emily" and "La siesta del martes." The five short stories set in "el pueblo" suggest incidents and delineate characters later to appear in *La mala hora,* a novel steeped in "la violencia" that swept over Colombia after the 1948 assassination of Jorge Eliécer Gaitán. "Un día de estos," the second story in the collection, appears in altered form in *La mala hora,* as do the incidents described in "La viuda de Montiel" and "Rosas artificiales."

"Los funerales de la Mamá Grande" is the longest and the most significant work in the collection. It is a pivotal story, precursory of the future form of García Márquez's novels, *Cien años de soledad* and *El otoño del patriarca.* Mamá Grande, the matriarch of Macondo, is a legendary figure whose power reaches even the Vatican and whose illness and death shake the very foundations of the nation and of the ecclesiastical world. Satire and gross hyperbole accompany the rhetorical style used to describe in mythical terms the demise of a social and economic order. Macondo moves from a historical realm as seen in *La hojarasca* into a timeless myth in "Los funerales de la Mamá Grande." This process will reach its climax in *Cien años de soledad,* where the apocalypse, vaguely perceptible in "Un día después del sábado," is finally realized. The matriarchal Mamá Grande is a prototype of the strong female characters who inhabit Macondo and who are the "glue" that holds together the pieces of Faulkner's Yoknapatawpha County. The reverse side of the coin is apparent in the title of *El otoño del patriarca,* but here the patriarch is a straw demon, feared by those who rarely see him, and ultimately a victim of the very reign of terror he so carefully designed.

With *Los funerales de la Mamá Grande,* the stage is set for *Cien años de soledad,* García Márquez's most successful novel. Here the maturity of the Colombian novelist is most evident, and Macondo achieves its broadest mythical dimensions before its final destruction. The magical realism through which its characters move is very different from Yoknapatawpha County. Yet at this stage it is possible to compare two writers at their prime who use similar techniques and motifs, different literary styles, and their own unique versions of particular myths.

With the 1967 publication of *Cien años de soledad* and its unprecedented popularity in Spanish America, Europe, and the United States, García Márquez passed from the ranks of an obscure secondary writer of contemporary Spanish American fiction to the spotlight of critical attention and the furor of public interest. Following the initial success of *Cien años,* critics began to evaluate such earlier works as *La hojarasca, Los funerales de la Mamá Grande, La mala hora,* and *El coronel no tiene quien le escriba* in terms of his most popular novel. Various collections of his earlier short stories and newspaper articles were published, but his readers were forced to wait until 1975 for the appearance of his most recent novel, *El otoño del patriarca.* At almost every turn, a Faulknerian tag was pinned to *Cien años,* and at times to *El otoño del patriarca,* in much the same way that critical opinion had correctly viewed *La hojarasca.*

In a conversation with Rita Guibert, García Márquez accepted Faulkner as a mentor, especially in his early works, but he rejected the notion that he consciously or unconsciously sought to imitate Faulkner. As he read Faulkner in Cartagena and later in Barranquilla, he found that the American South was very much like the Caribbean coast of Colombia. Later, travel through the South had convinced him of these similarities and cultural affinities. *Cien años* and *El otoño del patriarca* are mature works that stand alone and merit a comparison with Faulkner's Yoknapatawpha saga. Such a comparison of both writers' understanding of Macondo and Yoknapatawpha on a parallel mythical and conceptual level reveals the common factors that shape their view of human destiny.

Ronald Christ's perspective of the two writers is that the Colombian novelist is explicitly inspired by Faulkner and his evocation of life through his imaginary county. Christ goes on to state that *Cien años* has single-handedly mythologized a whole continent in telling the multiple story of guilt and innocence in a prototypical endeavor to establish a society. The founders of Macondo, José Arcadio Buendía and his wife Ursula Iguarán, establish the village with others who have accompanied them on a long journey through mountains and dense forest. In the first half of the novel, the village and the family move forward on an ascendant path. Decadence begins in the second half of the novel as civil wars degenerate into senseless conflicts, and the banana company, first viewed as the savior of Macondo, abandons it to the wiles of man and nature. The destruction of the village is parallel to the disintegration of the Buendía family. In the development of the narrative there are some fifteen primary figures, most of them members of the Buendía clan, but the principal figure is, without a doubt, Colonel Aureliano Buendía. His father, José Arcadio, and his mother, Ursula Iguarán, are also important characters. Ursula is the strength of the family. She lives to be one hundred and fifteen years old, and with her dedication to hard work and common sense, she serves as a counterpoint to the caprices of her husband and sons, who, for the most part, dedicate themselves to counterproductive experiments in a household laboratory, to internecine warfare, and to sexual exploits.

Subsequent generations sink deeper into the morass of solitude and despair in their confrontation with forces from the outside world and with deterioration from within. José Arcadio, the founder of the dynasty, dies tied to a tree in the central patio of the house where he has been left to spend the last years of his life. Years later, his son, Colonel Aureliano Buendía, totally disillusioned with the futility of the endless wars between liberals and conservatives, watches the annual parade of an itinerant circus and then leans against the same tree and dies. Near the end of the novel, the last Aureliano and his aunt, Amaranta Ursula, are the only Buendías remaining. Aureliano has never left Macondo, but he has taught himself to read Sanskrit, the language of the mysterious manuscripts in the family laboratory. Amaranta Ursula has been educated in Europe, and on her return to her decaying family home she fails to realize the exact blood relationship between herself and Aureliano. A torrid love affair between these last Buendías produces the child with a pig's tail. Amaranta Ursula dies in childbirth. As the red ants devour the forgotten child in the patio,

Aureliano reads the last sheets of the manuscript that describe recent events. Meanwhile, the inevitable hurricane approaches and obliterates Macondo from the face of the earth.

García Márquez's use of Macondo as a microcosm for the study of a whole society was also the technique used by Faulkner when he created his own locale in which to reexamine the South, its great tragedy, and its system of traditional values. Jefferson and Yoknapatawpha County were first delineated in 1929 in *Sartoris* and *The Sound and the Fury,* and ultimately this region was to be the home of his families and their subsequent generations. In *Cien años,* the development of the Buendía family through five generations parallels Faulkner's creations. Both novelists offer a panoramic view of the vicious circle of civil war and incestuous societal decadence. The primeval paradise of Yoknapatawpha as undeveloped Indian territory and of Macondo in its earliest years is lost when human exploiters come to violate the innocence of nature. Later intruders—carpetbaggers and the banana company—arrive to accentuate the decline through the exploitation of the "fruit" of the land. The history of Macondo, written by the ubiquitous gypsy Melquíades, who, like Virginia Woolf's Orlando, lives from century to century, is a tale that ends in an apocalyptic whirlwind of dust and rubble, spun by the wrath of the hurricane. Faulkners's creation did not suffer destruction, but he had planned as a grand finale a "Doomsday Book," after which he would break his pen and quit. *The Reivers,* Faulkner's last novel, certainly is not his "Doomsday Book," and shortly after its appearance, he died of a heart attack on 6 July 1962.

One of the most extensive and accurate comparative studies of Faulkner and García Márquez is to be found in the work by Florence Delay and Jacqueline de Labriolle. These French critics find so much in common between the two novelists that their case rests on the sound observation that "Faulkner aura été pour lui (García Márquez) un stimulant exceptionnel, un maître en lucidité, en hardiesse novatrice. Mais il ne saurait suivre plus longtemps les fantasmes d'un autre. Il veut faire entendre une voix proprement latino-américaine." A sense of fatal decadence, they believe, informs the writings of both novelists, and whereas the male protagonists are those primarily responsible for the fatal chain of events, strong female figures attempt and ultimately fail to hold the fabric of society intact. Ursula Buendía and the other cofounder of Macondo, the prostitute Pilar Ternera, are among the last to die as the inevitable hurricane nears Macondo. Miss Jenny of *Sartoris,* Rosa Coldfield and Clytie Sutpen in *Absalom, Absalom!,* and the black maid Dilsey in *The Sound and the Fury* furnish a sense of stability and continuity as the postwar South crumbles about them.

A counterpoint to the theme of decadence is Faulkner's obsession with incest in many of his most important novels and the Buendías' fear of incest itself—or the appearance of incest—as certain to cause the birth of a child with a pig's tail. The rational obsession in Faulkner and the folkloric, irrational fear in García Márquez are nevertheless equal in their power of control over the various protagonists. Faulkner's characters react against this taboo as an aberration, and, as in the murder of Charles Bon by his half brother Henry Sutpen in *Absalom, Absalom!,* as a means of preventing the double tragedy of incest and miscegenation. Ursula Buendía's fear is based on family tradition and augmented by the prediction of Melquíades that the last Buendía would fulfill the prophecy and would be devoured by a horde of red ants. On a second level, both Macondo and Yoknapatawpha County suffer a type of societal incest that is only exacerbated by isolation and spiritual solitude. New blood to rejuvenate both societies is never accepted, and decay from within continues its unmitigating advance.

Both novelists employ the repetition of names, suggesting thereby that the many protagonists are interchangeable pieces in the puzzle of life. These protagonists face a struggle against time which assumes a circular form. Events, names, and sequences seem to swirl about both created locales without any regard for chronological order. This duplication of circular time is the frame of reference in *El otoño del patriarca.* Time makes futile circles that result in a chronological and spatial fragmentation. The six circular divisions of the novel all begin at a point near the time of death of an unnamed patriarch who governs an unnamed Caribbean nation for an indeterminate time and who lives to an age of between one hundred and seven and two hundred and thirty-two years. This hyperbolic study of a Latin American dictator opens as vultures are circling the palace; cows munching velvet curtains are wandering through the vast rooms; the patriarch is dead. As his timid subjects enter the decrepit palace, there is an air of uncertainty, inasmuch as a previous "death" of the patriarch had turned out to be that of his perfect double. Because no one has really seen the man for many years, his identification is at first only provisional.

Within the circular divisions of the novel, the details of the patriarch's rise to power are offered in fragmentary reminiscences by the patriarch himself and by a series of unnamed witnesses. Some of these witnesses only retell bits and pieces of legendary materials passed down from generation to generation because none could have been witness in the true sense of the word to events that took place over a hundred years ago. His birth as the bastard son of a bird woman; his rise to power with the support of the British and later the Americans; the disappearance of his favorite mistress, Manuela Sánchez, during an eclipse of the sun; and the death of his wife and son, Leticia Nazareno and Emanuel, who are torn to bits in a public market by trained dogs, are events that gradually fall into narrative sequence as the past is recalled in fragmentary pieces. An additional technique is the interpolation of hyperbolic elements that give the work a tone of magical realism.

At first blush, it is apparent that *El otoño del patriarca* is quite different from *Cian años de soledad.* It is a meditation on the solitude of absolute power, a theme suggested in the presentation of the figure of Colonel Aureliano Buendía in García Márquez's earlier writings. Instead of a fictional town such as Macondo or Jefferson, García Márquez has created an entire fictional nation with a Caribbean setting, a nation the capital of which is reminiscent of Havana or Caracas. There is no lack of models for his prototype of a dictator. William Kennedy traces the genesis of the novel in the following manner: "In 1968 when he began to write this majestic novel, Gabriel García Márquez told an interviewer that the only image he had of it for years was that of an incredibly old man walking through the huge, abandoned rooms of a palace full of animals." Kennedy goes on to say that García Márquez, as he witnessed the downfall of Marcos Pérez Jiménez in Venezuela, mentioned to friends that he would one day write such a book. An earlier Venezuelan dictator, Juan Vicente Gómez, is the principal model used for the novel's dictator. The timeless, nameless, and imprecise qualities of the patriarch elevate him from the realm of the specific to the world of myth. There are antecedents to *El otoño del patriarca* in García Márquez's earlier fiction. The use of various narrators who recall the life of a person now dead is the method used in *La hojarasca* and in Faulkner's *As I Lay Dying.* The gross exaggerations of García Márquez's short story "Los funerales de la Mamá Grande" prefigure this most recent novel as do the fantastic, imaginative tales of the short-story collection, *La increíble y triste historia de la cándida Eréndira y de su abuela desalmada* (1972). And, of course, the style of *El otoño del patriarca* recalls what Kennedy describes as "a densely rich and fluid pudding that makes Faulknerian leaps forward and backward in time . . . making the novel a puzzle of pronouns, consistently changing narrative points of view in mid-sentence." It is precisely this change of style that is the most Faulknerian aspect of this novel. With the publication of *El otoño del patriarca,* it is necessary to reconsider the matter of style and Faulkner's possible presence.

Faulkner's better known novels are often described as "difficult" for the average reader. The presence of some fifteen narrators of *As I Lay Dying* demands constant shifts on the part of the reader to organize the sequence of events that describes the journey of Addie Bundren's body to Jefferson, where it was her wish to be buried. *The Sound and the Fury,* although it uses only four different points of view, is much more fragmented and complicated. These novels retell the past, combining the traditional narrative with a stream-of-consciousness technique. The scope of *Absalom, Absalom!* is much greater in that it covers a historical period from 1817 to an ambiguous present. García Márquez was especially interested in this latter novel, and its structure and technique are evident as models for *Cien años de soledad* and *El otoño del patriarca.* In 1929, when *The Sound and the Fury* appeared, Faulkner seemed to invite the reader to share with him in a search for order, truth, and significance. Much the same was in store for the readers of later Faulknerian novels. García Márquez first used this method in *La hojarasca.* In *Cien años,* there is a false sense of linear progression in story development, but many flashbacks are required to complete the picture of Macondo and its final destruction. *El otoño del patriarca* breaks what was a deceptively facile narrative style for chronological, narrative, and stylistic complexity. The repetition of the verb *vimos* allows constant shifts in point of view, but first, second, and third-person verb shifts make the task of the reader much greater as he sorts out chronology from such a multitude of material.

In many of Faulkner's writings and in *El otoño del patriarca,* the work begins at or near the end of the action, and flashbacks related by different narrators fill out the picture. Each point of view is incomplete; often it is the memory of the past as recalled in a nebulous present. Often there is an incompleteness at the end of the work, and the reader is called upon to "finish" the novel. The Civil War in Faulkner, the thirty-two revolutions that Aureliano Buendía lost, and the long dictatorship in *El otoño del patriarca* are the antecedents of a present sense of fatality. Time makes futile circles that result in chronological and spatial fragmentation. Clarity is achieved only after events pass into a distant historical perspective, only after the reader has had time to decipher their meaning. *Absalom, Absalom!* ends with Quentin Compson and his Harvard roommate, Shreve McCannon, attempting to decipher the meaning of events and motives that Quentin has related about his family in Jefferson. *Cien años* ends as the last Aureliano rapidly translates the manuscripts written much earlier by Melquíades; as he finishes the translation, the hurricane wipes the last vestiges of the Buendía family from Macondo. The timelessness of these novels permits the characters and events to achieve universal meaning on a mythical level. In this way, the regional characters of both novelists become protagonists with universal problems and concerns.

Magical realism, the introduction by a novelist of the improbable and the fantastic within a realistic world, is far more evident in García Márquez than in Faulkner. This element would seem, at first glance, to set *Cien años de soledad,* the short stories of the *Eréndira* collection, and *El otoño del patriarca* apart from the world of Faulkner, but it is only in the degree that García Márquez employs magical realism that the difference is marked. Faulkner found a sense of the marvelous and wondrous in nature; it is the central theme of *The Bear.* Kulin observes that in *Old Man* it is the elusive body of a deer that is the representation of the soul of the convict as the two desperately seek salvation in the swirling waters of the flood. An even greater sense of irreality informs *A Fable,* and there are moments of the magical in *As I Lay Dying* and *Light in August.*

García Márquez takes the marvelous to much greater extremes: gypsies with flying carpets, yellow flowers falling on Macondo like rain, the exaggerated sexual prowess of the Buendía males, and the apparent immortality of Melquíades and the ancient patriarch. But Delay and de Labriolle find a common ground in the worlds of Macondo and Yoknapatawpha: "Cet amour du billage, fût-il 'anachronique,' cette sympathie amusée pour les petits gens au milieu desquels il a grandi, voici peut-être la clé du 'merveilleux' qui a fait couler tant d'encre savante."

A final comparison is necessary. Although it is easy to see the presence of Faulkner in García Márquez's first novel, *La hojarasca,* and in his early short stories, it is less evident as the Colombian reaches artistic maturity. Both deal with similar societies at a time when they are attempting to survive the jolting effects of civil strife and exploitation. The labyrinthine prose so common in Faulkner does not appear in García Márquez until *El otoño del patriarca.* Yet in the final analysis, García Márquez's debt to Faulkner is undeniable. Faulkner left as part of his legacy a moral tone and standard by which human beings could judge his characters and ultimately themselves. His faith in man was evident in his Nobel address when he insisted that man would not merely endure but would prevail. The last sentence of *The Wild Palms,* "between grief and nothing I will take grief," reasserts his dedication to the struggle of humanity for survival. Whereas García Márquez ends *Cien años de soledad* with the unmitigated statement that races condemned to a hundred years of solitude do not have a second opportunity on earth, he concludes *El otoño del patriarca* with the ringing of bells announcing that the time of seemingly eternal dictatorship has come at last to a close. Both Faulkner and García Márquez seek a world of justice for a new generation. Macondo exists no longer, and death brought the end of the saga of Yoknapatawpha County, but a message of hope lingers propitiously above the ruin and ashes of destruction.

JOHN GERLACH

The Logic of Wings: García Márquez, Todorov, and the Endless Resources of Fantasy

Is fantasy dependent on certain themes, and, if so, might these themes be exhausted? My own response to one story, Gabriel García Márquez's "Very Old Man with Enormous Wings," a story in which theme and the atmosphere of fantasy that emerges from the theme are, if anything, negatively correlated, leads me to suspect that fantasy is not closely tied to theme, so that fantasies may be created in any age, without reference to theme.

The story might best be described by starting at the end. At the conclusion, an old man flaps like a senile vulture away from the village where for years he has been held captive. The woman who has grudgingly taken care of him watches him open a furrow in the vegetable patch with his fingernails in his first attempt to rise. She sees him nearly knock down a shed with his "ungainly flapping." As he gains altitude and begins to disappear, she watches "until it was no longer possible for her to see him, because then he was no longer an annoyance in her life but an imaginary dot." George McMurray, in his recent study of Gabriel García Márquez, focuses on this final image and concludes that for the reader (and the villagers) the story is a "cathartic destruction of antiquated myths." My own reaction was quite different: I had the prescribed catharsis, but I came away with my taste for myth and the supernatural intact. I could see how McMurray arrived at his conclusion, because this particular Icarus, with his "few faded hairs left on his bald skull" and the air of a "drenched great-

From *Bridges to Fantasy,* edited by George E. Slusser, Eric S. Rabkin, and Robert Scholes. Southern Illinois University Press, 1982.

grandfather," would hardly seem to inspire wonder. But I felt as if I had witnessed the beginning of a myth, not its end, and the story had evoked for me the sense of wonder and marvel that one associates with myth at its inception.

Whether the story is best designated as a myth or as a fantasy is another matter. Myths present "supernatural episodes as a means of interpreting natural events in an effort to make concrete and particular a special perception of man or a cosmic view," as *A Handbook to Literature* would have it. The old man of García Márquez's story does not stimulate the villagers to interpret anything. He is dropped into their existence unexplained, and leaves unexplained, clarifying nothing. It would be more accurate to consider the work a fantasy on the grounds that the story deals, to use the handbook's terms again, with an "incredible and unreal character." I will eventually apply a more contemporary definition of fantasy to the story, Todorov's definition, but for the moment I prefer to pursue further the consequences of McMurray's approach. His view implies that the subject of myth, or, as I will have it, fantasy, determines our reactions. If the text parodies a mythic subject, then the reader would appropriately respond, not with an elevated sense of wonder, but with amusement at the exposure of nonsense. Since the subject matter in García Márquez's story does not diminish my own appreciation of the marvelous, I am left to conclude either that McMurray has misread the text or that the effect of a fantasy is not dependent on the subject. I have concluded that both propositions are true. McMurray has misrepresented the text, and, even so, something other than theme or subject matter creates what the reader responds to in a fantasy. "A Very Old Man with Enormous Wings" can be used to show that, as Todorov has predicted, the manner of telling, not the matter, creates the fantasy.

McMurray's points should first be dealt with in more detail. His interpretation is brief, but his argument is easily extended. Part of García Márquez's strategy, as McMurray suggests, was undeniably to diminish the grandeur of this unearthly winged creature. Similes used to describe him do not even grant him human attributes: matched with the villagers who stood around his cage he looked "like a huge decrepit hen among fascinated chickens." Later it is said that he tolerates a child's "ingenious infamies with the patience of a dog who had no illusions." A complex simile, to be sure, for the narrator is saying not only that the old man is like a dog, but also that the dog with his patience and lack of illusions is like a human being. Nevertheless, the effect of the simile is to emphasize the analogy to an animal. The syntax of the sentence which reveals the old man's wings also diminishes rather than ennobles him. Pelayo, the man who found him, heard something moving and groaning in the courtyard that he had recently cleaned of crabs and the stench they left behind. Pelayo "had to go very close to see that it was an old man, a very old man, lying face down in the mud, who, in spite of his tremendous efforts, couldn't get up, impeded by his enormous wings." The long sentence, with its hesitations that duplicate in the reader the efforts of the old man, relegates the marvel of his wings to the terminal subordinate clause. Rhetorical decisions such as these have just as much effect on us as the content. It would seem that both the language and the content are pushing the reader in the direction that McMurray has outlined. The supernatural is described as something ordinary or, even more precisely, foul and repellent.

McMurray's analysis can be extended further. The narrator's motive in telling the story would seem to be satiric rather than inspirational. The credulity of mankind and greed—Pelayo's wife begins to charge admission to see the old man—are apparently the narrator's targets. The church is too, for the attempts of ecclesiastical bureaucrats to discover through correspondence with the resident priest whether or not the winged creature is an angel are bogged down by their desire to find out "if the prisoner had a navel, if his dialect had any connection with Aramaic, how many times he could fit on the head of a pin, or whether he wasn't just a Norwegian with wings." Furthermore, the narrator's exaggerated manner of description seems to undercut even further our response to the old man. When Pelayo and his wife Elisenda first speak to the old man, "he answered in an incomprehensible dialect with a strong sailor's voice." What it is that makes the voice sound like that of a sailor is not questioned by the narrator, who simply mirrors what is presumably the illogic of Pelayo and Elisenda. The narrator's complicity in this fabrication extends beyond mirroring. He notes that Pelayo and Elisenda "skipped over the inconvenience of the wings and quite intelligently concluded that he was a lonely castaway." Since wings are certainly more than an "inconvenience," and the logical processes of Pelayo and Elisenda are therefore something less than intelligent, we have a narrator who, instead of striving to establish the credibility of this supernatural creature, is emphasizing the credulity of the villagers.

Similes that demean, satire, playful logic—it would seem that García Márquez is not about to honor a myth. Yet none of these devices totally cancels out the mystery. The diminishing suggested by these devices does not represent all of the truth about the old man and his wings. However decrepit the old man is, he does renew himself. When he arrived he seemed close to death, and several years later a doctor listening to the old man's heart concludes that it is impossible for him to be alive; yet after his release from his cage and with the onset of sunny days, stiff feathers begin to grow on his wings. Although the narrator continues to denigrate, calling the new growth "scarecrow feathers" that look like "another misfortune of decrepitude," the feathers do allow the old man to fly away. Something about the old man is greater than the narrator's estimation of him.

Other devices that the narrator used to increase rather than decrease our respect for the old man also need to be considered. When compared to those around him the old man becomes the model of patience, trying the best he can to "get comfortable in his borrowed nest, befuddled by the hellish heat of the oil lamps and sacramental candles that had been placed along the wire." He refuses to eat the mothballs that one of the villagers thinks is the "food prescribed for angels," and subsists on eggplant mush. If he is "befuddled," that term has ironic value, for it is those that regard him who are confused.

Contrast with what seems to be even the sanest of mortals is illustrative. Father Gonzaga is the figure presented by the narrator as the most sane. He is not, as his parishioners are, ready to make the old man the mayor of the world or a "five-star general in order to win all wars," nor does he want to put him out to stud to create "a race of winged wise men who could take charge of the universe." Father Gonzaga "had been a robust woodcutter" and so by implication is more realistic. He soberly approaches the old man and says good morning in Latin. Father Gonzaga has "his first suspicion of an imposter" when he saw that the old man "did not understand the language of God or know how to greet His ministers," and it is at this point we realize that Father Gonzaga is the one who fails the test, not the old man. Father Gonzaga notices that "seen close up" the old man "was much too human," and so the priest warns his parishioners not to be taken in. In the light of Father Gonzaga's response, the comment that the old man is "too human" is particularly telling. Gonzaga's rationalism obscures his realization that although the winged gentleman may not meet doctrinal specifications, he still is miraculous. What begins to emerge is an image of the old man as someone possibly more human and reasonable than members of the wingless species.

The winged man's humanity is underlined by a foil the narrator creates, a woman who has been changed into a spider. Her presence distracts the villagers, and they cease to pay attention to the old man. Her exhibit costs less, and unlike the old man, she talks about her affliction. Where the old man refused, she encourages responses, readily accepting meatballs tossed into her mouth. There is nothing ambiguous or submerged about our perception of her. The old man's wings were slowly revealed; we are told bluntly that this woman is "a frightful tarantula the size of a ram . . . with the head of a sad maiden." Though the narrator does not exaggerate the catalogue of her strangeness, she is in fact more grotesque than the old man.

The narrator's description of the villagers' response to her is familiar: once again the logic of the villagers is suspect; the crowd regards her as a spectacle full of "human truth," a "fearful lesson." The facts of the lesson, however, are these: a lightning bolt of brimstone changed her form because she had been dancing all night without her parents' permission. The narrator's indirect exposure of the triviality of what the crowd considers a basic truth alters our response to the old man. We begin to admire more his silence and even his diet.

The way the villagers treat him is ultimately the best clue to how we should regard him. They poke, they prod, and at one point they burn him with a branding iron. Up until this point pain itself has seemed unreal. Those with ailments who come to be cured have only the most fanciful of afflictions, such as that of an old man "who couldn't sleep because the noise of the stars disturbed him" and that of "a poor woman who since childhood had been counting her heartbeats and had run out of numbers." But the old man with wings responds with true pain, ranting in his "hermetic language," tears in his eyes, flapping his wings to create "a whirlwind of chicken dung and lunar dust." The villagers take the old man as no more than a creature of fiction, hence not subject to pain. They may not see the old man's humanity, but the reader should.

What I hope is emerging is a more complete sense of the role of the narrator. His denigrations of the protagonist have been systematic but not exclusive. He distorts by alternately exaggerating and understating. What could be called the outer or secondary level of distortion is the product of the narrator's supposed sympathy with the viewpoint of the villagers. This level, whose function is basically satiric, leads the narrator to call wings "inconvenient" or to exaggerate the church's concern in terms of the medieval problem of calculating the number of angels on the head of a pin. The narrator takes the viewpoint of the villagers themselves, pretending to be alternately detached or supportive, but everywhere he exposes irrationality and superstition. Underneath this level, however, is another, an inner or primary level of distortion, which grows from one central fact—there is an old man with enormous wings. That conception embodies even in its grammatical form a paradox in the contrast between "old" and "enormous," for we would not expect anything so powerfully endowed to be so decrepit. Beyond this paradox is a kind of simplicity and unarguable solidity. The nature of the wings themselves does not change; what changes is our perception of their naturalness. By the end of the story, a doctor examines the old man and is surprised by "the logic of his wings," and the reader is prepared for a similar realization. These wings, as the doctor puts it, seem "so natural on that completely human organism that he couldn't understand why other men didn't have them too." This old man, with his muteness, his patience, is in some ways more human, more natural, and even more believable, than anyone else in the story. The secondary level of distortion playfully exposes human folly; the primary level by contrast defines more desirable human traits.

At this point it is appropriate to define the genre of the work more precisely. The definition will allow us to see how the two levels of distortion work together to create the effects we associate with fantasy. Within the last few years, several critics, in particular W. R. Irwin, Eric S. Rabkin, and Tzvetan Todorov, have attempted to describe fantasy as a genre. Of the three, Todorov's analysis provides the most instructive standards to apply to García Márquez's story. The fit is not perfect; Todorov, I believe, concludes that "fantasy" narrowly defined is hardly being written anymore. But even the divergence between "A Very Old Man with Enormous Wings" and Todorov's principles is in itself enlightening.

Todorov assumes that, first, fantasies produce the effect of hesitation. The reader is never wholly sure whether he is confronting a supernatural event or something that can be rationally explained. If the reader is able to conclude the event is explicable solely on the supernatural level, the story belongs to another genre, the marvelous, and, if the reader chooses the rational explanation, the story falls into the genre of the "uncanny." Second, the reader usually participates in the story through the medium of a character who believes in reason and order, so that the reader experiences the hesitation through the character's eyes. Third, the reader must not be able to explain away the supernatural events by considering them allegorical or poetic. In this case the reader would conclude that the supernatural is merely a shorthand for an idea, hence not to be taken literally. One of the clues to allegory is that no one in the story takes an aberration to be unusual, and so there is no sense of hesitation.

In the case of the García Márquez story, it is simpler to deal with the second point first. There is no character recounting for us his experiences.

There is an implied narrator, and this narrator is a direct inversion of the sort of character that Todorov has posited. This is no rational human, but a creator of exaggerations. The hesitation that Todorov speaks of as his first point, then, derives in this story not from the doubts of a character, but from our doubts about what the narrator is saying. Todorov's analysis allows us to see the ingenuity of what García Márquez has done. García Márquez has taken what would normally be the index of normality, the village folk, and made them the greatest of exaggerators. The unreal character, in contrast, begins to appear normal and harmless. García Márquez has managed to make his central contrary-to-fact situation, the old man with wings (what I have been calling the primary level of distortion), seem altogether more rational and ordinary than the villagers. Those who follow Rabkin's definition of fantasy should be pleased, for the effect that I have described is replete with what Rabkin calls 180-degree turns in perspective, the undermining of established expectations. As for the matter of allegory, it is possible that the wings themselves might be taken as allegorical evidence of the true dignity of man. What prevents us from taking the wings as allegory is the very insistence on the decrepitude of the old man, and elaboration of the reality of the wings, the "stellar parasites" in them. In the same way, the characters both are and are not taking the old man as unusual, so that the wings both are and are not allegorical. It is not that García Márquez is making hash of Todorov's categories. What he is doing by his exaggerations is creating the maximum doubt and hesitation about not only the supernatural but the natural as well.

We should now be able to reconsider some of the questions originally raised by McMurray's interpretation. Although it might be possible to contend that McMurray's reading of the text failed to take into account the double role of the narrator and the two levels of distortion, and hence he did not see the extent to which García Márquez has shifted our sympathies toward the old man and located the antiquated, exhausted view in the perception of the villagers, such a view does not fully account for the energy of the story. Arriving at the truth of the story and feeling its impact do not automatically result from peeling off the secondary layer of distortion and getting at the primary. It is not possible to take either level as the ultimate truth. The positive values may seem to be vested in the primary level, for García Márquez has made muteness and patience seem truly supernatural virtues, and by implication exaggeration the expression of human fallibility. But the center of the story is still an exaggeration. Men do not have wings. The process of distortion itself is the vehicle of our approach to the story. The very act of reading and interpreting the story rests not on muteness and patience, but on the appreciation of exaggeration. In reading the story the reader does not respond only to the truth of a particular idea, in the case of this story, for instance, the idea that there is an indestructible, winged aspect of man that can fly despite its own aging or the lack of appreciation from ordinary men. The story is a whole, not a set of levels, and what causes the reader to respond, in the terms that Todorov has established, is the reader's hesitation over what is real.

This hesitation is built up from the minutest details, as can be shown in one isolated segment, the ending. Even slight distortions in language are significant. The concluding phrase states that the old man "was no longer an annoyance in [Elisenda's] life but an imaginary dot on the horizon of the sea." The antithesis of "annoyance" and "dot," contrasting an abstraction with something at least barely visible, might make us grammatically uncomfortable, but the mismatch reproduces the quality of the story itself. It is as if there were a rather easy flow between our feelings and the things we find about us, so that a thought might suddenly take a substance as real as our own, or just as suddenly disappear. The energy created by unusual phrases works in the same way. The idea of modifying "dot" by the adjective "imaginary" is plausible in that the dot may be so small that it is nearly imaginary, but the conjunction of the two terms is also implausible; it has something of the force of an oxymoron, for Elisenda is simultaneously seeing and merely imagining. "Imaginary" is also apt in that the old man is by our standards rightly considered imaginary. Structurally the close is effective because it complements the opening—the character was visually constructed piece by piece for us, and now visually recedes into nothingness. Viewed from one perspective, humankind is relieved of a burden. Viewed from another, a creature more perfect, more logical than man has achieved his freedom. The fact that the old man has escaped from the perspective of the characters means to the characters that he does not exist, he may be ignored. But we have seen him endure over a period of time and can imagine him perhaps going back to whatever imaginary place it is that he lives in, one that has as much validity to it as this imaginary town into which he has fallen.

The cluster of possibilities here matches the possibilities advanced in the rest of the story. Clusters such as this give the story its power and create the effects we identify with fantasy; the clusters work much the same way as the hesitation over the natural and the supernatural. Because the effect of the story, the sense in which it is a fantasy, is created by the treatment, not by the subject or theme, the number of fantasies that can still be written should be endless. At one time myths may have been man's way of imagining the unimaginable, but now, even though literal myth-making is no longer used to explain the world around us, the sense of wonder that myth brings with it need not in consequence be abandoned. It does not matter that we cannot take the fanciful as literally as man might once have, nor does it matter that the subject of a myth is decrepit, toothless, and featherless. The sense of wonder that a myth or a fantasy evokes inheres not in the subject, but in the telling. Fantasy is more the how than the what.

Put in terms of Todorov's discussion, fantasy is created initially by something significantly contrary to the ordinary. The task of the reader is to naturalize, to recuperate, that is, to make intelligible, this break from the norms of the reader's experience. The most significant thing about the genre is that the break should not readily be bridged; the circuits must be kept open as long as possible. In Todorov's words, the hesitation must continue. What the reader ends up recuperating is ultimately the process, the broken circuit itself. It is not what the break is about, it is that there *is* a continuous break that makes a fantasy. Since fantasy is a process, not a result, its resources are endless, and it is in no way dependent on the fashion of the conventions it adapts.

The final matter to consider is the effect of parody in the genre. Does the parody of a myth or fantasy make the story a last gasp, as the Russian formalists have asserted in other cases, of a genre that is about to expire or assume a new form? I think not. Parody is not central to this story. The mention of stellar bugs and scratchings is only a way for the narrator to make the mystery of the old man more, not less, incredible. There are parodic elements, but this is not a parody as such. What one ultimately grasps in a fantasy is the potential of language to construct a world partly, but not wholly, like our own. Fantasy is the logical extension, the wings, of language itself. Literature in general and fantasy in particular are the magic which our customary language so dimly represents.

EDUARDO GONZÁLEZ

Beware of Gift-Bearing Tales: Reading García Márquez According to Mauss

Jésus se fût obstinément refusé à faire des prodiges que la foule en eût créé pour lui; le plus grand miracle eût été qu'il n'en fît pas; jamais les lois de l'histoire et de la psychologie n'e populaire n'eussent subi une plus forte dérogation. Les miracles de Jésus furent une violence que lui fit son siècle, une concession que lui arracha la nécessité passagère. Aussi l'exorciste et la thaumaturge sont tombés; mais le réformateur religieux vivra eternellement.

—ERNEST RENAN, *Vie de Jésus*

Speaking of the main task of his *Essai sur le don* (1925), Marcel Mauss says that he intends "to catch the fleeting moment when a society and its members take emotional stock of themselves and their situation as regards others." In the wake of recent structuralist burdens, Mauss's words appear heroically forthright and endowed with a kind of naive authority; his essay is the plain song that opens a vast and intricate symphony. Of particular interest is his emphasis on emotions and feelings as preeminent objects of analysis. In *The Gift,* Mauss rebuilt an instance of social being which was significant in that it seemed to be total and, in spite of its aberrant display of excess and waste, practical. He saw the act of gift-exchange, or total prestation, as that juncture in time and space where structure and event intercept each other. As an object of storytelling, the group *becomes,* it begins at such a moment: social reality originates as *kairos,* as an occasion overruled by its own pregnant disclosures.

From *MLN* 97, no. 2 (March 1982).

Behind Mauss's faith in rational analysis, there was a sober awareness of having to be timely in its exercise; for the surest attribute of social phenomena is not found in their constancy, but in how quickly the full force of their meanings stands to perish. The deftness of his dissertation creates the illusion that the practices it dissects and illustrates are being held hostage to inquiry within a fleeting measure of time which will not again be graspable. In this fashion, the accent and style of Mauss's explorations bring him closer to the storyteller than to the semiotician or other recent practitioners of the structuralist science whose beginnings he is believed to have fostered.

I would like to show the lasting exemplariness of Mauss's practice by reading Gabriel García Márquez's short tale, "La prodigiosa tarde de Baltazar," as if it were an occasion akin to the one that Mauss saw in gift-exchange. I shall outline a way of posing the story as a fable concerning the origination of the *social* as an alienating domain within a given literary narrative. With this exercise I hope to demonstrate how, without embedding stories in a particular ethnosocial context, our structural knowledge of them is bound to remain an empty formality. However, by context I shall understand, not so much the story's empirical setting (in this case the Colombian countryside), as the implicit links existing between a story and instances of ethno-social learning whose subject matter would qualify them as genealogical antecedents of a given tale. At issue will be what we might call the canonical significance of stories (or of narrative cycles) within specific sectors of a large domain of practical discourse aimed at disclosing the meaning of persons as social beings.

Readers of García Márquez's *One Hundred Years of Solitude* (*Cien años de soledad,* 1967), will be familiar with the elder José Arcadio Buendía's fondness early in that novel for wild experimentation and relentless tinkering, as he is driven by the spell cast on him by Melquíades, the Gypsy Magus. In Macondo's morning, objects and instruments of all kinds rise from their slumber when reached by the zeal of the elder José Arcadio turned into a demiurge. The plot of "La prodigiosa tarde" hinges on a similar act of creative frenzy. As the story opens, its protagonist, the humble and naive carpenter Baltazar, has just spent a small season of toil and disturbed sleep building a birdcage. His talents as craftsman have exceeded carpentry; on this occasion he has managed to fashion a prodigious object, worthy of the skills seen only among master artisans of older times.

Baltazar lives, unmarried and childless, with the level-headed Ursula. Upon its completion, the birdcage soon becomes the center of increasing polemics. From the start, Ursula is exclusively interested in the product's cash value, while on his part Baltazar seems to agree with her strong sense of profit, but in the end, a motive other than obtaining cash will rule over his actions. The town's children are the first to gather as celebrants of the cage's beauty, but soon a more keenly disposed observer makes the scene. Doctor Octavio Giraldo wants to offer the cage to his invalid wife, a bird lover. Giraldo's prodigality is spent in rhetoric. His speech, at once terse and hyperbolic, seizes the occasion. As he might have put it, his idioms seem to have gathered in sails attuned to harnessing the slightest drifts of cunning wisdom. He addresses the cage, and through it Baltazar, as if instead of buying it he were engaged in selling it to its maker. Giraldo's rhetorical elegance transforms the cage into a synoptic illusion; upon his celebration, the object becomes a tuning fork which, vibrating, registers and absorbs into measure its own expanding significance as a perceptual event. Meaning originates as a sort of metaphoric exodus transacted by means of rhetorical ploys which partake of keen superstition and gossip. Metaphor acts here as a kind of homeotropic gesture which shadows forth the cage's imminent tonality: Doctor Giraldo is the first executor of this tropism when he puts into play his gift for metonymic sympathy. There is no need, he says, to put birds in the cage, "It would be enough to hang it in the trees so it could sing by itself." Baltazar's contact with the cage's resonance is of a different sort, perhaps one nearer the object's tacit occupancy of space, a form of public dwelling which is meant to resist metaphoric seizures: he indexes the cage's intricacies and then sounds it with one definitive flourish of his wrist: "The measurements are carefully calculated—he said—pointing to the different compartments with his forefinger. Then he struck the dome with his knuckles, and the cage filled with resonant chords."

In the end, the good doctor's efforts are thwarted. According to Baltazar, the cage has already been promised to Chepe Montiel's son (Montiel enjoys the accursed reputation of being Macondo's rich man). Giraldo quibbles to no avail: can Baltazar prove that the cage is meant for troopials and not for other birds; did the child give him a blueprint to follow? During the bargaining Ursula supports Baltazar, moved by her desire to sell the cage to the richer Montiel.

It is to be noted also that it is Ursula, and not Baltazar, who first mentions Montiel as the buyer, when she estimates the best price which the cage is likely to command. The reader might surmise at least two things: that Baltazar has told her (in the implicit past of before the story) about the child's request; or that, led by her common sense and good business practice, she takes for granted that if Baltazar has ended up building such an extravagant cage, it better be for the only person in town with the means to buy it. The point is a crucial one since, as we are about to see, the story offers a minute account of the role played by inference in social affairs.

For instance, in strict discursive terms, the cage rises before the reader's imagination in full detail as if in seeming complicity with the doctor's arrival on the scene. His presence brings before our eyes the achieved object in full captivating complexity. Until then, the cage has existed as sheer inference, as rumor devoid of form; since then it becomes a visual and imaginary event.

The doctor's visit establishes several things: first, it forces both Ursula and Baltazar to declare that the sale to Montiel has in fact already taken place (which of course is not the case); second, it underscores the fact that selling a product involves more than the ability to exact the best possible price: social prestige and power (being a Montiel and not a Giraldo) might be stronger factors in creating commercial ties than just the amount of money exchanged; and last but not least, Giraldo's visit heightens the conflict between maker and user concerning the thing made, its value and contingent meanings. The first paradoxical outcome of the story's plot is to be found in Giraldo's odd victory over Baltazar: for the doctor's failure to obtain the sale through rhetorical ploys cannot match the lasting contagiousness produced by his diagnosis. As a failed owner, he still manages to prescribe the spreading force of word over deed, of unstable metaphor over the presumptive accuracy of action or labor (perhaps Giraldo is destined to own only a wealth of words in which the never-to-be-owned object lies buried in the shadows of rhetoric's dreamwork).

In a curious way which testifies to the depth of practical wisdom conveyed by the tale—in the manner of a medieval *exemplum*—Giraldo's devious attempt to buy the cage anticipates Montiel's subsequent refusal to even consider buying it. Both men would seem to regard the transaction as something of far greater import than a simple commercial deal.

Giraldo's quaint elegance and cunning give way to Montiel's beastly alertness. No matter how much his son raves there will be no deal. Here is where readers of Mauss's *The Gift* might see in Montiel's refusal to honor his son's request, as well as in his suspicion of Baltazar's motives, something more than just the fear of parting with some cash at the whimsies of a child.

Surrounding the meanness of Montiel with respect to exchange there lies an area of intertextual prodigality which in this particular case happens to deal with the unrestrained giving and taking of objects. As it is well known, Marcel Mauss understood communal gatherings such as the potlatch as affairs in which primitive groups engaged in prolonged bouts of gift-giving and taking, under the common and necessary belief that a pervasive force—a sort of "mystic cement" in the words of Marshall Sahlins—existed binding donor and recipient; a force conveyed in and by the thing given, a force whose flow could not be arrested: receiving meant giving in turn to a third party and so, relentlessly and sometimes for weeks, men bound themselves through reciprocity.

In refusing Baltazar, Montiel manifests a tacit and inadvertent sense of the logic mapped out in *The Gift.* His character becomes attuned, pretextually, to the knowledge of the central moral put forth by Mauss. Montiel seems aware of something in the sale which exceeds the mere notion of a transaction, something in the order of a reciprocal bond, more deeply rooted in human soil than the overt exchange of cash for object. In other words, and in line with Mauss's lexicon, it is fear of *connubium,* of a lasting dwelling in the other, and of the other in oneself, through the force held in what is given, it is such apprehension which haunts Montiel into breaking this act of attempted *comercium.*

Baltazar's excessive and, until now, unfocused zeal meets in Montiel's denial a fitting and complementary force. The clash of wills brings about a shift from market affairs to the older strictures of gift-exchange: Baltazar's zeal and frenzy (which remain mystifying and naive at a narrowly realistic level) point beyond selling, while Montiel's refusal grasps, negatively, the gift import dwelling in the thing, its poisonous talents, its gravity. Here I am of course alluding to Mauss's use of etymology to create his own sense of analytic contagiousness: in several languages, including German, *gift* and *poison* stand in neighboring complicity. In our story, Montiel's refusal to buy is followed by Baltazar's gift of the cage to the child, an act far more offensive and threatening to Montiel than the attempted sale itself.

In terms of the need to reciprocate shown by Mauss, Montiel gets away without buying because nothing like the gift relationship exists in Macondo. One must see the archaic norm of symbolic exchange as subjunctive, being the opposite of function, working in not working any longer. Existing, it would have answered Montiel's refusal with strife. But Baltazar's gift is as unreciprocal as Montiel's non-buying: it shows as the poison foreshadowed in the refusal. Montiel knew well, something archaic lurked beneath the blank mirror of the carpenter's face.

I have tried to show that our understanding of the meeting between Montiel and Baltazar is heightened when merged with the textual contingencies activated by *The Gift.* I would also argue that when Mauss brings under interpretation the act or institution of gift-exchange he is dealing with the phenomenon of heightening itself. In other words, he is dealing with whether or not the occasion can ever arise to grasp social phenomena at a heightened pitch of meaningfulness, an occasion at once so singular and general as to amount to a total social deed. Without such heightening of communal purpose, the structuralist project could not meet its proper object of study, an object both discrete and universal. "Nothing in our opinion," writes Mauss, "is more urgent or promising than research into 'total' social phenomena"; adding that "the advantage is twofold. Firstly there is an advantage in generality, for facts of widespread occurrence are more likely to be universal than local institutions or themes, which are invariably tinged with local colour. But particularly the advantage is in realism. We see social facts in the round, as they really are. In society there are not merely ideas and rules, but also men and groups and their behaviours. We see them in motion as an engineer sees masses and systems, or as we observe octopuses and anemones in the sea. We see groups of men, and active forces, submerged in their environment and sentiments."

These words should explain how the institution of gift-exchange became the inaugural structuralist construct. Lévi-Strauss sees *The Gift* as such a beginning when, in his introduction to the main writings of Mauss, he recalls experiencing "the entire gamut of emotions" upon reading the essay for the first time, comparing his experience with Malebranche's evocation of his first reading of Descartes: "a thumping heart," "the head boiling," in other words, a total seizure. From this we may gather that poets and storytellers are not the only creators ruled by the jubilant but also anxious discovery of their powerful predecessors.

Mauss's emphasis on the possibility of transcribing feelings, and of moving beyond ideas and rules, casts him in a heroic role, given the reductive and arid character of much of what nowadays pretends to offer a semiotic account of social action. At any rate, he aims at a total gathering of social means, feelings and imaginings held in normative concert. Such a total construct achieves both its integrity and logic by opposing, replacing or holding at bay other, equally encompassing and frequently lethal domains. In the case of *The Gift,* the adversary turns out to be war itself. Just as gift-exchange must become total in order to prevent strife, Mauss's reconstruction of it must also achieve analytical integrity and wholeness if it is to stem chaos and randomness in the realm of knowing.

As the American anthropologist Marshall Sahlins has so elegantly demonstrated, *The Gift* shows the savage state of constant "war against" "warre," amounting to a "new version of the dialogue between chaos and covenant." I would add that the integrity and logic which characterize structuralist constructs such as *The Gift* become legitimate insofar as they prove necessary in order to stem randomness, thus mirroring culture's own righteousness. The resources of interpretation, painstakingly applied, become self-sustaining tropes (like culture itself), rendering themselves as the ethical instruments of the subject's peculiar surrender to cultural meanings.

And, just as the anthropologist stems randomness in the very act of surmising how the savage stems war through the battle of the gifts, Baltazar defeats Giraldo, but only after the doctor erects before his eyes an already odd and prodigious cage wrapped in a veil of words. Thus the plot of the story unfolds as a series of polemics, it makes itself—or so is our illusion as readers—out of a primal ground of reciprocal contingencies. I am reminded of Paul Ricoeur's rhetorical exclamation when confronting the ingenuity of the structuralist who, like the Argonauts, builds his vessel as he sails on it. "Now," says Ricoeur, "this is quite a strange brand of imitation which comprises and constructs the very thing it imitates!"

Even critics not concerned with Marcel Mauss have read "La prodigiosa tarde" in terms of latent warfare. The Peruvian novelist Mario Vargas Llosa speaks of "la guerra que divide a la realidad ficticia"; and of "la pugna primordial" which, active at the heart of the story, transcends a narrowly defined socioeconomic understanding of its incidents. Following this notion of *pugna,* one could see how Baltazar prevails in his meeting with Doctor Giraldo only at the level of literal exigencies (he manages to preserve the cage for Montiel's child), while being bested at the level of metaphoric or figural value: the doctor prescribes norms of understanding which transcend the immediate, the practical and urgently useful, just as Baltazar did when creating the cage in all its sumptuousness, before he landed upon the business of having to sell it. In his meeting with Montiel, however, Baltazar deviates into transcendent significance, he falls for what in the cage remains the prodigy that is the gift; he defeats meanness in Montiel and, as a result, he engages ruin. His surrender of the cage seems to be at once ridiculous and magnificent. The reader is left with a heightened sense of the conflicting meanings held in abeyance by the notion of prodigality embedded in the title: is to be prodigal to be reckless, wasteful and even idiotic, or is it perhaps to exercise the noblest of human talents? (Answering this question involves addressing the complex issue of the frequently mentioned christological aspect of Baltazar's figure, but by placing emphasis on the theological and existential hiatus that separates *Jesus* from *Christ.*)

> So far we have been concerned with cases where Jesus is someone else's guest, and not himself the host.

(Edward Schillebeeckx, "Jesus as host: a copious gift of God," *Jesus: An Experiment in Christology*)

Baltazar will remain oblivious to certain metaphoric gains. Instead of proclaiming his triumph by basing it on the prestige of giving gifts to the children of the rich (thus acknowledging his failure to sell and to profit), he will accept his now numerous followers, hosting them while being acclaimed for defeating Montiel's meanness through a sale. Thaumaturgic generosity, and its embarrassment of symbolic riches, is thus defeated by a different sort of metaphoric excess. As such, Baltazar's flight into the realms of metaphor is inflationary. It is so at least in a triple sense: he pays for the celebration of his own heroics with money from a sale that never takes place; not having such money, he leaves his watch at the saloon as token of future payment to be made with wages not as yet earned; and, once drunk, he dreams of building thousands of cages until becoming a millionaire. One might ask if such inflation could not be something meant to imply the inherent fictiveness of both monetary and personal values, something that betrays the ill-begotten powers put into these tokens in order to abstract from flesh, toil and thing their specific talents, their concrete modes of being. This question might reflect that, perhaps at a deeper level of understanding, what prevails here is the allegory of a process which, being at work in the growth of each individual, reproduces in his or her life a similar alienation into the abstract: could it be that ours is like the fate of things which grow into commodities and, further, into tokens of exchange? Baltazar's fate tells us about feelings, about times lived and felt, time known in the deed, but it tells us about all of it becoming, in the long run, not a form of being, but one of having been, of having to lag behind ourselves, lengthening the hiatus of our own life told as a tale of dispossession.

A brief parenthesis is now needed to deal with the unfolding political economy latent in the allegorical drift of the individual towards abstraction and alienation. In fact, the growth towards the abstract just sketched amounts to the move on the part of both plot and character into the realm of political economy, and away from modes of exchange and symbolic value which would lie outside of it.

Jean-Pierre Vernant has described the status of artisans in ancient Greece in terms of utmost pertinence. Working under a system of values which raised the use of products over their making, artisans made objects whose worth depended on the designs of their intended users. The models provided by the latter were the ones which ruled over the product's significance and social place. Men acted only when they used and not when they made things; they stood free, on account of this reigning ideal, only when they acted as users and not as makers. In fact, according to Vernant making was denied the philosophical status of being an action.

But such had not always been the case. In archaic times, before the flowering of the *polis,* there were *thaumaturgoi* or wandering makers shrouded in demonic prestige. These men engaged in making marvellous *thaumata* or *agalmata,* objects as sumptuous in their intricacies as they were useless, which these magicians displayed before their audiences. Building such captivating devices rested on the faculty (demiurgic as well as, in a radical sense, poetic) to seize the right occasion, the *kairos* or pregnant moment when the maker's labors stood the best chance of achieving the rhythms linking them with the force and values latent in matter. It should be clear that the same principle of sumptuous excess and prodigality discerned by Mauss is at work here, in the art of the thaumaturgus.

Baltazar, too, inscribes his action as maker within a similar domain of values, although in his case the spellbinding uselessness of the cage proves ephemeral. His increasing failure to resist the encroachment of the contending forms of use value which others would impose upon the cage equals his own drift (as constant as his heartbeat) towards the politics of economics and the economics of politics. It seems that there is in the order of things a cunning sort of reciprocity which pays the tribute of awe before the thing made, only to exchange it immediately for the appropriation taxed upon it by use value. Nothing of value can exist free from two temporal modes of becoming: first, the one in which use value is found and, then, the one which marks the object's fate as exchangeable value, as it sets it adrift in the currents of circulation.

This temporal drift characterizes the strictures of political economy. In his *Le Miroir de la production* (Paris: 1973), Jean Baudrillard argues in favor of regarding political economy as a category set within the Western, European and, by extension, capitalist understanding of production. He goes on to theorize that the Marxian critique of economic modes reinforces the basic concepts of production which it attempts to demystify, being an extension of the very system of political economy that it sets out to subvert. In his view, the systems of symbolic exchange that characterize archaic or savage societies of the sort treated by Mauss, are not economic. In viewing them as such, Marxist and other theories of production perform an act of cognitive imperialism.

Regardless of the validity of Baudrillard's thesis in the realm of pure economics, I would like to point out its relevance to practical criticism along the following lines: to subject literary fictions to semiotic transcription might result in a similar act of imperial appropriation. Without necessarily having to return to a subjectivist or emotionalist approach to literary values (or, for that matter, without turning literature into the eternal savage within our midst), one might search for modes of understanding more in sympathy with that aspect of literary fictions which remains a wayward and excessive act, a gesture not exhausted upon being reflected in the atomistic mirror of semiotic jargons. This becomes truly urgent after being witness to how much current exercises in semiotics tend to adopt the air of universal legitimacy which other Western sciences have historically claimed for themselves. Finally, it is dubious that the best and only means to address literary fictions through critical discourse should be that of demystifying them. The current abundance of such exercises in lucidity betrays our professional fascination with technique more than it does demonstrate an unlikely surge in applied wisdom.

I should like now to cite some areas of meaningfulness in "La prodigiosa tarde" which I have been in the need of omitting. These are details in which one could see perspectives in flight, or the process of how the story resists economic closure.

For instance, there are the women, beginning with Ursula in whom I like to see a Penelope who awaits and keeps time slicing onions and who, like her namesake Ursula Iguarán from *Cien años de soledad,* joins each single day with the next to form an endurable measure of life. Also there is Giraldo's wife, the enigmatic invalid from the short novel, *La mala hora,* always silent, bird-like in her gilded isolation. And finally Montiel's wife, who is better known to us as the widow of "La viuda de Montiel," and whose only moment of graceful acquaintance with life seems to have been her welcoming of Baltazar into the house and her celebration of the cage. I also all but excluded her son, who is dismissed by most critics as just a spoilt brat, but who exceeds such a minor role, being perhaps twice an orphan: orphan to Montiel's callousness and to Baltazar's childless prodigality (between child and cage there is a transparent affinity—"The child jumped up, embraced the cage which was almost as big as he was, and stood looking at Baltazar through the wirework without knowing what to say"; both are contested objects: two marks of disownment, the cage in its joyous emptiness as the vanishing point of the tale's allegories, the child as the inheritor of the blessings through which his dual orphanhood twice denies him the chance of becoming prodigal).

Quite besides these and other avoidances, I tried to focus on the two meetings between Baltazar, Giraldo and Montiel. I hoped to fix the plot upon a given site, an imaginary point in time and space large enough to encompass the main deployments of the action and yet small enough to allow for coherence in procuring a central fable, that of passage, of passing from feeling and desire into symbol and, ultimately, into abstraction. Here I must replace Giraldo as diagnostician of Baltazar's predicament, offering neither a prescription nor a cure for his increasing isolation. Matching Giraldo's eloquence with some borrowed jargon, I would call Baltazar a *hysteresiac*. In other words, he might be said to suffer from belatedness, he lags behind the effects of his own willfulness and craft, vibrating to the tune that someone else plays with his creation. By hysteresis I do not mean a psychological malady, but rather I wish to imply a rupture of temporal and semantic immediacy taking effect between person and surroundings, an acute state of ontological displacement with respect to life, habits and common values. Baltazar's *prodigiosa tarde* is emblematic of his falling into literature, of the layered disclosure which heightens his being as an affliction open to reading. Only as such could these few hours be at once catastrophic *and* blissful. The plot that befalls Baltazar removes him from his social cradle, from the contrived manner of space and time which his craft carves out.

If there is a token of literature in the tale, or a critical point where this peculiarly modern domain or affliction is best registered, it might be found in the protagonist's resistance to make it as structure. For all that we are given to know, when at the end Baltazar lies by the wayside in death-like sleep ("The women who passed on their way to five-o'clock Mass didn't dare look at him, thinking he was dead"), he might be enjoying that exorbitant condition of abjectness which Georges Bataille places at the heart of the unassailable realm of meaning known to him as the *heterogeneous*. With Baltazar we obtain either the residual oddity left behind by a hero of everyday toil, or just a patient awaiting some disciplinary judgement of his ills.

Our search for an available subject (which the rigors of social specification would not acknowledge unless it came structured) meets in the last Baltazar a figure as exempt from willed expressiveness (as unanswering) as the early Cordelia was poor in tokens of wordly acknowledgment. Literature as fiction chooses to begin and end as a barely articulate residue of a wordless domain, of a person always not-yet-available. Ironically, this could be fiction's way of matching the savage fulfillment of total social means and its enforcement of unanimous group practice. Acting within a social context in which affairs such as gift-exchange would now amount to a form of individual alienation, the fictions of literature could repeat, and perhaps on occasions be impelled to reenact, those ancestral agreements among bygone groups by regressing to stages radically ignorant of individual identity, or to a point where the *social* would simply vanish. Such backward exodus could leave behind traces of a social agenda yet to be conceived, a truly indigent proposal to be taken up by future readers.

> Adam was but human—this explains it all. He did not want the apple for the apple's sake, he wanted it only because it was forbidden. The mistake was in not forbidding the serpent: then he would have eaten the serpent.
>
> (Mark Twain, *Pudd'nhead Wilson*)

In bringing tale and essay together, I tried to outline what should be regarded as a basic structuralist ploy, of which *The Gift* is a seminal example. It consists of arresting the flux of social phenomena at a virtual point in time, or at a moment of potential crisis when systems of belief as well as practices can be grasped in dualistic confrontation. When the ethics of structuralism is imagined, it becomes apparent how, perhaps manifesting its debt to Hegel, the method has invariably tried to break such dual confrontations by means of generating a third realm of synthetic resolutions. This moral fable is a persistent one in the history of structuralist discourse: beginning with the insoluble and crisis-laden bond of signifier/signified (or Symbolic/Imaginary, as in Lacan), continuing with the master split Nature/Culture (plus its endless derivations) and gathering an ever-growing lexicon of polarities, the method remains poised on the line which *must* separate seemingly alien and yet reciprocal spheres in need of mediation.

I then tried to suggest that both essay and tale heighten for us the perils of passing from randomness to culture, doing so through a sort of transactional cadence. The giving and taking of gifts liberated culture from what Mauss saw, in line with other French moralists, as a brutish and stagnant condition. But in so doing he altered the views of classical contract theories by demonstrating that chaos had not preceded commonwealth, that before civilization coercion had not been the price of order (such is the case made by Marshall Sahlins). Likewise, the tale helped us establish a minimum coefficient of sociability in Macondo's life. In both essay and tale culture swings precariously between confrontation, its risks, and the dispersal of energies. Culture is fragile, menaced by corruption and distrust, but in *The Gift* is still remains free from the force of the body politic. In the absence of such a powerful synthesizer as well as censor of options and energies (the State or Commonwealth), human beings spent their lives dealing themselves in promiscuous yet logical ways (so goes the illusion raised by Mauss's sober nostalgia; in his concluding remarks he seems to be calling for at least a partial return to such animistic approaches to symbolic exchange). García Márquez also tells the story of Macondo as a struggle to remain reciprocal, or believing in the alien graces of the other, welcoming the gift of his arrival, or sustaining what Melville calls in *Moby-Dick* "the Siamese connexion with a plurality of other mortals."

But sooner or later social affairs will break away from the gift's enclosure, Macondo will evolve from Eden-like hamlet to boom town to ghostly ruin. The gypsy Melquíades's early offerings (those marvellous toys which José Arcadio changed to the point of madness) become in the end the Book itself, the one gifted occurrence which some characters will have to unravel, making of their own lives a fitting tune for its mute script.

If, as Gerard Genette has said, structuralism views language as a process of inexorable degradation of the symbol into the sign, the transfer of gifts offers us one of the earliest instances of such a drift. For archaic symbolic exchange encompasses a struggle, a *pugna* where symbol and thing meet, as the former is being institutionally born. But before the motivated character of the symbol with respect to that which it embodies gives way to the unmotivated and arbitrary sign, a prior severance will have occurred: the thing would have been designated or named, all perceptive immediacy between person and world having thus been broken (a passage which structuralism can adopt or simply assume but could not describe without going beyond its own epistemological strictures).

The tale brings us closer to this primal scenario than does the essay, since for Mauss gift-exchange must amount to at least a rudimentary institution, while in García Márquez's text the birdcage would exceed all stable linguistic designations, being either an unnamable aspect of thinghood, or a generator of the most extravagant efforts to describe it.

The theoretical preoccupations of Jacques Lacan tell us how close gift-giving was to the earliest vestiges of symbolic practice known to humans. *Symbol,* or what might correspond to our notion of it, designates in several languages "bond," "intercourse," "twisting together," "knotting" and, in archaic Greek, "a contribution to a common meal or feast." In parallel terms, Vladimir Propp sees the origins of folktales as a narrative detachment from ritual, in which a story is cast off from a ceremony where an object or amulet played the central role of being transferred into story; the object was eventually lost or simply replaced by a nucleus-plot dealing with its search and recovery (a fitting if historically dubious genesis for stories such as "La prodigiosa tarde").

However, what seems at stake here is not history as such, but rather casting our knowledge of fable-making in terms of tale-telling itself, a project which leads to the nostalgic sense of having lost contact with objects whose making and ritual possession the stories uphold in remembrance. Walter Benjamin also left us a fable of the storyteller's craft and of its imagined historical origins. The narrative elements of his well-known essay heighten the loss and eventual recovery of an object which remains at the heart of the tale's origination. Thus at one point in his essay Benjamin speaks of how "traces of the storyteller cling to the story the way the handprints of the potter cling to the clay vessel." For him the teller of tales ventures "into the depths of inanimate nature," a thematic thread which gains in prominence as the essay nears the end, finding perhaps emblematic resolution in his retelling of Johann Peter Hebel's story where a would-be bride recovers the crystalized body of her deceased betrothed after years of burial at the bottom of a mining shaft, an outcome that lends to the human form, recovered in jewel-like perfection, the status of an object at once pristine and definitive, like those which the art of the storyteller is said to seek.

The ethnographic records favored by Lacan bear affinities with the views of Propp and Benjamin. In them, thought, action and discourse become available to the archaic mentality as extraneous additions and support of gifts circulated in ritual. What discourse replaces and supplements into eventual obliteration is a touchstone-like object which, in an even more primordial sense becomes a site-of-sites, a clinging-to-place, a holding-fast-place, a dwelling place in need of being rent or cast asunder from itself.

But structuralism must leave such primal grounds in haste, searching for other, more structurable terms. However, readers of literature may lag behind such flight into abstraction, holding fast to the gifted enigma that is the object in its givenness.

To conclude, the merging of gift-bearing tale and essay suggests that in what is likely to prove the most enduring aspect of structuralism there is at work a grand fable which narrates the untuning of savage harmonies and tells us how there used to be an active embedding of the individual in his communal and natural environments. These harmonies the fortunate ethnographer might arrest and transcribe before they fade out forever. What literature might have to offer in answer to such a stern nostalgia for a bygone integrity of thought, action and setting is its own problematic sense of structure. Problematic because, in spite of some recent critical efforts, object/texts such as "La prodigiosa tarde" have a structural character which might be at best dubious and at worst trivial. Critics bent on structuring (and even some trying to emulate deconstructions) do not seem to have learned the lesson conveyed in recent fiction (by writers as different as Carlos Fuentes, Manuel Puig, Thomas Pynchon, Michel Tournier and of course García Márquez). For them, semioticians of literary fictions would seem to be engaged in a rather ponderous removal of the Emperor's new clothes, a game long since preempted by the dream merchants of what used to be called "Pop Culture," and last but not least by these novelists themselves, who remain as much connoisseurs of randomness as they are counterfeiters dealing in structures.

It is in grasping the structural contingency and excess of literary fictions as well as of hermeneutical strategies, and not in redeploying them structurally, that the beginnings of the critical task should lie. In this sense, to heighten a tale by means of an essay should be understood as a fictive and allegorical retelling aimed at disclosing the grounds of the interpreter's choices and ploys, which I perceive as being caught in the need to answer an always unfulfilled call for reciprocity embedded in the fable's mute wisdom.

ROBERTO GONZÁLEZ ECHEVARRÍA

Cien años de soledad: *The Novel as Myth and Archive*

To most readers the Latin American novel must appear to be obsessed with Latin American history and myth. Carlos Fuentes's *Terra Nostra* (1976), for instance, retells much of sixteenth-century Spanish history, including the conquest of Mexico, while also incorporating pre-Columbian myths prophesying that momentous event. Alejo Carpentier's *El siglo de las luces* (1962) narrates Latin America's transition from the eighteenth century to the nineteenth, focusing on the impact of the French Revolution in the Caribbean. Carpentier also delves into Afro-Antillean lore to show how blacks interpreted the changes brought about by these political upheavals. Mario Vargas Llosa's recent *La guerra del fin del mundo* (1980) tells again the history of Canudos, the rebellion of religious fanatics in the backlands of Brazil, which had already been the object of Euclydes da Cunha's classic *Os Sertões* (1902). Vargas Llosa's ambitious work also examines in painstaking detail the recreation of a Christian mythology in the New World. The list of Latin American novels dealing with Latin American history and myth is very long indeed, and it includes the work of many lesser known, younger writers. Abel Posse's *Daimón* (1978) retells the story of Aguirre, the sixteenth-century rebel who declared himself free from the Spanish Crown and founded his own independent country in South America. As the title of the book suggests, Posse's fiction centers on the myth of the Devil and his reputed preference of the New World as residence and field of operations, a theme that had been important in two

From *MLN* 99, no. 2 (March 1984).

earlier Latin American masterpieces: Alejo Carpentier's *El reino de este mundo* (1949) and João Guimarães Rosa's *Grande sertão, veredas* (1956).

Given that myths are stories whose main concern is with origins, the interest of Latin American fiction in Latin American history and myth is understandable. On the one hand, American history has always held the promise of being not only new but different, of being, as it were, the only *new* history, preserving the force of the oxymoron. On the other hand, the novel, which appears to have emerged in the sixteenth century at the same time as American history, is the only modern genre, the only literary form that is modern not only in the chronological sense, but also because it has persisted for centuries without a poetics, always in defiance of the very notion of genre. Is it possible, then, to make of American history a story as enduring as the old myths? Can Latin American history be as resilient and as useful a hermeneutic tool for probing human nature as the classical myths, and can the novel be the vehicle for the transmission of these new myths? Is it at all conceivable, in the modern, post-oral period, to create myths? Latin American history is to the Latin American narrative what the epic themes are to Spanish literature: a constant whose mode of appearance may vary, but which rarely is omitted. A book like Ramón Menéndez Pidal's *La epopeya castellana a través de la literatura española* could be written about the presence of Latin American history in the Latin American narrative. The question is, of course, how can myth and history coexist in the novel? How can founding stories be told in this most ironic and self-reflexive of genres? It seems to me that the enormous and deserved success of Gabriel García Márquez's masterpiece *Cien años de soledad* is due to the unrelenting way in which these forms of storytelling are interwoven in the novel.

II

In order to explain why and how myth and history are present in *Cien años de soledad* I must first give a brief outline of the broad theory within which my arguments are couched, a theory that, I hope, will allow me to bring a new perspective to the study of the origins and evolution of the Latin American narrative. It is my hypothesis that the novel, having no fixed form of its own, assumes that of a given document endowed with truth-bearing power by society at specific moments in history. The novel, or what is called the novel at various points in history, mimics such documents to show their conventionality, their subjection to rules of textual engenderment similar to those governing literature, which in turn reflect those of language itself. The power to endow the text with the capacity to bear the truth is shown to lie outside the text; it is an exogenous agent that bestows authority upon a certain kind of document owing to the ideological structure of the period. In sixteenth-century Spain these documents were legal ones. The form assumed by the Picaresque was that of a *relación* (report, deposition, letter bearing witness to something), because this kind of written report belonged to the huge imperial bureaucracy through which power was administered in Spain and its possessions. The early history of Latin America, as well as the first fictions of and about Latin America, are told in the rhetorical molds furnished by the notarial arts. These *cartas de relación* were not simply letters nor maps, but also *charters* of the newly discovered territories. Both the writer and the territory were enfranchised through the power of this document which, like Lazarillo's text, is addressed to a higher authority. The pervasiveness of legal rhetoric in early American historiography could hardly be exaggerated. Officially appointed historians (*cronista mayor de Indias*) were assigned by the Crown and the Royal Council of the Indies a set of rules which included ways of subsuming these *relaciones* into their works. American history and fiction, the narrative of America, were first created within the language of the law, a secular totality that guaranteed truth and made its circulation possible. It is within this totality that Garcilaso de la Vega, el Inca, wrote his *Comentarios reales de los Incas* (1609), for one must not forget that the *mestizo*'s book is an appeal to restore his father's name to an honorable position.

In the nineteenth century Latin America is narrated through the mediation of a new totality: science, and more specifically the scientific consciousness that expresses itself in the language of travelers who journeyed across the Continent, writing about its nature and about themselves. This was the second European discovery of America, and the scientists were the chroniclers of this second discovery. Except for a ground-breaking article by Jean Franco, little attention has been paid to this phenomenon, whose dimensions can be glimpsed by looking at the recent *Travel Accounts and Descriptions of Latin America and the Caribbean 1800–1920: A Selected Bibliography,* compiled by Thomas L. Welch and Myriam Figueras, and published by the Organization of American States (1982). Though selective, this volume contains nearly three hundred pages of tightly packed entries. The names of these scientific travelers are quite impressive, ranging from Charles Darwin to Alexander von Humboldt, and including the likes of the Schomburgk brothers, Robertson, Koch-Grünbergh, and many others. Their fictional counterpart is Professor Challenger in Sir Arthur Conan Doyle's *The Lost World,* whose voyage to the origins of nature takes him to South America. A scientific consciousness that expresses itself in the language of the travelogue mediates the writing of Latin American fiction in the nineteenth century. Domingo Faustino Sarmiento's *Facundo* (1845), Anselmo Suárez y Romero's *Francisco* (1880), and da Cunha's *Os Sertões* (1902) describe Latin American nature and society through the conceptual grid of nineteenth-century science. Like the chronicles, which were often legal documents, these are books that have a functional value and begin outside of literature. *Francisco* was originally part of a report sent to the British authorities documenting the horrors of slavery in Cuba. Latin America's history and the stories of adventurers, who seek to discover the innermost secrets of the New World, that is to say its newness and difference, are narrated through the mind of a writer qualified by science to search for the truth. Both the self and science are, as Franco suggests, products of the power of the new European commercial empires. Their capacity to find the truth is due not to the cogency of the scientific method, but to the ideological construct that supports them, a construct whose source of strength lies outside the text. The "mind" that analyzes and classifies is made present through the rhetorical conventions of the travelogue. Sarmiento ranges over the Argentine landscape in a process of self-discovery and self-affirmation. In his book he dons the mask of the traveling savant, distanced from the reality that he interprets and classifies according to the intervening tenets of scientific inquiry. This particular mediation prevails until the crisis of the nineteen-twenties and the so-called *novela de la tierra.*

The modern novel, of which *Cien años de soledad* is perhaps the best known example, avails itself of a different kind of mediation: anthropology. Now the promise of knowledge is to be found in a scientific discourse whose object is not nature, but language and myth. The truth-bearing document the novel imitates now is the anthropological treatise. The object of such studies is to discover the origin and source of a culture's own version of its values, beliefs, and history through a culling and re-telling of its myths. Readers of Mauss, Van Gennep, Lévi-Bruhl, Frazer, Lévi-Strauss and other anthropologists will no doubt recognize the inherent complexity of such works. In order to understand another culture, the anthropologist has to know his own to the point where he can distance himself from it. But this distancing involves a kind of self-effacement, too. This dramatic process has been beautifully expounded by Lévi-Strauss in *Tristes tropiques,* a book in which he devotes a good deal of time to his stay in

Brazil. John Freccero and Eduardo González have studied how much this book has in common with Alejo Carpentier's *Los pasos perdidos,* a text to which we shall have to return shortly.

Anthropology is the mediating element in the modern Latin American novel because of the place this discipline occupies in Western thought, and also because of the place Latin America occupies within that discipline. Anthropology is a way through which Western culture indirectly affixes its own cultural identity. This identity, which the anthropologist struggles to shed, is one that masters non-historical cultures through knowledge, by making them the object of its study. Anthropology translates into the language of the West the cultures of the others, and in the process establishes its own form of self-knowledge through a kind of annihilation of the self. Existential philosophy, as in Heidegger, Ortega and Sartre, is akin to this process, because it is only through an awareness of the other that Western thought can pretend to wind back to the origin of being. The native, that is to say Latin Americans or in general those who could be delicately called the inhabitants of the post-colonial world, provide the model for this reduction and beginning. The native has timeless stories to explain his changeless society. These stories, these myths, are like those of the West in the distant past, before they became a mythology. Freud, Frazer, Jung, and Heidegger sketch a return to or a retention of those origins. Anthropology finds their analogon in the contemporary world of the native. The modern Latin American novel is written through the model of such anthropological studies. In the same way that the nineteenth-century novel turned Latin America into the object of scientific study, the modern Latin American novel transforms Latin American history into originary myth in order to see itself as other. The theogonic Buendía family in *Cien años de soledad* owes its organization to this phenomenon.

The historical data behind my hypothesis concerning the modern novel and its relation to an anthropological model are vast. Miguel Angel Asturias, as is known, went to Paris to study ethnology under Georges Raynaud, an experience that produced in 1930 his influential *Leyendas de Guatemala.* One of Asturias's classmates at La Sorbonne was none other than Alejo Carpentier, who was then writing *¡Ecué-Yamba-O!* (1933), a novel that is, in many ways, an ethnological study of Cuban blacks. Another Cuban writer was also preparing herself in Paris in those years: Lydia Cabrera, whose pioneering studies of Afro-Cuban lore would culminate in her classic *El monte* (1954). In more recent times Severo Sarduy has been a student of Roger Bastide, and his *De donde son los cantantes* is, among many other things, a sort of anthropological study of Cuban culture, seen as the synthesis of the three main groups inhabiting the island: the Spanish, the Africans, and the Chinese. Borges's 1933 essay "El arte narrativo y la magia," where the art of storytelling is compared to two kinds of primitive cures outlined in *The Golden Bough,* is but one indication of the wide-ranging impact of Frazer on Latin America. Traces of this influence are visible in Octavio Paz, Carpentier, Carlos Fuentes, as well as in many others. Lydia Cabrera is perhaps the most significant author here, for she stands for a very important kind of Latin American writer who sits astride both literature and anthropology. Cabrera is a first-rate short-story writer, just as she is a first-rate anthropologist. Her teacher, Fernando Ortiz, was also claimed by literature and his influence upon modern Cuban letters is vast. Examples of writers straddling literature and anthropology are plentiful. The most notorious in recent years is Miguel Barnet, whose *Biografía de un cimarrón* not only contains all the perplexing dualities and contradictions of that relationship, but is also the perfect example of a book whose form is given by anthropology, but which winds up in the field of the novel. But the Peruvian José María Arguedas is without a doubt the most poignant figure among these anthropologist-writers: a novelist, anthropologist, and raised by Indians, Arguedas whose first language was Quechua, not Spanish, carried within him the contradictions and the tragedy inherent in the relationship between anthropology and literature with such intensity that he chose suicide in 1969.

Arguedas's radical gesture is a literal version of the reduction of the self inherent in the process of re-writing Latin American history in the context of the anthropological mediation. It is a gesture that has its literary counterpart, as we shall see, in *Cien años de soledad.* Arguedas's radical effacement of self, like the one practiced by Barnet as he turns or pretends to turn himself into Esteban Montejo, is part of the "unwriting" involved in the modern Latin American narrative. For the modern Latin American narrative is an "unwriting," as much as it is a rewriting, of Latin American history from the anthropological perspective mentioned. The previous writings of history are undone as the new one is attempted; this is why the chronicles and the nineteenth-century scientific travelogues are present in what I will call the Archive in modern fiction. The new narrative unwinds the history told in the old chronicles by showing that that history was made up of a series of conventional topics, whose coherence and authority depended on the codified beliefs of a period whose ideological structure is no longer current. Those codified beliefs were the law. Like the Spanish galleon crumbling in the jungle in *Cien años de soledad,* the history in the chronicles is a voided presence. Likewise, modern novels disassemble the powerful scientific construct through which nineteenth-century Latin America was narrated by demonstrating the relativity of its most cherished concepts, or by rendering literal the metaphors on which such knowledge is based. The power of genealogy is literalized in *Cien años de soledad* by, among other devices, the stream of blood that flows from José Arcadio's wound to Ursula. The presence of the European travelers Robertson and Bonplant in Roa Bastos's *Yo el supremo* attests to this second voided presence. But the paradigmatic text among these unwritings is Alejo Carpentier's 1953 *Los pasos perdidos*. In this first-person narrative, a modern man travels up the Orinoco river in search of native musical instruments that will unveil the origins of music. As he travels upriver—clearly the river in which Melquíades dies many years later—the narrator-protagonist writes about his voyage as if it were a journey back not only through time, but through recorded history. Hence he passes through various epochs, the most significant of which are the nineteenth century of the traveling European scientists, who provide him with a way of interpreting nature and time, and the colonial period of Latin American history, characterized by activities such as the founding of cities, the indoctrination of Indians, the beginning, in short, of history in the New World as set down by the charters of those institutions—the *cartas de relación*. There are other epochs, reaching all the way back to prehistoric times, but the above are the most important ones, because they are present not only thematically, but through the mediating texts themselves: the era of the petroglyphs is narrated in the language of the scientific travelogue, and the founding of cities in that of the legalistic chronicles. The narrator-protagonist's text is organized according to a set of rhetorical conventions that reveal themselves as such in the process of reading. In the fiction of the novel, the narrator-protagonist cannot remain in what he has termed the Valley-of-Time-Detained, the origin of time and history, for he needs to secure enough paper to set down the music he has begun to compose. In the fiction the quest for that degree zero of time and history whence to inscribe a rewriting of Latin American history has not been found. But in the writing of the novel a clearing has been reached, a razing that becomes a starting-point for the new Latin American narrative. That razing involves the various mediations through which Latin America was narrated, the systems from which fiction borrowed truth-bearing forms, erased to assume the new mediation, which requires this level-ground of self and history. This is the point at which *Cien años de soledad* begins, and the reason why the world is so recent "that many things lacked names, and in order to indicate them it was necessary to point." It is also the point that the last Aureliano seeks at the very end when he discovers how to translate Melquíades's manuscripts. He reads in a frenzy "discovering the first indications of his own being in a lascivious grandfather who let himself be frivolously dragged across a hallucinated plateau in search of a beautiful woman who would not make him happy." What is left for fiction after *Los pasos perdidos?* Clearly, only fiction; but novels are never content with fiction, they must pretend to deal with the truth. So, paradoxically enough, the truth with which they deal in the modern period is fiction itself. That is to say, the fictions Latin American culture has created to understand itself, the myths about the origin of its history.

III

The importance of myth in *Cien años de soledad* was noticed by the first commentators of the novel and later studies have again taken up the topic. It seems clear that myth appears in the novel in the following guises: (1) there are stories that resemble classical or biblical myths, most notably the Flood, but also Paradise, the Seven Plagues, Apocalypse, and the proliferation of the family, with its complicated genealogy, has an Old Testament ring to it; (2) there are characters who are reminiscent of mythical heroes: José Arcadio Buendía, who is a sort of Moses, Rebeca, who is like a female Perseus, Remedios, who ascends in a flutter of white sheets in a scene that is suggestive not just of the Ascension of the Virgin, but more specifically of the popular renditions of the event in religious prints; (3) certain stories have a general mythic character in that they contain supernatural elements, as in the case just mentioned, and also when José Arcadio's blood returns to Ursula; (4) the beginning of the whole story, which is found, as in myth, in a tale of violence and incest. All four, of course, commingle, and because *Cien años de soledad* tells a story of foundations or origins, the whole novel has a mythic air about it. No single myth or mythology prevails. Instead the various ways in which myth appears give the whole novel a mythical character without it being a distinct version of one given myth.

At the same time, there is lurking in the background of the story the overall pattern of Latin American history, both as a general design made up of various key events and eras, and in the presence of specific characters and incidents that seem to refer to real people and happenings. Thus we have a period of discovery and conquest, when José Arcadio Buendía and the original families settle Macondo. There is in this part of the book little sense that Macondo belongs to a larger political unit, but such isolation was in fact typical of Latin America's towns in the colonial period. Even the viceroyalties lived in virtual isolation from the metropolitan government. The appearance of Apolinar Moscoso and his barefoot soldiers is the beginning of the republican era, which is immediately followed by the outbreak of the civil wars in which Colonel Aureliano Buendía distinguishes himself. Though Colombia is the most obvious model for this period, nearly the entire continent suffered from civil strife during the nineteenth century, a process that led to the emergence of dictators and *caudillos*. This period is followed by the era of neocolonial domination by the United States and the struggles against it in most Latin American countries. These culminate in the novel with the general strike and the massacre of the workers. There are, unfortunately, countless models for this last, clearly defined period in the novel. After the flood, there is a time of decay before the apocalyptic wind that razes the town at the end. The liberal priest and the various military types who surround Colonel Aureliano Buendía, are among the characters with counterparts in Latin American history. Lucila I. Mena has already demonstrated that some of the historical incidents in the novel can be documented, and a sedulous critic with time and the proper library can probably document many others. But to carry this sort of research much further than Mena has would be a rather gratuitous critical exercise. Set against the global, totalizing thrust of the novel are these historical details which, without being specific, are nonetheless true in a general sense. Each of the above mentioned epochs is evoked not only through major historical events, but also through allusion to specific minor incidents and characters. For instance, early Macondo is inhabited by a *de jure* aristocracy made up of the founding families, which is analogous to that of colonial Latin America, where conquistadores and their descendants enjoyed certain privileges and exemptions.

The blend of mythic elements and Latin American history in *Cien años de soledad* reveals a desire to found an American myth. Latin American history is set on the same level as mythic stories, therefore it too becomes a sort of myth. The lack of specificity of the various incidents, which appear to represent several related or similar events, points in this direction. The Latin American myth is this story of foundation, articulated through independence, civil war, struggle against U.S. colonialism, all cast within a genealogical line that weaves in and out, repeating names and characters. There is a Whitmanian thrust to the brash declaration of the existence of a literary language that underlies this mixture of historical fact with mythic story in *Cien años de soledad*. The novel is in fact intimately related to similar efforts in poetry, such as the ones by Neruda in his *Canto General* and Octavio Paz in his *Piedra de Sol. Canto General* in particular is one of the most important sources of García Márquez's novel. Framed by Genesis and Apocalypse, fraught with incest and violence, the story of the Buendía family thus stands as Latin American history cast in the language of myth, an unresolved mixture that both beckons and bewilders the reader.

This duality is present throughout *Cien años de soledad* separating the world of writing from the atemporal world of myth. But the play of contradictions issuing from this duality reaches a synthesis that is perhaps the most important feature of the novel. As we have seen, myth represents the origin. Latin America's history is narrated in the language of myth because it is the other, represented by incest, taboo, and the primitive act of naming. The novel's persistent preoccupation with genealogy and with supernatural acts performed by various characters belongs to this realm. History, on the other hand, is critical, temporal, and dwells in a special place: Melquíades's room in the Buendía house, which I have chosen to call the Archive. The room is full of books and manuscripts, and has a time of its own. It is here that a succession of characters attempt to decipher Melquíades's parchments, and the last Aureliano, in an epiphanic inspiration, orally translates the whole (or nearly the whole) manuscript and dies. What occurs here, the text of the novel suggests, is unrepeatable. In the fiction of the novel, on the other hand, there are many repetitions. Ursula, for instance, twice feels that time is going around in circles and that members of the family follow one or two patterns of behavior indicated by their names. Time is circular in the fiction, but not in Melquíades's room. The Archive appears to be linear and teleological, while the plot of the novel itself is repetitive and mythical. *Cien años de soledad* is made up of two main stories: one has to do with the family and culminates in the birth of the child with the pig's tail, while the other is concerned with the interpretation of Melquíades's manuscript, a linear suspense story that culminates in Aureliano's final discovery of the key to the translation of the parchments.

That there should be a special abode for documents and books in *Cien años de soledad* should come as no surprise to readers of modern Latin American fiction. In spite of its apparent novelty, there are such enclosures in *Aura, Yo el Supremo, El arpa y la sombra, Crónica de una muerte anunciada* and *Oppiano Licario,* to mention a few of the novels where it plays a prominent role. What is characteristic of the Archive is: (1) the presence not only of history, but of previous mediating elements through which it was narrated, be it the legal documents of colonial times or the scientific ones of the nineteenth century; (2) the existence of an inner historian who reads the texts, interprets and writes them; (3) and finally the presence of an unfinished manuscript that the inner historian is trying to complete. In *Cien años de soledad* the most tenuous presence is the legal texts, but one can infer it from the allusions to the chronicles that were in fact *relaciones,* and particularly in the founding of Macondo, for the founding of cities, primordial activity of conquistadores, was closely connected to the writing of history. The vagueness of this presence is only so in relation to the others, for at least two critics have convincingly argued in favor of the overwhelming influence of the chronicles in *Cien años de soledad.* The nineteenth-century travel books are evident in the descriptions of the jungle and at a crucial moment when José Arcadio Segundo hears Melquíades mumble something in his room. José Arcadio leans over and hears the gypsy mention the name of none other than Alexander von Humboldt and the word *equinoccio,* which comes from the title of the latter's book, which in Spanish is *Viaje a las regiones equinocciales del Nuevo Mundo.* In Macondo's Archive, there are in addition two key works: the so-called English *Encyclopedia* and *The Thousand and One Nights.* These two books play an important role in Melquíades's writing, and the *Encyclopedia* is instrumental in the decoding of his manuscripts. The existence in Melquíades's fiction of precisely these two books adds a peculiar twist to the Archive, one that points to its own literary filiation.

I do not think that it would be too farfetched to say that *The Thousand and One Nights* and the so-called English *Encyclopedia* together are allusions to that master of fictions called Borges. In fact, Melquíades is a figure of the Argentine writer. Old beyond age, enigmatic, blind, entirely devoted to fiction, Melquíades stands for Borges, the librarian and keeper of the Archive. There is something whimsical in García Márquez's inclusion of such a figure in the novel, but there is a good deal more. It is not too difficult to fathom what this Borgesian figure means. Planted in the middle of the special abode of books and manuscripts, a reader of one of the oldest and most influencial collections of stories in the history of literature, Melquíades and his Archive stand for literature; more specifically, for Borges's kind of literature: ironic, critical, a demolisher of all delusions, the sort of thing we encounter at the end of the novel, when Aureliano finishes translating Melquíades's manuscript. There are in that ending further allusions to several stories by Borges: to "Tlön, Uqbar, Orbis Tertius," in that Macondo is a verbal construct; to "The Secret Miracle," in that

Aureliano, like the condemned poet, perishes the moment he finishes his work; to "The Aleph," in that Aureliano Babilonia's glimpse of the history of Macondo is instantaneous and all-encompassing; and particularly to "Death and the Compass," for the moment of anagnorisis is linked to death. Like Lönnrot, Aureliano only understands the workings of his fate at the moment of his death.

The Archive, then, is Borges's study. It stands for writing, for literature, for an accumulation of texts that is no mere heap, but an *arché*, a relentless memory that disassembles the fictions of myth, literature and even history. The masterbooks in the Archive are, as we have seen, the *Encyclopedia* and *The Thousand and One Nights*. The *Encyclopedia*, which Aureliano has read according to the narrator from A to Z as if it were a novel, is in itself a figure of the totality of knowledge as conceived by the West. But how is it knowledge, and how has Aureliano read it? The moment we consider the order of knowledge in the *Encyclopedia* and the way in which Aureliano reads it, we realize the paradoxes inherent in the Archive as repository of history. The *Encyclopedia* is organized, of course, in alphabetical order, without the order of the entries being affected by any sort of chronological or evaluative consideration: Napoleon appears before Zeus and Charles V before God. The beginning is provided arbitrarily by the alphabet as well as by the sequence: apocalypse must appear in the first volume. *The Thousand and One Nights*, on the other hand, stands for a beginning in fiction, or beginning as fiction, as well as for a series of individual, disconnected stories, linked only by the narrator's fear of death. Aureliano is like Scheherazade, who tells her stories on the verge of death. Neither book seems to have priority over the other. Both have a prominent place within the Archive, providing their own forms of pastness, of documentary, textual material. The order that prevails in the Archive, then, is not that of mere chronology, but that of writing; the rigorous process of inscribing and decoding to which Melquíades and the last Aureliano give themselves over, a linear process of cancellations and substitutions, of gaps.

Writing and reading have an order of their own which is preserved within the Archive. It might be remembered that in Melquíades's room, it is always Monday and March for some characters, while for others his study is the room of the chamberpots, where decay and temporality have their own end embodied in the very essence of eschatology. The combination of feces and writing in the Archive is significant enough. Writing appears as an eschatological activity in that it deals with the end. Yet writing is also the beginning, insofar as nothing is in the text until it is written. Hence the prevalence of Monday and March in the secret abode of Melquíades, the beginning of the week and of spring respectively (March, not April, is the "cruellest month" in García Márquez). Melquíades is both young and old, depending, of course, on whether or not he wears his dentures; he presides over the beginning and the end. The Archive, then, is not so much an accumulation of texts as the process whereby texts are written; a process of repeated combinations, of shufflings and re-shufflings ruled by heterogeneity and difference. It is not strictly linear, as are both continuity and discontinuity, held together in uneasy allegiance. This is the reason why the previous mediations through which Latin America was narrated are contained in the Archive as voided presences; they are both erased and a memory of their own demise, keys to filing systems now abandoned, but they retain their archival quality, their power to differentiate, to space. They are not archetypes, but an *arché* of types.

This process is evident in the way in which Melquíades's manuscript is written and translated. Throughout the novel we are told that Melquíades writes undecipherable manuscripts, that his handwriting produces something that looks more like musical notation than script, that his writing resembles clothes on a line. Eventually José Arcadio Segundo discovers, with the aid of the *Encyclopedia,* that the writing is in Sanskrit. When Aureliano begins to translate from the Sanskrit, he comes up with coded Spanish verses. These verses have different codes, depending on whether they are even or odd numbered. Aureliano is finally illuminated when he sees the dead newborn being carried away by the ants and remembers the epigraph of the manuscript, which is supposed to read: *"The first of the line is tied to a tree and the last is being eaten by the ants"* (emphasis in the original). He realizes then that the manuscript contains the story of his family, and hurries on to translate it to discover his own fate and the date and circumstances of his death. We shall return to the significance of all this, but first let us complete our description of the manuscript and its translation, for it is very easy to leap to conclusions concerning Melquíades's writing. Aureliano begins to translate the text out loud, jumping ahead twice to get to the present faster. Once he reaches the present he has a second illumination: that he would die in the room where the manuscript is kept once he finished translating the last line of poetry ("el último verso"). Critics have been quick to say that what we have read is Melquíades's version of the history of Macondo, that is to say, *Cien años de soledad.* Even if in fact it is Aureliano's translation that we read, then some changes have been made. To begin with, the epigraph has been omitted, as we have seen. In addition, Aureliano's leaps to get to the present have either not been accounted for in this version, or the holes they left have been restored. But by whom? The only solution to this enigma is to say that our reading—that each reading—of the text is the text, that is to say, yet another version added or appended to the Archive. Each of these readings corrects the others and each is unrepeatable insofar as it is a distinct act caught in the reader's own temporality. In this sense, we, like Aureliano, read the instant we live, cognizant that it may very well be our last. This is the eschatological sense announced in various ways by the Archive.

The radical historicity to which the Archive condemns us belies its apparent atemporality and the bizarre order that the masterbooks within it have. It is a historicity that is very much like the one to which the narrator-protagonist of *Los pasos perdidos* is condemned at the end of that novel. In fact, Aureliano's reading of the manuscript in search of his origins and of an understanding of his being in the present is analogous to the reading performed by Carpentier's character in search of the origins of history and of his own beginnings. Such dearly achieved historicity in the face of the circularity and repetition of the family's history is somewhat ironic, given the sense of ahistoricalness with which many readers, intoxicated by the similarity of names and by Ursula's notion that time is going round and round, leave the novel. Such historicity, however, is needed to represent, within the anthropological mediation posited, the lucid consciousness of the West, able to understand itself by posturing as the other, but unable to abandon the sense of history to which writing sentences it. This is a sentence from which we can gain acquittal by means of a wilful act of delusion, but one that *Cien años de soledad,* for all its fictive force, does not allow the reader.

There is a curious fact that few readers of *Cien años de soledad* remark upon: even though the novel begins with Colonel Aureliano Buendía facing the firing squad, the one who dies at the end is not Aureliano the soldier, but Aureliano the reader. It seems to me that this displacement, plus the fact that Aureliano's moments of vision are flashes of insight parallel to those of the rebel, seem to suggest a most significant connection between the realms of history and myth, one that constitutes a common denominator between the repetitions of the family history and the disassembling mechanisms of the Archive. In the Archive, the presence of Melquíades and Aureliano (and in *Aura,* Felipe Montero, in *Yo el Supremo,* Patiño, etc.) is an insurance that the individual consciousness of a historian/writer will filter the ahistorical pretense of myth by subjecting events to the temporality of writing. But in *Cien años de soledad* the death of these figures is indicative of a mythic power that lurks within the realm of writing, a story that makes possible the Archive. In *Yo el Supremo* this is clearly indicated by Patiño's being a "swollen foot," that is, an Oedipus who pays a high price for his knowledge. In *Cien años de soledad* Aureliano suffers a similar fate. He commits incest with his aunt, engenders a monster with her and dies the moment he has a glimpse of his fate. Aureliano is the necessary victim for us to be able to read the text, for us to acquire the knowledge we need to decode it. He (we) is no Oedipus, but more likely a Minotaur, which would bring us back to Borges (and also Cortázar). The ritualistic death—which prefigures that of *Crónica de una muerte anunciada*—is necessary because of the incest committed both at the genealogical and the textual level. In both cases, what has been gained is a forbidden knowledge of the other as oneself, or vice versa.

As we have seen, the most salient characteristic of the text we read is its heterogeneity. However, this heterogeneity is made up of differences within similarity. The various versions of the story are all related, yet differ in each instance. Their difference as well as their relation is akin—*valga la palabra*—to the relationship between the incestuous characters and to the broader confrontation between writer and a primitive other who produces myth. Put differently, the self-reflexiveness of the novel is implicitly compared to incest, a self-knowledge that somehow lies beyond knowledge. A plausible argument can be made that the end results of both are similar, in the most tangible sense, or at least related. When the ants carry away the carcass of the monstrous child engendered by Amaranta Ursula and Aureliano, its skin is described in terms that are very reminiscent of Melquíades's parchments. The English translation blurs that similarity. It reads: "And then he saw the child. It was a dry and bloated bag of skin that all the ants in the world were dragging." The Spanish reads: "Era un pellejo (it was a skin) hinchado y reseco, que todas las hormigas del mundo iban arrastrando." I need not go into the etymological and historical kinship uniting skin and parchment because the novel itself provides that link. The parchments are once described as "parecían fabricados en una material árida que se resquebrajaba como hojaldres," and the books in the Archive are bound "en una materia acartonada y pálida como la piel humana curtida." The English reads, "the parchments that he had brought with him and that seemed to have been made out of some dry material that crumpled like puff paste," and "the books were bound in a cardboard-like material, pale, like tanned human skin."

The monster and the manuscript, the monster and the text, are the product of the turning onto oneself implicit in incest and self-reflexivity. Both are heterogeneous within a given set of characteristics, the most conspicuous of which is their supplementarity: the pig's tail, which exceeds the normal contours of the human body, and the text, whose mode of being is each added reading. The novel is a monster, engendered by a self-knowledge of which we too are guilty, to which we add our own pig's tail of reading and interpretation. The plot line that narrates the decipherment of the manuscripts underscores our own falling into this trap. Like Aureliano, we follow along in search of the meaning of the manuscripts, constantly teased by scenes where Melquíades appears scratching his incomprehensible handwriting onto rough parchment, by scenes where José Arcadio Segundo or Aureliano make preliminary discoveries that eventually lead them to unravel the mystery. But like Lönnrot in "Death and the Compass," and like Aureliano himself, we do not discover, until the very end, what the manuscripts contain. Our own anagnorisis as readers is saved for the last page, when the novel concludes and we close the book to cease being as readers, to be, as it were, slain in that role. We are placed back at the beginning, a beginning that is also already the end, a discontinuous, independent instant where everything commingles without any possibility for extending the insight, an intimation of death. This independent instant is not the novel; it is the point to which the novel has led us. By means of an unreading, the text has reduced us, like Aureliano, to a ground zero, where death and birth are joined together as correlative moments of incommunicable plenitude. The text is that which is added to this moment. Archive and myth are conjoined as instances of discontinuity rather than continuity; knowledge and death are given equivalent value.

It is a commonplace, almost an uncritical fetish, to say that the novel always includes the story of how it is written, that it is a self-reflexive genre. The question is why and how it is so at specific moments. Clearly, *Cien años de soledad* is self-reflexive not merely to provoke laughter, or to declare itself literary and thus disconnected from reality or from history. In García Márquez, and I daresay in all major Latin American novelists, self-reflexivity is a way of disassembling the mediation through which Latin America is narrated, a mediation that constitutes the pre-text of the novel itself. It is also a way of showing that the act of writing is caught up in a deeply rooted, mythic struggle that constantly denies it the authority to generate and contain knowledge about the other without at the same time generating a perilous sort of knowledge about one's mortality and capacity to know oneself.

What do we learn about Latin American history in *Cien años de soledad?* We learn that while its writing may be mired in myth, it cannot be turned to myth, that its newness makes it impervious to timelessness, circularity, or any such delusion. New and therefore historical, what occurs in America is marked by change, it is change. García Márquez has expressed this by tantalizing the reader with various forms of myth, while at the same time subjecting him to the rigors of history as writing, of history as Archive. He has also achieved it by making Borges the keeper of the Archive, for the figure of the Argentine ensures that no delusions about literature be entertained. In a sense, what García Márquez has done is to punch through the anthropological mediation and substitute the anthropologist for an historian, and to turn the object of attention away from myth as an expression of so-called primitive societies to the myths of modern society: the book, writing, reading, instruments of a quest for self-knowledge that lie beyond the solace mythic interpretations of the world usually afford. We can always use *Cien años de soledad* to escape temporality, but only if we wilfully misread it to blind ourselves of its warnings against it. American history can only become myth enmeshed in this very modern problematic that so enriches its most enduring fictions.

For it is not toward a high-pitched rationality that *Cien años de soledad* moves, but toward a vision of its own creation dominated by the forces that generate myth. This is perhaps most evident if we consider that the Archive may very well be the most powerful of cultural retentions. The Archive is, first of all, a repository for the legal documents wherein the origins of Latin American history are contained, as well as a specifically Hispanic institution created at the same time as the New World was being settled. As is known, the great Archive at Simancas, begun by Charles V, but finished by the King Bureaucrat Philip II, is the first and possibly most voluminous such storehouse in Europe. The same Herrera who designed the Escorial had a hand in planning the Archive, that is to say, in turning a castle that was originally a prison into the Archive. America was discovered by Columbus, but really became a historical entity as a result of the development of the printing press. Latin America was created in the Archive. It may very well have been Carlos Fuentes in his *Terra Nostra* who most clearly saw the connection, making Cervantes the inner historian in that novel. In terms of the novel's ability to retain and pass on cultural values, the message contained in books such as Fuentes's and *Cien años de soledad* is indeed disturbing, for they tell us that it is impossible to create new myths, yet bring us back once and again to that moment where our desire for meaning can only be satisfied by myth.

REGINA JANES

Liberals, Conservatives, and Bananas: Colombian Politics in the Fictions of Gabriel García Márquez

García Márquez once remarked that the reader of *Cien años de soledad* who was not familiar with the history of his country, Colombia, might appreciate the novel as a good novel, but much of what happens in it would make no sense to him. Such a reader is in danger of giving to the author's inventiveness what belongs to reality's own absurdity and the author's gift for perceiving, selecting, and heightening the impossible fact. The danger is García Márquez's own fault. Solitude and the operation of the imagination on life are the obsessions of his fiction, and neither is intrinsically political or social. The reader accustomed to García Márquez's smudging the line between the possible and the impossible can locate himself more or less comfortably and correctly when the references are to universal history or human psychology, but if he misses the specific historical allusions, he misses the intersection of the imagined and the real in the realm of the political where men meet to struggle for power. *Cien años de soledad,* with which we will be principally but not exclusively concerned, integrates personal obsessions, literary allusion, and political interpretation in a "total" novel, a kind of which Vargas Llosa has usefully remarked, "The novelist creates from *something;* the total novelist, that voracious being, creates from *everything.*"

It took García Márquez some time to discover how to integrate the political with everything else. In his earlier works, political issues are either allegorized or serve as an indistinct backdrop against which a conflict between characters or within a character is enacted. In *Cien años de sole-*

From *Hispanofila* no. 82 (September 1984).

dad and *El otoño del patriarca,* the political serves as an organizing principle for the work, providing the structure of the two central sections of *Cien años de soledad* and informing the whole of *El otoño del patriarca,* which blends the allegorical, satirical, and mythic in a manner reminiscent of the earlier short story "Los funerales de la Mamá Grande." In an early essay, "Dos o tres cosas sobre la novela de violencia" (1960), García Márquez discussed the problem of treating contemporary political issues in fiction and defined the way he was to handle them in his earlier works. The fault he found with most novels dealing with "la violencia" was that they were bad novels, and they were bad in large part because the novelists had forgotten that novels must deal with the living and not with the dead. They had put "la violencia" first and gone astray in descriptions "de los decapitados, de los castrados, las mujeres violadas, los sexos esparcidos y las tripas sacadas," forgetting that "la novela no estaba en los muertos . . . sino en los vivos que debieron sudar hielo en su escondite." He preferred the indirect mode of Camus's *La Peste* in which the horror is in the atmosphere men breathe and through which they move and not in piles of corpses. In his own early works, "la violencia" and the memory of the civil war occupy the prescribed place, a stifling backdrop of fear and insecurity, an atmosphere heavy with oppression affecting the lives of the characters but not at the center of the action of the fiction. In *La hojarasca* (completed in 1952, published in 1955), the conflict between the grandfather who would bury the dead doctor and the town who would have him rot in his house depends for its motivation on the civil wars and guerrilla activity, but the action of the fiction is the grandfather's determination to fulfill a promise. In *El coronel no tiene quien le escriba* (1958) the action is again centered on an old man's determination, a determination to continue waiting for the pension promised him at the end of the last civil wars as he struggles with the governmental bureaucracy, and his son and his son's friends die in guerrilla struggles. The rage of the waiting finally finds a focus and purpose in the care of his son's fighting cock, and it is his discovery of that purpose that forms the action of the fiction, while governmental lethargy and betrayal constitute a context, a backdrop on which he can have no effect, before which his struggles are futile, and because of which his struggles continue. In stories such as these, García Márquez takes fifty years of Colombian history for granted and expects his reader to recognize his references.

The same need for recognition occurs in stories written at about the same time in the fantastic mode. Historical realities are still recognizable but are now deformed by the imagination, and the effect of the stories depends on the reader's recognition of the truth of the deformity. Both "Los funerales de la Mamá Grande" and "El mar del tiempo perdido" are satirical allegories, the first like *El otoño del patriarca* (from which it differs most in the character of the narrative voice) packed with specific references; the second more general, making use of a symbolic action parallel to that of the foreign exploitation it satirizes. One of the triumphs of *Cien años de soledad* and *El otoño del patriarca* is the integration of the fantastic and the realistic in the interpretation of political history, and to appreciate that integration some sense of the realities on which it is based is necessary.

The principal events to which García Márquez refers throughout his fictions are the traditional opposition between political parties, the civil wars of the nineteenth century, "la violencia" of the twentieth century, and the banana strike of 1928 in the Santa Marta region. García Márquez has on occasion argued, following Carpentier, that the reality of Latin America is in itself marvelous, and while one may quarrel with the premise, Colombia seems to have done its best to be useful to its author both as a history and as a habit of mind.

In common with most Colombian historiography, García Márquez's work neglects the colonial period and confines itself to the period following independence and to the modern period. In the neglected period, there are at least two events that García Márquez might have invented but did not need to. Bogotá, the capital of Colombia, occupies part of a high plain separated from the Caribbean to the north by 400 miles of jungle and mountains; it is 200 miles due east from the Pacific with two Andean ranges and jungle intervening; to the east of the city, there are again mountains, a great desert plain, and more jungles. In pre-Colombian times, it had acquired some indigenous fame as the site of "El Dorado," "the gilded man," from the custom of the king's rolling himself in gold dust and going for a swim in a nearby lake. In 1538 this remote and inaccessible city was discovered simultaneously by three Spanish explorers coming from three different directions: one from the north (he arrived first by a week), one from the southwest, and one from the east. Colombia also contrived to double its wars of independence. With the lawful king of Spain ousted by Napoleon, Colombia declared itself independent in 1810. In 1815 the Spanish general Murillo effected a brutal reconquest of which the centerpiece was the siege of Cartagena where some 6,000 people died. In 1820, Bolívar reliberated the country. Murillo's initial victory had been facilitated by internal squabbling among the Colombians themselves, and that period is enshrined in Colombian historiography under the dubious title "la Patria Boba," "the Booby Fatherland." Somewhat unexpectedly for the home of the Buendías, Colombia has given itself seven different names.

The period prior to independence exists in García Márquez's fictions largely in the form of memories and relics. Drake's attack of Riohacha in 1568, the discovery of the skeleton in armor and the galleon in *Cien años de soledad,* the defeat of William Dampier's lombards in 1681 in *El otoño del patriarca* are memories of past incursions unconnected with the life of the present but preserved as talismans of an heroic past. The life of the colonial period surfaces briefly in the house that Ursula built in *Cien años de soledad.* It was constructed for the most aristocratic of purposes, to promote and arrange the marriages of marriageable daughters, and it is filled with imported objects, Viennese furniture, Bohemian crystal, tablecloths from Holland. With the guest list for the inaugural party, Macondo emerges as a town with an aristocracy and leading oligarchs, for the only people invited, we are told, are the descendents of the founders, with the exception of the scandalous and therefore excluded family of Pilar Ternera. The social pattern incarnated in that house can be called colonial, but it could as well be postindependence and early modern, for it is a pattern that was established early and has endured long in Colombian society, reputedly one of the most traditional, aristocratic, and closed in Latin America.

As soon as the house is finished, Don Apolinar Moscote materializes as magistrate to order it painted blue, the color of the Conservative party, for the celebration of national independence. José Arcadio Buendía tries and fails to throw him out of town in an early enactment of the futile resistance of local and apolitical caudillos to the power of the central authority impinging on their own. Shortly thereafter, Moscote explains the difference between the political parties to the incipient Colonel Aureliano Buendía:

> Los liberales, le decía, eran masones; gente de mala índole, partidaria de ahorcar a los curas, de implantar el matrimonio civil y el divorcio, de reconocer iguales derechos a los hijos naturales que a los legítimos, y de despedazar al país en un sistema federal que despojara de poderes a la autoridad suprema. Los conservadores, en cambio, que habían recibido el poder directamente de Dios, propugnaban por la estabilidad del orden público y la moral familiar; eran los defensores de la fe de Cristo, del principio de autoridad, y no estaban dispue-

> stos a permitir que el país fuera descuartizado en entidades autónomas.

Moscote is not a bad political analyst, and the father-in-law teaching the son agrees with one despairing scholarly analysis of party affiliation in Colombia—that it is inherited and passed on through the family.

Inadvertently echoing Gilbert and Sullivan, Milton Puentes began his history of the Liberal party in Colombia by saying that there are five kinds of human beings, but only two kinds of political beings: liberal and conservative. Hernández Rodríguez maintains that "among the most remote childhood memories of a Colombian are . . . those of political parties similar to two races which live side by side but hate each other eternally." Colombia's political parties came into being with independence but acquired their formal designations in the election of 1849. The ideological division between them has always been clear and distinct, the armed conflict bloody and recurrent. It was an axiom of Colombian historiography in the early twentieth century that unlike the revolutions in other parts of Latin America and other parts of the world, violent conflict and intestine broils in Colombia were caused not by conflicting economic interests or by a brutal drive for power, but by the opposition of political ideals. Abstract and principled, Colombia's conflicts were bloodier and longer lasting than those of other nations because they could not be satisfied with blood or bread or any material thing. Conflict was rooted in the national character, and with the nation embattled over abstractions there was not room for Burkeian compromise. This fatalistic and poetic rendering of the national history was facilitated by the vertical organization of the parties. Both included representatives from all social and economic strata instead of being organized horizontally to represent a single class interest.

But the relations between the parties are by no means so simple as that description would have it. The parties have consistently joined ranks to expel dictators; factions of one party have aided factions of the other in fomenting civil wars; both parties have joined together not only to oust dictators who threaten the hold of either party on political power, but also to quell social unrest rising from below. Perhaps the most bizarre arrangement anywhere in recent political history was the formation of the National Front in 1957, by which the two parties agreed to alternate in power for sixteen years with one term a Conservative president, the next a Liberal president, and balanced cabinets. Such an arrangement, possible only among those with a common class interest transcending ideology, gives some force to the cynical popular saying, quoted by García Márquez in *Cien años de soledad,* that "La única diferencia actual entre liberales y conservadores es que los liberales van a misa de cinco y los conservadores van a misa de ocho."

The ideological question that first divided the parties was the structural one that Moscote lists last: federalism versus centralism. Should the provinces of New Granada be united in a loose federation with a high degree of local autonomy or should there be a strong central government with a powerful executive exercising significant control over state governments? The quarrel arose from the bivalent structure of Spanish colonial rule and an ideological split with respect to the appropriate constitutional model. In the colonial period, there had existed a central authority sent from Spain and concentrated in the capitals of the viceroyalties. But the territories so ruled were vast, and effective control of the entire territory by the central authority was impossible. Thus there existed, as a product of the isolation created by distance and the difficulty of communication across mountain ranges and jungles, considerable autonomy of the local level in spite of the constitutional concentration of power. After independence it remained the interest of local magnates to retain their autonomy, and as a result such anomalies occurred as the Conservative support of the federalist constitution of 1863 when the Liberals were briefly the dominant party.

Linked to the question of structure were a number of other issues, and the conflict between the parties on those issues has found two principal outlets: civil war and the writing of new constitutions. Between 1821 and 1945 Colombia formulated eleven national constitutions, and in 1976 the president of the republic was calling for yet another constitutional convention. It is difficult to keep track of the number of civil wars. One source estimates that there were between seventy and eighty major uprisings between 1821 and 1930, with most of them occurring between 1821 and 1903, averaging a war every year and a half. In 1883 Rafael Núñez, twice president of the republic, complained that Colombia was morally and materially ruined by revolutions. Rather unkindly, he compared Colombian politics to the London zoo and quoted a North American minister to the effect that "In Colombia they've organized anarchy itself."

Although there are of course no constitutional provisions regulating marriage and divorce, the constitutions are the documents that define the structure of the government, the role of the church, and the extent of civil liberties. The first few constitutions (of 1811, 1821, 1830, 1832, 1843) were centralist, but in 1849 the Liberals assumed power, and the succeeding constitutions (1853, 1858, 1861, 1863) became progressively more federalist and, in the broader sense of the term, liberal. As García Márquez has pointed out, the Liberal constitution of 1863 provided for more fundamental civil liberties than does the constitution in effect in Colombia today. Looking for ideological support to the European revolutions of 1789 and 1848, the Colombian Liberals sought to ensure religious toleration and to secularize the state by removing education from the control of the church, by barring clerics from national office, and by depriving the church of state support and the right to acquire real property. They removed all property, income, and literacy qualifications for voting and for holding public office and maximized the number of officials elected directly by the people. That constitution also provided for free, secular, and obligatory primary education, unlimited freedom of the press, and the right to traffic in and possess arms. The provisions with respect to the church, as Moscote confirms, were particularly sensitive. The constitutions of 1861 and 1863 are the only constitutions not drawn up in the name of God; excluded from those proceedings, he has been recalled in subsequent deliberations. The provision for secular and obligatory primary education was the immediate occasion of the civil war of 1876–77, when the Conservatives of Antioquia and Cauca rose against the national government. Other uprisings were occasioned by the confiscations of church property and the closing or consolidation of religious houses. The status of the Jesuits provides something of a weathervane. García Márquez alludes to one wholesale expulsion of religious in *El otoño del patriarca* but the Jesuits have made more than one round trip out of and back into Colombia. Expelled in 1767 from all his dominions by the king of Spain, they returned to Colombia in 1844 by an act of 1815. Expelled again in 1850, they were allowed to return in 1858; expelled yet again in 1861, they returned in 1886 and are still there.

The provisions of the constitution of 1863 that allowed traffic in arms and rendered the states sovereign entities resulted in a period of such social unrest that it has been called the "era of the warlords." Riascos Grueso estimates that in the fourteen years between 1862 and 1876 there were forty-five local civil wars affecting almost every part of the country. That comes to better than three uprisings a year and should make Colonel Aureliano Buendía's thirty-two uprisings in almost twenty years appear rather modest, though by no means negligible. The continued turmoil occasioned a split in the Liberal ranks in which the "radicals" continued to support the constitution of 1863 and its provisions for state sovereignty and arms traffic, while the "independents" favored a new constitution that would fortify the central government and reserve the police power to it. Led by Núñez, the "independents" gathered support from 1878 on, and in 1884 Núñez was elected president. In 1884–85, the bellicose wing of the "radicals" (as distinct from the "pacific" wing which opposed war) rose against the "independent" government headed by Núñez. Núñez promptly called for and received support from the Conservatives, defeated the radicals, and established the National party, composed of Conservatives and "independent" Liberals. Núñez and his supporters, replaying on their own terms the convention of Rionegro that had put together the constitution of 1863 without a Conservative in the room, composed the constitution of 1886 at a convention to which no radicals were invited.

The constitution of 1886, which remains the basis of the constitution in effect in Colombia today, promptly abolished the states as substantive political entities, forebade the possession of arms and traffic in munitions except by the government, declared Catholicism the religion of the nation, enjoined the public authorities to protect and respect it, and ordered public education to be organized and directed in accord with the Catholic religion. Religious toleration was respected in that no one was to be required to contribute to the support of the church or to support its doctrines; clerics were still barred from public office, and the freedom of the press was guaranteed, with the wide proviso that the press was to be "responsible under law for injuries to personal honor and for disturbances of the social order and public peace." Indirect elections and the appointment of officials were reintroduced on a massive scale, and property qualifications for voting and for holding office were reinstituted. In effect, the constitution aimed to reassert the power of property in the state, to reestablish the privileged position of the church, and to tighten the control of the central government over the states by insuring that officials in state governments would be dependent upon the national government for their tenure.

Although marriage and divorce are not constitutional topics, there is a curious provision in the constitution of 1886 relating to legitimacy. Colonel Aureliano Buendía was, it will be remembered, much moved by the concern of Liberals for the rights of illegitimate children. In the articles treating of citizenship, the constitution of 1886 confined nationality by birth to those born in Colombia and to the "legitimate" children of Colombian father and mother born abroad. The illegitimate child of Colombian father or mother born abroad had to apply for nationality "by origin." No other constitution, earlier or later, contains such a provision, and it vanished in the next constitution or codification of 1936.

Moscote's representation of the positions of the political parties is then a relatively orthodox one, even to the association of the Liberals with the masons. It is a representation nineteenth-century Conservatives would have appreciated, though the Liberals might have been rather miffed. "Our ideals have been distorted, the blood we shed for liberty mocked," they might protest, and justly since the description of positions is given to a Conservative. But Moscote's schematic description is not the only way political positions are rendered in the fiction, and while the Liberals may object, the Conservatives have no occasion to crow. Even if there were no other evidence to dispute the conservative claim to superiority, Moscote's ideas are clearly anachronistic: the English reader cannot help remembering that the last political theorist to argue seriously that power was given directly by God was Sir Robert Filmer in 1680. In his rendering of inter-party conflict, García Márquez exposes the irrelevance of ideology to conflict, the corruption of both parties, and the way the parties have provided an identity for their adherents.

The irrelevance of ideology appears on several levels. Moscote identifies the Conservative party with the church, but it is the Conservatives who brutalize a priest and who shell the church. The Liberals, in the person of Arcadio rather than Colonel Aureliano Buendía, are anti-clerical, but as Amaranta remarks with sardonic wonder of Gerineldo Márquez, the Liberals go to war to destroy the church and give prayer books as presents, and it is the Liberals who rebuild the church destroyed by Conservative bombardment.

Colonel Aureliano Buendía's ideological base is, at the beginning of the conflict, nil, less even than that of the memorialists of the War of a Thousand Days who tell us that the fundamental liberties of the nation were threatened by the Núñez regime and that war was necessary to preserve Colombia's most basic freedoms but who never enumerate the freedoms or liberties or describe the character of the threat. Moved by a vague humanitarianism, offended by the stealing of elections, Colonel Aureliano Buendía takes his twenty-one men to war after a series of atrocities committed by the Conservative forces occupying the town, the summary execution of Dr. Noguera, the brutal beating of Father Nicanor, the murder of a woman by pounding her to death with rifle butts. The response is to the brutality of power, not for or against any abstract ideas or threats to liberty. When the Liberals possess power, their atrocities are less only because they are weaker: Arcadio is prevented from murdering Moscote only by the superior force of his grandmother. (The women of the town consistently support a stable social order, whether by curbing the excesses of an

Arcadio or defending the regime of the Conservative General Moncada.) When they are not weaker, they are fully as brutal. Colonel Aureliano Buendía connives at the murder of a general who threatens his position as leader of the Liberal forces, Teófilo Vargas, allows the execution of General Moncada, and destroys the house of Moncada's widow. In the background, politicians in black frock coats negotiate and compromise, jockey for places in a Conservative administration, and alter the ideological terms of the struggle. The Colonel himself finally embraces the conflict as a struggle for power alone, with which the terms of ideological conflict have nothing to do. For others, the possibility of absolute power never theirs or lost once held, party affiliation exists as a state of mind, a form of allegiance and personal identity, for Gerineldo Márquez throughout the struggle, for the Colonel in the long years after his defeat. Before the firing squad, when Arcadio shouts "¡Cabrones! ¡Viva el partido liberal!" he defines himself as a man, affirming a self he never had as he loses it.

But if ideology is irrelevant, why is the Colonel a Liberal? Could he not as easily be a Conservative, like the sympathetic Moncada, whose name is an anagram for Macondo? As a Liberal, the Colonel belongs to the party of the progressive left for his period, the party that would institute some social reforms, labor, and welfare legislation in the 1930's and that had been the defender of civil and political liberties throughout the nineteenth century. García Márquez himself is a liberal by family inheritance, a revolutionary socialist by modern conviction. He began his reportorial career writing for the liberal paper *El Espectador,* and the grandfather who raised him was a colonel in the forces of the Liberal General Rafael Uribe Uribe. Not accidentally, Colonel Aureliano Buendía's political development manifests an anachronistic radicalization. His wars are "the wars of the last century," but his final political positions belong to the twentieth century. He becomes an instigator of radical land reform repudiated by his party. The wars he fights correspond in duration not only to the incessant wars of the nineteenth century but also to the "almost twenty years" of "la violencia" from 1948 to, roughly, 1964. García Márquez has mingled the experience of his grandfather in the nineteenth century with his own experience as witness to the conflicts of the twentieth.

Colonel Aureliano Buendía's wars end after almost twenty years under a great ceiba tree with the Treaty of Neerlandia. The last war of the nineteenth century, the War of a Thousand Days, ended with two treaties, the Treaty of Wisconsin and the Treaty of Neerlandia at which Uribe Uribe surrendered to the Conservative government in the presence, among others, of García Márquez's grandfather, Colonel Nicolás Márquez. The War of a Thousand Days (1899–1902) was the explosive finale to decades of conflict, and it should not lead us to reduce the Colonel's years of war from a "fictitious" twenty to a "real" three. For the period 1863–1876, estimates of civil wars somewhere in the country range from forty to forty-five. In 1875 an uprising in the department of Magdalena, the coastal state where García Márquez was born and Macondo is located, required federal intervention; in 1876–77 civil war was general throughout the nation; in 1879 civil war was confined to three states, including Magdalena; and in 1880 only Antioquia had a civil war. From 1884 to 1902 there were three general civil wars, in 1884–85, 1895, and 1899–1902. Uribe Uribe outdid Aureliano Buendía in the length if not the intensity of his military career, since his lasted almost thirty years from his participation at the age of seventeen in the war of 1876–77 through the other conflicts to 1902.

Vargas Llosa has pointed out that the camaraderie between Colonel Aureliano Buendía and General Moncada is based on that between Uribe Uribe and the conservative General Pedro Nel Ospina. The two exchanged "tuteando" letters, lamented separation from their families, and entrusted the wounded to each others' good care, while reiterating the desire to civilize war. The same pattern marks the correspondence and public statements of the liberal General Benjamín Herrera, commander of the Liberal forces in Panama. But neither Uribe Uribe nor Herrera executed his correspondent in the name of the revolution, largely because neither conceived of himself as a revolutionary. The brutality of the nineteenth-century civil wars was considerable: Herrera issued so many proclamations in favor of civilizing war because he disliked the habit of murdering and mutilating wounded prisoners. But the brutality lacked theoretical justification.

In the history of Colonel Aureliano Buendía, García Márquez suggests not only the corrosive effects of power but also the brutalizing effects of ideology, even radical ideology. No direct connection is drawn between radicalism and brutality, but the two are consistently juxtaposed. As a youthful widower and sentimental liberal, Aureliano Buendía could not understand shedding blood for things that cannot be touched with the hands, and he rejected Dr. Noguera's politics of assassination as the politics of a butcher. As he becomes more effective as a military leader and instrument of political change, his humanity evaporates. The transformation is dramatized in his relations with General Moncada. Once a friend, he allows Moncada's execution against the wishes of the town and with a humanly impenetrable shifting of responsibility for the action: "—Recuerda, compadre—le dijo—, que no te fusilo yo. Te fusila la revolución." A page earlier, he had acted to redistribute property on a more equitable basis, annulling the legal outrages of his brother José Arcadio. Similarly, when he orders the house of Moncada's widow pulled to the ground, that act is juxtaposed to the revision of property titles and the joint opposition of Liberal and Conservative landowners to the radicalism of the Colonel. The distrust of political action is profound, but it is less a distrust of actions than of actors. Land reform does not become less necessary or less desirable because it is performed by a brute, but the character of the actor prevents a simple response of unconsidered satisfaction to the action. We approve without much thought José Arcadio Buendía's patriarchal and egalitarian distribution of property at Macondo's founding; Colonel Aureliano Buendía's redistribution occurs in more complex circumstances.

In addition to the colonel's commitment to land reform, other elements in the history of his wars seem to echo events more recent than the civil wars of the nineteenth century. He is declared a bandit; a price is put on his head; Conservative and Liberal leaders combine against him. These details point to the period of "la violencia," though the connection is less explicit in *Cien años de soledad* than it is in such other fictions as *El coronel no tiene quien le escriba, La mala hora,* and "Un día de éstos."

For almost twenty years, rural violence harried the Colombian countryside. In the names of the traditional political parties, small and large landowners were dispossessed, properties burned, men murdered, and women raped. Some called the perpetrators guerrillas; others called them bandits. It began in Bogotá with the assassination of the popular leader of the left wing of the Liberal party, Jorge Eliécer Gaitán, on April 9, 1948. Gaitán had originally come to prominence in 1929 by exposing the brutality of the army's suppression of the banana strike in Santa Marta. Named the "bogotazo," the riots that followed the assassination levelled large parts of the city, burned down the pension of a law student named García Márquez, and left thousands dead. Quelled in the city, violence spread to the countryside where, in widely separated geographical areas, independent bands of guerrillas rose in rebellion. Some of the bands were Conservative; some ten to fifteen percent were, it is estimated, Communist-led; but most were Liberals who rose against the Conservative regime, the local authorities, and the traditional enemy, Conservatives of all classes, from campesinos to landowners. Between 1948 and 1964, according to conservative estimates, some 200,000 Colombians died in this unofficial civil war. For ten years, the toll of civilian dead alone rose, reaching over 300 a month in 1958, when it leveled off at 200 a month for four years until

1963, and the rate began to fall. While some groups received support, material and moral, from Liberal leaders in the cities, they were for the most part disowned by the national Liberal directorate, which joined with the Conservatives to repudiate the "bandits" or *"antisociales."* In 1952 a national Conference of Guerrillas convened to formulate a program including agrarian reform and other radical goals, but the movement remained a guerrilla movement composed of largely autonomous bands. The atrocities committed by both sides, guerrillas, army, and police, were horrific, and one of the more significant elements in García Márquez's work is his deliberate refusal to enumerate horrors. One anonymous witness described the actions of the Conservative authorities:

> My eyes have seen many sights. I have seen men coming into the cities mutilated, women raped, children flogged and wounded. I saw a man whose tongue had been cut out, and people who were lashed to a tree and made to witness the cruel scene told me that the policemen yelled, as they cut out his tongue: "You won't be giving any more cheers for the Liberal Party, you bastard!" They cut the genitals off other men so that they wouldn't procreate any more Liberals. Others had their legs and arms cut off and were made to walk about, bleeding, on the stumps of their limbs. And I know of men who were held bound while policemen and Conservative civilians took it in turns to rape their wives and daughters. Everything was carried out according to a preconceived plan of extermination. And the victims of these bloodthirsty policeman were poor, humble country people who were members of the Liberal Party. Their wives, their old folk and their children were shot in the full light of day. The official police took possession of the property of Liberal farmers, killed the owners, requisitioned their barns and disposed of their money, their livestock; in a word, of all that had been the livelihood of their families. It was an avalanche of pillage and an orgy of blood. At times these atrocious crimes were committed under the cover of night, with the encouragement of high government officials. And all this in the false name of God, with holy medals jingling around their necks, and without remorse.

Fiction can add nothing to such scenes, and their force is capable of destroying the balance of any fiction. But it is important to be aware of the depth of hatred such actions illustrate and evoked. Liberals did not fail to reciprocate in kind. In 1957, after ten years of "la violencia," and recourse to the dictatorship of Rojas Pinilla, the leaders of the Liberal and Conservative parties formed the National Front to eliminate the dictator and to collaborate in exterminating the guerrillas. By the end of the sixties, with the active collaboration of the church and the increasing efficiency of the army, they were largely successful. While the guerrilla movement affected large parts of the country, it was essentially a rural phenomenon and failed to spread to the Atlantic coast and the department of Magdalena.

The traces of "la violencia" in García Márquez's fictions are relatively slight, a few situations, an atmosphere, an intimation of guerrilla activity, but no direct grappling with the violence of "la violencia." In "Dos o tres cosas" he argued that the writer should not try to treat what he has not actually experienced, what he has only at second-hand. Vargas Llosa, commenting on the essay, observes that it is imaginative and not actual experience that counts. The imagination must be able to digest its materials to put them to use. The raw material of "la violencia" is rather indigestible, but the reason García Márquez has chosen not to deal directly with those materials has more to do with the character of his imagination than with the innate intractability of the material. His stories grow from images; his novels are chains of stories; meanings and effects in both emerge not from authorial analysis but from the multiple levels of suggestion communicated by the plot line and details of the inset narratives. He consistently subordinates historical detail to the integrity of the anecdote. To deal directly with "la violencia" would require either accounting for it historically and analytically, not a mode with which García Márquez is comfortable, or putting it at the center of the narrative. But what would be its effect at the center of the narrative as the focal point? In themselves, the materials produce horror and outrage, but they cannot illuminate anything unless they are subordinated to some other end, and subordinating them means moving them away from the center. Thus, in the earlier short stories and novellas, the references to "la violencia" illuminate character in resistance; in *Cien años de soledad,* they illuminate character and condemn militarism; in *El otoño del patriarca,* they illuminate the character of despotism itself. Further, the attitudes called forth by "la violencia" can only be unambiguous; there is little room for complexity of response in scenes of rape, torture, murder, and mutilation. Now García Márquez is perfectly capable of unambiguous renderings, but they tend to occur in his reportage rather than in his fictions. The nearest approach to an historical event rendered without ambiguity of any kind is the banana strike of 1928 in *Cien años de soledad.* While "Los funerales de la Mamá Grande" and *El otoño del patriarca* let us know without much delving that our attitude towards the protagonist is to be disapproval, the effect of focusing on that pair of saurians is to create admiration for their energy and a strong sense of their superiority to their sycophants and even to the harmless, afflicted people whose passivity lets them continue. While the final attitude is perhaps a simple one, the attitudes experienced in reading the fiction are complex. The exception is the treatment of the banana strike, but even there García Márquez's treatment is more sophisticated and more complex than the interpretations placed upon that episode by some critics who praise it for its political message.

As Lucila Mena has pointed out, the banana episode could serve as a textbook illustration of "lo real maravilloso (the marvelous-real)." Rendered with scrupulous accuracy, the historical event seems incredible, as "marvelous" as Remedios the beauty's rising into the heavens holding on to the family sheets. The key to the marvelous in the episode is the real: García Márquez has told the episode as it happened, and it is scarcely accidental that other, non-fictional descriptions of the events in Santa Marta in 1928 produce comparable effects of absurdity. The presence and nature of the episode raise a number of interesting questions. In the first place, what is it doing in the fiction? García Márquez has said that experience must be lived, but having been born in 1928, he can scarcely be said to have lived through the banana strike. Then its tone: it is the only episode characterized in large part by a tone of simple outrage. Finally, associated with the question of tone is the question of genre: the reportorial character of the episode associates it with the genre of "banana novels" and protest literature. The most famous examples of the kind are Asturias's banana trilogy, but the twenties and thirties saw dozens of others, and García Márquez's friend Álvaro Cepeda Samudio wrote a novel on the subject of the strike in 1967, *La casa grande*. The episode of the banana strike is in part an example of generic allusion, parallel to the allusions to Borges, Carpentier, Fuentes, Rulfo, and others, but distinct in that the shape and matter of the entire section constitute the allusion. Other instances of generic allusion define the fiction's structure: bildungsroman, patriarchal epic, Biblical and mythic structures, fairy tale structures. That of the banana episode simply pertains more immediately to the national literatures of Latin America.

But what of the charge that against his own dictum the banana strike was not lived through? There are two principal kinds of significance in the episode of the banana strike: the events themselves and the official obliteration of the events. It is the latter that finally emerges as the more important: not that 3,000 people died, but that 3,000 people die *and no one believes it.* It will be remembered that the horror of the insomnia plague at the beginning of the novel is not wakefulness but the obliteration of the past and that many of the inhabitants "sucumbieron al hechizo de una realidad imaginaria, inventada por ellos mismos, que les resultaba menos práctica pero más reconfortante." In the same fashion, the horrors of the banana strike are the obliteration of the existence of the workers by the lawyers and the denial that the massacre ever took place by both the people of Macondo, "Aquí no ha habido muertos," and the official versions that eventually triumph: "La versión oficial, mil veces repetida y machacada en todo el país por cuanto medio de divulgación encontró el gobierno a su alcance, terminó por imponerse: no hubo muertos, los trabajadores satisfechos habían vuelto con sus familias, y la compañía bananera suspendía actividades mientras pasaba la lluvia." The final, fitting irony of the episode is that North American readers unfamiliar with the history of Colombia assume that the episode is one more fantastic invention. For them, the event is saved from oblivion by the novel itself, but it is not restored to reality.

The banana strike and its bloody aftermath were the major events in García Márquez's natal year in the area in which he was born. He has said that he remembers conflicting reports of the strike from friends and neighbors, some of whom claimed there were no dead, others said an uncle, a brother had died. The time and place of the event gave it a certain privilege in his imagination, and it serves as the locus for the fury with military repression that appears in so much of his non-fiction. The banana episode integrates the memories of childhood with the adult's outrage at the combined forces of foreign imperialism, domestic injustice, and military repression exerted against the legitimate desires of the people. It is an episode that belongs to the past, threatened with oblivion, unless it is rendered, saved, in words. A public event that became part of the personal past is now rendered public again through the medium of the fiction.

García Márquez's narrative traces the history of the banana company in Macondo from the arrival of the company and its physical and social transformation of the town, through the organization of the workers against the company, to the strike, the massacre at the train station, the final "mopping up" operation conducted by the army afterwards, and the expunging of the events from the secondary school history texts. The United Fruit Company was incorporated in New Jersey in 1899 in the merger of the Colombia Land Company and the Boston Fruit Company. In the first decades of the twentieth century, it established itself as a state within a state in the "banana zone" on the Atlantic coast of Colombia. The company constructed an irrigation network (the moving of the river in *Cien años de soledad*), maintained its own railroad, telegraph network, retail stores, and fleet to carry its cargoes to U.S. ports. The company owned 30,000 acres in the region and employed about 18,000 men. In addition to the company, there were independent growers, Colombian nationals, dependent on the company's irrigation network and transport facilities who do not appear in the novel. The development of the banana industry produced an influx of workers both domestic and foreign that acquired the contemptuous nickname "la hojarasca" from the longtime inhabitants. As two of the sons of Colonel Aureliano Buendía remark, "'Nosotros venimos . . . porque todo el mundo viene.'"

The period was a boom period, but the position of the workers was not altogether advantageous. Workers were paid on a piece-work system by the number of bunches of bananas cut or the amount of land cleared. For the most part, they were not employed directly by the company or by individual growers, but worked under foremen-contractors and migrated from one plantation to another. Part of their wages were paid in scrip for exchange at the company's commissaries, kept stocked by the ships of the banana fleet that must otherwise have returned empty from New Orleans. The system of contract labor allowed both native growers and United Fruit to evade the provisions of Colombian law intended to protect the workers by requiring employers to provide medical care, sanitary dwellings, collective and accident insurance. Since the contractors lacked capital, they were not legally required to provide those benefits; since the growers did not employ the workers directly, neither were they. In 1918, the workers of the region had exerted enough pressure on the company to persuade it to promise to consult its Boston home office on the complaints raised by the workers, principally demands for wage increases and the elimination of scrip payments, as well as fulfillment of the company's obligations under the labor laws for workers' conditions. Ten years later, the workers raised their demands again, and the company refused to bargain but again promised to consult.

In his account, García Márquez gives us two strikes, though they do not seem to be separated by ten years. The first occurs on Fernanda's return from incarcerating Meme and brings José Arcadio Segundo out of the houses of French whores into political action: "La huelga estalló dos semanas después y no tuvo las consecuencias dramáticas que se temían." The second, "La huelga grande," begins after a period of demonstrations, agitation, and fruitless pursuit of the authorities of the banana company that had begun when Aureliano, Meme's son, was a year old. The widespread support for the workers among merchants and newspapers in the region seems to be signified in the fiction by Father Antonio Isabel's approval of the workers' demands: "La petición pareció tan justa que hasta el padre Antonio Isabel intercedió en favor de ella porque la encontró de acuerdo con la ley de Dios." The incredible evasions by the banana company are represented in the fiction by the disappearances and multiple disguises of Mr. Jack Brown, but García Márquez closes that absurd and comical account not with an invention of his own but with the actual ruling of the courts that because labor on the plantations was temporary and occasional, the company had no workers: "se estableció por fallo del tribunal y se proclamó en bandos solemnes la inexistencia de los trabajadores."

In his account of the strike proper, García Márquez conflates a few events, drops others, and does not disguise the incipient violence in the workers' confrontation with the army. In García Márquez's account, the army arrives to break the strike, martial law is declared, the workers gather at the station to await a mediator, are fired upon by the army after having had read to them Decreto Número Uno, declaring them a "cuadrilla de malhechores," signed by General Cortés Vargas and his secretary Enrique García Isaza. José Arcadio Segundo wakes up to find himself on a nightmare train ride with thousands of corpses and returns to a Macondo in which no one believes anything has happened. The workers' demands have been reduced and accepted, but the rains have begun and the search for the assassins and incendiaries of Decree No. Four continues until the union leaders are eliminated. So much for the efficacy of grassroots organization.

The differences between García Márquez's account and that of General Cortés Vargas himself are relatively minor. Both agree that the workers were interfering with the work of scabs, stopping trains, and damaging cut fruit. Martial law was not declared, however, until the night at the train station in the Decreto Número Uno that ordered the workers to disperse. In Cortés Vargas's account, as in García Márquez's, after the order to disperse had been given and the crowd was told it would be fired upon in five minutes, "'Le regalamos el minuto que falta,' gritó una voz de entre el tumulto." At this point, the accounts diverge. Cortés Vargas's all male crowd falls to the ground and flees after the army fires, leaving behind nine dead and a litter of machetes and hats. García Márquez's mixed crowd of men, women, and children is brutally mown down in numbers that correspond to those given in North American newspaper accounts and those of the strike leaders. The next day, Cortés Vargas issued the notorious Decreto Número Cuatro that declared the strikers a "cuadrilla de malhechores" and marked the beginning of the army's "mopping up" operation, resulting in the jailing of hundreds of workers by his own account. In Cortés Vargas's version, most of the real violence occurred after the firing at the train station, but García Márquez uses the massacre at the train station as a climax and limits the bloodbath afterwards to a few sentences: "La ley marcial continuaba. . . . En la noche, después del toque de queda, derribaban puertas a culatazos, sacaban a los sospechosos de sus camas y se los llevaban a un viaje sin regreso. Era todavía la búsqueda y el exterminio de los malhechores, asesinos, incendiarios y revoltosos del Decreto Número Cuatro. . . . Así consumaron el exterminio de los jefes sindicales."

As to the concessions won by the strikers, García Márquez tells us that the workers' demands had been reduced to two points, the provision of medical services and the building of latrines, and indeed Cortés Vargas assures us that most of the demands were illegal, but the company graciously consented to raise wages slightly, to build two hospitals (instead of the one for every four hundred workers demanded) and "mejorar e higienizar las habitaciones de los trabajadores en las fincas."

At the end of the episode, the official obliteration of events receives as much if not more attention than the horrors of the events themselves, and Mercado Cardona has pointed out the passage in Henao and Arrubla, the standard secondary school text on Colombian history, that deals with the strike:

> El gobierno declaró turbado el orden público el día cinco del mes siguiente, como medio de defensa social, una vez agotados los recursos que indicaba la prudencia para ver de pacificar los ánimos, en la provincia dicha. Las vías de hecho adoptadas, mediante el imperio de la ley marcial, hicieron renacer la tranquilidad y volver al régimen legal. El orden público se restableció en la región el 14 de marzo de 1929.

There was admittedly a strike, but fortunately nothing much occurred except the restoration of public order.

Most of the narrative of the banana strike is told in the neutral narrative tone customary in the novel, but the description of the arrival of the army troops violates the usual convention:

> Eran tres regimientos cuya marcha pautada por tambor de ga-

> leotes hacía trepidar la tierra. Su resuello de dragón multicéfalo impregnó de un vapor pestilente la claridad del mediodía. Eran pequeños, macizos, brutos. Sudaban con sudor de caballo, y tenían un olor de carnaza macerada por el sol, y la impavidez taciturna e impenetrable de los hombres del páramo. Aunque tardaron más de una hora en pasar, hubiera podido pensarse que eran unas pocas escuadras girando en redondo, porque todos eran idénticos, hijos de la misma madre, y todos soportaban con igual estolidez el peso de los morrales y las cantimploras, y la vergüenza de los fusiles con las bayonetas caladas, y el incordio de la obediencia ciega y el sentido del honor.

The description is heavily freighted with hostility, from the "dragón multicéfalo" and "vapor pestilente" to "la vergüenza de los fusiles" and "la obediencia ciega," and it appears before anything has occurred to warrant the hostility as a projection of an attitude to be justified in the course of the narrative. The soldiers are of course the principal actors in the brutality to follow, but directing hostility at those who follow orders rather than at those who give them still seems odd. One of García Márquez's omissions clarifies the matter a little. In Cortés Vargas's account, the principal reason the people did not disperse when ordered was that the people were confident that the soldiers, common people like themselves, would not act against them but would throw down their arms and join them. A memory of that conviction lingers in the woman's murmured remark, "'Estos cabrones son capaces de disparar,'" which suggests that the discovery of the capacity to fire is new. The betrayal of the people by the people seems to arouse more anger in the narrator than the actual massacre, perhaps because the massacre can be allowed to have its own effect.

El otoño del patriarca cannot be attacked, as *Cien años de soledad* has been, for abandoning the politically committed or engaged novel in favor of the byways of myth and fantasy. In it, García Márquez has taken on one of the central problems of Latin American and indeed world politics, the endurance of the dictator. But he has been attacked for one aspect of his method, his failure to represent the people successfully resisting the dictator. Like Carpentier in *Recurso del método,* García Márquez has represented the experience of dictatorship from inside, from the perspective of the dictator himself. Unlike Carpentier, he provides no hints as to how the dictator may eventually be brought down. His means and his end are those of satire: not to provide a blueprint for action but to purge our vision by stripping bare the horror that exists in the fulness of its power. His initial intention for the structure of the book was to have the dictator brought before a tribunal for a people's trial. That plan was abandoned, fortunately if the puerile trial scene in Bertolucci's *1900* is any indication of what might have gone on in García Márquez's version. Instead of using a form based on polarization and judgment, he plunges the reader into a stew of allusions, anecdotes, and images culled from Colombian, Latin American, European, and classical history. Just as Pope keeps us fast within the realm of Dulness and her minions in *The Dunciad* to show us the all-pervading power of the anti-Christ of intellect, so García Márquez keeps us by the patriarch, the demon of his world, to force us to recognize the truth, the horror, and the black comedy of the world he inhabits, the sources of his power and his undeniable skill in holding on.

The principal satiric devices that García Márquez exploits are magnification, the hyperbolic length of the patriarch's career, equivalent in time to Swift's static, spatial magnification of the human body in *Gulliver's Travels,* and the persona of the naif. All the multifarious voices of the novel are those of innocents, whether the people who cannot believe that the patriarch is dead, the expelled dictators who arrive in their pajamas with their trunks full of press clippings, the mother who would have had her son learn to read and write had she only known he would become head of state, and the wily, cynical old man himself, fearful of assassination yet convinced the people love him, amorous, sentimental, and murderous. There is an authorial narrative voice distinct from the voices of the innocent, but it is not a judgmental voice. It is the voice of one who sees both sides of the tapestry of illusions of reality and who persistently turns the tapestry over to show both sides, juxtaposing what seems and what is. Both kinds of voice keep us fast within the patriarch's world, allowing us no perspective from which to feel superior or immune to that world, enacting the fundamental paradox of satire, that it imprisons us within a world it condemns.

As he did in *Cien años de soledad,* García Márquez plunders Colombian history and his own earlier fictions. Victorious federalists dismember the country; the Liberals sell the revolution, and the Conservatives buy it; the great noise, a mysterious subterranean blast that occurred in 1687, acquires a new explanation; the people of a high, cold, misty city (Bogotá) look like poets but are really "godos," "goths," the old nickname for Conservatives; a figure resembling either Bolívar or Colonel Aureliano Buendía wants to wipe out every conservative regime from Alaska to Patagonia. Names and episodes recur: Papa Montero's wake is celebrated; the patriarch possesses the fertilizing powers of Petra Cotes and the supernatural powers of the banana company, discards Aureliano Segundo's faded animal lotteries for a more scientific system using billiard balls, and another Iguarán runs afoul of him in a cock fight. Most centrally, the patriarch is Colonel Aureliano Buendía having won his wars instead of having lost them; as locked in solitude, he possesses the small glass ball of power that the colonel never managed to grasp and hold.

When García Márquez moves politics from the background to the foreground of his works, he abandons realism for suprarealism and becomes a satirist. The apolitical abandonment of realism in many of the short stories and much of *Cien años de soledad* pushes to a bitter contrast between the limitless powers of the imagination and the limitations of the body bound to death. Enacting solitude and death, those fictions offer the exuberance of imaginative play to soften that awareness and reconcile us to it. And sometimes to blind us to it: we forget the tragedies of the lives of the characters in the comedy of events. In the political fictions (including the political sections of *Cien años de soledad*) the same contrast operates but with the realm of experience narrowed to the world of power and a far bleaker view of human possibilities because there can be no escape by way of the imagination from the world imagined. The play of the imagination serves not to free us but to return us to the world of the powerful, and the only cheering, consoling invention of *El otoño del patriarca* is the patriarch's death from natural causes. Dictators, like other men, do die, but García Márquez reminds us that the species continues. A novel that showed the triumph of the people in action might be more optimistic, but García Márquez's revelation of the care, feeding, and endurance of the beast shows a preference of truth to wish, of perception to dream or desire. The satirist may no longer be able to kill rats, as Irish poets used to do, and he may no longer believe that his ridicule will change men's actions for the better, but he does know that unless we see clearly, we can have neither motive nor power for action.

RAYMOND WILLIAMS

The Autumn of the Patriarch

The publication of this novel about a dictator disappointed some of those readers who had associated García Márquez exclusively with the enchantment and accessibility of Macondo. It does not take place in Macondo and is more difficult to read than any of García Márquez's other novels. Judged strictly on its own intrinsic artistic merit, however, *The Autumn of the Patriarch* is a major book for both García Márquez and the field of the contemporary Latin American novel. It was one of several Latin American novels appearing in the 1970s dealing with a dictator.

The novel of the dictator is a venerable tradition in Latin America. The two best known initial novels of this type were *Tirando Banderas* (1926) by the Spaniard Ramón del Valle Inclán and *El señor presidente* (1946) by Miguel Angel Asturias. The decade of the 1970s saw the startling empowerment of military dictatorships in Latin America, particularly in the Southern Cone. As if by tacit agreement, major novelists, such as Alejo Carpentier, Augusto Roa Bastos, and García Márquez all published novels on dictators: Carpentier's *Reasons of State* appeared in 1974 and Roa Bastos's *Yo el Supremo (I, the Supreme)* in the following year. García Márquez had begun his project at the end of a dictatorship that preceded these sanguine *caudillos* of the 1970s, that of Pérez Jiménez, ruler of Venezuela during the 1950s. Upon arriving in Caracas from Europe in 1958, García Márquez witnessed the downfall of Pérez Jiménez and the concurrent spectacle created by the outburst of a national celebration in Venezuela. The figure of Pérez Jiménez, nevertheless, was just a point of departure. García Márquez began reading histories of dictators, books containing historical anecdotes that can make the most fantastic Latin

---

American fiction read like stodgy realism. For example, García Márquez has told of reading about a recent Haitian dictator, Duvalier, who ordered all black dogs in the country killed because he believed one of his political enemies had transformed himself into a black dog; Maximiliano Hernández Martínez of El Salvador invented a pendulum to weigh his food before eating to assure it was not poisoned. *The Autumn of the Patriarch* contains anecdotes from these history books. The author explains:

> My intention was always to make a synthesis of all the Latin American dictators, but especially those from the Caribbean. Nevertheless, the personality of Juan Vicente Gómez [of Venezuela] was so strong, in addition to the fact that he exercised a special fascination over me, that undoubtedly the Patriarch has much more of him than anyone else. In any case, the mental image that I have of both is the same. Which doesn't mean, of course, that he is the same character as the one in the book, but rather an idealization of his image.

The protagonist of this novel, of course, is a dictator. A more precise definition of the theme, however, is not dictatorships but power. From those days of Pérez Jiménez's fall García Márquez was intrigued by the "mystery of power," as he called it. He had dealt with this abstract notion in such stories as "Big Mama's Funeral" and several stories written between 1968 and 1972. The project on the theme of power was begun in the late 1950s, set aside, and then completed after *One Hundred Years of Solitude*. The result was a stunning and enormously complex performance in the craft of fiction.

One indicator of the change in García Márquez's fiction is the fact that this novel is not located in Colombia. The exact location of the dictator's realm is impossible to establish, although it is a nation in the Caribbean area. Some readers will find themselves locating the imaginary country in Venezuela, while others will envision an island. The text's ambiguities make both possibilities plausible. The problem is that there are references to locations that different readers will associate with specific areas of the Caribbean. García Márquez, who knows all the Caribbean intimately, explains the novel's locale as follows:

> Undoubtedly, it is a country in the Caribbean. But it is a Caribbean mixed with the Spanish Caribbean and the English Caribbean. You are aware that I know the Caribbean island by island, city by city. And I've put everything there. What is mine

> first. The bordello where I lived in Barranquilla, the Cartagena of my student days, the little port bars where I used to eat when leaving the newspaper at four in the morning, and even the ships that at dawn would leave for Aruba and Curazao filled with whores. In it there are streets that are like the Calle del Comercio in Panamá, street corners of the old section of Havana, of San Juan and of Guajira. But also places that belong to the English Antilles, with their Hindus, Chinese, and Dutch.

To speak of a plot is an equally ambiguous proposition, since there is no plot developed in a consistent fashion. The novel involves a series of anecdotes which relate to the life of a dictator identified as the General. The anecdotes do not appear in chronological order; in addition, they sometimes include such gross anachronisms as the presence of Christopher Columbus and American marines in the same scene.

The first chapter begins with the discovery of the General's rotting corpse in the presidential palace. The narrative moves quickly to anecdotes during his lifetime. The central anecdote in this chapter is what is identified as his "first death": his government-appointed double, Patricio Aragonés, dies. The General is able to observe the spectacle of popular celebration over his death. He learns a valuable lesson about the fragility of power, and consequently has those who had taken over his government assassinated, while he rewards those who mourned his death. At the end of the chapter he looks out the window facing the sea of his palace, and he sees that the marines have abandoned the dock and three Spanish ships are arriving.

The action of the second chapter is centered on the woman with whom the General falls obsessively in love, Manuela Sánchez. She is characterized somewhat like Laura Farina in "Death Constant beyond Love." Manuela, of working-class origins, has a stunning beauty which overwhelms the General, who is rendered helpless at her sight. The relationship between Senator Onésimo Sánchez and Laura Farina is also quite similar to the one between the General and Manuela Sánchez: both men are impotent and childlike figures; both women are more mother figures for these two men than potential lovers. Manuela Sánchez disappears at the end of the chapter, never to be found, despite the rumors of her having been sighted in different parts of the Caribbean, from Aracataca to Panama. The General realizes he is condemned to dying without her love, and envisions a death lying facedown between the ages of 107 and 232 years.

The third chapter deals with the politics of power. His power seems limitless, as he is capable of arranging the weather, and signaling with his finger so that trees give fruit, animals grow, and men prosper. A revealing scene with respect to the General's politics occurs when an idealistic young foreigner visits the General to request support. The young man needs logistic and political support for the conservative cause, for which he professes his willingness to die. Hearing these words, the General recommends that the young idealist not be a fool, for he should enjoy the country while he is alive. The patriarch does not aid this conservative idealist. One of the novel's most memorable scenes occurs at the end of the chapter when the General intuits a plot against his government. He decides the culprit is one of his most intimate friends, General Rodrigo de Aguilar. The guests wait an inordinate amount of time for Rodrigo de Aguilar's arrival, but he does finally arrive at the banquet. The chapter ends with his grand entrance:

> And then the curtains parted and the distinguished Major General Rodrigo de Aguilar entered on a silver tray stretched out full length on a garnish of cauliflower and laurel leaves, steeped with spices, oven brown, embellished with the uniform of five golden almonds for solemn occasions and the limitless loops for valor on the sleeve of his right arm, fourteen pounds of medals on his chest and a sprig of parsley in his mouth, ready to be served at a banquet of comrades by the official carvers to the petrified horror of the guests as without breathing we witness the exquisite ceremony of carving and serving, and when every plate held an equal portion of minister of defense stuffed with pine nuts and aromatic herbs, he gave the order to begin, eat hearty gentlemen.

The General's power begins to wane in the fourth chapter. His ability to understand either his loss of power or a diminishing contact with reality seems limited. His aging mother, Bendición Alvarado, becomes the object of an obsession on the part of the General to have her canonized. The result of his campaign is her being given the status of "civil sanctity" and being named patroness of the nation. Near the end of the chapter he initiates an intimate relationship with his future wife, Nazareno Leticia. The General becomes so terrorized by the prospect of physical intimacy with her, however, that he defecates in his shorts.

The last two chapters narrate his final demise. The General marries Nazareno Leticia and has a child by her. The wife and child are assassinated and dogs rip apart their corpses in a public plaza. The General hires a smooth and handsome henchman, Saenz de la Barra, to carry out the sadistic assassinations that the government needs. The supreme dictator celebrates his one hundredth anniversary in power, but thereafter his reign is one of decadence in all senses of the word. He dies unsure of the possession of the power that he exercised and by which he was tormented in the solitude of his dictatorship.

This basic anecdote as described above could be reduced to a nuclear verb: "A corpse is found." This simple anecdote is the point of departure and frame for the actual storytelling. Each chapter begins with this basic anecdote, describing the discovery of the General's corpse in the presidential palace. The total narrative content of the novel, however, is developed beyond this discovery: it relates the General's entire life by transforming this basic anecdote of the framework into a more complete biographical revelation.

The transformation of this anecdotal material to the actual story of the text can be described by considering the novel's six chapters as a system of progressive apertures. That is, the first chapter is developed on the basis of an aperture, the second on another aperture, and so on. The qualifier "progressive" underlines the fact that the apertures occur at an earlier point in each of the six chapters. These apertures occur in each of the six chapters on four levels. It must be noted, however, that each level will be discussed separately only for the clarity of analysis. In the novel's experience these levels occur simultaneously. The four levels of aperture are (1) the opening of the original situation, (2) the opening of the sentence length, (3) the opening of narrative focus, and (4) the opening of a "seen" reality. The structure of progressive apertures provides for a dynamic experience.

The first chapter establishes the basic circumstances involved with the discovery of the General's corpse, the original situation (first level) in the presidential palace. In this first scene an unidentified narrator within the story describes some vultures entering the presidential palace. With this sign, the narrator notes, he and some of his accomplices dare to enter the premises. Upon their entrance, the narrative describes the physical surroundings—for the most part decaying objects in the palace. After an initial two-and-one-half-page description of the physical surroundings, this narrator provides the first description of the General's body, an image that recurs throughout the novel: "y allí lo vimos a él con el uniforme de lienzo sin insignias, las polainas, la espuela de oro en el talón izquierdo, más viejo que todos los hombres y todos los animales viejos de la tierra y del agua, y estaba tirado en el suelo, bocabajo, con el brazo derecho doblado bajo la cabeza para que le sirviera de almohada, como había dormido noche tras noche durante todas las noches de su larguísima vida de déspota solitario (and there we saw him, in his denim uniform without insignia, boots, the gold spur on his left heel, older than all old men and all old animals on land or sea, and he was stretched out on the floor, face down, his right arm bent under his head as a pillow, as he had slept night after night every night of his ever so long life of a solitary despot)." At approximately this point the narration changes from exclusively a description of the immediate surroundings to the telling of the General's story: "Sólo cuando lo volteamos para verle la cara comprendimos que era imposible reconocerlo aunque no hubiera estado carcomido de gallinazos, porque ninguno de nosotros lo había visto nunca. (Only when we turned him over to look at his face did we realize that it was impossible to recognize him, even though his face had not been pecked away by vultures, because none of us had ever seen him.)"

By noting that none of them had ever actually seen the General before his death, the narrator has changed from a description of the physical surroundings to relating *past* circumstances. This is the point in the first chapter that may be identified as the "aperture" in the narrative—an opening of the original situation into a broader story.

Each of the five remaining chapters establishes the original situation as described above and follows it with an aperture to narration of the General's past. In the second chapter the narrator begins to integrate the elements of the General's story almost immediately upon beginning the description of the original situation in the presidential palace. The first sentence of the second chapter reads as follows: "La segunda vez que lo encontraron carcomido por los gallinazos en la misma oficina, con la misma ropa y en la misma posición, ninguno de nosotros era bastante viejo para recordar lo que ocurrió la primera vez, pues siempre había otra verdad detrás de la verdad. (The second time he was found, chewed away by vultures in the same office, wearing the same clothes and in the same position, none of us was old enough to remember what had happened the first time, but we knew that no evidence of his death was final, because there was always another truth behind the truth.)" The sentence may be divided into three parts that demonstrate the way the structure of the novel functions. The first part, to the word "posición," refers to the original situation, the corpse. The second part, from "ninguno" to "primera vez," refers to that part of the story already learned by the reader, in addition to the original situation. In the third part, the story opens to present new information—that is, information other than the original situation and what the reader has already learned. By the second page of this chapter, however, the narrator has returned to the original situation, employing a short sentence that makes reference to it: "Tampoco el escrutinio meticuloso de la casa aportó elemento válido para establecer su identidad (Nor did the meticulous scrutiny of the house bring forth any valid element to establish his identity)." (It is important to note the use of short sentences at the beginning of the chapters and also for reference to the original situation.) Then the narrator describes more of the physical surroundings—Bendición Alvarado's room. After approximately two and a half pages the complete opening can be identified, changing the focus from the original situation to telling the General's story: "Al contrario de la ropa, las descripciones de sus historiadores le quedaban grandes (Contrary to what his clothing showed, the descriptions made by his historians made him very big)." From this point in the chapter there is no more description of the physical surroundings, and the narrative opens exclusively to the narration of the General's story. By the third chapter the transformation from the revelation of details concerning the original situation to reference to the known story occurs earlier, and the original situation is less important than in the two previous chapters (again, stressing the "progressive" nature of the structure).

The first sentence refers to the cadaver: "Así lo encontraron en las vísperas de su otoño, cuando el cadáver era en realidad el de Patricio Aragonés, y así volvimos a encontrarlo muchos años más tarde en una época de tantas incertidumbres que nadie podía rendirse a la evidencia de que fuera suyo aquel cuerpo senil carcomido de gallinazos y plagado de parásitos de fondo de mar (That was how they found him on the evening of his autumn, when the corpse was really that of Patricio Aragonés, and that was how we found him again many years later during a moment of such uncertainty that no one could give in to the evidence that the senile body there gouged by vultures and infested with parasites from the depths of the sea was his)." In this sentence there is one reference with a scope beyond the original situation: "during a moment of such uncertainty." The second sentence refers to the physical (his hand), and from this point the sentence moves toward the past. By the third sentence, there are no references to the immediate physical surroundings, and the chapter has opened up to narration of the General's story. The fourth sentence and the fifth sentence make no reference to the physical environment, and mention the corpse only as a point of departure for relating to the story beyond this situation. These two sentences can be identified as the point of definitive opening of the chapter from the original situation to narration of the General's story. There are no more references to the original situation, and the opening has occurred on the second page of the chapter. The original situation has now become less important, being used more as a technical point of departure.

The first sentence of the fourth chapter deals with the General's story, making no reference to the original situation. The second sentence does refer to the corpse, and then continues beyond this original situation to relate popular opinion concerning the General: "Sin embargo, mientras se adelantaban los trámites para componer y embalsamar el cuerpo, hasta los menos cándidos esperábamos sin confesarlo el cumplimiento de predicciones antiguas, como que el día de su muerte el lodo de los cenegales había de regresar por sus afluentes hasta las cabaceras, que había de llover sangre (Yet, while the plans for reassembling and embalming the body went forward, even the most candid among us waited without so confessing for the fulfillment of ancient predictions, such as the one that said that on the day of his death the mud from the swamps would go back upriver to its source, that it would rain blood)." The third sentence makes no reference to the General's physical environment. It continues relating the rumors and versions about his life. At this point on the first page the opening to narration of the General's past takes place.

In the fifth chapter the first sentence refers specifically to the original situation: "Poco antes del anochecer, cuando acabamos de sacar los cascarones podridos de las vacas y pusimos un poco de arreglo en aquel desorden de fábula, aún no habíamos conseguido que el cadáver se pareciera a la imagen de su leyenda (Shortly before nightfall, when we finished taking out the rotten husks of the cows and putting a little order into that fabulous disarray, we were still unable to tell if the corpse looked like its legendary image)." The second sentence also refers to this original situation; the narrator explains the attempts made to prepare the General's corpse. The third sentence functions as a bridge between relating the original situation and opening to the past. It remains within the framework of the original situation, but extends the immediate present (the specificity of the corpse) by relating the meeting of officials in a nearby room ("salón de consejo") in which they begin to decide upon the division of power: "Mientras tanto, en el salón de consejo de gobierno invocábamos la unión de todos contra el despotismo de siglos para repartirse por partes igulaes el botín de su poder, pues todos . . . (In the cabinet room meanwhile we called for the unity of all against the despotism of centuries so we could divide up the booty of his power in equal parts, because everyone . . .)."

The "salón de consejo" is not precisely within the scope of the original situation, and thus serves as a physical link between this situation and the relating of the General's story. The fourth sentence creates the actual opening of this narrative: "Nos encontrábamos inermes ante esa evidencia, comprometidos con un cuerpo pestilente que no éramos capaces de sustituir en el mundo porque él se había negado en sus instancias seniles a tomar ninguna determinación sobre el destino de la patria después de él, había resistido con una terquedad de viejo a cuantas sugerencias se le hicieron desde que el gobierno . . . (We were defenseless against that evidence, compromised by a pestilential corpse that we were incapable of replacing in the world because he had refused in his senile insistence to take any decision concerning the destiny of the nation after he was gone, with the invincible stubbornness of an old man he had resisted all suggestions made to him ever since the government . . .)." At the beginning of the sentence the narrator makes note of the "pestilential corpse." Then, however, the sentence begins to describe the General's actions (having refused to make any provisions for what was to be arranged after his death) previous to this basic situation, and thus marks the point of opening in the narrative: the chapter continues as the story of the General and there are no more references to the original situation.

In the last chapter, the sixth, the aperture occurs on the first page. Several parts of the sentence refer to the original situation: "Ahí estaba, pues, como si hubiera sido él aunque no lo fuera, acostado en la mesa de banquetes; . . . más temible muerto que vivo con el guante de raso relleno sobre el pecho (There he was, then, as if it had been he even though it might not be, lying on the banquet table; . . . more fearsome dead than alive, the velvet glove stuffed with cotton on a chest)." Toward the end of the first page the narrator changes the focus to a previous discussion, which, in turn, leads to opening the narrative to related matters: "discutíamos palabra por palabra el boletín final con la noticia que nadie se atrevía (we were discussing the final bulletin with the news that no one dared believe word by word)."

Both tradition and innovation are descriptive of the effect of this aperture on the first level, or the original situation. The manner in which physical space functions in this novel corresponds in a sense to the realist-naturalist tradition: the beginning of the novel focuses more precisely on the physical space; then, after the physical environment has been described at the outset of the novel, the narrator elaborates the anecdotal material with less background provided for the reader in terms of setting. On the other hand, the reader does not experience place in exactly the same manner as in the traditional novel. García Márquez manipulates physical space to such a degree that the reader finds himself progressively more limited in terms of physical space and background setting, and at the same time progressively more involved in the elaboration of the General's life.

These apertures that function as points indicating change from the original situation to the General's story are supported technically by the use of a progressive opening of the length of the sentence. This is the second level of aperture. The sentences lengthen at approximately the same point in each of the chapters as the noted point at which the transformation from the original situation to the General's story occurs. In each chapter the beginning sentences might be identified as a normal length. The sentences then expand in length as the chapter continues. The progressive nature of this development is evidenced by the fact that each chapter has fewer sentences: chapter 1 has thirty-one sentences; chapter 2, twenty-four sentences; chapter 3, nineteen sentences; chapter 4, eighteen sentences; chapter 5, fifteen sentences; and chapter 6 is a single sentence.

In the first chapter the sentences on the first page might be described as a "normal" length—that is, of eight, eight, and five lines, respectively, in the text. The fourth sentence expands to twenty-one lines. Throughout the next seven pages the length of the sentences varies, but remains approximately within the limits of the sentences on the first two pages, ranging from a few lines in length to a full page (thirty-five lines in the text). Then, on page 12, the first significant opening of the length of the sentence takes place, with the sentence on pages 12 and 13 being sixty-four lines in length. From this point, sentences become progressively longer, or at least tend to maintain the length of the longer sentences observed (about a page or slightly more).

The change in sentence length is abrupt in the second chapter. On the first two pages the sentences tend to be relatively short. As in the first chapter, the first sentence is eight lines. The second sentence, the longest in the beginning pages, consists of thirty lines (slightly less than a page); the remainder of the sentences on the first two pages range from three to twenty-one lines. At approximately the same point where the narrative changes its focus from the original situation to the General's story, the sentence length expands to a page or more. The change from the original situation to past description has been noted on page 50 in this second chapter (in Spanish text). The initial expansion of the sentence also takes place on page 50; the sentence on pages 50–51 is thirty-five lines, or a full page, in length. From this point the narrative opens (both in its circumstance and in sentence length), and the remaining sentences of the chapter tend to be longer than a page rather than shorter than a page.

The progressive nature of the openings in sentence length is equally evident in the third, fourth, and fifth chapters. In the third chapter there are three sentences before the extension of the length, and the fourth and fifth chapters contain two sentences and one sentence of normal length, respectively. The sentences that mark these openings in the three chapters are of twenty-eight lines, forty-nine lines, and twenty-two lines. In each case the change in sentence length is noted at the same place in the text that marked the change from the original situation as discussed.

The last chapter begins "Ahí estaba, pues como si hubiera . . . (There he was, then, as if it had been . . .)." This is a reference to the corpse and the immediate situation. Within this same sentence the chapter opens to related matters on the first page ("we were discussing"). The opening in terms of sentence length reaches the extreme; the entire chapter is one sentence of one thousand eight hundred and twenty-five lines (in Spanish text). This change is in accordance with the progressive nature of the structure as it has been discussed. Although more extreme than in the previous chapters, this length is a logical step in the development: sentences have become progressively longer in each chapter.

The progressive and precise manner of organizing the sentence length in correspondence with the opening of the original situation contributes to the formation of the narrative system García Márquez constructs in this novel. Although apparently lacking in punctuation (in the first reading), this novel employs punctuation in a manner different from its traditional function in prose; the specific placement of the period corresponds to the poetic use of textual space. Such technical precision supports García Márquez's contention that this novel is a "poem about the solitude of power."

The third level of aperture, also corresponding to the first two, is the opening of narrative focus. The narrative focus in which each chapter begins is relatively limited; then it opens to other points of view, and in some cases to multiple points of view within the same sentence. This variation of the narrative's focus, by use of the apertures to be described, has various effects and is a particularly important aspect of the experience of the novel.

An unidentified narrator within the story recounts the beginning pages of the first chapter. He and other unidentified accomplices enter the presidential palace to discover the rotting corpse. For this reason this narrator will be referred to as the "narrator-discoverer." Thus, the initial pages are narrated in the first-person plural ("we saw"). The first sentence does not identify a narrator as necessarily within the story, and technically it could be told by a narrator outside the story: "Durante el fin de semana los gallinazos se metieron por los balcones de la casa presidencial, destrozaron a picotazos las mallas de alambre de las ventanas y removieron con sus alas el tiempo estancado en el interior, y en la madrugada del lunes la ciudad despertó de su letargo de siglos con una tibia y tierna brisa de muerto grande y de podrida grandeza (Over the weekend the vultures got into the presidential palace by pecking through the screens on the balcony windows and the flapping of their wings stirred up the stagnant time inside, and at dawn on Monday the city awoke out of its lethargy of centuries with the warm, soft breeze of a great man dead and rotting grandeur)."

From the beginning of the next sentence the position of the narrator within the story is evident: "Sólo entonces nos atrevimos a entrar (Only then did we dare go in)." For approximately the next three pages the narrative remains within the scope of this narrator who enters the palace in the company of others. By the fourth page, however, the narrative begins to open to other speakers. The first change occurs on page 9 in the Spanish text (page 11 in English text) in which the narrator inside the story is relating details about the physical environment, and suddenly the narrative changes to several words that originate from another speaker: "y una tarde de enero habíamos visto una vaca contemplando el crepúsculo desde el balcón presidencial, imagínese, una vaca en el balcón de la patria, qué cosa más inicua, qué país de mierda (and one January afternoon we had seen a cow contemplating the sunset from the presidential balcony, just imagine, a cow on the balcony of the nation, what an awful thing, what a shitty country)." The "just imagine" interrupts the original narrator's account through the use of this conversational style. In this case the narrative has changed from pure narration to inferring a live dialogue. This point in the narrative, noted as the opening of the narrative focus (transcending the limits of the narrator-discoverer), occurs in the same situation already discussed, changing from the original situation to the story of the General. Later in the chapter, as the sentences lengthen, the length of the communications by other speakers is extended.

The second chapter begins once more with the relatively "closed" narrative focus of the narrator-discoverer. The first change in this focus, an expansion beyond the limits of this narrator, occurs in the place identified as the point of aperture on the two other levels, on the fourth and fifth pages of the chapter. Here, the narrator changes his scope from a general knowledge to the specific words of the General. The key sentence in which this change takes place reads as follows: (I quote it through the first change in narrative focus): "Esta certidumbre parecía válida inclusive para él, pues se sabía que era un hombre sin padre como los déspotas más ilustres de la historia, que el único pariente que se le conoció y tal vez único que tuvo fue su madre de mi alma Bendición Alvarado a quien los textos escolares . . . (That certainly seemed valid even for him, as he knew that he was a man without a father like the most illustrious despots of history, that the only relative known to him and perhaps the only one he had was his mother of my heart Bendición Alvarado to whom the school texts . . .)." The words "se sabía (it was known)" exemplify the level of communication identified as general knowledge—that which everybody (or all the inhabitants) knows. Later in this sentence the first opening beyond the limits of this narrator and general knowledge is noted with the word "mi," either the actual speech of the General or the narrator's imitation of his words. Three additional parts of this sentence express a focus beyond general knowledge. First, the narrator states: "a quien él proclamó por decreto matriarca de la patria con el argumento simple de que madre no hay sino una, la mía, una rara mujer de origen incierto (and whom he proclaimed matriarch of the land by decree with the simple argument that there is no mother but one, mine, a strange woman of uncertain origins)." Later in the same sentence the first longer opening of narrative focus in the chapter takes place in the voice of the General's mother:

> Ni podía soportar que había dicho en una fiesta diplomática que estoy cansada de rogarle a Dios que tumben a mi hijo, porque esto de vivir en la casa presidencial es como estar a toda hora con la luz prendida, señor, y lo había dicho con la misma verdad natural con que un día de la patria . . .
>
> (Nor could they bear the fact that at a diplomatic party she had said I'm tired of begging God to overthrow my son, because all this business of living in the presidential palace is like having the lights on all the time, sir, and she had said it with the same naturalness with which on one national holiday . . .)

At the end of the sentence another phrase changes to the mother's actual words, and the last two words are of the General. From this point in the chapter the focus of the narrative has been opened, and the voices continue to vary as the chapter proceeds, such changes becoming more frequent and lengthy.

In accordance with the progressive nature of the structure, the opening of focus occurs at an earlier point in the third chapter than in the first two. The narrator-discoverer who begins the chapter has entire control of the narrative for only the first page. In the fourth sentence the chapter opens, in sentence length and likewise into the past beyond the original situation. It is also this fourth sentence that opens the narrative to speakers other than the narrator-discoverer. This takes place on the second page of the chapter and in the words of Palmerston. Palmerston's voice continues for eighteen lines: at this point in the novel the opening of narrative focus not only occurs earlier than in the previous chapters, now there is an *extensive* opening from the beginning of the chapter. The sixth sentence, the longest of the chapter (207 lines in Spanish), contains numerous changes in speaker.

The fourth chapter is structured quite similarly to the third, contains approximately the same number of sentences, and does not vary significantly from the procedures noted in the third chapter. The chapter opens, in sentence length, in the third sentence (forty-nine lines, in Spanish). With the fourth sentence, of forty lines, the focus expands with the use of short phrases in the voices of characters other than the narrator-discoverer. Thus, on the third page of the chapter a character says "adiós" to the General, and later in the same sentence we find the short phrase: "al pasar con un pañuelo blanco, adiós mi general, adiós, pero él no oía nada desde los lutos crepusculares (with a white handkerchief when he passed, hello general sir, hello, but he didn't hear, he had heard nothing since the sunset mourning rites)." From this point, the sentence that opens the narrative focus, the fourth chapter continues with at least short interruptions of the narration of the narrator-discoverer. The opening of the narrative focus takes place slightly earlier in the fifth chapter than in the fourth. The opening to the General's story has been seen in the fourth sentence, and this is the point at which the narrative focus opens beyond the narrator-discoverer. This chapter also contains another of the rare, extensive uninterrupted monologues by the General (thirteen lines). It is significant both in theme and structure: (1) the subject of this monologue is his "mar," an object very important to the General's power, and (2) as in the extensive monologue in the previous chapter, it occurs near the end of the chapter where the length of the sentence is extended and in the second longest sentence of the chapter (214 lines).

The last chapter carries the progressive nature of the structure to its extreme by opening to the General's story on the first page and extending the sentence to constitute the entire chapter. The use of various speakers also takes place earlier than before, beginning immediately after the first page of the chapter: "un teniente que iba de puerta en puerta ordenando cerrar las pocas tiendas que empezaban a abrirse en la calle del comercio, hoy es feriado nacional gritaba (a lieutenant going from door to door ordering people to close the doors of the few shops that were beginning to open on the commercial street, today is a national holiday they shouted)." Other brief changes in the narrative voice follow on the same page and immediately thereafter. The variety of narrative voices present in this one-sentence chapter makes it the most complex of all. These speakers appear more frequently and their communication is more extensive than in the preceding chapters. At the beginning of the chapter the first extensive change in narrative focus is communicated in the words of an adolescent girl whom the General seduces, an act described by her in a monologue of twenty-seven lines. The second monologue on the following page is by another of his lovers. It also describes the general's sexual preferences from the point of view of a woman, a monologue of nineteen lines. Afterward and throughout the chapter, there are numerous short dialogues by the General and other characters, such as José Ignacio Sáenz de la Barra, Commander Kitchener, Consul Macdonnal, Bendición Alvarado, Ambassador Kipling, unidentified officials close to the General, and unidentified citizenry.

One function of the changing narrative focus is to provide a more complete characterization of the General, which, in turn, is responsible for humorous effects in this characterization. A common technique is to place emphasis on the General's omnipotence (usually the "exterior" view of the General) in contrast with his fundamental simplicity (usually the "interior" view of him). Power is expressed from the first page as something intangible but perceived by all under the General's rule. The narrator-discoverer reveals the generalized perception of the General's power by professing to believe in the General's power to order trees to bear fruit: "power was still not the shoreless bog of the fullness of his autumn but a feverish torrent that we saw gush out of its spring before our very eyes so that all he had to do was point at trees for them to bear fruit and at animals for them to grow and at men for them to prosper." As this passage suggests in both its content and style, according to the "exterior" and distanced view, the General is a God-like figure.

The inside view of the General and his power supports this God-like characterization, and also creates humor by showing the pettiness of his conception of power (in contrast with the grandiosity of the God figure), and his paranoia and puerility. Once the first chapter has opened beyond the generalized view, an omniscient narrator communicates the General's God-like understanding of his capacity to decide "destiny." When he justifies the assassination of officials who betray him, he does so with a God-like expression of being their creator.

In contrast with the God-like power that he manipulates both in the view of the citizenry and in his own self-esteem, the inside view consistently emphasizes his pettiness and puerility. Throughout the novel the General carefully and repetitively locks an elaborate combination of "the three crossbars, the three locks, the three bolts" in his room, thus underlining his paranoia. Despite his God-like self-confidence, his friend Rodrigo de Aguilar is the only person "authorized" to defeat him in dominoes. The General's simplicity is an aspect of his characterization not revealed by the narrator-discoverer. The General is characterized as such after the narrative focus has opened to other speakers beyond the voice of the citizenry. In the first chapter, after the narrative opens beyond the narrator-discoverer, an omniscient narrator explains that the General oversees the milking of the cows each day in order to measure the exact amount of milk the presidential carts carry to the city, providing a humorous contrast with the grandiose figure seen by the citizenry, and even with the interior view of himself as a God figure. When the General decides to find his love, Manuela Sánchez, his search for her resembles an adolescent experience: he looks for her in the neighborhood, nervously asks various people for directions to the home he describes, and after introducing himself to her mother, waits anxiously in the living room while her mother knits.

His characterization as a child figure is developed from the beginning of the novel when he is described as a "decrepit child." At one point he joyfully plays with his live siren, wind-up angel, and giant shell. In general, the relationship between the mother and son tends to be a mother-child relationship. For example, she reprimands him about his health and informs him that he must stay home for dinner. After his mother's death, he marries Leticia Nazareno and she assumes the mother role. She teaches him to read and write, the important factor here being the infantile methodology she uses: he recites children's songs.

The technique of contrasting the exterior and interior views of the General is particularly effective in certain passages in which a particular anecdote changes from the exterior to the interior focus within one sentence. For example, an attempted assassination is foiled by the General when, as the potential assassin holds him at gunpoint, he confronts the man and screams: "atrévete cabrón, atrévete (I dare you you bastard, I dare you)." When the assassin hesitates, the General attacks him, calls his guards, and orders the victim tortured. After the narration of this anecdote by an omniscient narrator (with occasional interjections by the General), the story is completed by providing at the very end of the sentence the interior focus (of which those who saw him were not aware): "desapareció en la sala de audiencias como un relámpago fugitivo hacia los aposentos privados, entró en el dormitorio, cerró las tres aldabas, los tres pestillos, los tres cerrojos, y se quitó con la punta de los dedos los pantalones que llevaba ensopados de mierda (he disappeared into the hearing room like a fugitive lightning flash toward the private quarters, he went into the bedroom, shut the three crossbars, the three bolts, the three locks, and with his fingertips he took off the pants he was wearing that were soaked in shit)." Until the narrator reveals the General's reactions in the last three words, the reader's view has been exterior and similar to that of the people observing the General's reactions. The last three words provide the interior contrasting characterization of the General and thus create the humor.

The fourth, and final, level of aperture in the structure of *The Autumn of the Patriarch* is the opening to a "seen" reality; or one could say that this fourth level is an opening of the dimensions of reality experienced in the novel. Each chapter begins with defined limits of reality—that which can be seen. The reader experiences this manipulation of visible and invisible reality in conjunction with the three other levels of aperture.

In the first scene of the novel, vultures are entering the presidential palace. The first suggestion that the General is dead is thus provided by visual means. From this sentence and throughout the novel, it becomes apparent that only that which is seen may possibly be believed: the General, the citizenry, and the reader learn to believe only what they can see. This problem of visible and invisible reality is fundamental to the main theme of the novel—the General's power—and to the reader's experience. After the description of the vultures, the visible sign of death, the narrator-discoverer emphasizes the importance of what can be *seen:* "y las cosas eran arduamente visibles en la luz decrépita (and things were hard to see in the decrepit light)." He follows with an elaboration of his realm of the visible, using the verb "to see" repetitively. The final use of the verb "to see" at the beginning of the chapter takes place when they discover the General's corpse. Appropriately, upon describing this visible image of the General, the narrative opens to beyond what this narrator can see—the point of aperture in the chapter. In the sentence following the description of the General, for example, the conjugated verbs are "comprender (to understand)" and "saber (to know)." The narrative changes from what can be seen to what is understood, and to what has been related.

The first sentence of the second chapter sets forth the actual theme—

the problem of the visible versus illusion—thus discussing the experience of living under the General's power and the process elaborated by the novel's structure: "La segunda vez que lo encontraron carcomido por los gallinazos en la misma oficina, con la misma ropa y en la misma posición, ninguno de nosotros era bastante viejo para recordar lo que ocurrió la primera vez, pero sabíamos que ninguna evidencia de su muerte era terminante, pues siempre había otra verdad detrás de la verdad. Ni siquiera los menos prudentes nos conformábamos con las apariencias . . . (The second time he was found, chewed away by vultures in the same office, wearing the same clothes and in the same position, none of us was old enough to remember what had happened the first time, but we knew that no evidence of his death was final, because there was always another truth behind the truth. Not even the least prudent among us would accept . . .)." After this initial suggestion of one of the novel's fundamental themes, the narrator-discoverer once more describes the experience of entering the palace by relating exclusively what he sees: "vimos un sillón de mimbre mordisqueado por las vacas . . . vimos estuches de pinturas de agua . . . vimos una tinaja (we saw a wicker easy chair nibbled by the cows . . . we saw watercolor sets . . . we saw a tub)." When they enter the General's bedroom the verb employed is "to find (encontramos)," rather than "to see," but stress continues to fall on the tangible. At this point in the chapter the emphasis changes from what is actually seen to what has been said.

In the third chapter the opening takes place on the first page of the chapter. The verb "to see" is not employed, but the verb "to find" functions similarly, indicating something tangible. The narrator-discoverer describes the General in the first sentence of the chapter: "y así volvimos a encontrarlo muchos años más tarde en una época de tantas incertidumbres que nadie podía rendirse a la evidencia de que fuera suyo aquel cuerpo senil carcomido de gallinazos y plagado de parásitos de fondo de mar (and that was how we found him again many years later during a moment of such uncertainty that no one could give in to the evidence that the senile body there gouged by vultures and infested with parasites from the depths of the sea was his)." The second sentence also describes the strictly visible. The next sentence changes the emphasis from the visible: the narrator explains what it *seemed* like and what they doubted.

The first sentence of the fifth chapter refers to the problem of the visible versus the invisible General, the latter being the one that has been imagined, the one that has been created through general knowledge, that is, "se dice (it is said)" or "se contaba (it was told)": "we were still unable to tell if the corpse looked like its legendary image." In this instance the narrator-discoverer is in the presence of the visible General, but an attempt is being made to change him so that he might correspond to the reality—his legend—that has superseded the real and tangible. The second sentence involves the actual physical process through which reconciliation of these two realities is attempted. The theme of the visible versus the invisible reality is abandoned by the third sentence and the chapter opens beyond this problem to a meeting of officials after the General's death.

Just as in the previous chapters, the last chapter uses as its point of departure the theme of the visible General versus the popular legend. The first words of the first line emphasize his visual image: "Ahí estaba, pues como si hubiera sido él aunque no lo fuera . . . (There he was, then, as if it had been he even though . . .)." At this point the theme of the visible versus the invisible has become problematical: it appears to be the General even if it is not, and it is impossible to make any definitive statement concerning the matter. Later in the first page there is another direct reference to the problem of the visible General versus the invisible, in this case affirming the importance of the visible within this fictional world. By the last chapter the characterization of the General only affirms the observation made concerning the reiteration of the verb "to see" in the beginning chapters of the novel: only the visible offers the possibility of being believable, although it certainly does not assure credibility.

This fourth level of the structure is fundamental to the novel's experience not only because this experience is based considerably on the manipulation of the visible and the invisible, but also because the General controls power and the image he projects by manipulating what is visible. Thus, there is a correlation between characterization and character and also between them and technique. When the General actually sees his own death (that of his double) in the first chapter, the experience changes him profoundly. This anecdote is described by means of a repetition of the verb "to see." The intensity of this experience is based on the fact that he *sees* death. Just as death becomes a reality for the General after he sees it, he confides only in reality as he can observe it, and becomes a victim of the circumstances he has created through his power. When he falls in love with Manuela Sánchez, he attempts to attract her with the visible manifestation of his power. Logically, the maximum gift for his maximum love, then, is the most impressive visual spectacle possible. Thus, his gift for Manuela Sánchez is a comet.

Maintenance of power is determined by the General's ability to manipulate the visible and the invisible. After a potential assassin fails to kill him, the General not only orders the man put to death, but more significantly in the context of his own understanding of the importance of the visible, he orders that the different parts of the assassin's body be exhibited throughout the country, thus providing a visible manifestation of the consequences of questioning the General's power. When he feels the necessity for exerting maximum control of his power, he visibly observes its functioning. This also explains the General's bizarre insistence in observing the milking of the cows each morning. On the other hand, when his power is threatened by the church (it denies sainthood to his mother), the General takes direct control of the situation, declares "civil sainthood" for his mother, and, given the seriousness of the situation, visibly oversees the fulfillment of his orders. In one description the General is portrayed as most content when he has a complete view of his country through his window. Similarly, he considers himself less responsible for that which he does not see. He feels no compunction about ordering the massacre of two thousand children, because he does not observe the actual killing, and the brutal maneuvers of Sáenz de la Barra are of little consequence to him because they are covert. Being aware of this importance of the visible, one of the General's officials suggests that Sáenz might be eliminated from the government if there were some way the General could *see* the atrocities taking place.

The question of the visible and the invisible and its relation to the novel's main theme, power, is also elaborated through the presence of the sea ("mar") in the novel. As the superb visible object in the General's daily life, the "mar" is his most treasured possession. The "mar" is first mentioned in the first chapter when, after a reiteration of the verb "to see," the narrator-discoverer ends a sentence on the third page of the novel as follows: "vimos los cráteres muertos de ásperas cenizas de luna de llanura sin término donde había estado el mar (we saw the dead craters of harsh moon ash on the endless plain where the sea had been)." Early in the novel such a reference to the "mar" seems inexplicable. In the context of the novel and the General's concept of power, it is understood that, since the General conceives of his "mar" as lost, it is naturally perceived as such by the citizenry, which is totally indoctrinated by him. In the first chapter the "mar" also becomes closely associated with his window, and from this point his window and his "mar" are inseparable in the novel. Technically, this association is established through the use of the preposition "de" ("of"): "oyó por la ventana abierta del mar los tambores lejanos las taitas tristes (through the open windows facing the sea he could hear the distant drums)." When the General condemns some political prisoners to death, international pressure is placed upon him to annul the order. In such moments of crisis, he contemplates from his window. As he gradually loses control of his power, he turns to his window more often. At the end of the fifth chapter, decrepit and in his hundredth year of power, he goes to his window and watches the sea, seemingly observing his very loss of power: "iba viendo pasar el mismo mar por las ventanas (he went along seeing as he passed the same sea through the windows)."

His window, his "mar," and his power become so intimately associated that the General insists upon maintaining possession of his window and "mar" as persistently as he does with reference to maintaining his power. When he is in the process of losing his power, he is adamant about not losing his "mar." In one of his extensive dialogues with an ambassador, he defends his position concerning the sea:

> Trying to explain to him that he could take anything he wanted except the sea of my windows, just imagine, what would I do all alone in this big building if I couldn't look out now as always at this time at what looks like a marsh in flames, what would I do without the December winds that sneak in barking through the broken windowpanes, how could I live without the green flashes of the lighthouse, I who abandoned my misty barrens and enlisted to the agony of fever in the tumult of the federalist war, and don't you think that I did it out of patriotism as the dictionary says, or from the spirit of adventure, or least of all because I gave a shit about federal principles which God keep in his holy kingdom, no my dear Wilson, I did it all so I could get to know the sea.

He has a similar response later for Ambassador Stevenson. When yet another ambassador attempts to make a deal, the General once more refuses. The sign that the General has lost his power is the selling of his sea at the end of the novel: "I granted them the right to make use of our territorial waters in the way they considered best for the interests of humanity and peace among peoples, with the understanding that said cession not only included the physical waters visible from the window of his bedroom to the horizon but everything that is understood by sea in the broadest sense, or, the flora and fauna belonging to said waters." The General has lost his maximum view and all that was significant for him: "they carried off everything that had been the reasons for my wars and the motive of his power."

The four levels of the novel's structure as described above are functional in the elaboration of the novel's themes. The opening of the original situation into the General's story provides a complete characterization of the General not limited by traditional subordination of the narration to the requirements of space and time. The latter are subordinate, in *The Autumn of the Patriarch,* to the act of narrating itself. The opening of the sentence supports this first opening technically, and is a specific device that provides for a progressively more elaborate textual presentation of the story. The opening of the narrative focus provides for a multiplicity of views of the General, and this is significant not only in the complexity and completeness of the characterization of him, but also in establishing the novel's tone—the humor that is fundamental to the experience of the novel. On the final level, the opening of a seen reality into a confluence of the visible and the invisible, the experience of the novel becomes similar to the principal theme it develops: the illusion of reality and power. To a considerable extent, the universalization of this theme through specific techniques creates the reader's experience. Although the cycle of novels focused on Macondo is finished, the universal experience created in *The Autumn of the Patriarch* is a continuation of the transcendent regionalism so evident in García Márquez's previous work, especially *One Hundred Years of Solitude.*

VERA M. KUTZINSKI

The Logic of Wings: Gabriel García Márquez and Afro-American Literature

Night is an African juju man
weaving a wish and a weariness together
to make two wings.
—ROBERT HAYDEN, "O Daedalus,
Fly Away Home"

One of the main differences between the work of those writers who comprise the so-called literary "mainstream" in the United States and that of major Latin American authors from the Caribbean is the way in which the latter group accepts Afro-American culture as a vital part of its cultural identity. Nicolás Guillén once wrote that the African element brings the definitive mark to the cultural profile of (Latin) America, and we only have to look at the writings of Alejo Carpentier, Guillermo Cabrera Infante, Miguel Barnet, Antonio Benítez Rojo, Lydia Cabrera (who may well deserve to be called Cuba's Zora Neale Hurston), and even Adalberto Ortiz to recognize the validity of such a claim. The following citation from Lydia Cabrera's introduction to her famous *El monte* further corroborates this. "There is no doubt," she writes, "that 'Cuba is the whitest island of the Caribbean.' But the impact of the African influence on that population, which regards itself as white, is nonetheless immeasurable, although a superficial glance may not discern this. You will not be able to understand our people without knowing the blacks. That influence is even more evi-

From *The Latin American Literary Review* no. 25 (January–June 1985).

dent today than it was in colonial times. We cannot penetrate much of Cuban life without considering that African presence, which does not manifest itself in skin color alone." The validity of Cabrera's comments extends far beyond Cuba, and I intend to substantiate that proposition by examining the uses of Afro-American myth and history in the writings of Gabriel García Márquez. One may well ask what the work of García Márquez has to do with Afro-American culture and literature, and justly so, since there appears to be very little evidence in his novels and stories of such a connection. Unlike Carpentier, for instance, García Márquez never wrote *about* blacks. He belongs to a generation of Latin American writers who arrived on the scene well after the heyday of the Afro-Antillean movement in the twenties and thirties, but for whom questions about Latin America's cultural identity and about an authentic Latin American literature nevertheless remain issues of no less importance now than fifty or sixty years ago. Afro-American culture continues to occupy a fairly prominent position when it comes to those questions, and this is nowhere more evident than in the Caribbean, of which García Márquez is undoubtedly a part.

Although his work is strongly indebted to the modern offsprings of the *novela de la tierra,* as is revealed by the similarities between Rómulo Gallego's *Doña Bárbara* (1929) and "Big Mama's Funeral" (1962), there is also another, more distinctly Caribbean, aspect to García Márquez's writings. This already becomes apparent when we consider "Big Mama's Funeral" in connection with Cabrera Infante's *Three Trapped Tigers* (1967) and his "Meta-final," which although initially conceived as the end of *Three Trapped Tigers,* was published separately in 1970. What is important here is not only the remarkable resemblance between the voluminous black singer Estrella, "the Queen, the Absolute Monarch of Cuban music," and Big Mama, "absolute sovereign of the Kingdom of Macondo," but the way in which this resemblance renders accessible the source from which both of these female figures spring: the legendary black Dominican Ma' Teodora Ginés. The famous "Son de la Ma' Teodora" is, as Roberto González Echevarría has pointed out in his excellent discussion of the subject [in "Literature of the Hispanic Caribbean,"] "a synthesis of the Spanish, African and *taíno* (Arawak) cultures that composed the Caribbean." As such, the "Son" is perhaps the earliest cultural ritual (it dates back to the second half of the sixteenth century) which celebrates the breakdown of ethnocentrism in the Caribbean by establishing a kind of contrapuntal coherence that later writers, notably Carpentier in his *Explosion in a Ca-*

thedral (1962), will attempt to develop into a fully fledged theology.

Gabriel García Márquez very consciously places himself within the historico-cultural framework represented by the "Son de la Ma' Teodora." His following remarks, taken from a recent interview, leave no doubt about this.

> My grandparents were descendants of Spanish immigrants, and many of the supernatural things they told me about came from Galicia. But I believe that this taste for the supernatural, which is typical of the Galicians, is also an African inheritance. The coast of the Caribbean, where I was born, is, like Brazil, the region of Latin America where one most feels the African influence. In this sense, the trip I made to Angola in 1978 was one of the most fascinating experiences I have ever had. I believe that it divided my life into two halves. I expected to encounter a strange world, completely foreign, and from the moment I set my feet down there, from the moment I smelled the air, I found myself immediately in the world of my childhood. Yes, I found myself face to face with my entire childhood, customs and things which I had forgotten. This also included the nightmares I used to have as a child.
>
> In Latin America we have been trained to believe that we are Spaniards. This is true in part, because the Spanish element forms part of our peculiar cultural make-up and cannot be denied. But I discovered during that trip to Angola that we are also Africans. Or better, that we are *mestizos.* That our culture is *mestizo,* that it is enriched by diverse contributions. Never before had I been conscious of this. . . . In the Caribbean, to which I belong, the boundless imagination of the black African slaves mixed with that of the native pre-Columbians and then with the fantasy of the Andalucians and the supernatural cult of the Galicians. This ability to view reality in a certain magic way is characteristic of the Caribbean and also of Brazil. From there has evolved a literature, a music and a kind of painting like that of Wifredo Lam, all of which are aesthetic expressions of this part of the world. . . . I believe that the Caribbean has taught me to see reality in a different way, to accept supernatural elements as something that is part of our daily life. The Caribbean is a distinctive world whose first magic piece of liter-

> ature is *The Diary of Christopher Columbus,* a book which speaks of fabulous plants and mythical worlds. Yes, the history of the Caribbean is full of magic.

What García Márquez is proposing here as the founding principle of his writings is a kind of magic realism that is strongly suggestive of the Carpentierian concept of a "marvelous American reality" in that it presupposes a certain faith, an acceptance of the supernatural as part of one's daily life. There are faint allusions to this in an earlier interview, but they are by far not as revealing, or even as serious, as the above pronouncements. What is indeed most striking about the above passage is that García Márquez describes his experiences in Angola in terms which suggest a kind of homecoming, a return to the forgotten, but yet very familiar, world of his childhood in the Caribbean. His image of Africa is that of a native land, and the symbolic value of such a statement should not be underestimated. Shall we then dismiss this as a case of fanciful nostalgia simply because it comes from a writer with no black ancestry in the strict genealogical sense?

I have said earlier that there appears to be little evidence in the work of García Márquez of a connection with and possible indebtedness to Afro-American culture. It is true that such a link is difficult, if not impossible, to discern as long as we keep searching for the kinds of explicit references and allusions we encounter for instances in Carpentier's *The Kingdom of This World,* Barnet's *Autobiography of a Runaway Slave,* César Leante's *Capitán de Cimarrones,* or Adalberto Ortiz's *Juyungo.* With very few minor exceptions, there are no black characters in García Márquez's texts, but that fact alone, as I have already suggested in my brief remarks about "Big Mama's Funeral," is misleading given the sources from which figures such as Big Mama spring. What I would now like to examine in some detail are two stories, which more than likely were among those childhood memories rekindled by García Márquez's visit to the African continent: his own "A Very Old Man with Enormous Wings" (1968), which, in the translation, is subtitled "A Tale for Children," and Juan Rodríguez Freyle's story of Juana García, which appears in *El carnero* (1636) and has been widely anthologized under the titles of "Las brujerías de Juana García" or "Un negocio con Juana García."

There appears to be no immediate connection between those two texts outside of the obvious fact that both their authors are Colombian. On closer look, however, we find that both stories share not only the same geocultural space (that of the Caribbean coast of Colombia), but also, even more importantly, cluster around the same fundamental trope: that of flying. Interestingly enough, this key metaphor is almost completely obscured in the English translation of the story of Juana García, who is introduced as a freed Negress who "was something of a witch," whereas the original reads, "Esta negra era un poco *voladora*" (my italics), which literally means, she "could fly a little bit." On the one hand, Juana García is, as Enrique Pupo-Walker has pointed out, undeniably a variation on Fernando de Roja's Celestina. But on the other hand, the association of sorcery with flying, brought about by the use of "voladora" and "volatería" instead of "bruja" and "brujería," which are the more common terms for witch and witchcraft, adds to Rodríguez Freyle's character a dimension which is even more distinctly Afro-American than the fact that Juana García is black. To be sure, Pupo-Walker's point that the story of Juana García is "a precursor text of the Afro-Hispanic narrative" is well taken, but for even more profound reasons than he himself may suspect.

The metaphoric link between flying and sorcery (or magic) is of vital importance to the entire Afro-American literary canon. There are numerous tales about and allusions to flight in Afro-American folklore, all of which are, in one way or another, versions of what is commonly known as the myth of the flying Africans. "Once all Africans could fly like birds; but owing to their many transgressions, their wings were taken away. There remained, here and there, in the sea-lands and out-of-the-way places in the low country, some who had been overlooked, and had retained the power of flight, though they looked like other men." In this sense, those who have retained the gift of flight are the guardians of Afro-America's cultural tradition. These keepers of traditional values and beliefs are the sorcerers and conjure-(wo)men, almost archetypal figures of notable prominence in Afro-American literature. One of those figures is that of the old man, who appears in the following version of the folktale "All God's Chillun Had Wings."

> The overseer and the driver ran at the old man with lashes ready; and the master ran too, with a picket pulled from the fence, to beat the life out of the old man who had made those Negroes fly. But he old man laughed in their faces, and said something loudly to all the Negroes in the field, the new Negroes and the old Negroes. And as he spoke to them they all remembered what they had forgotten, and recalled the power which had once been theirs. Then all Negroes, old and new, stood up together; the old man raised his hands; and they all

> leaped up into the air with a great shout; and in a moment were gone, flying, like a flock of crows, over the field, over the fence, and over the top of the wood; and behind them flew the old man. The men went clapping their hands, and the women went singing; and those who had children gave them their breasts; and the children laughed and sucked as their mothers flew, and were not afraid.

The function of the old man in this traditional Afro-American tale corroborates Lydia Cabrera's observation that the practices and rites of the black sorcerers are directed toward the well-being of their community. That this community, specifically in the Caribbean, also includes a large number of white members, who are not necessarily converts to *santería,* voodoo, or any of the other Afro-American religions in that region, but nonetheless avail themselves of the special knowledge and services of the "brujos" or "brujas," is quite evident from the story of Juana García. We are told that the Negress's confession to the Archbishop, who is also the Chief Inquisitor, "implicated various other women . . . and rumor had it that many had been caught in the net, among them ladies of importance." Enrique Pupo-Walker has aptly pointed out [in *La Vocación*] that this tale "confirms—on the most intimate planes of the cultural process—the presence of blacks as a basic factor of the new social context." Similarly, the kind of sociocultural interpenetration or syncretism here is substantiated by the fact that Juana García, also admitting as part of her confession that she had "flown" to Bermuda at the time of the sinking of the *Capitana* and the subsequent drowning of the two *oidores* which is mentioned at the beginning of the story, "had taken wing [echó a volar] from the hill behind the Church of Nuestra Señora de las Nieves, where one of the crosses stood." The hill, ever since known as "the hill of Juana García," is a symbolic space that accommodates both the official religious emblem and popular magic. But it is not without a certain irony that Juana García should choose, as point of departure for her flight, that is, for the practice of powers which literally surpass those of the officially recognized religion, the very same place where the Catholic Church had erected the symbol of its imperial authority. The Negress's powers defy, if not outrightly mock, such institutional authority, in much the same way as her punishment for such open defiance re-creates an image which perpetuates and significantly solidifies that mockery: "[The Archbishop] imposed on her as a penance that she be placed on a raised platform in Santo Domingo at the hour of high mass, with a halter around the neck and a burning candle in her hand." Even Juana García's lament that she alone was made to pay while all the others had been absolved to save the face of the viceroyalty, cannot distract from what is also suggested by her standing on that platform with a halter around her neck (doubtlessly to keep her from flying away!) and a lighted candle in her hand. What is intended as punishment ultimately yields an image that surreptitiously asserts the very powers whose existence it is supposed to crush: not only does the halter around Juana García's neck indirectly verify her power of flight by attempting to restrain it. In addition, the burning candle in her hand recalls a phenomenon associated, according to Lydia Cabrera, especially with the black sorcerers from Haiti and Jamaica, whose victims are said to carry a lighted candle in their hands as a warning to other mortals. This is quite appropriate given that the sorceress had been carried off to Santo Domingo, where the punishment is administered.

It is not entirely coincidental that this particular scene should evoke a famous historical incident which also occurred in Santo Domingo about a hundred years later: the burning of Macandal in 1758, which is one of the key events in Carpentier's *The Kingdom of This World*. The analogy between these two punishment scenes as described by Rodríguez Freyle and Carpentier respectively is obvious enough and need not be discussed in any great detail. What is most relevant to our topic is the striking recurrence in the scene of Macandal's execution of the flight metaphor: "The bonds fell off and the body of the Negro rose in the air, flying overhead, until it plunged into the black wave of the sea of slaves." Although Macandal's body was indeed consumed by the fire, the black slaves were undeterred in their belief that he had saved himself through his "volatería": "That afternoon the slaves returned to their plantations laughing all the way. Macandal had kept his word, remaining in the Kingdom of This World. Once more the whites had been outwitted by the Mighty Powers of the Other Shores." Macandal's flight, like Juana García's, constitutes an undisguised mockery of institutionalized authority and its feeble attempts to impose shackles on something that has no *body* to bind. In the story of Juana García, this corrosive mockery is subtly reinforced by the fact that the notice she admits to having posted on the walls of the *cabildo* in Bogotá imitates an official document: It is complete with the exact date, only lacking the "proper" signature. It may be argued that one of the functions of the story of Juana García within that particular chapter of *El carnero* is to explain the origin of that mysterious notice, which, although seemingly peripheral, serves as a kind of supplement to the actual plot, the "deal" with the pregnant woman.

Supplements also play an important role in García Márquez's tale about "A Very Old Man with Enormous Wings," which is, as we shall see, part of the literary canon generated by the trope of flying. This story differs from Rodríguez Freyle's and Carpentier's versions in that its curious protagonist, if he can be called that at all, is not black. In fact, there is a great deal of confusion about who or what this strange winged creature actually is: "The light was so weak at noon that when Pelayo was coming back to the house after throwing away the crabs, it was hard for him to see what it was that was moving and groaning in the rear of the courtyard. He had to get very close to see that it was an old man, a very old man, lying face down in the mud, who, in spite of his tremendous efforts, couldn't get up, impeded by his enormous wings." While the huge buzzard wings of this "drenched great-grandfather," now "forever entangled in the mud," substantially impede his own physical movements, they seem to have exactly the opposite effect on the inhabitants of this unidentified town, which is another version of Macondo—but with a difference. Macondo, as we know from *One Hundred Years of Solitude,* is located in the interior of Colombia, whereas the town we encounter in this story is clearly situated on the Caribbean coast. This is not only evident from the very beginning of the text, where we hear about Pelayo throwing the dead crabs into the sea; García Márquez is careful throughout the story to remind his readers of that specific location. Unfortunately, these more or less subtle reminders—references to Martinique, the Caribbean, and Jamaica—have been, for some reason, either changed or completely removed from the text of the translation. Furthermore, it should not be overlooked that the old man speaks "an incomprehensible dialect with a strong *sailor's* voice" (my italics). At first glance, all these details may appear relatively insignificant to the actual narrative. On closer look, however, they indicate the importance García Márquez attributes to the Caribbean as a cultural context within which to cast the winged old man.

The "inconvenience" of the wings gives rise to all kinds of speculation about the stranger's identity: some regard him as the victim of a shipwreck; others claim that he is angel knocked down by the three-day rain; and Father Gonzaga almost predictably suspects that he is one of the devil's carnival tricks.

> The parish priest had his first suspicion of an impostor when he saw that he [the old man] did not understand the language of God or know how to greet his ministers. Then he noticed that seen close up he was much too human: he had an unbearable

> smell of the outdoors, the backside of his wings was strewn with parasites, and his main feathers had been mistreated by terrestrial winds, and nothing about him measured up to the proud dignity of angels. Then he came out of the chicken coop and in a brief sermon warned the curious against the risks of being ingenuous [sic: simple-minded]. . . . He argued that if wings were not the essential element in determining the difference between a hawk and an airplane, they were even less so in the recognition of angels.

Yet these wings, parasite-infested as they may be, are of crucial importance not so much for determining the actual identity of the fallen freak, but for comprehending how and why García Márquez employs the trope of flying as a foundation for his own particular version of a more or less "marvelous" American reality.

Described and examined in quite some detail in this story, the wings are the visible metaphoric extensions of the Afro-American myth of flying. They almost literally grow out of that myth, which itself is an appendage, a *supplement* in the Derridean sense, to the body of Hispanic culture in the Caribbean. It is quite telling in this regard that the doctor, who could not resist the temptation of examining the "angel," should be struck by "the logic of his wings"—"They seemed so natural in that completely human organism that he couldn't understand why other men didn't have them too." The *logic* of the wings, as it were, is the logic of the supplement, which is at once complementary and additional; it is both a part of as well as apart from the cultural and textual context in which it appears. This ambiguity is precisely what characterizes the position of the bird/man within that community into which he has been accidentally thrown. He is a stranger, yet he is familiar; he appears to be human, yet he is more than that; he is, in short, a being which cannot easily be contained within noncontradictory definitions. In this sense, the old man's ambiguous anatomy is already sufficient to place him, much like Juana García and also Macandal, in direct opposition to the kind of authority to which Father Gonzaga appeals for "a final judgment on the nature of the captive." The priest "promised to write a letter to his bishop so that the latter would write to his primate so that the latter would write to the Supreme Pontiff in order to get the final verdict from the highest courts." Clearly, Rodríguez Freyle's Juana García, Carpentier's Macandal, and García Márquez's old man with enormous wings are all mythical figures which exist outside and in defiance of the authority of the law, which in all three cases attempts, rather unsuccessfully, to confine them within the limits of a fixed definition or identity, to make them adhere to the conceptual categories officially employed to define reality and truth.

It is important to note that intimate connection between the law, which assures permanence and identity, and the kind of writing which may be called "legal" in the sense that it does not tolerate contradictions and ambiguities. This writing is used as a means of social control in that it seeks to impose indelible marks of the official authority vested in it by the bureaucratic apparatus of either Church or State. In García Márquez's story, this link is most evident in a passage that emphasizes the inherently violent nature of such inscriptions of authority. The particular act of violence we witness significantly assumes another, very specific, cultural dimension once we consider that it was a common practice among slaveholders in all parts of the New World to brand their slaves as punishment for certain offenses. This form of punishment was most frequently administered to recaptured runaways, so that they could easily be identified by their mark of possession.

> The only time they [the curious gathered in front of the chicken coop] succeeded in arousing him [the old man] was when they burned his side with an iron for branding steers, for he had been motionless for so many hours that they thought he was dead. He awoke with a start, ranting in his hermetic language and with tears in his eyes, and he flapped his wings a couple of times, which brought on a whirlwind of chicken dung and lunar dust and a gale of panic that did not seem to be of this world. Although many thought that his reaction had been one not of rage but of pain, from then on they were careful not to annoy him, because the majority understood that his passivity was not that of a hero taking his ease but that of a cataclysm in repose.

Again, this scene is somewhat reminiscent of Macandal's execution in *The Kingdom of This World,* which I have mentioned earlier in connection with the end of the story of Juana García. There is a remarkable figurative analogy here between Macandal's moving the stump of his arm in a "threatening gesture which was none the less terrible for being partial" at the very moment that the flames were beginning to lick his legs and the old man's flapping his wings when touched by the hot branding iron. Both gestures cause a panic among the crowd of spectators, who are instantly reminded of the destructive powers latent in the kind of magic ascribed in similar ways to these two characters as well as to Juana García. This invites us to consider in more detail an important quality shared by these three figures: They are all believed to be sorcerers and as such invested with special curative powers. It is not an exaggeration, then, to describe each as what Derrida has called a *pharmakos* (healer, wizard, magician, sorcerer). The term is particularly appropriate because of its ambiguity, which results from the continuous vacillation of its meanings between all kinds of positive and negative connotations.

The characteristic ambiguity of the *pharmakos* is perhaps most apparent in the case of Macandal, whose acquired knowledge of plants and herbs enables him to orchestrate a large-scale poisoning of the white slaveholders and their families, thus "curing" the blacks from the pains of their bondage. In contrast, Juana García's poison is much more subtle: By offering the promiscuous young wife of a Spanish merchant concrete evidence of his husband's own infidelity in the form of a sleeve from his mistress's dress, she enables the woman to conceal, and even legitimize by way of blackmail, the accidental result of her adultery (the child who is born and disowned during her husband's long absence). Juana García's services implicitly sanction such marital transgressions and thus pose a threat to the moral order as well as to the public image of the colony. Her magic poisons not the bodies, but the minds of the residents of Bogotá. The ambiguous powers of García Márquez's mysterious old man are suggested in a variety of ways. Both the fact that the sick infant of Pelayo and Elisenda recovers almost immediately after the "angel's" appearance in their courtyard as well as the arrival of pilgrims from all over the Caribbean in hope of miraculous relief from their illnesses and deformities indicate that he might possess the positive qualities of a healer. "The most unfortunate invalids on earth [sic: of the Caribbean] came in search of health: a poor woman who since childhood had been counting her heartbeats and had run out of numbers; a Portuguese man [sic: a Jamaican] who couldn't sleep because the noise of the stars disturbed him; a sleepwalker who got up at night to undo the things he had done while awake; and many others with less serious ailments." But all the winged sage offers those invalids, whose unusual, if not absurd, afflictions cannot but strike us as somewhat Borgesian, are "consolation miracles, which were more like mocking fun" than serious remedies: "the few miracles attributed to the angel showed a certain *mental disorder,* like the blind man who didn't recover his sight but grew three new teeth; or the paralytic who didn't get to walk but almost won the lottery, and the leper whose sores sprouted sunflowers" (my italics).

Those extraordinary "consolation miracles" are, of course, further manifestations of the same kinds of supplementarity which, as we have seen, determines the logic of the old man's wings. This logic in its characteristic ambiguity is akin to the inherently contradictory nature of the *pharmakos;* in fact, the wings are a synecdochial representation of the *pharmakon,* which is the magic power of transformation earlier described as "volatería." What we are dealing with, in short, is not a condition of mental disorder, but a method capable of both enriching and at the same time endangering the stability of the accepted, official version of an historical reality and an historical process which, in each of the three texts, is represented by a figure of public authority: the Governor of Santo Domingo in *The Kingdom of This World;* the Chief Inquisitor in *El carnero;* and Father Gonzaga in "A Very Old Man with Enormous Wings." This conceptual method, which avails itself of the paradoxical logic of the supplement or *pharmakon* in order to disrupt and destabilize conventional Western ideas of order as well as the formulaic language in which these ideas are cast, significantly links Macandal's poison, Juana García's sleeve, the wings of the old man and his consolation miracles.

Although it might be argued that the Platonic/Derridean concepts of the *pharmakos* and the *pharmakon* as applied to these texts lift them out of their specific cultural and literary context by reducing their figurative properties to universals, it ought to be noted that the inseparable bond between *pharmakos/pharmakon* and flight already preempts such a reading. The *pharmakos* as "volatería" is endowed with irreducible culture-specific meanings, and as such verifies the continued existence of distinct Afro-Americanisms in twentieth-century Latin American literature. These Afro-Americanisms are pronounced enough to generate a separate canon, but at the same time it has to be emphasized that this canon, unlike its North American counterpart, does not simply consist of texts produced by a clearly defined "minority." Rather, it is composed of texts which add Afro-American myth and history to Latin America's repertoire of founding fables. Afro-America thus becomes an integral part of the literature of the Hispanic Caribbean, but it is integrated into this larger cultural and literary context without losing its distinctiveness or authenticity. Viewed from this perspective, it is not all that surprising that even a writer like García Márquez should, among other things, lay claim to the same cultural heritage as a black writer from the United Sates. Afro-America constitutes a bridge between Latin America and the United States, and it is certainly no coincidence that the relationship between those groups which comprise the cultural/literary establishment in the United States and particularly the Hispanic Caribbean is quite similar to that between so-called white America and its black community. This has been historically true approximately since the turn of the century.

Such generalizations of course require at least some evidence. Without leaving the immediate realm of our discussion, which has been predominantly but not exclusively literary so far, I would thus like to call attention to a poem by the late Robert Hayden entitled "For a Young Artist," which, as indicated by the author himself, is a tribute to García Márquez's "A Very Old Man with Enormous Wings." That an Afro-American poet like Hayden should single out this particular short story as the basis for one of his best-known poems at a time when literary critics and historians were for the most part very much preoccupied with cutting the American literary canon into thin ethnic slices, is a statement of some importance which, if nothing else, indicates the existence of a substantial lag between American literature and its criticism. Without overstating the importance of Hayden's symbolic gesture, it is safe to say that the relationship between his poem and García Márquez's story is, in many ways, representative of a larger pattern of cross-cultural interpenetration in modern American literature. Hayden is by no means an exception in this regard, and it is worth noting that the work of other contemporary black writers from the United States—among them the poets Jay Wright and Michael Harper as well as the novelist Gayl Jones—reflects a similar interest in Latin America.

But let us look more closely at the textual relationship between "For a Young Artist" and "A Very Old Man with Enormous Wings." Obviously, what attracted Hayden most to this story was García Márquez's peculiar practice of the traditional Afro-American flight metaphor. For Hayden, as for García Márquez, the gift of flying is intimately associated with the poetic power to unsettle and transform language by making it referentially and representationally ambiguous, by freeing it from the constraints of singular, fixed meanings. Like the old man in both the poem and the story, this language "*twists* away/from the cattle-prod" (my italics), and, in doing so, assumes a semantic multiplicity or plurivalence that is as elusive as the "angel," who, after finally dragging himself out of the chicken coop, "seemed to be in so many places at the same time that they grew to think that he'd been duplicated, that he was reproducing himself all through the house." This elusiveness, which is significantly figured as a process of multiplication, of endless supplementation, already anticipates the ultimate achievement of flight at the end of both texts.

> He strains, an awk-
> ward patsy, sweating strains
> leaping falling. Then —
>
> silken rustling in the air
> the angle of ascent
> achieved.

The preparatory intensity of movement created by the verbal cluster "sweating strains/leaping falling" builds up toward a similar kind of elusiveness, which is prefigured by the hyphen ("Then—") and culminates in the complete disappearance of the persona in the poem's final stanza. It is interesting that in neither one of the two texts do we actually witness the moment of flying. We only hear the "silken rustling" of the wings and Elisenda's "sigh of relief, for herself and for him, when she saw him [the old man] pass over the last houses." The moment of flight is clearly a moment of depersonalization: The winged old man ceases to be a presence, in Elisenda's life as well as in the texts themselves, and becomes an "imaginary dot on the horizon of the sea." What remains in the text, *as* text, is the "angle of ascent" which, as a metaphor for the textual representation of flight, significantly replaces what we may call the "ascent of the angel." Hayden's seemingly playful pun, the turning of "angel" into "angle," is the key event in the poem: It signals the transformation of character into trope, and thus comments on García Márquez's text—and by extension on the execution of Macandal and the story of Juana García—in a most profound way. The trope is what supplements mere representation by adding to it an allegorical dimension, so that representation can become a vehicle for allegory. This, in and by itself, is nothing new or unusual. But Hayden's realization that certain texts in Latin American literature are vehicles for specific Afro-American myths and allegories is an insight that opens many new possibilities for studying processes of canon-formation in American literature(s).

HUMBERTO E. ROBLES

The First Voyage around the World: From Pigafetta to García Márquez

venient annis
saecula seris, quibus Oceanus
vincula rerum laxet et ingens
pateat tellus Tethysque novos
detegat orbus nec sit terris
ultima Thule.
—Seneca, *Medea,* 2.374–79

Antonio Pigafetta's account of the first voyage around the world (1519–22) is of manifold significance. On the one hand, it is an allusive compendium of cartographic, historical, political, religious and economic components. On the other, it transcends its time and establishes itself as a primordial text that directly or indirectly has affected the interpretation of the New World by such varied authors as Peter Martyr, Montaigne, Shakespeare, Vico, De Pauw and others. Moreover, Pigafetta's relation of Magellan's voyage is equally germane to the understanding of apposite cultural and aesthetic concerns and practices evident among some distinguished contemporary Latin American writers, not the least of whom is Gabriel García Márquez. Thus envisaged, Pigafetta's text is not merely a document where one can examine the historical contact of early sixteenth-century Europe and a "wider world," but also one where the seeds of modern literary practices and conventions of Spanish America can be discerned.

From *History of European Ideas* 6, no. 4 (1985).

I

Understandably, much ink and erudition have been expended on the problem of the textual history of Pigafetta's Relation. The four extant manuscripts, three in French and one in the Venetian dialect of Italian, have been subjected to lengthy debates as to accuracy, dates and the question of the language in which Pigafetta first rendered his account. Nationalism appears to have inevitably entered in reference to this last issue. A similar reason seems to be the cause of the contention between those who bestow preeminence for the overall accomplishment of the expedition to either Magellan or El Cano. Symptomatic of the polemics and even provincialism that have surrounded Pigafetta's work was the publication by the editorial house Calpe of *Primer viaje en torno del globo* (Madrid, 1922), in commemoration of the fourth centennial for the completion of the first circumnavigation. It is illustrative that the aforesaid text bears two prominent portraits of El Cano, while Magellan's is conspicuously absent. Furthermore, the reader is first party to a longer and more detailed biographical sketch of El Cano, then a succinct and perfunctory one of Magellan, and finally a few lines on the author of the book, Pigafetta.

Although the reception and fortune of Pigafetta's record is not the sole concern of this essay, it is pertinent to consider several factors regarding the historical unfolding of his text. Editors, translators and historians have been inclined to view Pigafetta's voyage account as ancillary to the extraordinary deed of Magellan and his men. Whether this has been prompted by the scant biographical material on Pigafetta—citizen of Vicenza, Knight of Rhodes—or because the fundamental interest of the interpreters has been the determination of an objective and accurate history of such a portentuous undertaking is not the issue. Indeed that is as it should be with a text that "as the first-hand narration of one of history's three greatest voyages . . . rivals Columbus's *Journal* and da Gama's *Roteiro.*"

What should be underlined, however, is that historical necessity—the unrelenting search for evidence, causes, processes and explanations—has largely restricted the interpretation of Pigafetta's narrative to those aspects that confirm his "*esattezza scientifica*" and substantiate the reliability and authenticity of his report. The rest is discarded as myth or, at best, glossed derogatorily as an exaggeration. Thus, hardly any effort has been devoted to discern the sense of form that guides the narrative, nor to assess the marvellous encounter between a reasonably well-educated Renaissance mind, such as Pigafetta's, with an unknown and unfamiliar reality. Very little has been written on how he makes use of language and metaphor to make the unfamiliar familiar. Metaphors are crucially necessary when a culture or social group encounters phenomena that either elude or run afoul of normal expectations or quotidian experiences.

Another significant feature in the reception of Pigafetta's text is how it has fared in the literary world and in the context of the history of ideas. Here the situation is tantamount to a conspicuous oversight of the identification of text and author. And this in spite of the fact that Pigafetta's depictions have enjoyed relatively good fortune insofar as they have been borrowed and elaborated upon to suit aesthetic and ideological purposes. Peter Martyr's *Decades* (5.7) surely profited from the report of our voyager. The same could be said, with less certainty, of Montaigne's "Of Cannibals" (*Essays,* 2.31), although in this case López de Gómara was his most likely documentary source of inspiration. It should be stressed nonetheless that Gómara's *Historia de las Indias* is indebted to Pigafetta for those sections descriptive of Magellan's expedition. Notwithstanding, some of Montaigne's comments on the way of life of the newly discovered world, which he interpreted and advocated as an ideal primitive commonwealth, faintly echo passages found in the Italian's work.

Shakespeare's influential drama, *The Tempest,* has been linked to Montaigne and to voyage literature in general. In fact, one of the better-known excerpts of Pigafetta's narrative, that of the Patagonian giants' god, Setebos, found its way into the play. Caliban mentions and invokes it more than once. Critics, however, have generally identified Richard Eden's *History of Travayle* (1577) as Shakespeare's source, without ascertaining that Eden's book, as he indicates himself, is essentially a compilation and translation of the accounts of chroniclers and travellers, with bits of Pigafetta among them. The inevitable conclusion is that Pigafetta's presence has been unjustly displaced and relegated to anonymity. In this light, one of Pigafetta's declared reasons for wanting to join Magellan's expedition—"so that I might be able to gain some renown for later posterity"—appears ironically foreboding. It seems that the "document" has acquired an autonomy of its own, subject only to the Western mind's need for abstraction and historical form.

Witness, for instance, how the *Patacones,* as Magellan presumably called the Patagonian giants because of their enormous feet, fared in Vico's *The New Science.* Antonello Gerbi has summarized Vico's interpretation of them as "prototypes of a barbaric and heroic humanity." He goes on to observe that "the Patagonian giants filled a prominent role as exemplars of the indigenous people, and they were exploited by authors who defended America's virgin and robust nature against slanders of weakness and degeneration." Although in principle we agree with these statements, it is questionable whether the giants were exclusively used to defend the New World against indictments of weakness and degeneration. Peter Martyr and Gómara, to cite two instances, would be inclined to agree with Vico, but only to the extent of seeing the *Patacones* as "gross wild creatures." What Gerbi has in mind, of course, is the social polemics of the eighteenth century, and in particular Cornelius de Pauw's debased theories about the monstrousness and inferiority of the primal people of America. The possible existence of a robust indigenous population, such as the Patagonians, was contrary and intolerable to the derisive contentions of De Pauw.

But it must not be overlooked that in the various debates we have roughly outlined, the Indian was not the real issue—be it whether the point of contention was between the relative nature of barbarism when mirrored against the shortcomings of "civilised" Europe, as deduced from Montaigne; or between Prospero and Caliban, as evident in *The Tempest;* or amidst advocates of the Noble Savage or the Wild Man in the eighteenth century. What was ultimately in question was the European social order: "The Noble Savage was a concept with which to belabor 'nobility,' not to redeem the 'savage' . . . the amelioration of the natives' treatment was not a primary consideration of those who promoted the idea of their nobility. The principal aim of the social radicals was to undermine the concept of 'nobility.'" In that sense, Pigafetta's book, invariably unidentified, did nothing more than provide data for longstanding ideological polemics.

To be sure, Pigafetta's account has had an impact as a documentary source for concrete historical research and it has made its presence felt in literary texts; it also has functioned as a stimulus for diverse social arguments, and has been used to sustain or oppose the theoretic needs of thinkers of different persuasion. What is lacking in that context are three factors: (1) the need to salvage Pigafetta from surrogate authors; (2) the real absence of interpretations of the Relation by American minds, Latin American to be more precise; (3) a scrutiny of the text that would hence focus more rigorously on its formal aspects and beliefs rather than the accuracy of its historical components.

If a recent article, "Shakespeare y América," is any indication, the first point has begun to be corrected. The study discusses Shakespeare's sources, Eden for instance, but not without directing the reader in unmistakable terms to the authentic matrix. In reference to the second point, as we will see presently, García Márquez has most recently called attention to

Pigafetta's text and read it from a different vantage point than that of the Europeans. But first the text.

II

In the preface of his *The Journal of a Voyage to Lisbon* (1775), Henry Fielding sets forth what could be described as a theoretical statement on the responsibilities of the voyage-writer to his reader, and on how travel accounts "might and ought to be" written. Such books, Fielding argues, should be entertaining, instructive and selective. He further contends that the narrator should dispense with the unnecessary accumulation of irrelevant detail and should be unobtrusive to the extent of leaving most observations to the office of the reader. Fielding's comments on what he understands to be the primary motivation of the voyage-writer as well as his ideas on the "true source of the wonderful" are of consequence here:

> The vanity of knowing more than other men is, perhaps, besides hunger, the only inducement to writing, at least to publishing, at all. Why then should not the voyage-writer be inflamed with the glory of having seen what no man ever did or will see but himself? This is the true source of the wonderful in the discourse and writings, and sometimes, I believe, in the actions of men.

In retrospect, the main thrust of Fielding's premises recalls the sense of purpose and scope voiced by Pigafetta in the prefatory remarks to his account. Addressing Lord Philippe de Villiers L'Isle Adam, to whom the book was dedicated, Pigafetta proceeds swiftly to establish the tone and character of his narrative, the circumstances which led him to join Magellan's expedition, and the reasons that induced him to embark on such an adventure and to record it for posterity.

Pigafetta saw his wanderings as singular and unique. The underlying concern of his Relation, he observes, will be "the great and wonderful things which God has permitted me to see and suffer during my long and dangerous voyage." That the extraordinary and marvellous stamp the record of the first voyage around the world is further suggested by Pigafetta's assertion that what prompted him to go to sea was his acquaintance with books and reports that told of uncommon experiences. A man of his era, Pigafetta was evidently not satisfied with merely having read or heard of unwonted deeds and things, but preferred to look for confirmation himself to be able thereby to write about them and, thus, gain future honour: "having learned many things from many books that I had read, as well as from various persons, who discussed the great marvellous things of the Ocean Sea . . . I determined . . . to experience and go see those things for myself, and so that I might be able thereby to satisfy myself somewhat, and so that I might be able to gain renown for later posterity."

While it is clear that the reportage of unconventional and extraordinary encounters is Pigafetta's primary interest, it is also evident that preconceived ideas and forms guide the principle of selection of the material incorporated in the narration. Indeed, it could be safely deduced that the world of books was not far from Pigafetta's mind when he was composing his record. A cursory reading of Pigafetta's text would suggest affinities in tone and narrative strategies with such widely read classics of the genre as the travel accounts of Marco Polo or Sir John Mandeville. The information may differ, but the mode of presentation is essentially the same. The dividing line between fact and fiction appears blurred.

To read the Relation solely in search for objective detail is to ignore that tradition and to discount Pigafetta's contention that he is writing about his personal "vigils, hardships, and wanderings." In this light, it would be fruitful to inquire how that private perspective affects the overall organisation of the account, and what it discloses therein on the encounter of a man such as Pigafetta with a widening world. This, of course, raises questions on taxonomy and on the relationship between history and fiction which are beyond the scope of this study. It should be stressed, however, that because of the format of Pigafetta's book, there could be some inclination to indiscriminately identify it as a diary or a chronicle.

A diary it is not, despite the many dated entries that permeate the pages of the volume, and despite Pigafetta's claim that upon his return to Spain he "presented to his sacred Majesty, Don Carlo, neither gold nor silver, but things very highly esteemed by such sovereign. Among other things I gave him a book, written by my hand, concerning all the matters that had occurred from day to day during our voyage." This document remains lost, and unless Pigafetta made a copy of it, which is most unlikely, there is no evidence that the text at hand is a diary. On the contrary, everything suggests that it was written after the author's return to Italy in 1523, and at the urging of Lord Philippe de Villiers L'Isle Adam: "you . . . told me that you would be greatly pleased if I would write down for you all those things which I have seen and suffered during my voyage."

We could further discount the idea of a diary by examining the temporal perspective employed in the Relation. The sense of immediacy associated with a diary is absent. The verbal tenses used reveal the point of view of someone looking back on past events, intent on shaping and arranging them. This is instructive for it betokens Pigafetta's concern with form. Various devices are indicative of a narrator who is aware of his reader and of the need to be entertaining, and who is also apprised of narrative progression and of organisation in general, as these examples attest: "I omit other particulars in order not to be tedious"; "We heard of Malucho there before the death of the captain-general"; "As we shall return to that island again, I shall say nothing further [now]."

The presence of anticipatory motifs and other techniques precludes calling the account a diary and even questions whether it is a chronicle in an absolute sense. Hayden White has distinguished among several "levels of conceptualisation in the historical work." The differences he proposes between "chronicle" and "story" are of particular interest in this essay:

> First the elements of the historical field are organised into a chronicle by the arrangement of the events in the temporal order of their occurrence; then the chronicle is organised into a story by further arrangement of the events into the components of a "spectacle" or process of happening, which is thought to possess a discernible beginning, middle, and end.

Elements of a story are evident in Pigafetta's presentation of episodes and in his overall conception of the account, which is self-contained and has a beginning and an end.

We are not suggesting that there is a tight organic relationship among the parts. Yet there is a semblance of structure inasmuch as it has been possible for some editors to prescribe section and even chapter divisions for the text. The Spanish edition of 1922, for instance, divides the narrative into four parts. The first, from 10 August 1519, the day of the departure from Seville, to 28 November 1520, when the sailing vessels debouched from Magellan's Straits. The second includes the crossing of the Pacific until the death of Magellan, on 27 April 1521, in what we now call the Philippines. A third section comprises navigation in the Pacific and the relentless search for the Moluccas or Spice Islands which, as we know, was the primary objective of the expedition. A final part encompasses the trip from the Moluccas, begun on 21 December 1521, to Seville, where they arrived on 28 September 1522. Eighteen of the original two hundred and thirty-seven men returned.

The first circumnavigation is so full of vicissitudes and of incidents so different in character and nature that it would be better understood if we arrange it according to the tone and inner tensions prevalent in the different moments of the text's linear progression. The four major divisions outlined above, to which we in general adhere, can be identified more precisely if we follow a lexicon derived from the rhetorical terminology employed to classify voyage literature.

Within that framework, the first section of the account is a "journey," given that we move "from one locale to another" without "implication as to the nature of [the] movement." In this segment there is an aura of delight and freshness triggered no doubt by the encounter with a pristine and extraordinary reality, a reality without precedent in the author's experience. These are the pages most pertinent to America and to which we shall return later.

The second subdivision corresponds to the crossing of the Pacific and can be properly labelled an "odyssey," since it "has no particular ostensible spiritual significance" and yet there is a sense of purpose, and an overriding desire to arrive at a destination. This is the portion of the narrative where a feeling of suffering, doom and failure is most in evidence. Interminable days elapse marked only by the limitless presence of sea and sky. Man appears dehumanised, but sufficiently resilient to endure at any cost. Obsessed with wanting to reach land and the Moluccas, Magellan and his crew march on, ingesting leather and even rodents to stay alive.

The third part encompasses the search for the Spice Islands. The peregrination—first with Magellan and then without him after his death—turns into an assiduous and quixotic "quest." The voyage acquires at this time a "sense of mission" and a "consciousness of purpose" that is not as prevalent elsewhere in the text. The Marianas, the Philippines, Borneo, Java, and Timor are among the sites visited. It is instructive that the depiction of life on these islands does not appear nearly as alien and anomalous as the reality described in the first part of the account. This no doubt is related to the better organised and more advanced nature of the societies encountered, and also to ulterior ideological and economic motives that tinge the descriptions. Pigafetta seems intent on conveying signs of untapped riches, propitious to future mercantile gain. In doing so, he was making more attainable the land of aromatics and affirming the success of the expedition.

The final part of the Relation has all the attributes of a "pilgrimage." Laden with cloves and other spices, and with a weary and fatigued crew, the "Victoria," the only one of the five original vessels to accomplish the circumnavigation, strives "to reach" its Spanish destination. The men are ostensibly moved by one overriding objective, to thank God: "Monday, September eight, we cast anchor near the quay of Seviglia, and discharged all our artillery. Tuesday, we all went in shirts and barefoot, each holding a candle, to visit the shrine of Santa Maria de la Victoria, and that of Santa Maria de l'Antiqua."

Journey, odyssey, quest and pilgrimage constitute, respectively, the four sections of Pigafetta's narrative and each is illuminating, but it is the third and first parts that are illustrative of the unique encounter between a Western mind of the sixteenth century and a widening world.

As a consequence of the almost excessive accumulation of detail, the descriptions that figure in the third part tend to be monotonous. The same scenario is repeated time and again—the Europeans coming in contact with the Islanders of the Pacific. But it is precisely that repetition that brings into focus Pigafetta's and his comrades' beliefs and ideas. Expansive images of the natives' pomp and ceremony, which betray Western lucrative interests, are juxtaposed with inadvertently allusive portrayals of the Europeans' cunning use of symbol and gesture, indicative of their world-view.

Consistently, the use of symbol is one of the most revealing features of the Western mind's attitude toward the indigenous people. The sense of power and of economic and evangelical mission is communicated in carefully encoded messages. The Europeans project icons of invincibility and strength designed to assert their right of conquest. A pattern of superiority is set. The "manifest destiny" and pre-eminence of the West are established as a matter of course and dictated by means of suggestive images and expressions. The native population, superficially observed, is blatantly manipulated and subjected by instilling in them a mythical fear of awesome weapons and incomprehensible technology:

> Then the captain showed him cloths of various colors, linen, coral [ornaments], and many other articles of merchandise, and all the artillery, some of which he had discharged for him, whereat the natives were greatly frightened. Then the captain-general had a man armed as a soldier, and placed him in midst of three men armed with swords and daggers, who struck him in all parts of the body. Thereby was the king rendered almost speechless. The captain-general told him through the slave that one of those armed men was worth one hundred of his own men. The king answered that that was a fact. The captain-general said that he had two hundred men in each ship who were armed in that manner. He showed the king cuirasses,

> swords, and bucklers, and had a review made for him. Then he led the king to the deck of the ship, that is located above the stern; and had his sea-chart and compass brought. He told the king through the interpreter how he had found the strait in order to voyage thither, and how many moons he had been without seeing land, whereat the king was astonished.

There is no reason to question Pigafetta's authentic rendering of such encounters. The issue becomes more complicated, however, when we look at descriptions of the manner in which the Europeans treated the natives on the subject of religion. Is Pigafetta operating here with equal candor, or is he imposing preconceived ideas on the events? Is he recording incidents as they occurred or is he organising his narrative to adhere to the religious policy of the Spanish crown? We are persuaded that the latter is the case. He must have been aware, and certainly Magellan, that the question of how to affect the conversion of heathens into Christians was and had been highly debated in Spain. To be sure, circa 1513–14, at the instruction of King Ferdinand, Juan López de Palacios Rubios had written a treatise, *De las Islas del mar Océano,* that contains this instructive declaration: "De lo anterior se infiere primeramente que los infieles no deben sólo por motivo de su infidelidad y sin mediar otra causa justa, ser privados de sus bienes, ni moverles guerra en que los Cristianos se apoderen de lo que poseen."

Thus, when Pigafetta renders passages of how Magellan approached the primal people, such as the one that follows, we cannot help deducing that he is making certain that Magellan is in no way indicted for not adhering to the policy of the kingdom, especially if we consider that the Portuguese captain, highly admired by Pigafetta, was then being discredited in some circles. "The captain-general then told them that they should not become Christians for fear or to please us, but of their own free wills; and that he would not cause any displeasure to those who wished to live according to their own law; but that the Christians would be better regarded and treated than the others."

Personal and collective political concerns, to be sure, do play an underlying role in informing and organising portions of the third part of the account. Actual experience appears subordinated to concept. Pigafetta is as imprisoned as anyone else in the beliefs and formulas of his time. Moreover, his text does not escape tradition and convention in another respect. As in much of the travel literature that preceded him, in this section of the narrative he resorts without diffidence to hearsay and fantasy, as when he speaks of the fantastic bird *garuda* or when he reports that an old pilot from "Maluco" told him of "men and women [who] are not taller than one cubit, but who have ears as long as themselves. With one of them they make their bed and with the other they cover themselves." Notwithstanding Pigafetta's faith in such fabulous phenomena, we are inclined to ponder if Pliny's *Natural History* (7.2) is not a more likely source than the old pilot from Maluco?

If the third part is imbued with preconceived ideas, conventions and possible bookish inspiration, the first, in contrast, rings of authenticity. There is hardly any room for hearsay in this section. Only a scarce few had preceded Pigafetta along the coastline of Brazil and the rest of the subcontinent. Thus, the world he encountered was pristine and essentially undivulged. The marvellous derives not from undocumented tales, accepted on faith, but from viewing for the first time something "no man ever did . . . see but himself," to borrow Fielding's words.

The nature of that encounter inevitably betrays a feeling of alienation and impotence, and (why not?) of modernity. Authoritatively prescribed presuppositions and certainties appears to crumble in lieu of a plural and expanding world that refuses to conform to patrician European norms and expectations. Pigafetta is faced with the need to translate unconventional and disturbing experiences into the realm of the quotidian. He must do this not only to comprehend, but to reduce and confine the unwanted and the unknown within the limits of his own demands for coherence and harmony. To accomplish this he has to resort to figurative language—to metaphor.

It is worth noting that while a large portion of the lexicon used in the description of the first voyage around the world is precise and devoid of tropes, such is not the case when Pigafetta stumbles on unrecorded phenomena, be it the flora, fauna or the people and things of the newly discovered lands. In those situations, reality is subjected to the transforming tenor of language. Thus, "the potatoes resemble chestnuts in taste, and are as long as turnips." And the oars used by the primal people to propel their canoes are likened to "blades like the shovels of a furnace." We could proliferate the number of examples and arrive at the same conclusion. Pigafetta's device in each instance is to make an alien New World familiar by means of analogies inspired in the Old.

But there are occasions nonetheless when language and observation prove deficient. So much so that the encounter between Europe and America appears taxed by the incapacity of language to apprehend and convey the unfamiliar. The result is at times a monstrous combination of elements prompted by the urge of making comprehensible the anomalous: "un monstruo no es otra cosa que una combinación de seres reales," Borges notes. This is precisely what transpires in some of Pigafetta's descriptions, that of the guanaco for example, as we will see in due course.

III

It is that limitation of language in translating America's reality that will continue to attract the attention of interpreters of new-world circumstances. How is a writer to make attainable to people from distant regions the characteristics of a strange and marginal world such as Latin America? Alejo Carpentier asserts that the problem stems from the lack of universality of the experience conveyed. It is not an easy charge to make someone see that which he has not seen before. To achieve this exacts not only a special talent, but also stylistic demands on the nature of the language employed. It is one thing for a writer, observes Carpentier, to name or allude to items and icons which are part of an established tradition and of a shared universal cultural heritage such as that of Europe. But that privilege is not often granted the Latin American narrator who, finding himself at the periphery of Western culture, and yet a part of it, is repeatedly in need to reach a public other than his own:

> La palabra *pino* basta para mostrarnos el pino; la palabra *palmera* basta para definir, pintar, mostrar, la palmera. Pero la palabra *ceiba*—nombre de un árbol americano al que los negros cubanos llaman "la madre de los árboles"—no basta para que las gentes de otras latitudes vean el aspecto de columna rostral de ese árbol gigantesco, adulto y solitario, como sacado de otras edades, sagrado por linaje.

We may deduce from Carpentier's remarks that of necessity the Latin American writer has to recur to tropes and figures, to minute detail and to a baroque style in order to apprehend his reality, to define it and thus make it universal and attainable to the unacquainted and uninformed. Independent of this baroque question, it seems clear that Pigafetta was faced with the task of naming a world. And this he did, and at times with considerable success. Notice how he *showed* us the then not so conventional fruit of the palm tree of which Carpentier speaks:

> The palm bears a fruit . . . which is as large as the head or thereabouts. Its outside husk is green and thicker than two fingers. . . . Under the husk there is a hard shell, much thicker

> than the shell of the walnut. . . . Under that shell there is a white marrowy substance one finger in thickness, which they eat fresh . . . and it has a taste resembling the almond. . . . There is a clear, sweet water in the middle of that marrowy substance which is very refreshing. When that water stands for a while after having been collected, it congeals and becomes like an apple.

It is Pigafetta's method and skill in recording an unknown and fabulous reality that has attracted the attention of Latin American interpreters, rather than his undisputed value as a source of historical fact. In 1933, the Ecuadorian story teller José de la Cuadra wrote an essay on Pigafetta that is exemplary for its concision and its embryonic aesthetic implications. One of the critical concerns of the essay addresses the question of naming and founding a world. What could there be more extraordinary, asks Cuadra, than to go "de isla en isla, en son de confirmar, como obispo en campo, dándolas nombres pintorescos y atrabiliarios, de acuerdo con la ilusión del momento, con el patrono o santo del día, con el tiempo marino, con la característica aparente." As Pigafetta recounts, this is exactly what Magellan and his men did: "The captain-general called those people Patagoni"; "The captain-general wept for joy, and called that cape, Cape Dezeado, for we had been desiring it for a long time"; "We saw no land except for two desert islets, where we found nothing but birds and trees, for which we called them Ysolle Infortunate." Textual references like these give credence to the opinion that the Europeans did not discover a world but invented it.

A second point Cuadra advances concerns the presence of the marvellous in new-world reality. After comparing Pigafetta's adventures with those of Simbad the seaman, and thereby indicating that in the chronicle of the Italian there is a propensity to fantasise, he cautions in the most emphatic terms that the truly marvellous in the Relation does not derive from those episodes transformed by the rich imagination of its author, prone to exaggeration out of convenience or naïveté, but from the authentic reporting of what he saw:

> Mas, que no quede en mi lector la impresión de que sólo fantasías iluminan la crónica del caballero Pigafetta, como fuegos fatuos en un pudridero. Sólidas realidades, más luminosas aún que las más deslumbrantes fantasías, se entrecruzan y contraponen en ella. Es que esas realidades son, de suyo, en esa hora de la vida humana que le tocó vivir a Pigafetta, tanto o peor de

> increíbles que las máximamente exageradas obras de la imaginación creadora. ¡Realidades de abracadabra!

On two recent occasions, García Márquez has made reference to Pigafetta and arrived at essentially the same conclusion, that the unearthly dimensions of the Latin American world are such that they rival and surpass any interpretative effort attempted by the imagination. Let us discount immediately any possible influence from Cuadra on García Márquez. What they share is a similar tropical environment, a corresponding attitude to and understanding of their circumstances, and a confirmed admiration for Pigafetta's work. In the case of García Márquez, that admiration, which has been longstanding, was most directly voiced in 1979 in an article that anticipated by approximately three years most of the ideas and even language discernible in his Nobel lecture: "Uno de mis libros favoritos de siempre ha sido *El primer viaje en torno del globo,* del italiano Antonio Pigafetta."

It is not surprising, then, that as Nobel laureate designate, García Márquez began his acceptance address with these suggestive words:

> Antonio Pigafetta, a Florentine [sic] navigator who went with Magellan on the first voyage around the world, wrote upon his passage through our southern lands of America, a strictly accurate account that nonetheless resembles a venture into fantasy.
>
> In it he recorded that he had seen hogs with navels on their haunches, clawless birds whose hens laid eggs on the back of their mates, and others still, resembling tongueless pelicans, with beaks like spoons. He wrote of having seen a misbegotten creature with the head and ears of a mule, a camel's body, the legs of a deer and the whinny of a horse. He described how the first native encountered in Patagonia was confronted with a mirror, whereupon that impassioned giant lost his senses to the terror of his own image.
>
> This short and fascinating book, which even then contained the seeds of our present-day novels, is by no means the most staggering account of our reality in that age.

Pigafetta's book thus becomes a point of departure for broad political and aesthetic contentions. Having established that the unwonted character of Pigafetta's Relation is not unique, but one more account among many subscribed by the Chroniclers of the Indies, García Márquez goes on to cite facts and figures from the historical past and present of Latin America to provide documentary evidence of an "outsized reality." Outlandish yet authentic images of delirious conquistadors, nurtured like Don Quixote in books of chivalry, of monstrous and eccentric dictators, capable of the most outrageous and grotesque acts, of rampant poverty and unimaginable infant mortality rates, fervently substantiate a view of an "unbridled reality" that asks "but little of the imagination, for our crucial problem has been a lack of conventional means to render our lives believable." These remarks call for a solution to Latin America's shocking social ills; and, they are also suggestive of García Márquez's thoughts on the role of the imagination in the artistic creations of his continent.

This last aspect is an underlying concern in the aforementioned article of 1979. The subject is unavoidably anchored in a discussion of Latin American reality. Pigafetta is once more cited to attest to the defiant superiority of reality's creations over the meekness of those of the imagination. Under those circumstances, what is the creative artist to do, what are the problems that face him, how is he to solve them? Those are some of the questions that García Márquez raises and attempts to answer. He reiterates that the most difficult endeavor facing the artistic mind is that of making believable the incredibly real:

> En América Latina y el Caribe los escritores han tenido que inventar muy poco, y tal vez su problema ha sido el contrario: hacer creíble su realidad. Siempre fue así desde nuestros orígenes históricos, hasta el punto de que no hay en nuestra literatura escritores menos creíbles y al mismo tiempo más apegados a la realidad que nuestros cronistas de Indias. También ellos—para decirlo con un lugar común irremplazable—se encontraron con que la realidad iba más lejos que la imaginación. . . . Toda nuestra historia, desde el descubrimiento, se ha distinguido por la dificultad de hacerla creer.

The problem is further compounded, argues García Márquez, by the lack of a language that would effectively render the hyperbolic dimensions of the Latin American world: "Un problema muy serio que nuestra realidad desmesurada plantea a la literatura, es el de la insuficiencia de las palabras." The solution would be to "crear todo un sistema de palabras nuevas para el tamaño de nuestra realidad." But beyond the expediency of formulating a nomenclature equal to the task, García Márquez does not offer concrete suggestions as to what path to follow in order to realize that objective. Or does he? All we would have to do is examine the narrative means elaborated in such works as *One Hundred Years of Solitude.*

Carpentier, Cuadra and García Márquez share prevailing concerns—to come to grips with the marvellous quality of Latin American reality, and the need to name a world whose colossal magnitude escapes the limitations of language. They understand that in surroundings where the teratological is an everyday occurrence, the demands on the imagination are not to invent, but to make believable an unbelievable, yet authentic reality. Given that situation, García Márquez comes to this humble conclusion: "Los escritores de América Latina y el Caribe, tenemos que reconocer, con la mano en el corzaón, que la realidad es mejor escritor que nosotros. Nuestro destino, y tal vez nuestra gloria, es tratar de imitarla con humildad, y lo mejor que nos sea posible."

IV

The ostensible attraction of Pigafetta's account for García Márquez rests on the assertion that it upholds his interpretation of Latin American reality. But we are persuaded that Pigafetta's text has also drawn his curiosity because it contains a narrative device that, however rudimentary, merited emulation. Several images from the Relation would illustrate this contention.

There are relatively few Amerindian documents indicative of the manner in which the primal people perceived the Europeans. More often than not, we have to recur to European sources, like Pigafetta, for instances of their grasp of reality. We may wonder how that information was acquired, but the fact remains that such instances are the only access we have to gain some inkling of the indigenous perspective of the encounter with the Western mentality. In this regard, Pigafetta recounts with evident relish the Indians' perception of the Europeans' sailing vessels: "At first those people thought that the small boats were children of the ships, and that the latter gave birth to them when they were lowered into the sea from the ship, and when they were lying alongside the ship (as is the custom), they believed that the ships were nursing them." We cannot help detecting in Pigafetta's amused attitude a presumptuous superiority toward what he judges to be the simplicity and lack of understanding of the primal people. After all, how could anyone mistake ships for animated beings!

An equally revealing image, in a similar yet ironic sense, is the description of a nameless animal, never seen before by Pigafetta, but which we recognise as the guanaco. "That animal has a head and ears as large as those of the mule, a neck and body like those of the camel, the legs of a deer, and the tail of a horse, like which he neighs, and that land has very many of them." We do not have a record of how the natives viewed the guanaco. What we have now is a word, a Quechua word, that identifies it as a concrete animal. Needless to say, in reference to the image of the ships, the situation is reversed, and the question must be asked whether Pigafetta's description of the guanaco would have been equally amusing and simplistic to the Indians as the Europeans' reaction to their view of the sailing vessels?

The images betray the two peoples' mutual lack of understanding as well as their drastically different perception of reality. From our current vantage point, we humorously contemplate the discrepancy of taking ships for animated beings, but only to find it similar to the permutation of the guanaco into a fantastic monster. After all, how different is Pigafetta's description of the guanaco from this of the unicorn?: "el unicornio, semejante por el cuerpo al caballo, por la cabeza al ciervo, por las patas al elefante, por la cola al jabalí. Su mugido es grave; un largo y negro cuerno se eleva en medio de su frente." None whatsoever, except that the unicorn belongs to the world of fantasy, while the guanaco exists.

But, paraphrasing Borges, let us move from the zoology of reality to that of mythologies and dreams. In Pigafetta's account there are images that instead of deriving from the world of facts transport us to the realm of fantasy and myth: "They . . . told us [of] a very huge tree . . . in which live birds called *garuda*. Those birds are so large that they carry a buffalo or an elephant to the place . . . of that tree." Never mind that the *garuda* is a mythical animal of the Buddhist faith, versions of which we can read in *The Arabian Nights,* Marco Polo and others. What is of consequence here is that in this instance Pigafetta is deficient on hard evidence that would sustain his report, and yet, instead of discarding it as unexplainable, he presents it as hearsay, and accepts it on faith.

If we return to the images outlined, we find that the freshness of the first two stems from the dislocation of our habitual perception of the objects observed. Depending on the point of view, the conventional in one world is made anomalous in the other. For us, in turn, the ships and the guanaco function as chiastic images whereby, simultaneously, the real is "made strange" and the strange is made real. In both instances the phenomenon described appears anew. Whatever the perspective, the familiar is "defamiliarised." Culturally, the two images in question document the immense gap separating Indians and Europeans. Yet they also suggest to the contemporary reader that the contact between the two peoples has resulted in a symbiosis of dissimilar frames of reference that ultimately have altered and enriched his experience. Aesthetically, the images, including that of the *garuda,* direct us to narrative strategies evident in such works as *One Hundred Years of Solitude.*

The transformation of the quotidian into something prodigious, which in Pigafetta was not intentional since his aim was to be informative, becomes in García Márquez a very conscious artistic device. So much so that it is feasible to state that it constitutes a major aspect of the narrative method of *One Hundred Years of Solitude.* Everyday objects and phenomena such as magnets, telescopes, telephones, false teeth or ice, which can be rudimentarily, not to say scientifically, explained, appear as marvellous and extraordinary by dislocating our customary sense of perception. Witness the Buendía family's discovery of ice in a pirate chest:

> Al ser destapado por el gigante, el cofre dejó escapar un aliento glacial. Dentro sólo había un enorme bloque transparente, con infinitas agujas internas en las cuales se despedazaba en estrellas de colores la claridad del crepúsculo. Desconcertado, sabiendo que los niños esperaban una explicación inmediata, José Arcadio Buendía se atrevió a murmurar:
>
> —Es el diamante más grande del mundo.
>
> —No—corrigió el gitano—. Es hielo.
>
> José Arcadio Buendía . . . puso la mano sobre el hielo, y la mantuvo puesta por varios minutos, mientras el corazón se le hinchaba de temor y de júbilo al contacto del misterio. . . . Embriagado por la evidencia del prodigio. . . . y con la mano puesta en el témpano, como expresando un testimonio sobre el texto sagrado, exclamó:
>
> —Este es el gran invento de nuestro tiempo.

Needless to say, and burlesque aside, the technique employed recalls Pigafetta's description of the guanaco and the sailing vessels.

But not all aspects of the extraordinary discernible in *One Hundred Years of Solitude* are so firmly grounded in everyday reality. There are also passages which transport us to the realm of the mythical and unexplainable. Remedios the Beauty's miraculous ascent to heaven is illustrative:

> Una tarde de marzo . . . Fernanda quiso doblar en el jardín sus sábanas de bramante, y pidió ayuda a las mujeres de la casa. Apenas había empezado, cuando Amaranta advirtió que Remedios, la bella, estaba transparentada por una palidez intensa.
>
> —¿Te sientes mal?—le preguntó.

> Remedios, la bella, que tenía agarrada la sábana por el otro extremo, hizo una sonrisa de lástima.
>
> —Al contrario—dijo—, nunca me he sentido mejor.
>
> Acabó de decirlo, cuando Fernanda sintió que un delicado viento de luz le arrancó las sábanas de las manos y las desplegó en toda su amplitud. Amaranta sintió un temblor misterioso en los encajes de sus pollerines y trató de agarrarse de la sábana para no caer, en el instante en que Remedios, la bella, empezaba a elevarse. Ursula, ya casi ciega, fue la única que tuvo serenidad para identificar la naturaleza de aquel viento irreparable, y dejó las sábanas a merced de la luz, viendo a Remedios, la bella, que le decía adiós con la mano, entre el deslumbrante aleteo de las sábanas que subían con ella . . . y se perdieron con ella para siempre en los altos aires donde no podían alcanzarla ni los más altos pájaros de la memoria.

Whether García Márquez was attempting a parody of the Virgin Mary's Ascension does not detract from the particular that, as in the case of Pigafetta's *garuda,* he is rendering one more version of a myth intelligible only through faith.

We can safely conclude that García Márquez's admiration for Pigafetta extends beyond the contention that the Italian's Relation gives credibility to a view of Latin American reality as outsized and unimaginable, though authentic. The chronicle of the first voyage around the world, and others like it, also point to a method of how that reality can be made believable. It is this last factor that substantiates the claim that the early chronicles contain "the seeds for our present-day novels."

Pigafetta's account is of central interest to Latin American interpreters not only for its historical accuracy or its possible use in wide-ranging ideological polemics, but because they see in it the roots of their need to name, define and discover their circumstances, and thus assert their spiritual identity and incorporate themselves into a wider world. The *ultima Thule* the Latin American writer aspires to overcome is the sense of dislocation and solitude, of alienation, that was already in gestation, however incipiently, in the first encounters between the Europeans and the primal people. To make the world see the emblematic guanaco for what it is, a reality, and not a monstrosity, would be to affirm that reality, to be.

PATRICIA TOBIN

The Autumn of the Signifier: The Deconstructionist Moment of García Márquez

One Hundred Years of Solitude arrived as a boon to the North American heart. So captivated were we with our first introduction to an exotic world, wider and wackier than our own, that we did not inquire of the genie out of the bottle whether the superabundance was due to the innocence of Latin American consciousness or the sophistication of Latin American art. Much of our elation was due to the imperturbability with which Gabriel García Márquez fashioned a fictional universe unfettered by the laws which, the new structuralism had taught us, governed our language, thought, behavior, disciplines, and institutions—the rules of identity and opposition, hierarchy, cause and effect, substitution and combination. And just as people were becoming thoroughly sick of daddies, Jacques Lacan had disclosed, as the origin and stabilizer of all representation, the Biggest Daddy of them all: the Phallus—Signifier of signifiers, Authorizer of the Word, Law, Truth, and the Symbolic order. How giddy we felt, then, as we witnessed the dynastic rut and romp of seven generations of Buendías, with not a Symbolic patriarch among them, but riddled with incestuous, alchemic, bastardly, celibate and pig-tailed sons escaping the system and exceeding the Father! We cheered for the lawless mesh of "*mágico realismo*" and "*lo real maravilloso,*" laughing our heartiest at the wholesale erasure of the boundaries that sustained our own precise categories of difference. It is the moment in which the laughter bursts from Michel Foucault, in his preface to *The Order of Things,* as he sees Western logic shattered by the unthinkable classifications of Borges's Chinese ency-

From *The Latin American Literary Review* no. 25 (January-June 1985).

clopedia. It was the last moment of pure glee we were to enjoy before literary theory turned unholy and *unheimlich* on us. It is the moment when rule-constrained structuralism is brought low by rule-breaking deconstruction.

The Autumn of the Patriarch is a book for the head, a book that allows us to think the thought of our times. It is the great contemporary novel written from the place of the Big Stud, the site from which García Márquez perpetuates a creative outrageousness fully compatible in its decentering effects with the systematic deviancy of post-structuralist deconstruction. It is the book that *Cien años* would have been, had its author crossed the ten-foot chalk circle drawn around Colonel Aureliano Buendía and punctured the solitude and craziness at the empty seat of power. *The Autumn of the Patriarch* is grounded in Foucault's second moment directly following the laughter when, gazing at the *Las Meninas* of Velázquez, Foucault suddenly becomes very serious and springs his uncanny codicil: Representation works, only when/because the Sovereign Signifier is absent. The Sovereign—he who is sitting for the painting within a painting, around whom it is all centered—must be invisible, inaccessible, exterior to it, faintly present merely in the mirror and in the directed gazes of the others. Only when the very site of representation, the point of all perspectives, is nowhere to be found, can representation inaugurate and sustain itself lawfully. Thus originates the unequal reciprocity between word and image: He who sees cannot signify, and he who signifies cannot see. To become Sovereign, the Signifier must disappear; for the Symbolic Father to authorize our discourses, the Real father must fade from view. What King Philip IV felt about his exile we do not know, but there is no mistaking the protest of the patriarch in his autumn when he cries out, "Who the hell am I because I feel as if the reflection in the mirror is reversed?"

Now there is nothing *unheimlich,* either scary or familiar, about the structuralist Signifier removed to extraterritorial space. The Symbolic Father, after all, is the dead father, the Phallus is not a penis, and everything circulates in an orderly system of exchange. However, when the deconstructionists deterritorialize the founding center into the locus of indeterminacy, inconsistency, and noise; or when García Márquez locates there a Señor Signifier, metamorphosed as a wild card, alive and well and thriving on catastrophe—then we suffer the awesome discomposure of the *unheimlich* third moment. If the Center does not hold, is the Symbolic order which it upholds then a fiction? Is it the crackbrained Center itself that looses anarchy upon world and word? What kind of grotesque Sublime grounds our linguistic and social orders? It is the Patriarch, in His autumn, who forces on us these disconcerting intuitions of the uncanny, and it is his history that maps the anatomy of these three moments.

Structuralism tells us that the world of discourse is an orderly space, stabilized by perpendicular distinctions between sameness and difference, which regulate our metaphorical substitutions and metonymical combinations, our grammar and our syntax. Everything circulates in a system of mutually exclusive and reciprocal exchange, because the Center that holds the poles apart is fixed and immobile. We begin by noting that this Signifier of signifiers enjoys the traditional attributes of godhead—omnipotence, eternality, invisibility. So also does the "undoer of dawn, commander of time, repository of light" of García Márquez. Our patriarch is "the one who can do everything . . . the one who gives the orders," and his indestructability is the star that guides the lesser lives of his children: "The only thing that gave us security on earth was the certainty that he was there, invulnerable to plague and hurricane, invulnerable to Manuela Sánchez's trick, invulnerable to time, dedicated to the messianic happiness of thinking for us, knowing that we knew that he would not take any decision for us that did not have our measure." Of an age so ancient that it can be computed only within a range of error of a hundred years, the Patriarch has killed death once, has risen on the third day, and if he dies again, who is not to believe that he will rise again? During the long reign of the Patriarch one gets used to repetition without variation, and temporal difference begins to look like eternal sameness. Everything returns in the commemorative calendar of the Patriarch—the year of the plague, the time of the comet, the anniversary of August 12, the victory of January 14, the rebirth of March 13. Emptied of its dialectical content, its unique and real events, history may come to seem like no history at all, like myth in fact. In the kingdom of the Patriarch, "time passes—but not so much."

Omnipotent and eternal, the Patriarch is also invisible, rarely seen, and then on a palace balcony distantly, through a touring car darkly. To his people, "general sir . . . you yourself were only an uncertain vision of pitiful eyes through the dusty peepholes of the window of a train, only the tremor of some taciturn lips, the fugitive wave of a velvet glove on the no man's hand of an old man with no destiny with our never knowing who he was, or what he was like, or even if he was only a figment of the imagination." Having already refused to die the literal death demanded by the Symbolic order, this patriarch also disallows any literal representation of himself. No words can be matched to such an elusive object, no mimesis pertain with any reliability. Indeed, only faked images of this disembodied god are allowed to circulate. What makes the rounds are counterfeited portraits, fabricated newscasts, false medals of imaginary victories, and even an "official impostor," Patricio Aragonés, who mimes the master just well enough to die his death for him.

Later on, many of his people will more or less cynically agree that these official images are untrustworthy, yet earlier these were the same folk who began to fabricate a sublime discourse around him: "All he had to do was point at trees for them to bear fruit and at animals for them to grow and at men for them to prosper, and he had ordered them to take the rain away from places where it disturbed the harvest and take it to drought-stricken lands, and that was the way it had been, sir, I saw it, because his legend had begun much earlier than he believed himself master of all his power." An unseen, absent Father apparently presents no obstacle to belief as it is elaborated in language; to the contrary, a vacuum, void, empty set seems to some to exist only to be filled back in with the fertile stuff of legend. When the whole man is unavailable for literal representation—when he is known only through his parts, a hand, his lips, his eyes—then this metonymical incompletion leads to metaphorical escalation. How rapid and absolute that escalation can become is seen in this wholly mythical description of the Patriarch at the height of his power: "Official schoolboy texts referred to him as a patriarch of huge size who never left his house because he could not fit through the doors, who loved children and swallows, who knew the language of certain animals, who had the virtue of being able to anticipate the designs of nature, who could guess a person's thoughts by one look in the eye, and who had a secret of salt with the virtue of curing lepers' sores and making cripples walk." For he who appears from nowhere, there is provided the origin myth of the son-of-no-father; and for he who is everywhere, there is the predictable apocalypse associated with his imagined demise "that the mud from the swamps would go back up river to its source, that it would rain blood, that hens would lay pentagonal eggs, and that silence and darkness would cover the universe once more because he was the end of creation." In such an economy, where visual representation and verbal imitation are all but impossible, words are worth a thousand images; and discourse, without the negative feedback of the Real, becomes destabilized, on runaway. Although such unauthorized mythologizing authorizes the Father and legitimates the Center, from a meta-perspective it also allows us to understand that Father as a generator of excess as well as a stabilizer of order. His very absence from reality dictates his ascent into myth.

We have heard what his people say, but what would they see if—like the reader or the deconstructionist—they invaded the space of the Patriarch? A silly, sullied, senile Sublime. A deaf and amnesiac Phallus dragging around a gigantic herniated testicle. The Signifier stripped down to a portable latrine, a pallet on the floor, and a common soldier's uniform *sans* insignia. The Emperor, shouts the irreverent poststructuralist, has no clothes! An illusory monarch, this poor, imperfectly forked animal is also a captive monarch, a slave to the power of which he should be master. García Márquez intends this minimalist emphasis, I think, to define the seat of power as a limbo, as a claustrophobia-inducing prisonhouse that suffocates its vassal. The suggestion is that the patriarch, caged up and cast away, maintains a certain site of innocence and gains courage from an endured victimage. This captive of power, nonetheless, is also a vicious wielder of power whenever he extends himself beyond his cage. The old bison suffering in his solitude, the locus of his nation's lives and legends, is likewise a volcano-god whose hot lava erupts over the land, flooding it to the peripheries. Our patriarch is a Papa Stalin, keeping his lonely vigil in the Kremlin out of concern for his children; but whether he chooses to confer parades or purges, shifts or gulags, whenever he reaches out, he is a devastating destabilizer. It seems clear that García Márquez is also insisting, significantly, that the safely exiled Signifier is but a consoling structuralist fiction.

This is a man who carries disorder in his bones and leaves a trail of devastation in his wake, even within his own privileged space. In his palace, at the heart of power, there are cripples on the stairs, whores in the laundry rooms, cows on the carpet, lepers in the rosebushes, hens pecking away at the government files. Into the house of power has seeped a folk-flood, eroding spatial orders and hierarchal proprieties. Outside the palace, the patriarch's most clearly intended reforms are deformations, as when the sweeping schools, instituted to provide employment and clean up national litter, issue in the Sisyphean practice of trundling a nation's rubbish from province to province; or when the massive urban renewal of the Dogfight District results in thousands of displaced refugees. The site of power begins to look like a carnival presided over by a clownish, captious lord of misrule, who upturns and overturns the rectilinear distinctions of his extensive domain.

If order leaks out of space, time fares no better in the kingdom of the patriarch. Temporality loses the serial punctuation that would permit gradualism and regularity, and is made instead to submit to the exclamatory mark of the catastrophe. We begin to realize what the world must have been like when gods were taken seriously. Our invisible patriarch has a sudden, brutal way of being noticed, of making a large, abrupt difference. The Catholic Church refuses to confer sainthood upon my dead mother? Herd every nun and priest out of the country, naked as the day of their infamous births, expropriate the Church properties, beat up the Papal Anuncio, and declare war on the Holy See! My old friend, the minister of defense, is plotting against me? Stuff him with herbs and pine nuts, and serve him for dinner to the other potentially traitorous Cabinet members! The children who draw for the national lottery threaten a very profitable swindle? Ship all 2,000 of them out to sea, and dynamite the raft into silence!

Not only is the patriarch a disruptive child at play and a victimizer of his people, but any strategy he chooses to insure order inevitably issues in increasing disorder; any attempt at correction simply exacerbates the noise and escalates the static in the system. The lottery-drawing children are a case in point. Instructed to pick from the bag only the billiard ball that is iced, the children must be removed from their families after each drawing to insure their silence. Protesting parents begin to fill up the nation's jails, and the children to overpopulate the dungeon beneath the harbor. As public indignation spreads, an international commission is sent to investigate. Now the children must be shuffled back and forth in boxcars to the uninhabited swamps, mountains, and rain forests until the investigators depart in defeat. With their departure the patriarch is free to massacre the children, but then the population must be decimated in the general insurrection that follows. And all for the lack of an honest lottery. For the want of a Symbolic Father, the Symbolic order is lost.

Excess is in fact mandated in the Signifier that refuses to die a literal death. With no one to say no, no off-button to stop him, no negative feedback to halt the snowball effect—the patriarch puts any system on runaway. Soon enough, his secret wishes and commands will be carried out before he can utter them: A nun will be kidnapped for his future wife, the soap operas on television will be rewritten to afford him happy endings, waterfront whores will be passed off as innocent schoolgirls to serve his aged lust. When silence authorizes definitively, copying errors increase, chance may become necessity and mistakes law, as when one diplomat's waving, white handkerchief becomes everyone else's protocol for attracting the attentions of the deaf patriarch. In or out of his bottle, the patriarch is an imp of catastrophe, a perverse clown, a sorting demon gone wild, a lightning rod for violence and excess.

Traditionally, the hero has been conceived in a condition of mediation, the third party between us and the gods, our official stand-in for those difficult negotiations. Yet this Daddy, unfit as a Center and emphatically disqualified for rational mediation, cannot be the fated hero of tragedy. If he is an Oedipus at all, he is the Oedipus of farce. Full of bluff and bluster, given to the immorality of ruinous waste, he is the criminal-as-detective who initiates national witch hunts for the perpetrators of the crimes again humanity he himself has committed. When their jobs are done, his hired assassins are hunted down and shot, quartered, beheaded electrocuted. Confronted with an atrocity apparently not his own, the patriarch typically escalates his feverish search for an arbitrary scapegoat into a national reign of terror. To discover who commanded the pack of dogs that tore apart his wife and son in the marketplace, he establishes a secret police force and thereafter, each time more cynically and wearily, signs individual receipts for the 918 severed heads that are delivered to the palace. Like Oedipus—who will accuse Creon, then Tiresias, then the messenger, and finally his shepherd foster-father—the patriarch may have initially thought he was seeking out the Truth. You must speak out, he tells his children, when the apostolic representative begins his investigation into the miraculous powers reputed to his dead mother, Bendición Alvarado. And speak out they do, dutifully and for pay, through seven volumes of testimony taken from the dropsy victims cured and the dead men raised—by the mother lying in state who "had been stuffed according to the worst skills of taxidermy" to provide relics for enterprising dealers. For such a grotesque national conspiracy against the Truth, whose is the ultimate responsibility? "Everything had been a farce . . . a carnival apparatus that he himself had put together without really thinking about it when he decided that the corpse of his mother should be displayed for public veneration on a catafalque of ice long before anyone thought about the merits of her sainthood." In the country where the lie is king, the Oedipus of farce lets the lie live (civil sainthood for Bendición), banishes the Church and the Truth, and he himself and his eyes stay put.

Near the end of his eternal reign, the only truth surviving in the country of the patriarch is the anonymous graffitti scrawled on the walls of the palace toilets. As one for whom virtue and love are impossible, the "general of the universe" has come to the determination that "a lie is more comfortable than doubt, more useful than love, more lasting than truth." He has arrived, this Signifier of signifiers, at "the ignominious fiction of commanding without power, being exalted without glory, being obeyed without authority." Yet even though the Center has been eroded, emptied out, dilapidated—the absolutes of command, exaltation, and obedience remain. How is it that nothing has stayed pure—that absolutes are grounded in the shakiest relativisms, the sublime in grotesqueries, Truth in farce?

According to Michel Serres, steps were taken very early in Western culture to insure that it couldn't happen here. In the first stunning volume of his *Hermes,* Serres engages in two brilliant pieces of theoretical speculation concerning a relation of similarity between the dialogues of Plato and the geometry of Parmenides. Customarily, the two interlocutors in a Socratic dialogue are supposed to be opposing each other in a dialectical search for the Truth. In the newer view of communication theory, they are on the same side, tied together by a mutual interest: the elimination of the noise that threatens to interrupt the communication. Mathematics likewise presents itself as a successful communication, in firm command of a code that is maximally purged of any interference. Serres calls this common enemy "the third man." The third man may be background noise, static, the chronic transformations of language-as-Babel, irrational numbers—in short, the entire empirical domain that can overwhelm any formal system. With Plato and the geometers Western thought begins it massive, concerted campaign to render an ideal form independent of its empirical realizations, to isolate it from the noise of the world, to eliminate everything that hides form. The structuralist Signifier is a contemporary manifestation of this hard-fought Western battle against noise and for formalization. The empirical domain, Lacan's Real, must be eliminated if a formal system, such as language, is to be born; the Real father must die, in order to inaugurate the Symbolic domain for the Signifier of signifiers. It is only in this exclusionary, restricted, formalized space that we conduct our searches and support their results as Truth.

Kurt Gödel in his famous Theorem tried to warn us that we couldn't win. In refuting the symbolic logic of Whitehead and Russell, he demonstrated mathematically the impossible coexistence of consistency and completeness within any formal system. If a system of thought is consistent, then it is so because it is incomplete; if it is complete, it will necessarily be inconsistent. Or, in Serres's formulation: If you successfully exclude the third man, you will have a neat formal lie; if you allow the background static in for the sake of completeness, you will have a tiger by the tail. The West has almost always opted for the first alternative, faking completeness in order to maintain consistency. Consistency has been as important to our thinking as unity to our sense of self, as continuity to our sense of time, as order to our sense of space. Remove one brick from that edifice, the house that Plato and Parmenides built, and you have a system in ruins.

García Márquez has removed all four—consistency, unity, continuity, and order. He has taken the second, infrequent way out of Gödel's theorem, deciding to go for the completeness and let the consistency go. He chooses not to exorcise the demon of noise, but rather to show how it is the necessary origin and end of all our systemizations. In *The Autumn of the Patriarch* he has taken us to the kingdom of the third man who refuses to be excluded. His patriarch is the empirical fact of contradiction that threatens the consistency of formal systems, at the same time that it grounds such systems as the background noise. In Serres's memorable metaphor, the patriarch is a spinning top: "The top spins, even if we demonstrate that, for impregnable reasons, it is, undecidably, both mobile and fixed. That's the way it is." Fixed, i.e., dead, the Symbolic Signifier thus establishes a boundary that doesn't shift, a bottom-line to representation, an ultimate sticking-place for referentiality. Captive of his power, the Patriarch enables the orderly circulation of words and goods, the proper distribution of functions, the stability of structuration—all because he doesn't move. But, like Galileo's earth, he *does* move, and catastrophically, undoing his own ordering powers and promoting the uneasy suspicion of a ground-that-shifts at the center of things, a ground itself decentered and decentering. Not to observe the boundaries is to erode the ground of representation, is to make verification and falsification impossible, is to destroy Truth and literality at the same blow. By taking the patriarch out of the mimetic portrait for which he is supposedly sitting firm, García Márquez measures the potential for havoc in the Signifier, exposing it in a mirror of the Real where contradiction and undecidability within Symbolic systems are escalated from formal inconsistencies to the empirical wilderness of "that's the way it is."

The imaginative intelligence of our author is decidedly post-Einsteinian. After Einstein, that perpetuator of relativity, God is the third man, a joker of "invisible power whose dice decided the fate of a nation." Márquez's patriarch is the demon of noise that actively works to disrupt successful communications. He knew "the secret of maintaining parallel services to stir up distractive rivalries among the military . . . identical organisms that he made look different in order to rule with more relaxation in the midst of the storm making them believe that some were being watched by others, mixing beach sand in with the gunpowder in the barracks and confusing the truth of his intentions with images of the opposite truth." The patriarch is that *unheimlich* vortex where contraries whirl, mix, and displace one another, where the only symbolic laws that pertain are Planck's randomness, Heisenberg's uncertainty, and Schrödinger's undecidability. It is this vortex—where Señor Signifier shits as he fucks—that is the ultimate focus of the deconstructionists. Probing and prodding only those nodes of a text where the Center shifts from stasis to static, the deconstructionist critics, appalled by its indeterminacy, themselves prolong the rigorous task of the text almost infinitely, steadfastly refusing to recuperate for system and theory the various entropies of the Real. Like García Márquez, they are suspicious of premature closures, embarrassed by any complacent conviction of completeness, and bored by the convention of consistency.

Against those who would argue for the interpretive Truth of a text, the deconstructionists employ their most radical strategy: the literalization of metaphor, and the metaphorization of the literal word. With this move, they effectively reduce to absurdity the notion of a ground. And where there is no ground, there can be neither mimesis nor antithesis, but merely figure after figure after figure, each one a surface without a depth. This, in Serres's phrase, is the "chronic transformation" that prevents the completion of communication and casts suspicion upon the existence of Truth. The patriarch's people learn this mistrust early, which García Márquez explicitly connects to his death which was a nondeath, suffered only by his double, the official impostor: "We knew that no evidence of his death was final, because there was always another truth behind the truth."

Not only does García Márquez adopt the literalizing/metaphorizing tactics of deconstruction, as we shall presently see, but he also makes his patriarch's life a literalization of one of deconstruction's own central metaphors. I refer here to the trade-off between insemination and dissemination, as elaborated in the thought of Jacques Derrida. The inseminating Father is the reliable Signifier of the structuralists, he who respects the past as a legacy, guarantees the legitimacy of his progeny, and stands securely for a calculable future. The patriarch of García Márquez neither inherits nor confers such dynastic credentials. The origin myth affirms that "a wandering birdwoman at the beginning of time had given difficult birth to a no man's son who became king." Further testimony about Saint Bendición reveals that she "was languid, went about dressed in rags, barefoot, and had to use her lower parts in order to eat, but she was beautiful, father, and she was so innocent that she fitted out the cheapest lory parrots with tails from the finest cocks to make them pass for macaws, she repaired crippled hens with turkey-feather fans and sold them as birds of paradise." The bastard son of an impoverished, possibly retarded con-woman who survives by disseminating confusion, the patriarch is himself a scatterer of his seed, wasting it on the large number of illegitimate seven-month runts he fathers. The herniated testicle that causes him continual pain and shame concretizes the antistructuralist metaphor of deconstruction's crippled Phallus, and accounts in the narrative of his life for the kind of furious impotency that propels his "rooster love" with the unending train of females he summons to his presence. His is an impotency realized empirically in the political sphere, where his absolute power is converted to absolute powerlessness, as when his *Doppelgänger* taunts the patriarch with "You're president of nobody," and his executioner reminds him impassively, "You aren't the government, general, you're the power." The disseminating father so scatters and squanders his seed that neither appearance nor reality, neither cause nor effect can be legitimated within the formalizations that Western Truth demands.

Throughout *The Autumn of the Patriarch* there are authorial techniques that deconstructionists would recognize as their own. For instance, there are the abrupt shiftings of pronouns that revise and add to the truth-tale of the farcical Oedipus, the foreign perspective of the third man that causes orderly narrative to leap its tracks and follow after local surprises. Still, deconstructionists have never followed their structuralist predecessors in their exclusive fascination with syntax. Much more challenging to them are the devious ways of metaphor, particularly in its folding-back into the literal, and vice versa, where the weaving of the symbolic and mimetic most resembles the double helix or gold braid which contains simultaneously all possibilities, every interpretation.

If we follow to the end one of these woven strands in the patriarch's history, we can readily see how it turns back on itself, so that "end" and "beginning" lose their significance as terminal points in a biography. Already we know that, in the moment of inauguration, eternity was conferred upon the Signifier simultaneously with his entrance into profane temporality. We might well suspect, then, that with whatever temporal journeying his life offers him, he will never move from where he is. We are now prepared to notice how García Márquez has through the play of rhetoric implemented the following formulations, which would create static in any formalized system: The end is in the beginning; secular temporality is all the eternity we have; the waters of indifferentiation are from whence we spring and whither we go; the feminine principle is but the female anatomy, the "oceanic feeling" and the womb merging in the indeterminacy of metaphorical and literal inscription.

"I did it all so that I could get to know the sea," confesses this old man from the backlands, who has sold the seacoast of his landlocked country to foreign exploiters, to ease the huge national debt. The ultimatum from his creditors is, "Either the marines land or we take the sea." What follows is this incredible writing, no deciding its identification as either metaphor or literalness, that runs away with the "take" metaphor/literality, twining the sublime with the grotesque: "So they took away the Caribbean in April, Ambassador Ewing's nautical engineers carried it off in numbered pieces to plant it in the blood-red dawns of Arizona, they took it away with everything it had inside, general sir, with the reflection of our cities, our timid drowned people, our demented dragons." Almost every word gives us cause for pause. The linguistic signs that point to precise, unambivalent signification—the proper names, the details of agency, time, and place—are evenly countered and cancelled by the enumeration of the mythical contents of the patriarch's sea. This is the ultimate dispossession of the Signifier. The Center is revealed as the primal soup; at the source of all circulation is not a male center of differentiation, but a female reservoir of undifferentiation; and the sea-womb is a tomb, the resting-place of both the pre- and post-individual. We are, already and always, where we are going to. Bracketing, as we must, the absurdity of this language, we can see that it encompasses both completeness and consistency. There is the consistency of the human condition within time and its accompanying lament for "this meatbeating life that goes only in one direction"; and there is completeness in the before/after symmetry of timelessness with which the temporal consistency is braided, tracked, and traced.

The patriarch of mythical birth, moreover, has been given the prophecy of a death that sounds very literal—he will die as "a solitary drowned man"—until we begin to extrapolate metaphorically by saying that this apparently means the embryonic waters will return to reclaim him. This is a rather comforting notion when pitched at the sublime level of the archetype, but the literalizing account of the patriarch's death in Ambassador Kipling's memoirs is a distinct downgrading to the grotesque: "He told how he had found him soaked in an incessant and salty matter which flowed from his skin, that he had acquired the huge size of a drowned man and he had opened his shirt to show me the tight and lucid body of a dry-land drowned man in whose crooks and crannies parasites from the reefs at the bottom of the sea were proliferating, he had a ship remora on his back, polyps and microscopic crustaceans in his armpits." Undecidability is multiplied here with almost every phrase. Might the salty matter be sweat rather than seawater? Huge on the outside and tight on the inside is both for and against a literal drowning. There aren't any crustaceans that are microscopic, are there? And perhaps, "a dry-land drowned man" is a metaphor for the power-victimized patriarch? Faithful readers of García Márquez will recognize this typical play on deconstructionist territory, where Truth can be neither confirmed nor disconfirmed. I myself like the quiet thud of the sentence Márquez writes for the minister of health's examination of the dead patriarch: "(It) revealed that his arteries had turned to glass, he had beachsand sediment in his kidneys, and his heart was cracked from a lack of love." It is the "lack" at the source of things—the repressed castration-wound whose first cut becomes our first boundary-limit—that makes of our lives a rehearsing over and over of the birth trauma. Perhaps the wisest intuition of the patriarch is that we can do nothing else but go home again. He voices it in the circular metaphor that his life has literalized: "Seas are like cats, he said, they always come home."

If it is womb/woman from whom and to whom we journey without moving, she is surely not one of Jung's archetypes, all of whom circulate within, not prior to, the economy of lack. Available to rational thought because they follow inauguration, the archetypes have no place outside of human consciousness and the neuroses of temporality. By their very differentiation into types, the virgin and the whore, wise crone and witch, madonna and matron are tainted with the marks of human longing and desire. If we seek the pre-embodiment woman, we are more likely to find her through Jacques Derrida's meditation upon Nietzsche's meditation on woman, as "one name for the untruth of truth." There, one finds Derrida strenuously opposing both philosophical and hermeneutical recovery of the text, through their devaluation of metaphor as the lying art that disrupts both logical thought and literary representation. There is nothing verifiable, of course, about Derrida's and Nietzsche's equivalency of woman and the swerve away from logic that is figurative language, of sexuality and nontruth. However, with the equation as a model for reading, he would have us adopt a tangential, and therefore perverse, relation to our texts, one that cuts across the normal conventions and dissolves our categorical languages along the slope of the diagonal. Put simply, the challenge is whether or not we can conceive the truth as skepticism, whether we can accept a ground that shifts beneath our stable foundations.

Originally, that stability was guaranteed by the purity of the concept, basic to philosophic thought, the Platonic idea. But in the fallen, ontological world the concept becomes contaminated with images of undecidability, evoked through the incessant human oscillations between the spiritualization and sensualization of love and hostility. The Platonic idea becomes woman; the becoming-female is a "process of the idea" (*Fortschritt der Idee*). Derrida's text is Nietzsche's *Twilight of the Idols,* specifically that section called "History of an Error" which immediately precedes his story of truth. There, Nietzsche says of the idea that "it becomes female . . . Christian," a statement which Derrida transposes as "she castrates (herself)," noting the Christian Church's preference for the excision and extirpation of passion, for "curing" through castratism, for seizing consistency through exclusion. Hostile to life, the Church and the concept are hostile to its invasion of their purity through woman, who is life. In the reactive position, either as truth or nontruth, woman is debased, censured. She eludes her conceptualized identity as sexual antagonist only when, as Derrida says, "she affirms herself, in and of herself, in man" as the dionysiac and artist, whose multiple styles render the idea "subtle, insidious, incomprehensible" and suspend "the decidable opposition of true and non-true." Hence, the heterogeneity of the womanly text, the entropy within sexual differentiation.

Now let us return to the patriarch of García Márquez. In all *his* castrated delusions of virility, in *his* dangerous delight in playing the thunder-god, in *her* seductive distance and captivating inaccessibility, in *her* tantalizing promise of transcendence—our *his/her* patriarch enacts the becoming-female of the Platonic idea, of the structuralist Signifier. Indeed, in his advanced age, he bears a striking resemblance to the eternal, sceptical Úrsula Buendía. His life given over entirely to domestic duties, he moves through his household with the lurching gait and the slovenly appearance of a slattern, counting the heads, covering the birds in their cages, burning the cow plops, turning out the lights, locking up for the night—without eliminating the disorder that disrupts, but also without arranging anything that will not be undone once again with the morning light. In accommodating the mess of his palace, the patriarch-as-Úrsula evinces a style, as passive as it might appear, that nonetheless makes the meshing of sexual difference intractable to hard-and-fast coding.

Whether his stylistic manifestations are active or passive, in the funhouse mirror of the deconstructionists, the Sovereign is this man-dressed-as-a-woman. His inaugural appearance must surely have been early, quite possibly in *The Bacchae* of Euripides. In that Greek tragedy we see the two genders in their active and passive orientations, uncastrated and castrated—as power, powerful impotence, impotent power, and impotence. There the already dilapidated Signifier appears through a principle of doubling, in the two-in-one of Pentheus, the sacrificial victim, and Dionysius, the god of misrule and intoxication. Arrayed in curls and gown, eager for his debut as a voyeur, Pentheus the king acts out the prelude of dedifferentiation that is necessary for the Dionysian rites of undifferentiation. The catastrophe occurs in the midst of carnival, with the dismemberment of Pentheus by his unseeing mother and the other women empowered and crazed through their shared communality of excess. The final scene features—not a responsible *deus ex machina* come to purge the city of its Dionysiac impurities—but rather a monstrous bull-man-god, smiling down from the top of the temple at the noise he has literalized at the hearts and hearths of the Greeks. With this supplement, tragedy is born.

Tragedy (here we might substitute Western history, logic, narrative) has always been the story of our resistance to an entropic heterogeneity that leaks out order through an inscription tangential to its own declamations of thesis and antithesis. It is not smart to choose sides within a non-organic totality. It is much better to find a style that undoes the fetishes and reifications of rationalized representation. My own choice among the Greek models of style-setters is not the Dionysius/Pentheus of Euripides, but rather the Hermes of Michel Serres. I like this jokester, this forever mobile, fleet-footed messenger of the gods. I like the seductiveness of his tricks, feints, ruses, and disguises. I like the way he keeps turning up as the god of commerce and exchange, of the crossroads, of thieves and secrets, of comedy. I like the zero-degree of reductionism implied by his caduceus rod, which looks so much like the double helix of DNA. Without being terrorized by the Dionysius who is Nietzsche's father of tragedy, we can appreciate Hermes as the background noise that precedes and founds our differentiations and individuation. To confront Hermes is to imagine at the Center the uncastrated woman, the (wo)man of the universe. In taking the structuralist Signifier straight, we were futilely countering the cosmic drift of entropy, trying once more to command nature without first obeying her. Now, in the autumn of the Patriarch, we should be prepared cheerfully to embark upon our unstable practices, assured that we are moving—and not moving—with the universe.

ISABEL ALVAREZ-BORLAND

From Mystery to Parody: (Re)Readings of García Márquez's Crónica de una muerte anunciada

Crónica de una muerte anunciada presents the critic with a text which, by way of a complex system of narrative and temporal levels, explores why an entire town allows a senseless murder to occur in the name of hypocritical honor codes. A sociological reading of *Crónica* traces the backward mentality of small towns in Latin America and elsewhere. The rich system of *presagios* and the biblical symbolism in the names of the main participants would support the interpretation of the story as a biblical myth, Santiago Nasar as its Christ figure, a scapegoat for the town's bloodthirstiness. Although helpful in the understanding of the text's didactic message, these interpretations only look for solutions in the mimesis of the text, leaving the reader with many unanswered questions regarding the direct references to the creative process contained in Márquez's tale. Analysing these allusions from the standpoint of the detective story as the perfect model of the "hermeneutic tale," the present study envisions this novel as a questioning structure rather than as an answer-providing construct. An analysis of the detective conventions as well as of their aesthetic effect is necessary in the appraisal of a work which has been labeled by reviewers as a "simplistic murder mystery," inferior in quality to the author's previous writings.

García Márquez's text is indeed a detective story which subverts the conventionality of its genre, but which at the same time takes advantage of the genre's inherent traits. *Crónica* exhibits what, according to Frank Kermode, makes the detective novel the perfect hermeneutic tale: a hermeneu-

From *Symposium* 38, no. 4 (Winter 1984–85).

tic preoccupation at the expense of depth, undifferentiation of characters, a turbulent temporal flow, and an ambiguity of clues. In fact, Kermode's descriptive categories become extremely important in García Márquez's subversion of the genre as they invite the reader to make inferences about an entirely new system of interpretation.

The tale centers around an unnamed *cronista,* who early on announces his intentions to "recomponer con tantas astillas dispersas, el espejo roto de la memoria." There seem to be no secrets left to discover in this so called mystery. The reader is told who killed Santiago Nasar twenty-seven years before, the manner in which he was killed, and even the exact time of the murder. The reader's first impression is one of confusion: if this is a mystery, what exactly is the narrator looking for? The book's investigative structure thus convinces the reader that he, along with the narrator, is on a hunt—although the reason for the search is never expressed.

Further confusion is introduced when the narrator dramatizes the recollections which more than fifty witnesses have of the murder. The ironic language used to narrate the events surrounding Nasar's death serves to hide rather than to reveal facts, and functions exclusively to distance the reader from the events he is seeking to resolve. The potentially illuminating function of language is constantly undermined, as is illustrated by the *cronista*'s description of Bayardo San Román, an enigmatic figure who exhibits "una manera de hablar que más bien le servía para ocultar que para decir." The contradictions in the townspeople's versions, as well as their simplistic evaluation of the events as predetermined acts of fate, are manifested by a narrator who himself is guilty of the same fatalistic line of reasoning. Faced with a multiplicity of accounts lacking any kind of specificity and coherence, the reader is forced to surmise, to read between the lines, careful not to interpret the townspeople's declarations in a literal fashion.

The text's discourse changes, however, in those passages which advance the action as well as provide the background of the protagonist. Here the language is transparent, straightforward, and gives the text its direct, mimetic quality. The text's linguistic duality causes the reader to be at once distanced from the events he is seeking to resolve, and seduced by the apparent clarity and simplicity of the tale unfolding before him. As demonstrated by the investigation, this dual language reveals *Crónica* as a two-tiered novel, with simultaneous plots metaphorically related by the conventions of the detective story.

At least two temporal levels can be distinguished in the narrator's account: the time contemporaneous with the murder, that is, twenty-seven years before, and the present of the *crónica,* the time in which the narrator decides to reconstruct these events. The first temporal level involves the declarations of the witnesses recorded in the instructor's summary as well as the memories the *cronista* has of the events, for he was in town the day of the murder. The second temporal category includes the retrospective memories of the multiple witnesses, as well as the narrator's own reminiscences of the crime. The intermingling of these two temporal levels is unsettling to the reader, since the narrator never distinguishes one from the other.

For further temporal ambiguity, we have only to look at the order in which the narrative events are reported. The text of the chronicle is divided into five unnumbered segments which reveal the events of Santiago Nasar's death in a most peculiar manner:

1. Recreation of the events immediately before Santiago Nasar's death
2. Background of Angela Vicario and Bayardo San Román (the defiled virgin and the wronged husband)
3. Background of the bride's twin brothers, the perpetrators of the crime
4. Morbid description of the autopsy of Santiago Nasar's body
5. Recreation of the events immediately before Nasar's death; graphic rendition of his death; poetic description of his death

A traditionalist analysis of the five segments would indicate that if the first three can be considered the exposition of the murder and the background of its main perpetrators, parts four and five could be interpreted as the implied author's indictment of the townspeople (including the narrator). The gloomy descriptions of the autopsy and the murder can thus be viewed as a motivation for the reader to realize, with the implied author, the dire consequences of stale and hypocritical honor codes. The fact that the point of view in the fifth segment changes from "I" to "We" can be taken as further evidence of the condemnation by the author of the narrator *and* the townspeople, thus presenting a scathing comment on the corruption of their moral values as well as their institutions. After this interpretation, however, many questions remain unresolved, two of which are fundamental to our investigation: What is the relationship between the narrator and his reconstructive sources, especially the instructor's text? Why is the narrator interested in revisiting the scene of the crime in the last segment; why the double rendition of the death of Santiago Nasar?

These two questions constitute the premise for an interpretation of *Crónica* based on the understanding by the reader of the text's narrative patterns. To begin to understand this text is to accept the book's process, and to move beyond what may seem to be the centers of the book—a parody of rigid conventions, even a tragedy.

As has been suggested by my comments regarding the narrator's categories of order and the ambiguity of his language, the overall pattern of this text strives against satisfactory closure of the issues that it raises. If at the mimetic level the reader is involved in the injustices of the gratuitous murder of Santiago Nasar, then on the level of discourse the reader must exert his own interpretative role. Viewed in this manner, the questions created by the text become incentives for the reader to examine its narrative process further. The complex relationship between the narrator and his written sources is a crucial aspect of this examination.

In addition to the reports of the townspeople as well as his own firsthand knowledge of the events narrated, the *cronista* uses as his reconstructive sources the official records of the Summary. These documents were recorded by a *juez / instructor* who does not appear on the scene but who, nevertheless, becomes an important presence in this text. The instructor's *sumario* becomes important to the *cronista* not for its contents—which many times are not different from the meaningless utterances remembered and quoted by the narrator—but for the record's literariness, the way in which the *cronista* "reads" the instructor's language. For instance, when the record mentions the fateful door, which could have been Nasar's salvation, the *cronista* dwells on the instructor's style: "la puerta estaba citada varias veces con un nombre de folletín: *La puerta fatal.*" On other occasions, the *cronista* seems to forego the contents of the record only to comment on the marginal notes of the instructor, and even on the drawings which the instructor made of the knives used in the murder. Moreover, in the last segment of the text, the instructor is described by the *cronista* as, "un hombre abrasado por la fiebre de la literatura," as the *cronista* continues to ponder over the enigma of his marginal notes: "Las notas marginales, y no sólo por el color de la tinta, parecían escritas con sangre. Estaba tan perplejo con el enigma que le había tocado en suerte, que muchas veces incurrió en distracciones líricas contrarias al rigor de su oficio. Sobre todo, nunca le pareció legítimo que la vida le sirviera de tantas casualidades prohibidas a la literatura, para que se cumpliera sin tropiezos una muerte tan anunciada." The instructor's *distracciones líricas* mentioned in the above passage also extend to his special liking for proverbs, a fact which might imply that the proverb appearing at the beginning of the text, "La caza de amor es de altanería," could be the work of either the *cronista* or the instructor. Intentional blurring of identities is suggested here, one which will be of crucial importance in our understanding of the role of the *cronista* as the reader of the *pliegos* as well as the author of this chronicle.

Of additional interest in the above citation is the analogy the *cronista* makes between literature and the story's main events. The confounding of life and art clearly indicates a commentary on the author's craft, and makes the reader aware of the text's conscious fictionality. Similar allusions can be found interspersed throughout the text, such as the *cronista*'s description of Angela Vicario, 23 years after the murder: "Al verla así, dentro del marco idílico de la ventana, no quise creer que aquella mujer fuera la que yo creía, porque me resistía a admitir que la vida terminara por parecerse tanto a la mala literatura." Such comparisons between the text's reality and the literary reality indicate a playful subversion of the concepts of life and art, and point towards the impossibility of ever arriving at factual truth—in this case the truth behind Santiago Nasar's murder.

Coupled with the *cronista*'s unusual interest in the literary quality of his reconstructive sources is the important issue of the *sumario*'s fragmented condition, for he found these *pliegos* in the disordered and abandoned archives of his hometown: "Yo mismo exploré muchas veces con las aguas hasta los tobillos aquel estante de aguas perdidas, y sólo una casualidad me permitió rescatar al cabo de cinco años de búsqueda unos 322 pliegos salteados de los más de 500 que debió tener el sumario." The fact that the *pliegos* are incomplete not only parallels the unfinished quality of the *cronista*'s text (our text) but also points towards the possible origin of yet another *pliego,* a mysterious piece of paper mentioned only twice in the narrative. In the first segment, this piece of paper is mentioned as a forgotten document, which, had it been found by the victim, could have prevented his death: "Alguien que nunca fue identificado había metido por debajo de la puerta un papel dentro de un sobre, en el cual le avisaban a Santiago Nasar que lo estaban esperando para matarlo, y le revelaban además el lugar y los motivos, y otros detalles muy precisos de la intriga." The use of the word *intriga* is of extreme importance here, as is the fact that, in a manner reminiscent of the Melquíades manuscripts in *One Hundred Years of Solitude,* this paper contains the story of Santiago Nasar, that is, a replica of our text. Actually, it is not until the last segment of the narrative, when the narrator revisits the scene of the crime, that the paper is mentioned again: "Plácida Linero vio entonces el papel en el suelo, pero no pensó en recogerlo, y sólo se enteró de lo que decía cuando alguien se lo mostró más tarde en la confusión de la tragedia." This piece of paper, like the marginal notes of the instructor, never figures directly at the level of the anecdote, although both play an important role in revealing the text's insistence on its literary nature. The paper also serves to thematize literary self-consciousness and functions to call attention to the repetitive, un-lifelike nature of the story. Because it contains the details of the plot, it can be considered a duplication of our text, a perfect example of what Dällenbach defines as a *mise en abyme.* This curious mirroring effect is not limited to just one incident, but can be encountered in other instances within the story. A good example is the equal but contradictory relationship between the twin brothers Vicario who, consistently, assume opposite physical and ideological postures throughout the tale.

Mirrors also function within the story as devices which enhance the characters' perspectives. For instance, they play a crucial role in the encounter between Angela Vicario and Bayardo San Román many years after the tragedy: "Pura Vicario pidió un vaso de agua en la cantina. Se lo estaba tomando, de espaldas a la hija, cuando ésta vio su propio pensamiento reflejado en los espejos repetidos de la sala. Angela Vicario volvió la cabeza con el último aliento, y lo vio pasar a su lado sin verla, y lo vio salir del hotel." In this instance, the mirror serves to reveal a new perspective, one that will lead Angela Vicario to the man she has loved for so many years. Sadly, the reflection of Bayardo is all she obtains, for the real Bayardo had gone by without really seeing her.

Mirrors have always been crucial to self-conscious texts as novelistic devices enhancing the problematic relationship between reality and its literary representation. In *Crónica,* the narrator is not only our mediator between the facts and his *crónica,* but he also seems to mirror a multiplicity of fictional roles going beyond his explicit task of reporting the facts. If the *cronista* becomes the reader and thus the interpreter of the *pliegos* and of the mysterious piece of paper, his role is also that of an author. He is our link between the events and the townspeople's declarations, and he is the only one who has control of the information we receive as readers. Indeed, the *cronista* plays with narrative truth, tells us that his *crónica* is only his personal impressions, introduces playful intertextual references such as the names of Aureliano Buendía and Gerineldo Márquez as his relatives, and lastly mentions Wenefrida Márquez, his aunt, as one of the last persons to have seen Santiago Nasar alive.

This invitation to equate the *cronista* with García Márquez is further complicated by the similarities between characters since the *instructor* and the *cronista* also share a common penchant for literary descriptions. For instance, the *cronista*'s description of Angela Vicario and that of Alejandrina Cervantes are clear products of a literary rather than a detectivesque mind. Even the witnesses seem to be well versed in the language of literature, for when Angela Vicario is questioned about Santiago Nasar's culpability, she answers with an enigmatic: "Fue mi autor." Thus, while narrating an apparently objective account of a murder, the chronicle is permeated with literary allusions and with descriptions which betray any desire to present a faithful account of the facts.

The *cronista*'s literary penchants become more evident when he revisits the scene of the crime in the last segment of the text. His recreation deserves close attention because it points to the literary theme while demanding that the reader reflect upon the book's artistic process.

At the anecdotal level, the morbid description of Nasar's stabbing, as well as the stylized description of this "double" death, can be interpreted as repetitions or amplifications of the same event mentioned in the text's first pages. In a very general sense the first segment of the text (part 1) is not different from the last (part 5). If at the literal level this description does not advance the action, or shed new light on the story, then its purposes must be interpreted as artistic. The reader knows Nasar is dead; he has known it since the very first lines. Nevertheless, he is presented once again with a naturalistic, gloomy account of the stabbing: "En realidad Santiago Nasar no caía porque ellos mismos lo estaban sosteniendo a cuchilladas contra la puerta. Desesperado, Pablo Vicario le dio un tajo horizontal en el vientre y los intestinos completos afloraron con una explosión. . . . Santiago Nasar permaneció todavía un instante apoyado contra la puerta, hasta que vio sus propias vśceras al sol, limpias y azules, y cayó de rodillas." The information that follows is crucial because it is out of character with the somber, grotesque mood pervading the account of the stabbing of Nasar. After his brutal experience, Santiago Nasar "se incorporó de medio lado, y se echó a andar en un estado de alucinación, sosteniendo con las manos las vísceras colgantes." The character continues to walk and manages to greet Wenefrida Márquez, who becomes the final reporter of his death: "contó que Santiago Nasar caminaba con la prestancia de siempre, midiendo bien los pasos, y que su rostro de sarraceno con los rizos alborotados estaba más bello que nunca. . . . Tropezó en el último escalón, pero se incorporó de inmediato. 'Hasta tuvo el cuidado de sacudir con la mano la tierra que le quedó en las tripas,' me dijo mi tía Wene." Nasar's second death, although tied to the book's events by the important detail of the fatal door, can be considered totally unnecessary from a mimetic or anecdotal perspective. This passage represents García

Márquez's right to artistic selection, and his power over his textual reality. The segment could thus be interpreted as a playful ending, an invitation for the reader to experience the book's essentially artistic nature.

If the reader is perpetually led away from closure as he grapples with the facts presented to him, then we must remember that, even at the anecdotal level, the book is not about *what* happened, but about arriving at an *understanding* of what happened (*why* a town became the silent accomplice to a murder committed by the brothers of a defiled virgin). Taking into consideration the important questions raised here regarding the narrator's sources as well as the text's artistic finale, a parallel emerges between the anecdotal and the artistic readings of this text, for they both become an invitation to *understanding* rather than knowing. Facts, temporality, events become muddled, for they are not important even if we have them. Ironic parody, the main impediment to a comfortable reading of this slippery text, can thus been seen on two levels: as a parody of the institutions and morals at the textual level, and as a parody of the classic detective structure at the artistic level. The text suggests multiple readings and should be viewed as a structure seeking pluralism. Thus it is possible to appreciate not only the meanings indicated by the narrator, but also the meanings implied by the novel's narrative discourse. Just as the text's ironic language forces the reader to read between the lines, so the narrative's duality invites him to understand the acts of reading and writing better by means of an intentional blurring of the three fictional components: the author, the reader, and the text.

MORTON P. LEVITT

From Realism to Magic Realism: The Meticulous Modernist Fictions of García Márquez

It was the extraordinary international success of *One Hundred Years of Solitude* (1967) which made "Magic Realism" a poplar term and, at the same time, provided the impetus to his North American publishers to translate and issue García Márquez's earlier fictions. These were not notably successful when they first appeared in Spanish—"until I was forty years old," he has said, "I never got one cent of author's royalties though I'd had five books published"—and reading them now makes clear to us how much lesser they are than their more famous successor. Yet these early stories and novels remain interesting to us today because they offer insight into the origins of the mature work—the fabled town of Macondo and some of its best known residents appear here in embryonic form—and, more important, because they reveal something of the roots and nature of Magic Realism as a literary mode. Some critics have argued that the Magic Realism of García Márquez is fundamentally different from the narrative art of other writers—a product, that is, not of "organization," as in the case of Vargas Llosa, but rather of "pure invention," as Raymond L. Williams has put it. "In the case of the *Cien años de soledad,*" adds John S. Brushwood,

> it is a very strange reality, but it is entirely accessible to the reader since there are no barriers created by difficult narrative techniques. . . . He seems to write from inspiration, using

From *Critical Perspectives on Gabriel García Márquez,* edited by Bradley A. Shaw and Nora G. Vera-Godwin.

> what he remembers combined with what he thinks of during the process of writing. His novel has a high level of spontaneity; it does not have a carefully worked pattern of meaning.

Reading these early works now, however, proves rather conclusively how large a role technique does play in the later development of so seemingly natural and artless a form. It speaks also of the subtle interplay of indigenous and borrowed, modernist sources in both *One Hundred Years of Solitude* and its still more powerful successor, *The Autumn of the Patriarch.* For Magic Realism—at least as García Márquez practices it in his mature works—is a function not just of vision but of narrative technique.

In Evil Hour (1962), only five years but another lifetime before *One Hundred Years,* begins objectively, early on a hot morning in a town not far from Macondo:

> Father Ángel sat up with a solemn effort. He rubbed his eyelids with the bones of his hands, pushed aside the embroidered mosquito netting, and remained sitting on the bare mattress, pensive for an instant, the time indispensable for him to realize that he was alive and to remember the date and its corresponding day on the calendar of saints. Tuesday, October fourth, he thought; and in a low voice he said: "St. Francis of Assisi."
>
> He got dressed without washing and without praying. He was large, ruddy, with the peaceful figure of a domesticated ox, and he moved like an ox, with thick, sad gestures. After attending to the buttoning of his cassock, with the languid attention and the movements with which a harp is tuned, he took down the bar and opened the door to the courtyard. The spikenards in the rain brought back the words of a song to him.
>
> "'The sea will grow larger with my tears,'" he sighed.

Father Ángel is observed from close by but never very intimately or from within, as it were, over his shoulder. He is seen—as are all the characters of the novel—as essentially a creature of the physical world. Only the last line of his description, "'The sea will grow larger with my tears,'" and another which follows shortly (and which he does not "sigh" aloud but simply "remembers"), "'This bark will bear me to your dreams,'" promise something more than the surface realities of a man—a priest—awakening, dressing, thinking of the date, smelling ("He urinated abundantly, holding his breath so as not to inhale the intense ammonia smell which brought out tears in him"), speaking aloud to himself, remembering the sounds of the previous night. But even these promisingly metaphoric lines exist solely on the surface; they are drawn not from the priest's imagination or vision after all, but only from a neighbor's new song. They are sentimental, inflated, clichéd in this context, not metaphoric at all. Many of the episodes of *In Evil Hour* give similar promise of a reality higher than mere physical presence, but they too in the end fall back to the quotidian: this is not our familiar daily life, of course, but one just as mundane within its own context. García Márquez's narrative technique is not yet capable of capturing that higher, what we have learned to call magical reality: a reality not limited to the representation of the surface of things or even to exploring the depths of the human psyche, a reality which defies the conventions of Realism and which offers somehow, in the process, deeper meaning, deeper insight into both surface and psyche.

In Evil Hour, however, remains a story of small town Colombian life, in a town beset by poverty, casual murders, periodic floods, sexual tensions, political rivalries, movie theatres and lampoons posted mysteriously on guarded doorways—some of the same elements, that is, that will soon ascend to the magical in nearby Macondo. This is not to suggest that García Márquez comes to abjure the realistic in his later work. No subject could be more plebian, more tied to the surfaces of reality than politics, and few novels are more intensely political than *The Autumn of the Patriarch* (1975). Yet it somehow transforms those local banalities—almost magically, it would seem—to the level of universal myth. It demonstrates wonderfully the movement in García Márquez from Realism to Magic Realism.

The difference is primarily a matter of perspective. The movie theatre in this unnamed town of *In Evil Hour* is a business enterprise merely, the single escape aside from politics, sex and gossip from the pervasive poverty and boredom, but it is boycotted by the residents when the church bells toll that the current film has not been approved for family viewing. In Macondo, in *One Hundred Years,* the movies seem so full of life to their viewers that they break up the theatre when they learn that they are mere illusion,

> for the character who had died and was buried in one film and for whose misfortune tears of affliction had been shed would reappear alive and transformed into an Arab in the next one. . . . The mayor . . . explained in a proclamation that the cinema was a machine of illusions that did not merit the emotional

> outbursts of the audience. With that discouraging explanation many felt that they had been victims of some new and shiny gypsy business and they decided not to return to the movies, considering that they had already too many troubles of their own to weep over the acted-out misfortunes of imaginary beings.

The leap between Father Ángel's boycott and this one is enormous; it goes to the very nature of realism in fiction and to the role of perception in ascertaining and evaluating such a reality. It provides, in a sense, the working definition of Magic Realism in the world of García Márquez, a mode as much linked to narrative technique—to the means of envisioning the world—as it is to the world itself. And that technique he adapts from the very different-seeming world of the European Modernists.

The point of view of *In Evil Hour* is only occasionally omniscient in the broadest sense of the term, but it often feels the need to explain events, particularly those uncertain events which appear to demand explanation. In *One Hundred Years,* there are few explanations, and those that there are come not from outside with certainty—from the omniscient author, that is—but from within the community, and they add thereby to the uncertainty of what may be accepted as real and what may remain something else. Fully explained, such phenomena as the mysterious lampoons and motion pictures would become further examples of simple exotica in a strange, distant, isolated town—and nothing more; left as they are, seen solely through the eyes of some resident or even of the town as a whole, largely ambiguous, promising of metaphor, they may reach beyond the normal bounds of the Realistic and toward the universal.

One of the opening images of *One Hundred Years of Solitude* illustrates the point very well. Crossing northward through the jungle as they search for the sea, the founders of Macondo, led by José Arcadio Buendía, pass into a primal world and are "overwhelmed by their most ancient memories in that paradise of dampness and silence, going back to before original sin, . . . like sleepwalkers through a universe of grief." And there, in the midst of the jungle, untold miles from the sea (it later proves to be a four-day march), "surrounded by ferns and palm trees, white and powdery in the silent morning light, was an enormous Spanish galleon." They do not question its provenance, and there is no rational, definitive voice here to explain it. What it evokes for its viewers is some other reality, a universe of timelessness and myth and the origins of the race, "protected from the vices of time and the habits of the birds."

On one level, this striking scene is a simple matter of vision and voice: we see this threatening, arcadian, unexplained image through the unquestioning eyes of men close to nature and their physical senses but removed from alien intellect. The finders are curious, but they seem never to question the strange presence, and there is no one here to rationalize it for them. After five years of not writing—"I had an idea [after *In Evil Hour*] of what I always wanted to do, but there was something missing and I was not sure what it was until one day I discovered the right tone"—García Márquez has at last developed the narrative voice appropriate to his vision.

> It was based on the way my grandmother used to tell her stories. She told things that sounded supernatural and fantastic, but she told them with complete naturalness. . . . I discovered that what I had to do [as a teller of tales] was believe in them myself and write them with the same expression with which my grandmother told them: with a brick face.

On another but connected level, the ship in the jungle serves as metaphor of a way of life that will as suddenly appear and—precisely with the century—as suddenly vanish, inexplicable, perhaps irrational, subject to the forces of nature if not to reason, at once beyond reason and thoroughly human, testimony both to the power of nature over history and to the regenerative power of men within nature. It offers resonances, that is, far beyond those that a rational, external voice could conceivably provide: the "brick face" of the narration is as important to the meaning of the metaphor as is the strange image itself. And we outsiders have little real trouble accepting them as real and not merely as "fantasy."

The tendency to consider such an approach as "fantastic"—whether in praise or dismissal—is as limiting as the insistence that it must also be spontaneous and unplanned. "The trouble is," says García Márquez, that many people believe "that I'm a writer of fantastic fiction, when actually I'm a very realistic person and write what I believe is the true socialist realism." The political implications of his comment aside for the moment, there is a certain demonstrable historicity about the events of *One Hundred Years,* although this is obviously not the reality of a Dickens (yet there are echoes here of the Victorian family chronicle) or a Robbe-Grillet. As Mario Vargas Llosa has pointed out in a knowing essay (there cannot be many such cases of a major novelist writing so extensively about the work of a contemporary), the pattern of rise and fall in the fictional Macondo, of prosperity, strife and collapse, is the historical pattern also of

Aracataca, Colombia, where García Márquez was born and where he was raised by his grandparents, "his most solid literary influences." By that time, however, activity in the town "had almost stopped . . . Aracataca—like so many Latin American towns—lived on remembrances, myth, solitude and nostalgia. García Márquez's entire literary work [this was written long before the appearance of *The Autumn of the Patriarch*] is built with this material which fed him throughout childhood." One factual episode may serve as illustration of how the author's creative imagination works in this context. As Vargas Llosa continues,

> The grandfather of García Márquez used to sing: "Mambrú has gone to war/how painful/how sad." Years later, García Márquez would discover that this song was a Castillianized version of a French song ("Mariborough s'en va-t'en guerre") [sic] and that "Mambrú" was in reality "Marlborough." Since the only wars his grandfather had known were the Colombian civil wars, García Márquez decided that a Duke of Marlborough had been a protagonist in the Colombian violence. Hence the phantasmagoric warrior who in five of García Márquez's books presents himself at the military camp of Colonel Aureliano Buendía; disguised in tiger furs, claws and teeth, he turns out to be the Duke of Marlborough.

Such incidents in themselves are realistic, even mundane. What raises them to the level of metaphor and the fantastic is, paradoxically, the matter-of-fact tone in which they are told. Theirs is a voice coming, as it were, from within: told not simply with a brick face but from a perspective at once intimate and detached, highly subjective in what it sees, coolly objective in the way that it sees: a point of view capable of presenting both the most simple and the most extraordinary events with the same involved but dispassionate, unexplaining voice, so that all such events become equally fantastic and equally natural. It is a studied, conscious, articulate simplicity, not nearly as artless as it seems, and its model is not the novelist's grandmother alone but his literary experience as well.

> One night a friend [at the university] lent me a book of short stories by Franz Kafka. I went back to the pension where I was staying and began to read *The Metamorphosis*. The first line almost knocked me off the bed. . . . I didn't know anyone was allowed to write things like that. If I had known, I would have

> started writing a long time ago. So I immediately started writing short stories.

These early efforts, however, "are totally intellectual short stories because I was writing them on the basis of my literary experience and had not yet found the link between literature and life." His storytelling Colombian grandmother and the European Modernist Kafka are equally essential to the creation of García Márquez's world—a world, like those of its sources, at once so substantial and so fantastic.

The novelist acknowledges certain other debts as well, although somewhat more reservedly. From Joyce, he "did learn something that was to be very useful to me in my future writing—the technique of the interior monologue." (However, "I later found this in Virginia Woolf and I like the way she uses it better than Joyce.") And in Faulkner, so often cited as a primary influence, he found, he says, principally an analogue. "Critics have spoken of the literary influence of Faulkner but I see it as a coincidence: I had simply found material that had to be dealt with in the same way that Faulkner had treated similar material."

With Faulkner, as with Woolf and Joyce and in a certain sense with Kafka as well—with the European Modernists in general—García Márquez shares a vision of a world cut off from traditional values yet informed still by mythic potential. Rooted in the reality of a specific time and place (usually a place representative of its time but just outside its center: imperial Dublin rather than London, Jewish Prague instead of Vienna, the stagnant rural American South and note the industrial North or expansionist West), they nonetheless reach beyond their reality toward some other potentially deeper truth. Objective reality is first established (note the comparatively mundane style and events of the opening chapters of *Ulysses*) and then undercut in this world (note the "Circe" episode), so that "no one knew for certain where the limits of reality lay." We might argue that the assaults on objective reality in *One Hundred Years of Solitude* are principally the products of an unsophisticated, literal imagination (witness the destruction of the movie theatre). But reality in Macondo appears to dwindle of itself. When a siege of insomnia afflicts the town and memory begins to vanish along with sleep, Aureliano Buendía, José Arcadio's son, posts signs everywhere to remind the people of the names of objects and of their functions:

> *This is the cow. She must be milked every morning so that she will produce milk, and the milk must be boiled in order to be mixed with coffee to make coffee and milk.* Thus they went on

> living in a reality that was slipping away, momentarily captured by words, but which would escape irremediably when they forgot the values of the written letters.

The seemingly objective eye which views this reality and the detached, seemingly uninvolved voice which reports it merely add to the breakdown of objective reality, undercutting belief in a continuing, universally, accepted physical world with its implications immediately apparent to all.

Such a dwindling reality is linked inevitably to time, another prime Modernist concern, and diminished further by it: to human and therefore failing memory, to nostalgia for a vanishing past, to the Buendía family's futile efforts to comprehend history and master the future. "Time passes," we are frequently told, but not as it used to. Metaphors emerge that promise momentarily a means of evaluating time's force (a photograph fastening the family "for an eternity"; an "innocent yellow train" bringing in the terrible future and uprooting the past; a perpetual motion time machine), but they too prove ephemeral. Various epochs of time become virtually interchangeable for the Buendías—past and present inescapably confused, the future indefatigably sought after—so that for them a history forms that is "radically opposed to the false one that historians had created and consecrated in the textbooks." Their very family name speaks of their need to incorporate time in their lives, and the mysterious chronicle which several males of the family dedicate their lives to deciphering proves to be the tale of their lives and a prediction that they would spend their lives trying to unravel the parchments rather than living them. The act of deciphering and the act of living become coterminous, so that Aureliano Babilonia, the last male Buendía, after many years of effort, at last "began to decipher the instant that he was living, deciphering it as he lived it, prophesying himself in the act of deciphering the last page of the parchments, as if he were looking into a speaking mirror," recognizing now

> that he would never leave the room, for it was foreseen that the city of mirrors (or mirages) would be wiped out by the wind and exiled from the memory of men at the precise moment when [he] would finish deciphering the parchments, and that everything written on them was unrepeatable since time immemorial and forever more, because races condemned to one hundred years of solitude did not have a second opportunity on earth.

The last of the Buendías understands at least the interpenetration of reality by time.

Thus, it is the familiar Modernist perception and usage of time that we find in *One Hundred Years:* circular in its development (the circle completed with the decipherment), simultaneous rather that merely chronological in its enactment (so that the Buendías of one generation inevitably recall their ancestors and descendants), a function ultimately of the mind and not of the clock (not simply a measure of life's passing, but a force in men's lives). Seen so generally, time in Macondo echoes the time in *Ulysses* or *The Waves* or *Absalom, Absalom!* But there is a significant difference: this time is not a phenomenon of the individual psyche alone, as in Woolf, or of the community at large, as in Joyce, or of the history of a region, as in Faulkner. Time here seems still broader, more inclusive, more Jungian, that is, than Freudian (or Bergsonian or Proustian), connected intimately to nature and to myth. It is in this context that what appears to be the preordained fate of the Buendías may turn out, after all, to be strangely redemptive.

For nature remains beyond all else in this primal place: as the first José Arcadio becomes part of the chestnut tree to which he is tied, as Aureliano Segundo sleeps with a neighbor so that the animals will be fertile, as the inhabitants of the town are turned almost to plants by a preternaturally long rain ("feeling unbroken time pass, relentless time, because it was useless to divide it into months and years, and the days into hours, when one could do nothing but contemplate the rain"), as the Buendía home falls gradually back into the jungle. And we may feel almost as if we have been present at the Creation. For myth, too, remains, sometimes in familiar, almost Biblical manifestations (the great flood, the ash crosses which mark the foreheads of the seventeen sons of Colonel Aureliano Buendía), sometimes in new, strikingly original yet recognizable analogues: in the beginnings of Macondo ("built on the bank of a river of clear water that ran along a bed of polished stones, which were white and enormous, like prehistoric eggs. The world was so recent that many things lacked names, and in order to indicate them it was necessary to point"); in the pursuit of knowledge by the male Buendías, encouraged and aided by the gypsy Melquíades (whose tribe "had been wiped off the face of the earth because they had gone beyond the limits of human knowledge"), who had himself "lost all of his supernatural faculties because of his faithfulness to life"; in the pursuit of death in this Eden.

All of the Buendías' deeds, including their effort to decipher their fate, are part of and lead to the eventual enactment of that fate. And so they may seem mere victims of their environment, no more in control of their lives than are the inexplicable swarms of dead birds at the funeral of old Úrsula Buendía or the striking banana workers whose bodies are thrown casually into the sea. Yet the Buendías may be redeemed because of the vitality with which they invest their lives, however brief, because they remain so close to nature and to natural myth, because—despite the similarities in their names and sometimes in their deeds—they remain individuals with recognizably human traits and concerns, and because we react to them and feel for them as fellow human beings whose lives, foreign as they are, may have some bearing on our own. We must not be misled by the distanced, objective narrative voice into assuming that these people are as natural as the animals around them. Each of the Buendías behaves as if he were responsible for what he makes of his life, and they are all dignified as humans by that responsibility which they so naturally bear. If they are not quite representative of modern, urban, industrial life in the West—as Leopold Bloom or even Gregor Samsa may be thought representative—they nonetheless offer valuable insight into what we have lost and also into our surviving potential.

Equally foreign, equally evocative, as much a product of this historical record as of the author's imagination, is the individual life marked out in *The Autumn of the Patriarch,* a compound of images familiar to dreams, of widely known Latin American political realities and of an exceedingly complex and inventive narrative technique. The title again suggests the pre-eminence of time and myth in this seemingly magical, still primal world, and the theme of human responsibility for human life is again at the center. The Patriarch whose life and name defines these events, who is both petty Caribbean despot and archetypal fertility god, serves as a true representative of his people and times, at once source and symbol and principal subject of their less than magical yet somehow inspired lives.

Despite García Márquez's abjuration of the political novel—"I believe that sooner or later the world will be socialist; I want it to be so and the sooner the better. But I am also convinced that one of the things which may delay the process is bad literature"—despite his implication that political literature is necessarily "bad literature," *The Autumn of the Patriarch* is directly and undeniably political. But it is more; its realm stretches to the farthest reaches of Magic Realism.

In the tradition of Asturias's *El señor presidente* (1946), its protagonist is a composite of such Latin American dictators as Estrada Cabrera (Asturias's principal model), Batista, Duvalier and Trujillo; his crimes, like theirs, are directed against his own people, who both fear and revere him; although they may die at his hands, it is through him that they live. There is, says Asturias, an "intuition" about such figures, "a sort of sense of smell or power of divination that dictators have, and which means that it's not everyone who can be one." He moves, says Joseph Campbell of this manifestation of *The Hero with a Thousand Faces,* "in a dream landscape of curiously fluid, ambiguous forms, where he must survive a succession of trials" in his "perilous journey into the darkness." Like Leopold Bloom before him, he is our truly, ambiguously, paradoxically eponymous hero.

His journey is both mythic and historical, involving factual or potentially factual or at least representative political events in this presumably representative, if fantastic, state. And so the Nicaraguan poet and diplomat Rubén Darío can appear alongside the King and Queen of Babylonia at the Patriarch's court, while Columbus, "admiral of the ocean sea," can become his contemporary. North American battleships and marines have occupied his land in the past, allegedly to civilize it ("they turned our artists into fairies, they brought the Bible and syphillis, they made people believe that life was easy"), and now, like modern conquistadors, they threaten to carry off the sea:

> So they took away the Caribbean in April, Ambassador Ewing's nautical engineers carried it off in numbered pieces to plant it far away from the hurricanes in the blood-red dawns of Arizona [presumably close to London Bridge], they took it away with everything it had inside . . . with the reflection of our cities, our timid drowned people, our demented dragons.

Given the history of the United States' involvement in Central American affairs over the past century or so, this act seems somehow less than fantastic and largely consistent with the mythopoesis which informs the novel.

The principal failing of North American political life in the novel is not that it is rapacious or supportive of dictatorships in Latin America but that it lacks in itself the life-giving potential of myth available even to the latter. The General, for instance, is obviously a despot, a recognizable contemporary figure and not at all Christlike ("long live the stud," shout his subjects), yet he bears with him the burdens and consequences of his Martyr's and Savior's role. Fatherless (because his mother was a whore, and many men might have fathered him), the child of a cult figure who recalls Mary, though hardly a Virgin (the cult, of course, created by her Son), appearing soon after several signs of chaos in the land and marked by his own sign of divinity ("his right testicle . . . the size of a fig"), compared overtly to Christ (by himself) and father himself of a son called Emanuel ("which is the name by which other gods know God"), he knows well the price of bearing mythic power and is the prisoner of that power which he bears. In his great old age, his advisers insulate him from the political realities of his land, with a

> newspaper which they printed only for you general sir, a whole edition of one single copy with the news you liked to read, . . . they had built the palm-lined avenue to the sea so that I wouldn't notice that behind the Roman villas with identical porticoes the miserable slums devastated by one of our many hurricanes were still there, . . . and they were not deceiving him in order to please him as had been done in the later years of his times of glory . . . but to keep him the captive of his own power in the senile backwater of the hammock under the ceiba tree in the courtyard where at the end of his years even the schoolgirl chorus of the petite painted bird perched on a green lemon limb wasn't to be real, what a mess.

In the messiest of times—even those created by him—he serves as measure of continuity for his people, "for the only thing that gave us security on earth was the certainty that he was there, invulnerable to plague and hurricane . . . invulnerable to time." The life and death of nature are associated with his life and death, as in the "ancient predictions . . . that on the day of his death the mud from the swamps would go back upriver to its source, that it would rain blood, that hens would lay pentagonal eggs, and that silence and darkness would cover the universe once more because he was the end of creation." He seems, then, this petty provincial dictator, a true fertility god: a true force of nature ("the corrector of earthquakes, eclipses, leap years and other errors of God"); the very source of life ("he had ordered them to take the rain away from places where it disturbed the harvest and take it to drought-stricken lands"). He has "the virtue of being able to anticipate the designs of nature" and can reverse its designs: after a great hurricane, "we saw the sad eyes, the faded lips, the pensive hand which was making the sign of the cross in a blessing so that the rains would cease and the sun shine, and he gave life back to the drowned hens, and ordered the waters to recede and they receded," "because they said I was the all-worthy one who filled nature with respect and straightened the order of the universe and had taken Divine Providence down a peg, and I gave them what they asked of me." Even an attempt to assassinate him becomes a kind of fertility rite.

But he does not die then, perhaps cannot die then when he is merely old, ancient even, but not yet his appointed five or ten score or more (actually "an indefinite age somewhere between 107 and 232 years"). He is no Annual King, according to Frazer's conception, to die for his people when his fertility is spent and thereby to redeem them and bring them new life. He journeys, like Campbell's related archetype, "through a world of unfamiliar yet strangely intimate forces, some of which severely threaten him . . . , some of which give magical aid." But when he "arrives at the nadir of the mythological round [and] undergoes [his] supreme ordeal," unlike his prototype he will gain no reward: neither union with the Earth Mother nor recognition by the Father nor his own "divinization." At no point does he as hero "reemerge from the kingdom of dread"; he bears no "boon . . . [to] restore the world."

There is nothing Realistic, of course, about the General's great age, and he is no mythic hero after all to induce our admiration and empathy. The genius of the narrative is that we identify with him nonetheless, despite his despotic acts, knowing that he is no redeemer nor even truly a martyr, because he is a convincing suffering human being and in his extreme and perilous condition we may find something of our own. Bearing the burdens and consequences of his position and life, wrapped in mythic expectation if not a true nature god, he seems singled out to learn, as we must all perhaps learn, the ephemerality of our humanity, "when after so many long years of sterile illusions he had begun to glimpse that one doesn't live, God damn it, he lives through, he survives, one learns too late that even the broadest and most useful of lives only reach the point of learning how to live." Only in his great old exalted but abandoned age, within the realm of the people whom he serves as a god, terrifying and sustaining, does he learn "of his incapacity for love" and of its significance.

> He had known since his beginnings that they deceived him in order to please him, . . . he had arrived without surprise at the ignominious fiction of commanding without power, of being exalted without glory . . . when he became convinced in the trail of yellow leaves of his autumn that he had never been master of all his power, that he was condemned not to know life except in reverse, condemned to decipher the seams and straighten the threads of the woof and the warp of the tapestry of illusions of reality without suspecting even too late that the only livable life was one of show, the one we saw from this side

> which wasn't his general sir, this poor people's side with the trail of yellow leaves of our uncountable years of misfortune and our ungraspable instants of happiness, where love was contaminated by the seeds of death but was all love general sir, . . . this life which we loved with an insatiable passion that you never dared even to imagine out of fear of knowing what we knew only too well that it was arduous and ephemeral but there wasn't any other, general.

In his failed but persistent humanity, the General serves us to affirm our own.

Central to this discovery is the interplay between the hero-king-General and his subjects, between the reader and his narrator(s), among the shifting narrative voices, a function of the most complex and evocative point of view in García Márquez's—and perhaps in post-Joycean—fiction. The narration begins with "we," an eyewitness to the General's death yet not quite an eyewitness ("because none of us had ever seen him"), revealed finally as a member of the General Staff and named (but with different names—and perhaps not a general). More significantly, the "me" as witness turns somehow to "me" as actor, the General himself, speaking and thinking of himself as both protagonist and outsider, with passionate self-involvement and a strange objectvity (as "I," "he" and "you"), across a great span of time, in singular and plural forms, as male and female alike: his voice seems that of both the General and his people, mutually involved, an internalized chorus at once national and private. This constantly shifting, near-universal point of view is a reflection, in part, of the General's status as a myth-connected figure of great age and failing memory, free of conventional bonds, acting desperately and unsuccessfully to order his reality as he has always seemed to order it, unsure to the end of his own identity ("who the hell am I," he shouts, "because I feel as if the reflection in the mirror is reversed"); in part also, these shifts are a sign of the political state of affairs.

For how can the hero define himself fully when his principal role is not as redeemer of his people but as a failed presence, not as man but as symbol?, and how can the citizen-reader, after abiding for so long under so great a shadow, understand who in truth he is? "Commander of time," his people call him, controller of history, able to alter time at his will, his own lifespan ordered "not . . . by human time but by the cycles of the comet," an eternal seeming figure in a land of many presidents for one day; in the end he loses control of his memory (taking "spoonfuls of candlewax to plug up the leaks in my memory"), his control over reality, his understanding of what his life has meant or what he has lost. And so he suffers.

But there are uncertainties and problems for us, too: if memory has failed, if history is suspect and mythmaking a fiction, if surface reality has been consciously and consistently amended to suit transient political needs, if mythos turns to senility and the senile General can himself lose control over the world he has made, "where the hell was the truth in that bag of contradictory truths that seem less true than if they were lies"? If there is no objective reality that we can all accept as lasting and real, if we have no confidence that some other reality can replace what we have been shown is transient above all, what sort of certainty remains?; what part of our humanity survives? We are left—for all our distance and uncertainty and scorn—with the General's narrated experience: with his lifelong sense that he has been the victim of his own power, with his recognition late in his life that he cannot change reality and the nature of life despite his great power, despite his great age, with his discovery and ours that what has seemed most permanent in the face of a changing reality is, in fact, as ephemeral as all that passes for real. His identity is uncertain, his career despicable, yet we are moved by the old man's predicament. We appreciate the truth of the burden he has borne all these years, however false it may be. We perceive that he is at times capable of feeling, enough at least to sense what he has lost. We understand the banal lesson of his life for our own perhaps autumnal age: that we all bear burdens that we cannot understand; that we all experience passions that we cannot control; that none of us can master this life whose reality we cannot comprehend or even name; but that we must continue to feel if we are to be human; and that we remain responsible for our lives.

It is a lesson derived not only from the experience of García Márquez's Latin America but from the Modernist literary example as well: from Modernist narrative techniques, from Modernist renderings of time and myth and a dwindling reality, from the Modernist vision of man adrift in the universe, redeemed not by some force outside himself but by his acceptance of his own humanity and of the responsibility which that entails.

This is the persistent lesson of all of García Márquez's art, from his early Realistic fictions, through the magical leap of *One Hundred Years of Solitude*, where for the first time he achieves a reality higher than simple physical presence, to the peak of *The Autumn of the Patriarch,* in which local political realities, the most pedestrian of sources, are transformed into universal truths. That the lesson is more powerful in the later works, that their characters and ideas are so much more compelling, is the result not of vision alone but of their meticulously crafted narrative technique. It is through this union of vision and technique, of indigenous and borrowed sources, that we are able to progress, along with the author, from Realism to Magic Realism.

And so we may feel with the General, as we feel with Leopold Bloom, caught up in the flow of his narrative and the rhythm of his prose, nurtured by his creator's demanding technique, despite politics, beyond history, outside the redeeming forces of myth. Our ability to feel his pain attests to his humanity and perhaps also to our own.

MICHAEL PALENCIA-ROTH

Prisms of Consciousness: The "New Worlds" of Columbus and García Márquez

Modern hermeneutic theory of interpretation is founded on the commonsense notion that what we see depends on what we are prepared to see and that what we understand depends on what we already understand. What one already understands may be called, in Heidegger's terminology, the forestructure of the understanding: it determines the structure of our understanding before we begin to understand. Or, to follow Gadamer (himself a pupil of Heidegger), whatever one is at a particular time—and that includes one's education and upbringing, one's culture and intelligence, one's prejudices, presuppositions, motives and ambitions—decides the "horizon" from which one views and interprets the world.

The horizons of the two figures juxtaposed in this essay, Christopher Columbus and Gabriel García Márquez, are vastly different. The one is a navigator and supposedly concerned with "truth," the other a novelist and therefore concerned with "fiction"; the one a man of the fifteenth century, the other of the twentieth. The first is a European who discovered the part of the world which the second calls home. These two so disparate figures are, however, comparable in interesting ways. It is not so much that both are undeniably central in the history of Latin American literature and culture, as important to an understanding and appreciation of its tradition as, say, Sophocles, Dante and Shakespeare are to theirs. It is, rather, that both Columbus and García Márquez shed light, from opposite directions, on the history of the colonization of Latin America. In addition, as shall

From *Critical Perspectives on Gabriel García Márquez,* edited by Bradley A. Shaw and Nora G. Vera-Godwin.

be made clear subsequently, both are fascinated by the same moment in that history: the first intercivilizational encounter in the New World.

The subject of colonialism—and particularly the study of the *processes* by which one culture colonizes another—is of abiding interest to those scholars who, like myself, are "comparatists," whether it be in Comparative Literature, in comparative civilizational analysis, or in any of the other "comparative" disciplines. Colonialism and its processes are not trivial topics; indeed as Herbert Lüthy writes, "the history of colonization is the history of humanity itself." Furthermore, although we need not share the opinion of the sixteenth-century historian Francisco López de Gómara that "the most important event in the world, after its creation and excepting the incarnation and death of Him who created it, is the discovery of the Indies, that is, the so-called New World," we cannot doubt the importance of Columbus's venture for European and, of course, "American" history. Therefore, whenever we are offered the opportunity to gain insight into the dynamics of his discovery and to reflect on a process (colonization) which is fundamental to historical change, we should not pass it up. Columbus and García Márquez together, as we shall see, provide just such an opportunity.

Colonization—the term which Lüthy prefers over "colonialism" because it possesses fewer negative connotations—has two concurrent histories: outer and inner, or the conventionally historical and the psychological, or, in the words of the twentieth-century Mexican humanist Alfonso Reyes, "lo institucional (the institutional)" and "lo humano (the human, personal side)." All too often, the inner, psychological, "human" history of colonization is ignored in the historian's concern to document facts and figures, or to describe institutions. Yet that inner history, my subject here, is as important as the outer.

In my view, the inner, psychological history of colonization in Latin American letters passes through three major stages, the last of which has not yet been completed. (A similar history may be explored concerning American letters.) The first stage, of course, consists of the initial confrontation between two cultures, a confrontation which I will analyze by focusing on Columbus. Here the attempt is made to assimilate the new culture or the new reality within the framework of the colonizer (the Indies are "Europeanized"). Ironically, the attempt sometimes results in the colonization of the colonizer, despite the cultural arrogance which seems invariably to be his principal psychological trait at this point. During the second stage the colonial mentality is internalized; this occurs in succeeding generations, once the colony is well established and its people have known no other reality but the colonial one. The outstanding example of this second stage in Latin American letters is El Inca Garcilaso de la Vega, son of an Inca princess and a Spanish conquistador. The principal psychological characteristic during this stage seems to be ambivalence and duality. Poised between two worlds and insecure in a dual cultural identity, El Inca and others like him spend their lives either attempting to mediate between their cultures or alternately identifying with one culture and then with another. Unfortunately, I have neither the time nor the space to deal with this transitional stage. The third and final stage in the inner history of colonization is rebellion and the attempt at emancipation, both of which involve rejection of the colonial mentality. The psychological emancipation from the colonial mother culture (in this case, Europe and Spain) tends to occur long after the political emancipation. Thus even Simón Bolívar, political liberator that he was, advocated the adaptation of British political systems to Latin American circumstances in his famous "Address at Angostura" and elsewhere. Throughout the nineteenth century, from Andrés Bello to Domingo Faustino Sarmiento, from Mexico to Argentina, the struggle for emancipation from psychological colonialism obsessed Latin American men of letters. Where the struggle continues in the twentieth century, American imperialism sometimes replaces European colonialism as the culture against which to react. In any case, what is most important in the fight against psychological colonialism is the reversal of the colonial perspective. In other words, the same reality must be reinterpreted—seen, heard—through the "native" prism of consciousness; in this way the native mentally ejects the colonizer and wins back his land. Later in this essay I will analyze an instance of the reversal in a novel by García Márquez, *The Autumn of the Patriarch*, published in Spanish in 1975 and translated into English in 1976.

COLUMBUS

The prism of Columbus's consciousness—his horizon, to use Gadamer's term—included his deeply religious nature; his being an Italian on a mission for Spain; his obsession with finding an ocean passage to the Orient; his "training" and skill as a navigator and cartographer; his medievalism; his unsystematic erudition in current myths and in religious literature (the Bible and some of the Church Fathers), in travel literature (Marco Polo, among others), in cosmography both classical (for instance, the comments of Aristotle and Ptolemy) and medieval (especially the *Imago Mundi* by Pierre d'Ailly and the *Historia Rerum Ubique Gestarum* by Aeneas Piccolomini). He applied directly to himself Seneca's prophecy in *Medea* that one day the ocean would be the key to the discoveries of new worlds. Driven as well by a desire for fame and fortune, he was haunted by the fear of failure. It is therefore understandable that he would do everything in his power to succeed, even if it required, as shall be seen, exaggerating the reports of certain aspects of his enterprise. Columbus's hunger for wealth and fame is immediately evident to anyone who peruses the two agreements—or capitulations—that Columbus obtained from Ferdinand and Isabella, on April 17 and on April 30, some months before his departure from the port of Palos. Not only is Columbus to be named "Admiral of the Ocean Sea," a title of nobility and an office to be passed, in perpetuity, to his heirs and successors, but he is also to be declared "Viceroy and Governor General" of all the "islands and mainlands" he might "discover or acquire." In addition, one tenth of all the profits of his venture will belong to him. However skeptical we might be concerning the "seriousness" of these promises (after all, the king and queen of Spain, for all they knew, were granting dominion over what could very well turn out to be nothing at all, and it is history which has given these capitulations their overwhelming significance), they reveal not only how determined Columbus was to secure certain social, political and economic rights and privileges, should his dream be made real, but also how important he himself considered his venture to be. Ennoblement, especially, is not something to be taken lightly, and for a commoner to make it the stated reward for a successful mission (and to get the king and queen to agree to it) is indicative of unusual pride, enormous self-confidence, and enviable powers of persuasion. Clearly, then, much was at stake when Columbus left Spain in late summer in 1492.

In the diary of Columbus's first voyage, the process of colonization unfolds in the following sequence. First, we notice a bare chronology: the listing of facts, of distances travelled, of atmospheric conditions, etc. Then, as the new reality begins to manifest itself, we notice an increase in the detail and in the volume of Columbus's observations. These document his desire to classify the new reality and to bring it within his familiar horizon through comparison and contrast. As the newness wears off, his observations depend less on rhetorical figures of similitude (e.g. "trees as green and as leafy as those of Castile in the month of April") and dissimilitude (e.g., "many trees very unlike ours"). His observations also become less obviously Europocentric. Upon further assimilation of this new world, even some of the vocabulary changes. And when Columbus expresses himself in terms belonging only to the New World we may say that the colonizer has begun to be colonized. At those moments his horizon may be said to have been extended or changed.

Let us now flesh out this process. In Columbus's diary, minimal record keeping mostly occupied him through the months of August and September. By mid-September, however, two important characteristics of his mind have become evident. The first is a willingness to tell less than the whole truth, even to create a "fiction," in order to ensure that his chances of success not be jeopardized. On September 9, Columbus decided to keep two accounts of the distance travelled, one for himself (a "true" account) and the other for his crew (a "false" account designed, Columbus said, to keep them from becoming too restless). If Columbus was willing to stretch the truth for his crew, is it not reasonable to infer that he would also be willing to do so in his report to the king and queen of Spain? After all, what they concluded about his venture was vitally important to his future. The other important psychological characteristic of these early journal entries—and a prefiguration of things to come—is Columbus's "comparative" frame of mind. On September 16, for instance, he compared the weather to "April in Andalusia." Another comparison is fanciful. "The savor of the mornings was a great delight," he wrote, and "the only thing wanting was to hear nightingales." Nightingales, of course, neither are ocean birds nor are they indigenous to the Caribbean. Some time later in his voyage Columbus reported actually having heard nightingales, a "report" which a number of critics have commented on. Not only, then, did Columbus's eye transform American sights into European ones, but his ear also transformed American sounds.

On October 12, 1492, and during the following days and weeks, Columbus described—and saw—not only what he was prepared to see and to understand, but also what he wanted *others* to comprehend. In part, he was struggling to appropriate the new reality by making it familiar to himself and to others. In part, also, he wanted to cast the best possible light on the results of his journey. The first step in this appropriation was, of course, the physical one. Upon landing on what has come to be known as Watlings Island, Columbus raised the royal standard and took possession of the island in the name of the king and queen of Spain. Then he made the "required declaration" to people who hadn't the faintest idea what he was saying and Guanahani, as the natives called it, legally became a colony of Spain. The next step seems to have been that of the island's "spiritual" colonization, for Columbus's first words in the diary about the natives themselves were religious: "They were," he wrote, "a people who could better be freed and converted to our Holy Faith by love than by force." A European cultural arrogance, however, is evident in what Columbus wrote next: he "gave to some of them red caps and to others glass beads, which they hung on their necks, and *many other things of slight value*, in which they took much pleasure." Columbus thus criticized by implication the native ignorance in matters important to Europeans.

Columbus and his successors were generally ambivalent about the natives' ignorance, an ambivalence which suggests the complexity of the European mentality concerning the New World. On the one hand, Europeans considered themselves superior to the natives precisely because the natives were ignorant of European ways. Cultural arrogance is a constant characteristic not only of Columbus's journals but also of the works of almost all the other conquistadors and colonists. It was arrogant of Columbus to assume, for example, that the Indians would make good servants (Oct. 12); to think that they would benefit from being converted to Christianity (Oct. 12); to consider that they could be easily conquered because they were so "inept" in the art of war (Oct. 14). On the other hand, ignorance and nakedness (for they *were* "quite as naked as their mothers bore them"—Oct. 12) had long been identified in the European imagination with the innocence of man before the fall. Therefore, the natives were somehow "purer," less "tainted," than the Europeans, and a number of Old World myths concerning purity, innocence, and youth eventually found a home in the New World.

Columbus's readiness to entertain the New World in terms of Old World traditions and myths—especially the more positive and optimistic ones—is apparent in his account of his experiences during the first two or three days on Guanahani, in which he borrowed from the "edenic" and golden age tradition, from the pastoral tradition, and from the legends of the fabled Orient. In his first descriptions, the men were all young, tall, and clean-limbed; no one was older than thirty. The men bore no arms and—out of ignorance—cut themselves on the Spaniards' swords. This last act meant that symbolically, in the eyes of some critics, the natives had not degenerated from the Age of Gold. In a number of mythological accounts of the history of the world (e.g., Hesiod, Ovid) iron is the last and lowest of the ages of man, the first three being gold, silver, and bronze. The landscape of these first islands is also seen in terms of the Old World, for it is richly pastoral, bringing to mind that Virgilian inspired tradition in European literatures which Cervantes would satirize extensively in *Don Quixote*. The weather was mild; the birds were always singing and the trees were always so lush that it was pure pleasure to gaze on them. The season, too, was eternally Spring. At the end of the entry for October 13, the oriental frame of reference appears, for there Columbus reported on his intention to "lose no time" in finding the island of Cipango (another name for Japan). Even before he sailed, he was obsessed by Cipango and the Great Khan. Indeed much of that first voyage was spent in search of the Great Khan, to whom Columbus carried letters of introduction from the king and queen of Spain. Until the day he died he thought that his voyages had taken him to the westernmost reaches of the Khan's kingdom.

These multiple frames of reference are fascinating, complex, and worthy of detailed and prolonged study. I do not have the space to indulge in that study here, however, and wish to conclude these brief remarks on Columbus by focusing on another aspect of colonization: the linguistic one. I will analyze but one example: the term for "dugout." The first time that Columbus came across a dugout he described it in sufficient detail to make it clearly imaginable to Europeans who had never seen such a thing:

> Ellos vinieron a la nao con *almadías*, que son hechas del pie de un árbol, como un barco luengo, y todo de un pedazo, y labrado muy a maravilla según la tierra, y grandes en que en algunas venían 40 ó 50 hombres, y otras más pequeñas, fasta haber dellas en que venía un solo hombre. Remaban con una pala como de fornero, y anda á maravilla; y si se les trastorna luego se echan todos á nadar, y la enderezan y vacían con calabazas que traen ellos.
>
> (They came to the ship in *dugouts* which are fashioned like a long boat from the trunk of a tree, and all in one piece, and wonderfully made [considering the country], and so big that in some came 40 or 50 men, and others smaller, down to some in which but a single man came. They row with a thing like a baker's peel and go wonderfully; and if they capsize they all begin to swim and right it and bail it out with calabashes that they carry.)

Almadía, the word for *dugout* here, belongs to two nations of the Old World, both of them colonizers: the Portuguese and the Arabs. The Portuguese used the term to describe dugouts from West Africa and, after 1498, from India. The Arabs, who independently of the Portuguese had also used the term to describe African dugouts, were responsible for bringing it into Spain during the Middle Ages. By Columbus's day it had become part of the Spanish language. From its first uses, then, *almadía* seems to have been a word associated with more recent colonial ventures. Perhaps by using it rather than, say, *barca* or *nave* (both of which have Latin roots), Columbus somehow sensed that its colonial associations, its double refraction through Portuguese and Arabic, made it the most appropriate term. Yet it did not remain the most appropriate term for long.

The next time Columbus used *almadía* at the end of the same diary entry, he used it without comment: "Ahora como fue noche todos se fueron a tierra con sus *almadías* (Now, as it was night, all went ashore in their *dugouts*)." He continued to write *almadía* without comment for the next few days. Then, on October 26, he penned the native word for *almadía* for the first time:

> Dijeron los indios que llevaba que había dellas á Cuba andadura de día y medio con sus *almadías* que son navetas de un madero adonde no llevan vela. Estas con las *canoas*.
>
> (The Indians on board said that to Cuba it was a journey of a day and a half in their *dugouts*, which are little boats of a single tree, without sail. Such are the *canoes*.)

The next time the Arauaco or Arawak word *canoa* appears, it is accompanied by *almadía*. Columbus noted, on October 28, that as he was setting ashore with his ships, "dos *almadías* ó *canoas* (two *dugouts* or *canoes*)" set out to meet him. From this point on, Columbus usually wrote, without comment or description, the native word *canoa* rather than the European *almadía*.

A similar process occurs with other words in the Columbus diary. For instance, for a while he referred to the native regional chieftains as *reyes* (kings). Finally, on December 17 and 18, 1492, he began to use the Arawak word *cacique*. In general, the fifteenth and sixteenth century colonization of the New World involved the intellectual, linguistic "Europeanization" of American reality. For example, Mexico was first known as *Nueva España* (New Spain); Haiti-Santo Domingo was *Isla Española* (Spanish Island). And Europeans quite frequently gave *their* names to American wildlife: *leones* (lions), *tigres* (tigers), *osos* (bears), *lobos* (wolves), *truchas* (trout), *águilas* (eagles). The list could be extended almost endlessly.

Linguistically, the process of colonization involves not only the absorption of the new reality within the horizon of the colonizer. It involves also, and perhaps paradoxically, the merging of the colonizer's horizon with that of the colonized, for the new reality is being described with—and on—its own terms. Gadamer would label this process that of *Horizontverschmelzung*, horizon-fusion. Symbolically, then, the linguistic colonization of the colonizer is shown in the transformation of an *almadía* into a *canoa*, or a *rey* into a *cacique*. One should remember, however, that such evidence of reverse colonization or horizon-fusion does not actually signal a profound change in Columbus's case. His values and perspective remained resolutely European. Although the inner history of the first stage of the colonial experience seldom develops in the orderly sequence I have described, Columbus's example prefigures other similar sequences in the writings of later conquistadors and colonists. His is a universal experience in the history of colonization.

GARCÍA MÁRQUEZ

In writing *The Autumn of the Patriarch*, García Márquez uses the figure of Columbus to deliver a blistering attack on the process of colonization and to demythify both the myth that Columbus had become and that of the New World which he feels Columbus had been instrumental in creating. Columbus's account is generally considered to be *history;* García Márquez thinks of it as *fiction*, in both the positive and negative sense of the word. García Márquez's prism of consciousness therefore includes not only a profound anticolonialism and even a feeling of resentment against Columbus himself, but also the following characteristics: he is a man of the Caribbean and of mixed blood; he is a novelist who is at ease both in creating and in debunking myths; and he is deeply proud of the Latin American "New World."

García Márquez's knowledge of Columbus, both of the man and of the work, is extensive and largely accurate. For him, Columbus, being the first European to have landed on American shores, is both a legend to all Latin Americans and the creator of the first work of Latin American letters. Consider the following characterization by García Márquez in an interview:

> The first masterwork of the literature of magical realism is the Diary of Columbus. From the first it was so contaminated by the magic of the Caribbean that even the history of the book itself makes an unlikely story. Its most moving moments, that is, the moments of the discovery itself, were written twice, and we do not possess either version directly. A few nights before he returned to Spain on the first voyage, a tremendous storm lashed his ship near the Azores. He thought that none of his

> crew would survive the gale and that the glory of his discovery would belong to Martín Alonso Pinzón, whose ship was sailing ahead. In order to make sure that the glory would belong to himself alone, Columbus hastily wrote down a history of his discoveries, placed the sheaf of papers in a water-proof barrel and commended it to the waters. He was so mistrustful that he did not confide in a single one of his sailors but instead made them believe that the barrel contained a prayer to the Virgin Mary to make the storm abate. The one surprising thing is that the storm did abate, and the other is that the barrel was never found, which means that if Columbus's ship had gone down, his account would never have seen the light of day. The second version, written down at greater leisure, has also been lost. What we know as *The Diary of Columbus* is, in reality, its reconstruction by Father Las Casas, who had read the original manuscript.

Allusions to Columbus the man, whom García Márquez's hero, the patriarch, seems to have known personally, appear throughout *The Autumn of the Patriarch*. At one point we read that Columbus has given the patriarch a golden spur to be worn on the left heel as a sign of the highest authority. At three different points in the novel we read details concerning Columbus's three tombs and his posthumous existence. Once he appears dressed in a Franciscan habit, a detail so bizarre to most readers that it sounds as though García Márquez invented it. Yet after his second voyage, and then again after his fourth, Columbus actually dressed in this way.

The most important allusion, however, is not to Columbus the man but rather to his famous—or infamous—diary. That allusion, a long passage of intertextuality found at the end of the first chapter of *The Autumn of the Patriarch,* is directly based on Columbus's diary entries of October 12, 13, and 14, the ones which I focused on earlier. The scene represents the patriarch's experience in reliving "that historic October Friday" when Columbus discovered America. Upon leaving his room that morning, the patriarch is startled to see almost everyone wearing red caps. Taken aback, he decides to investigate what had happened in the world while he had slept. Seeing some newcomers, he notes their strange speech, observes their puzzling behavior and their attitude toward clothing, and remarks on their ignorance concerning the significance of native gestures. By simply reversing the perspective from which the events of that historic day are seen, García Márquez ridicules Columbus's arrogance and colonial mentality.

Let us consider this reversal of perspective in more detail. The newcomers talk "funny," making the "word for sea feminine and not masculine, [calling] macaws poll parrots, canoes rafts, harpoons javelins" ("no decían el mar sino la mar y llamaban papagayos a las guacamayas, almadías a los cayucos y azagayas a los arpones"). "Cayuco," of course, is a Caribbean synonym for "canoa." Ironically, the non-existent Spanish language of the New World in the fifteenth century is considered culturally superior—and more correct—than that of the Old World! A bit later in the day, the patriarch again "compares" the two languages:

> [Los españoles] gritaban que no entendiámos en lengua de cristianos cuando eran ellos los que no entendían lo que gritábamos, y después vinieron hacia nosotros con sus cayucos que ellos llaman almadías, como dicho tenemos.
>
> ([The Spaniards] shouted that we didn't understand them in Christian tongue when they were the ones who couldn't understand what we were shouting, and then they came toward us in their canoes which they call dugouts, in our way of speaking.)

García Márquez here uses some of Columbus's characteristic phrases (e.g., "como dicho tenemos"); and he even focuses on the same contrast in terminology which so fascinated Columbus: the European *almadía* versus the native *cayuco* or *canoa*. The only thing that has been changed is the perspective. But that, as a hermeneutic theorist might say, is everything: when the horizon changes, so too does the reality.

The newcomers' behavior and reactions also strike the natives as bizarre. For instance, when the natives swim out to receive the Spaniards, which for García Márquez is a gesture of courtesy in the New World, the Spaniards, instead of joining the natives in the water, get excited and climb onto the yardarms like monkeys and shout to each other like silly parrots: "look how well formed, of beauteous body and fine face, and thick-haired and almost like horsehair silk." Gregory Rabassa's archaic touches in his translation are quite appropriate here, for such descriptions in the novel are taken almost word for word from Columbus's diary.

Clothes, or their absence, fascinate both the natives and the newcomers. The natives cannot "understand why the hell [the Spaniards are] making so much fun of us general sir since we [are] just as normal as the day our mothers bore us and on the other hand they [are] decked out like the jack of clubs in all that heat." One item of clothing, a silk doublet, receives great attention. In the diary, Columbus had promised a silk doublet to whomever should see land first. In the novel, however, the silk doublet is put to a rather different use: the natives marvel at the stupidity of the Europeans, who want "to trade a silk doublet for one of us to show off in Europeland, just imagine general, what idiocy." The irony is twofold: not only is it foolish to trade a human being for a piece of clothing, but it is doubly foolish to trade him for an item that is totally useless. What is the point of clothing in a culture where everyone is naked?

There is a deeper irony as well in the two passages cited in the paragraph above. In them the natives refer to the patriarch as "mi general" or "general sir." In the pre-columbian New World, however, there were no "generals." In fact, there were no "patriarchs," either, for the term properly belongs to the world of the Old Testament and its values, hence to the Judeo-Christian West. The use of these two designations for García Márquez's hero illustrates just how difficult the problem of colonial emancipation is when even the language of the colonizers has become fully the language of the colonized. Fully aware that he must write in a colonial language, indeed that, being monolingual, he has no choice, García Márquez tries in this scene to distance himself linguistically from his mother tongue through irony, parody, and humor. These modes aid him in reversing the colonial perspective.

In his novel, García Márquez also "documents" an instance of the cross-cultural misunderstanding of gestures on the part of the visiting Spaniards. He fabricates a different story than Columbus did of the natives' delight at being given little glass beads. The natives, simply to be polite and knowing the beads to be of little value, hang them around their necks in order to please their visitors. The latter, after all, must have valued these gifts highly, for they had transported them such a long distance. Columbus, as we have seen, interpreted the native gesture of friendship and courtesy as a sign of ignorance. For García Márquez, it could just as easily be said that it is the Spaniards rather than the natives who are the ignorant ones.

Such is the course of the patriarch's investigation of these strange intrusions in his world. At the end of the chapter he looks out of one of his palace (!) windows and sees, at anchor in the bay, the three caravels. It is the dawn of the European day in the New World.

García Márquez's humor and irony are both bitter and profound in these pages. It is as though he wished to rid Columbus's enterprise of *all* its heroic, legendary content; to destroy the historical validity of his observations; and to show how empty all rhetoric of colonial superiority, all colonialism, truly is. There is always, as García Márquez writes in *The Autumn of the Patriarch*, "another truth behind the truth." One man's truth is another man's lie, and the same may be said for the history of nations. One nation's colonialism is another's humiliation; one nation's emancipation, another's defeat.

García Márquez is suggesting, I think, that we are wrong if we believe Columbus's version to be true and accurate; that we are wrong, in sum, if we naively consider the diary to be "history." For García Márquez, historical and cultural truths are at best individual, relative and psychological, not universal, objective and scientific. To put it another way, the European historical tradition is but one of several, and what we are taught in school or what we have learned from most European historiographers is, to put it mildly, one-sided. Being one-sided, it is far from the whole truth. Granted: the attainment of the whole truth is of course a hermeneutical impossibility. Nevertheless, in any process like colonization, which by definition involves the interaction of at least two different "realities," García Márquez reminds us that there are at least two sides to its history and to its interpretation.

Up to the present the "schools" of comparison in both history and literature in the West have tended to be Europocentric. This unquestioned Europocentrism sometimes startles those who come to the Europeanized West from the so-called Third World, and not only from Latin America. In Salman Rushdie's *Midnight's Children*, for instance, a novel which treats the colonization and decolonization of India, one of the main characters travels to Europe to complete his medical training and suddenly learns that "India—like radium—had been 'discovered' by Europeans." Upon learning further of the Europeans' "belief that he was somehow [their] invention," this character is "knocked forever into that middle place" between both worlds. Although the European colonization of India differs substantially from that of Latin America, García Márquez and other like-minded Latin American novelists struggle against the same kind of Europocentrism which haunts Rushdie and his characters. All, novelists and characters alike, are but trying to find their way between the colonizing and the colonized worlds. Part of the way for García Márquez consists in reversing the European colonial perspective.

One of the objects of hermeneutical criticism is to make explicit those cultural and personal perspectives or assumptions which tend to remain implicit and unexamined. This I have tried to do in the case of Columbus and García Márquez, using colonization and decolonization as my focus. It is clear, I think, that in describing his experiences Columbus translated them not only into his own cultural idiom but also into the myths that fueled his desires, even as his own horizon was being changed in the process. The prism of his colonial consciousness and of his personal ambition shaped his vision and his language decisively. It should also be equally clear that for García Márquez, as driven in his way as Columbus was in his, the prism must lead to a completely different vision and language, for the process of colonization has almost run its course. García Márquez's prism of consciousness reflects not only a deep desire for independence but also a commitment to the emancipation from psychological colonialism in any form. In passionately advocating a decolonized New World, he demythifies the myths of the old colonial power. In doing so, however, he creates new myths which, one day, will in turn be reinterpreted from the newer horizons of newer worlds.

CARLOS J. ALONSO

Writing and Ritual in Chronicle of a Death Foretold

Gloomy Orion and the Dog
Are veiled; and hushed the shrunken seas.
—T. S. ELIOT, "Sweeney among the Nightingales"

If one were to take to the letter *Chronicle of a Death Foretold*'s avowed generic filiation as reportage, one would have to acknowledge immediately that the narrator's performance in its entirety constitutes nothing short of a scandal. For, as is made evident throughout the novel, the investigator was a member of the community in which the events took place, a circumstance that puts in check the objectivity that his rhetorical posturing demands. Even if the narrator takes pains to establish early on that he was asleep when tragedy struck, his "participation" is implicitly recognized in the text when he himself refers to Santiago Nasar's death as a crime "for which we all could have been to blame." As if to underscore this fact, the novel is quite careful in establishing the complex web of relationships that tied the narrator to all the protagonists of the tragic plot. In addition, the narrator time and again expresses his agreement with a given witness's opinion in a formula that arises from shared communal experience: "'One night he asked me which house I liked the most,' Angela Vicario told me. 'And I answered, without knowing what he intended, that the prettiest house in town was the farmhouse belonging to the widower Xius.' *I would have said the same*" (my emphasis). Nevertheless, cloaked by the dispas-

From *Gabriel García Márquez: New Readings,* edited by Bernard McGuirk and Richard Cardwell. © 1987 by Cambridge University Press.

sionate and measured tone that the inquest seemingly imposes on him, the narrator affords us few details about his person or motivations. Thus, the investigative framework of the novel may serve paradoxically to nurture the secret at the core of the events, since of all the ambivalent, mysterious and contradictory figures in *Chronicle of a Death Foretold*, none is more perplexing than the narrator of the story himself.

Moreover, when examined further from this generic perspective, *Chronicle of a Death Foretold* would appear to be an exercise in futility. After all the repeated interviews, corroborations and painstaking archival research, the narrator cannot produce any new concrete facts on the circumstances that determined the death of Santiago Nasar. Indeed, when considered in the light of the original official investigation, there seems no justification for the narrator's report on his new inquest since it repeats the failure of the preceding one. If he manages not to fall prey to the despondence and frustration that were repeatedly expressed by the civil magistrate in his report, the result is yet the same: the intervening years have not disentangled the "ciphered knot" around which the narrator weaves the weft of his own interpretive enterprise. This failure must be recognized even if we take the object of the investigation to be not the discovery of the truth but rather the determination of how such a publicized death could have taken place irrespective of the town's purported desire to prevent it. For what we are left with in the end is a series of coincidences, moments of personal weakness and false assumptions whose heterogeneity precludes the possibility of an overarching explanation or understanding of the crime. The only significant fact not available to the hapless first magistrate, the final reconciliation between Bayardo San Román and Angela Vicario some twenty years after the murder, does not illuminate unambiguously the tragic events and has exasperated more than one critic for its apparent lack of consequence. Nevertheless, the investigative framework of the novel forever seems to imply the imminent uncovering of some hitherto unknown datum that will bestow coherence upon the fateful events of that distant February morning. In particular, the repeated intimations of Santiago Nasar's innocence encourage the belief that the identity of the person responsible for Angela's dishonor will finally be revealed. And yet, the novel constantly thwarts all expectations of revelation through what seems a perpetual game of deferrals, extremely detailed but inconsequential information and contradictory affirmations. In fact, one could characterize the narrator's discourse with a phrase used in the text to describe Bayardo San Román's speech: "He had a way of speaking that served more to conceal than to reveal." These textual circumstances should have rendered superfluous the critical obsession with the referential status of *Chronicle of a Death Foretold*, manifested in the myriad attempts to confront the events depicted in the novel with a similar incident in Colombian *petite histoire*. Such a concern, and the critical enterprise that it has engendered, however, are symptomatic of a widespread critical conceit regarding the entire *oeuvre* of García Márquez, one that would characterize his work as devoid for the most part of the metaliterary concerns that characterize contemporary Latin American literature.

The difference between the rhetorical specificity of the novel and the text's failure when viewed from this perspective is significant, and should perhaps alert us to the fact that the development of the text is guided primordially by a performative rather than by a logical or teleological drive. Only from such a performative perspective can the narrative be said to *mean* something, given the evident inconsequence of its self-designated hermeneutic project. In other words, we are led to the realization that the logic that underlies the production of the text appears to be at odds with the logic inaugurated by the novel's avowed rhetorical model. This *décalage*, this differing of the text from itself, will constitute the space and subject in and on which the present commentary on the novel will dwell.

If the text makes entirely problematic its relationship to the *generic* application of the term "chronicle," an interpretation of the word that is attuned to its *etymological* charge proves no less of a misnomer, given the novel's non-linear chronological structure. It is not my intent, however, to detail the multiple ways in which the temporal displacements of the narrative render ineffective rigorous chronological succession in the novel. I would propose, on the other hand, to arrive at an examination of the performative dimension described above by exploring initially the paradoxical and yet relentless presence of repetition in the fabric of a text that invokes for its self-definition the rubric of "chronicle."

It could be argued that the superfluity of the narrator's investigation vis-á-vis the original inquest is emblematic of the narrative as a whole, inasmuch as it signals the overwhelming occurrence of repetition in the entire text. It would perhaps be more accurate to propose that instances like it attest to the untrammeled and unproblematic status of repetition in *Chronicle of a Death Foretold*. If the novel in its entirety can be perceived as a reenactment of the preceding inquiry, it is also true that the text itself is assembled from instances of repeated information. At the most general level, *Chronicle of a Death Foretold* is constituted by an orchestrated collage of quotations, paraphrases and summaries. In this regard, Raymond Williams has [in *Gabriel García Márquez*] established in very precise terms that "the narrator-investigator's total 'record' of his chronicle consists of nine citations from the written record and a total of 102 quotations from the thirty-seven characters." But more importantly, the novel itself can be shown to be organized through a succession of internal repetitions and restatements, whose cumulative effect is to give the text an overall sense of redundancy and familiarity. This aspect of the text determines, for instance, that the last pages of the novel should constitute a thoroughly anticlimactic moment. The depiction of Santiago Nasar's death with which the book closes has been rendered at that point entirely superfluous by the text's own dialectics. All its circumstances and gruesome particulars are thoroughly known at that juncture; we anticipate and recognize each thrust of the murderers' knives, since they and the damage inflicted by them were first inscribed in the autopsy report before they ever scarred the body of Santiago Nasar. This mechanism is what deprives the murder scene of its potentially ghastly impact. At the same time, the detachment that it produces renders it impossible not to notice the painstaking manner in which the description endeavors to account for each of the blows that had been previously detailed in the postmortem examination. This quality becomes apparent when the two passages are confronted with each other:

> Seven of the numerous wounds were fatal. The liver was almost sliced by two deep cuts on the anterior side. He had four incisions in the stomach, one of them so deep that it went completely through it and destroyed the pancreas. He had six other lesser perforations in the transverse colon and multiple wounds in the small intestine. The only one he had in the back, at the level of the third lumbar vertebra, had perforated the right kidney. . . . The thoracic cavity showed two perforations: one in the second right rib space that reached the lung, and another quite close to the left armpit. He also had six minor wounds on his arms and hands, and two horizontal slashes: one on the right thigh and the other in the abdominal muscles. He had a deep puncture wound in the right hand.

> The knife went through the palm of his right hand and then sank into his side up to the hilt. . . . Pedro Vicario pulled out his knife with his slaughterer's savage wrist and dealt him a second blow almost in the same place. . . . Santiago Nasar twisted after the third stab . . . and tried to turn his back to them. Pablo Vicario, who was on his left with the curved knife, then gave him the only stab in the back. . . . Trying to finish

> the task once and for all, Pedro Vicario sought his heart, but he looked for it almost in the armpit, where pigs have it. . . . Desperate, Pablo Vicario gave him a horizontal slash on the abdomen, and all his intestines exploded out. Pedro Vicario was about to do the same, but his wrist twisted with horror and he gave him a wild cut on the thigh.

Examples like these could be garnered almost at random from the text. It might be argued that repetition is unavoidable in a narrative of this sort, where the overlapping of strands of evidence and accounts has a confirmatory value. But given the generic ambiguity and intractability of *Chronicle of a Death Foretold* as well as the performative intention identified earlier, perhaps a more meaningful realization awaits us.

I should like to propose that the intricate web of repetition and restatements in the text seeks to duplicate effectively at the level of the narrative the same structure of foreknowledge that characterized the events leading to the assassination of Santiago Nasar. Surely, as the narrator affirms in reference to Nasar's murder, "there was never a death so publicized." The town's collective knowledge of the crime-to-be, and its unbearable guilt, is built on discrete instances of individual foresight: Hortensia Baute sees the knives dripping blood before they have performed their murderous task; Santiago's hand feels like a dead man's to Divina Flor; Pedro Vicario says that warning Santiago will not make any difference in the final outcome: "Don't bother. . . . No matter what, he's as good as dead already." And later, when reminded that Santiago usually went about armed, he shouts, "Dead men can't shoot"; to Margot, the narrator's sister, Nasar already had the countenance of a dead person some time before the murder actually took place. And when asked for the whereabouts of Santiago Nasar, the narrator's brother Luis Enrique answers inexplicably, "Santiago Nasar is dead." The same sense of foreknowledge that surrounded the murder of Santiago Nasar is incorporated by the narrative in its own coming into being through the pervasive presence of repetition in its structure. This parallelism advances the proposition that there exists a very significant relationship linking the events that led to the murder of Santiago Nasar to the text of *Chronicle of a Death Foretold*, the narration that recreates those same events. The novel appears to posit a homology between the way the crime takes place and the manner in which the narrative about the crime is constructed. In this fashion, the organization of the text would seem to recall the process that many years earlier had culminated in the assassination of Santiago Nasar. The recognition of this analogy will allow us to explore comprehensively the powerful and totalizing role of repetition in *Chronicle of a Death Foretold*.

Given the homology just described, one could adduce that the narrative would like to project itself as a reenactment of the murder of Santiago Nasar. More exactly—and as I will argue below—the text would endeavor to constitute a sort of ritual repetition of the crime. There are in fact many characteristics of the novel that would attest to this ritual dimension. To begin with, one would have to point out the "sacral" nature of the text's discourse. It is this aspect of the novel that clashes most violently with the rhetorical conventions of the model to which *Chronicle of a Death Foretold* ostensibly belongs, particularly the hermeneutical demands imposed by the genre: it is ultimately not a matter of understanding or accounting for the murder of Santiago Nasar, but of reenacting it. This explains why the text of the novel is rife with instances of apparent redundancy, digressions and extraneous information, all of which are nevertheless deemed essential for the textual reconstruction of the sacrificial *mise en scéne*. Take, for instance, the following passage:

> My brother Luis Enrique entered the house through the kitchen door. . . . He went to the bathroom before going to bed, but he fell asleep sitting on the toilet, and when my brother Jaime got up to go to school he found him stretched out face down on the tile floor and singing in his sleep. My sister the nun . . . could not get him to wake up. . . . Later, when my sister Margot went in to bathe before going to the docks, she managed with great difficulty to drag him to his bedroom. From the other side of sleep he heard the first bellows of the bishop's boat without awakening. Then he fell into a deep sleep . . . until my sister the nun rushed into the bedroom, trying to put her habit on as quickly as she could, and woke him up with her frantic cry: "They've killed Santiago Nasar!"

The fragment does not provide any privileged information regarding the murder of Nasar; and, given the particulars of the account provided, it would be difficult to claim that it describes a character's "participation" in the events. But from within a conception of the text as ritual repetition there is no meaningless or wasted action; no fleeting gesture is unworthy of being consigned to writing. Given the conventionality and rigidity that characterize it, ritual language has by its very nature this leveling effect that can be identified in the novel, paradoxically, as the apparently indiscriminate bringing together of data. There has been no attempt to sort out what is meaningful from what is extraneous in the information gathered; on the contrary, the pertinence and significance of every fact or event seems to be underwritten by its very presence in the narrative. Almost as if to call attention to this aspect of the text, there is a series of patent contradictions that plague the various depositions, and which are left to stand as such in the narrator's account. The most glaring of these leads to the inability to establish with any degree of precision something as elementary as the state of the weather during the morning of the crime.

In this ritual reenactment it is not surprising to encounter specific verbal constructions that through repetition acquire an almost incantatory quality. Such is the case of expressions like "On the day they were going to kill him," "They've killed Santiago Nasar" and "It was the last time they saw him alive," phrases that in their periodic appearance in the text would seem to mark the beat of the ceremonial proceedings. To this, one would have to add the clearly antiphonal structure that is so predominant in the novel. An intervention by the narrator will be followed by a "response" offered by one of the witnesses, as in the following case:

> No one would have even suspected . . . that Bayardo San Román had been in her [Angela's] life constantly from the moment he had brought her back home. It was a *coup de grâce*. "Suddenly, when Mother began to hit me, I began to remember him," she told me. The blows hurt less because she knew they were because of him. She went on thinking about him with a certain surprise at herself as she lay sobbing on the dining-room sofa. "I wasn't crying because of the blows or for anything that had happened," she told me. "I was crying because of him."

From this ritual perspective the entire narrative assumes a preparatory and propitiatory function for the sacrificial murder of Santiago Nasar with which the novel ends. The performative drive alluded to earlier would become a manifestation of this ritual dimension of the text. Its incongruity with the epistemic project of the investigative model is represented by the fact that the avowed inquest into the murder should end paradoxically with the repetition of the original crime. That the *telos* of the narrative is this reenactment of the assassination is confirmed with enigmatic precision by García Márquez himself in the course of a recent interview: "The story really ends almost twenty-five years after the murder, when the husband returns to the scorned wife, but to me it was always evident that the end of the book had to be the painstaking description of the crime."

In addition, the homologous relationship between the murder and the narrative is underscored by a series of similarities between the two registers. There is, for instance, a most telling scene in which the morning of the murder and the beginning of the investigation are explicitly equated: "She [Santiago Nasar's mother] had watched him from the same hammock and in the same position in which I found her prostrated by the last lights of old age when I returned to this forgotten town, trying to put back together the broken mirror of memory from so many scattered shards. . . . She was on her side, clutching the cords at the head of the hammock in an attempt to get up, and there in the shadows was the baptistery smell that had startled me on the morning of the crime." By the same token, Santiago Nasar's obsession with determining the cost of the wedding festivities parallels the many references made by the narrator to the "cost" of his investigation. By gleaning relevant fragments from the novel, a rigorous account of the chronological investment and of the effort spent on the construction of the narrative can be obtained. Take, for instance, the following: "There was no classification of files whatever, and more than a century of cases were piled up on the floor of the decrepit colonial building. . . . The ground floor would often be flooded by high tides and the unbound volumes floated about the deserted offices. I myself searched many times with water up to my ankles in that reservoir of lost causes, and after five years of rummaging around, only chance let me rescue some 322 random pages from the more than 500 that the brief must have contained." And closely related to this parallel tallying is the all-too-precise scansion of the temporal framework of the investigation, which usually assumes the formulaic expressions "x years later" or "x years afterwards." One could plausibly argue that its presence in the narrative is strongly reminiscent of the relentless chronological indexing of Santiago Nasar's murder, and of which the very first sentence of the novel may be the most appropriate example: "On the day they were going to kill him, Santiago Nasar got up at five-thirty in the morning to wait for the boat the bishop was coming on."

All of these similarities attest to the performative intention that rules the novel, that is, the desire to constitute the narrative as a ritual repetition of the murder of Santiago Nasar. There are a number of fashions in which such a reenactment could itself be understood as a function of the events depicted in the novel. As Freud suggested in *Beyond the Pleasure Principle*, the restaging of an unpleasant event allows for the possibility of achieving mastery over—or at the very least some degree of accommodation to—its disturbing consequences. This possibility would reside in the passage from passive experiencing to the active reenactment of the unsettling circumstance. In *Chronicle of a Death Foretold* the need to internalize the murder of Santiago Nasar goes from the individual (the narrator) to the collective (the entire town), and can be identified in at least two of its manifestations: as the compulsion to understand the events that transpired and as a desire for absolution and catharsis. The following passage incorporates the two succinctly:

> For years we could not talk about anything else. Our daily conduct, dominated until then by so many linear habits, had suddenly begun to spin around a single common anxiety. The cocks of dawn would catch us trying to give order to the chain of many chance events that had made absurdity possible, and it was obvious that we were not doing it from a desire to clear up mysteries but because none of us could go on living without an exact knowledge of the place and the mission assigned to us by fate.

In the projection of the narrative as a ritual reenactment of the murder there is an attempt to endow the crime with the prescribed order of ceremony, thereby overcoming the centrifugal and fortuitous character of the original events. The narrative repetition of the murder would subsume the multiplicity of discrete and heterogeneous facts surrounding the tragedy under the homogenizing mantle of ritual discourse and performance. In this context, the novel would seem to give an almost literal rendition of the following phrase by Victor Turner [in *The Drums of Affliction*]: "The unity of a given ritual is a dramatic unity. It is in this sense a work of art." The passage quoted earlier, in which the narrator describes his intention as that of "trying to put back together the broken mirror of memory from so many scattered shards," becomes particularly significant here. Thus, understanding in this instance would not reside in a privileged moment of epiphany but rather in the solace attained through the recognition of an efficacious teleology. Acting as a sort of officiant, the narrator would reassemble the collectivity once again through his narrative, seeking to achieve in the end the equilibrium and resolution of tension that according to Lévi-Strauss is the paramount concern of ritual ceremony:

> Ritual . . . conjoins, for it brings about a union (one might say communion in this context) or in any case an organic relation between two initially separate groups, one ideally merging with the person of the officiant and the other with the collectivity of the faithful. . . . There is an asymmetry which is postulated in

> advance between profane and sacred, faithful and officiating, dead and living, initiated and uninitiated, etc., and the "game" consists in making all the participants pass to the winning side.
> (*The Savage Mind*)

This project, based on a conception of writing as an efficient instrument for ritual closure and redemption, would seem to underwrite the entire novel. And yet, if *Chronicle of a Death Foretold* appears to exhibit the attributes of a cathartic ritual, its status from this standpoint becomes entirely problematic: there is no unpolluted agent in the text, no person who can legitimately conduct the ceremonial proceedings and certify the effective cleansing of the collectivity. This fact is a repostulation in a different sphere of the difficulty identified earlier when considering the novel as an investigative treatise. More importantly, the attempt to achieve cathartic release through the repetition of the original murder would carry with it the possibility of an endless cycle of contamination and atonement: the ritual to cleanse the crime would become itself a source of collective anxiety in need of purgation. We are therefore led to an impasse that can be resolved only by reexamining the homology identified earlier that conjoins the murder and the narrative.

In its desire to fashion itself as a reenactment of the murder of Santiago Nasar, the text simultaneously establishes a relationship between the processes that yielded the two, that is, between victimage and writing. From this perspective, rather than functioning simply as the vehicle for purgation envisaged above, writing is revealed as sharing essentially in the attributes of the violent act it is supposed to master and transcend. This contamination is signaled pointedly in the text by the fact that there is structurally someone for whom the death of Santiago Nasar always occurs for the first time: the reader. For us, forced symbolically to witness the murder in an analogous position to that of the townspeople in the original crime, writing cannot provide any solace or redemption. Indeed, rather than engaging in a ritual cleansing, what *Chronicle of a Death Foretold* accomplishes is a process of ritual pollution, one that is repeated time and again with each successive reading of the text. It should not be surprising, then, to find that the novel itself had provided all along a metaphoric structure that established unambiguously the relationship between writing and violence that has been proposed. It is an association that is not preserved by the English translation, but which becomes readily apparent when the appropriate fragments from the original Spanish text are confronted. Santiago Nasar's autopsy, which is significantly referred to as a murder beyond murder, includes the following passage: "El cascarón vacío, embutido de trapos y cal viva, y *cosido* a la machota con bramante basto y agujas de enfardelar, estaba a punto de desbaratarse cuando lo pusimos en el ataúd nuevo de seda capitonada." The English version of Gregory Rabassa reads: "The empty shell, stuffed with rags and quicklime and *sewn up* crudely with coarse twine and baling needles, was on the point of falling apart when we put it into the new coffin with its silk quilt lining." If we follow the thread of this metaphoric yarn, we find that it weaves its way through a number of specific allusions to writing and textuality in the novel. Thus, when Bayardo returns to the wife he had originally spurned, "he was carrying a suitcase with clothing in order to stay and another just like it with almost two thousand letters that she had written him. They were arranged by date in bundles *tied* [i.e., sewn] with colored ribbons, and they were all unopened." The English rendition blurs the perfect concordance that the Spanish original posits between this fragment and the previous quotation: "Llevaba la maleta de la ropa para quedarse, y otra maleta igual con casi dos mil cartas que ella había escrito. Estaban ordenadas por sus fechas, en paquetes *cosidos* con cintas de colores, y todas sin abrir." The same relationship surfaces during the narrator's account of his research in the archives of the Palace of Justice in Riohacha. The first floor, we are told, "se inundaba con el mar de leva, y los volúmenes *descosidos* flotaban en las oficinas desiertas." Once again, the English version obscures the metaphoric link. It reads: "The ground floor would be flooded by high tides and the *unbound* [i.e., unsewn] volumes floated about the deserted offices." Finally, while describing Bayardo San Román's almost mysterious disappearance after the events, the narrator reports that "there is a declaration by him in the brief, but it is so short and conventional that it seems to have been *put together* [i.e., patched up] at the last minute to comply with an unavoidable requirement." The Spanish text, however, is relentless in its metaphoric consistency: "Hay una declaración suya en el sumario, pero es tan breve y convencional, que parece *remendada* a última hora para cumplir con una fórmula ineludible." Also, one could note in this regard that the forlorn Angela Vicario divides her days between the nocturnal and surreptitious correspondence with Bayardo and an equally accomplished dedication to embroidery by daylight.

Thus, the relationship between victimage and writing that is implicitly posited by the novel is distinctly underscored by the metaphoric structure identified above. Both the crumbling body of Santiago Nasar and the text show their seams, as it were, the crude remainders of their shared violent history. For through the establishing of this association the text reveals its own necessarily concealed foundation in violence and suppression. I am alluding, in the terms offered by J. Derrida, to the imposition of a closed order of signification in the text, and the violent, expulsive "logic of the supplement" that it inevitably sets in place. This awareness of the supplement is expressed in the novel at both levels of the metaphoric association that confounds body and text. At the conclusion of Santiago Nasar's autopsy we read: "Furthermore, the priest had pulled out the sliced-up intestines by their roots, but in the end he didn't know what to do with them, and he gave them an angry blessing and threw them into the garbage pail." Just as Nasar's entrails become a surplus, a supplement that must be discarded, the text repeats the same violent gesture by turning each reading, as was seen earlier, into an ever-renewed act of pollution. Writing, the suggestion appears to be, cannot serve as the instrument for redemption and cleansing that the novel envisions, since it is itself constituted and sustained through a violence that traverses it to the very core.

This knowledge, I would argue, also appears to be incorporated in the novel as a persistent attempt to eradicate the structure of differences on which the text is constructed. Seen in this light, *Chronicle of a Death Foretold* seems to be forever on the verge of reverting to a state of undifferentiation that would jeopardize the system of differences that rules the text. Instances of this desire to abolish difference are myriad. For example, the narrator is twice confused with Santiago Nasar, and he comes to the town manifestly from the outside, just as Bayardo San Román had many years earlier. Bayardo's supposed antagonist, Santiago Nasar, is alluded to in the narrative as a *boyardo* (master, lord), a transformation that could also yield *Bedoya*, the last name of the narrator's closest friend, as one of its permutations. The onomastic similarities—whether literal or semantic—seem almost to dominate the text: The twins *P*edro and *P*ablo Vicario; *Divino* Rostro, *Divina* Flor, *Angela* Vicario; Divina *Flor*, *Flora* Miguel, don Rogelio de la *Flor*, *Hortensia* Baute; Luisa *Santiaga*, *Santiago* Nasar; Father *Carmen* Amador, Purísima del *Carmen*. In addition, there is a dimension in the novel that appears to indicate the possibility of an interpretation of the events that would hinge specifically on the differentiation between the two meanings of the term *altanería:* haughtiness vs. falconry. This reading would center on the epigraph to the text, borrowed from a poem of Gil Vicente, and which reads: "The pursuit of love / is like falconry (haughtiness) (La caza de amor / es de altanería)." A fragment of the same poem is quoted later in the novel by the narrator: "A falcon that chases / a warring crane / should expect no gain (Halcón que se atreve /

con garza guerrera, / peligros espera)," thereby proposing the existence of interpretive possibilities based on an explicit relationship with a previous text. But an examination of Vicente's poem reveals that it is itself sustained by the willful ambiguity and oscillation between the two meanings that the novel seems intent on maintaining. Moreover, Santiago Nasar, the person in relation to whom all the events and characters in the text delineate themselves, is depicted as a disassembler of identities, a veritable disseminator of nondifference:

> Santiago Nasar had an almost magical talent for disguises, and his favorite entertainment was to confuse the identities of the mulatto girls. He would plunder the wardrobe of some to disguise the others, so that they all ended up feeling different from themselves and like the ones they were not. On a certain occasion, one of them found herself repeated in another with such exactness that she had an attack of tears. "I felt like I'd stepped out of a mirror," she said.

This quality in turn assimilates him even more to Bayardo San Román, of whom it is said that he "not only was capable of doing everything, and doing it extremely well, but also had access to inexhaustible resources." Examples like the foregoing could be multiplied almost endlessly. What must be emphasized is that in the drive to abolish the differences that constitute it, the text motions towards its own violent essence, demonstrating that it must speak the contradictory knowledge that it embodies even at the expense of its very being.

In sum, then, the novel's attempted passage from violence to the ritual containment of that violence is compromised by the text's awareness of its own primordial inscription through another kind of violent act. One could propose that in attempting such a passage the novel becomes a perfect analogue of writing, since it traces the unfolding of the inevitable self-mystification in which every instance of writing indulges. Finally, in the text's unmasking of a violence that precedes and underpins all subsequent violence, one can perhaps find the most literal, yet possibly the most significant interpretation of the title *Chronicle of a Death Foretold*.

ANIBAL GONZÁLEZ

Translation and the Novel: One Hundred Years of Solitude

The concept of the definitive text *belongs only to religion or to exhaustion.*

—BORGES, "The Homeric Versions" (1932)

Cela [l'histoire du Babel] inscrit la scène de la traduction dans un espace qui est justement celui de la généalogie des noms propres, de la famille, de l'endettement, de la loi, à l'intérieur d'une scène d'héritage.

—DERRIDA, *L'Oreille de l'autre* (1982)

Gabriel García Márquez's *One Hundred Years of Solitude* stands today as an undisputed classic of Latin American letters, and, like all classics, it has been subjected to countless readings, from source studies to formal analyses to readings oriented by the latest critical theories. Like Cervantes's *Don Quixote*—to which it has been compared many times—*One Hundred Years of Solitude* offers a richness and a density that allows succeeding generations of readers to add further comments to its already abundant critical legacy. It is not altogether delirious to see in García Márquez's masterpiece, as one critic [Samuel García] has done, a kind of synthesis of "three thousand years of literature"; a novel that deals with such basic issues related to writing, history, and literature as *One Hundred Years of Solitude* does, cannot but evoke a good portion of the literary tradition that has preceded it. One of the many fundamental issues that are addressed in *One Hundred Years of Solitude* is that of translation, and of translation's links with the writing of this particular novel as well as with the novel as a genre. Few critics have failed to observe, of course, that the action in *One Hundred Years of Solitude* is inextricably linked to the process of decoding Melquíades's prophetic manuscript, and that such a decoding involves a translation; but the interpretation of this aspect of the novel has tended to revolve around theories of reading and more general questions about the nature of writing, and little attention has been paid to the implications of the act of translation itself. Yet, a consideration of what translation implies in the context of *One Hundred Years of Solitude* can provide us not only with insights about this contemporary Latin American classic but also about the role of translation in literary history and in the constitution of the novel as a genre. Starting from a rather simple (not to say simplistic) thematic reading, my purpose in the following pages will be to show how, by foregrounding the topic of translation and relating it to other fundamental topics such as those of genealogy and the incest prohibition, *One Hundred Years of Solitude* suggests that translation is at the very heart of the problematics of the novel as a genre, and that it is one of the key defining characteristics of that most undefinable of literary genres.

Besides the well-known scene at its end (to which I will, of course, return), the text of *One Hundred Years of Solitude* abounds with "scenes of translation" and references to learning and speaking foreign languages. And when I say "translation" here, I am referring to the ordinary usage of the term as "interlinguistic translation," to use Jakobson's formulation, and not to any etymological or broadly conceived meaning (there will be moments later in this essay when I will make use of an expanded meaning of the term). For the moment, I would just like to enumerate some of the more interesting instances of translation, and of allusions to it, in the novel's text, leaving detailed comments for later. The first direct allusion to translation in the novel occurs in the second chapter, when José Arcadio goes to bed with the gypsy girl: "José Arcadio felt himself lifted up into the air toward a state of seraphic inspiration, where his heart burst forth with an outpouring of tender obscenities that entered the girl through her ears and came out of her mouth translated into her language"; shortly afterwards, as we know, José Arcadio leaves with the gypsies. In the third chapter we learn that Arcadio and Amaranta, who were brought up in the care of Visitación, the Guajiro Indian woman who had come to Macondo fleeing the plague of insomnia, "came to speak the Guajiro language before Spanish," and "went about all day clutching at the Indians' cloaks, stubborn in their decision not to speak Spanish but the Guajiro language." When Rebeca arrives, along with the clucking bones of her parents, she too speaks the Guajiro language, and when Ursula tries to get her to drink some medicine against her vice of eating earth, she replies with "strange hieroglyphics that she alternated with her bites and spitting, and that, according to what the scandalized Indians said, were the vilest obscenities that one could ever imagine in their language"; however, "it was soon revealed that she spoke Spanish with as much fluency as the Indian language." Language loss and language reacquisition occur somewhat later on a collective scale, of course, during the plague of insomnia and its accompanying loss of memory (an episode full of enticing details about writing and memory on which, for the moment, I will not dwell). An even more significant episode closely related to translation is that of Melquíades's last days, when, already in an advanced stage of decrepitude, "he would answer questions in a complex hodgepodge of languages." All the while, he is writing his "enigmatic literature"; on one occasion, Aureliano "thought he understood something of what Melquíades was saying in his groping monologues, and he paid attention. In reality, the only thing that could be isolated in the rocky paragraphs was the insistent hammering on the word *equinox*, *equinox*, *equinox*, and the name of Alexander von Humboldt." It is during that same episode that Melquíades makes Aureliano "listen to several pages of his impenetrable writing, which of course he did not understand, but which when read aloud were like encyclicals being chanted": here we have the first of a whole sequence of encounters of the Buendías with Melquíades's cryptic inscriptions, which will culminate in the final decipherment of the manuscript. Another significant episode is that of José Arcadio Buendía's insanity, in which he no longer speaks Spanish but "a high-sounding and fluent but completely incomprehensible language" that later turns out to be Latin. A particularly graphic—so to speak—instance of plurality of languages in the novel is given in the younger José Arcadio's enormous penis, which was "completely covered with tattoos of words in several languages intertwined in blue and red." In contrast, Pietro Crespi's contribution to the topic of translation in the novel is of a more classical nature: "he would translate Petrarch's sonnets for Amaranta." It is interesting that the first member of the family who tries to decipher Melquíades's papers is the despotic Arcadio (son of José Arcadio the younger by Pilar Ternera), who, we are told, "never succeeded in communicating with anyone better than he did with Visitación and Cataure in their language. Melquíades was the only one who really was concerned with him as he made him listen to his incomprehensible texts and gave him lessons in the art of the daguerreotype. No one imagined how much he wept in secret and the desperation which with he tried to revive Melquíades with the useless study of his papers." The second intense assault on Melquíades's manuscript is that of Aureliano Segundo, who, after reading a book that is obviously the *Arabian Nights* (though the title is never mentioned), "set about deciphering the manuscripts" only to find that "it was impossible. The letters looked like clothes hung out to dry on a line and they looked more like musical notation than writing." Melquíades then appears to him, and "tried to infuse him with his old wisdom, but he refused to translate the manuscripts. 'No one must know their meaning until he has reached one hundred years of age,' he explained." José Arcadio Segundo is the second member of the Buendías' lineage to devote himself to the manuscripts, and the one who makes the most progress in deciphering them before Aureliano Babilonia manages to crack their code; it is he who manages "to classify the cryptic letters of the parchments. He was certain that they corresponded to an alphabet of forty-seven to fifty-three characters, which when separated looked like scratching and scribbling, and which in the fine hand of Melquíades looked like pieces of clothing put out to dry on a line." Finally, it is Aureliano who discovers that the language in which Melquíades had written his text is Sanskrit, but that is still not enough, "because the text in Spanish did not mean anything: the lines were in code"; thus, despite having learned "English and French and a little Latin and Greek" in addition to Sanskrit, Aureliano still lacks the key that will enable him to recognize the text's meaning. That key is not to be found in a text, but in something that looks like a text: the body of his pig-tailed child by Amaranta Ursula, "a dry and bloated bag of skin" (in Spanish, "un pellejo hinchado y reseco") not unlike Melquíades's parchments.

If my somewhat tedious enumeration has served any purpose, it is to show that, first of all, the topic of translation forms a thread that runs through the novel and gives it its underlying coherence: translation could almost be said to be the *telos* of this narrative, its finality; secondly, we can see that translation runs parallel in the novel to genealogy: the task of translating the manuscripts is handed down from one generation to the next, to selected members of each generation, in much the same way as Melquíades's ghost appears to those who are fit to deal with the manuscripts' enigma. Nevertheless, thus far I have merely surveyed the question of translation in the novel from a thematic point of view; I must now consider what is the meaning of translation in the broader context of the novel: why is translation foregrounded in *One Hundred Years of Solitude*? What makes translation so important? What is its relationship with genealogy and the incest prohibition?

To try to answer some of these questions, it is necessary first to address ourselves to the context of the theory of translation, and specifically to certain theoretical pronouncements which are, I think, quite relevant to any reading of *One Hundred Years of Solitude*. The first of these pronouncements belongs to Jorge Luis Borges, who is without a doubt the most important source for García Márquez's literary ideology. In his essay on "The Homeric Versions" (1932), Borges declares that "no problem is as intimately connected with literature and its modest mystery as that proposed by a translation. . . . Translation . . . seems destined to serve as an illustration for esthetic discussion." Borges reminds us here, as he does also in his short story "Pierre Menard, Author of the *Quixote*," that the notion of translation is intimately linked to the nature of literature, and that translation can serve as an instrument of critical inquiry into the workings of literature. In his comments on several different versions of Homer's *Iliad*, Borges stresses translation's power to somehow "purify" our understanding of a text by letting us see which elements of the original text are superfluous and which are part of its basic, underlying structure: "The facts of the *Iliad* and the *Odyssey* survive in full, but Achilles and Ulysses have disappeared, as well as what Homer was trying to represent when he named them, and what he really thought about them. The present state of his works resembles a complex equation which sets down precise relationships between unknown quantities." Borges's ideas on translation are akin to those of another important twentieth-century writer, Walter Benjamin; in his well-known introduction to his translation of Baudelaire's *Tableaux parisiens*, titled "The Task of the Translator" (1923), Benjamin gives further development, in his characteristically condensed style, to ideas very similar to Borges's. Like Borges in "The Homeric Versions," Benjamin prefers not to speak of "translation" in an abstract sense, but rather about the work of the translator and what it can reveal about translation and language. For Benjamin, as for Borges, the activity of translation involves a search for—in Benjamin's terms—"pure language," in other words, language "which no longer means or expresses anything but is, as expressionless and creative Word, that which is meant in all languages." It is interesting that both Benjamin and Borges use the metaphor of the "equation" in referring to translation, though valorizing it very differently; Benjamin says, "translation is so far removed from being the sterile equation of two dead languages that of all literary forms it is the one charged with the special mission of watching over the maturing process of the original language and the birth pangs of its own." One fundamental difference between Borges's and Benjamin's approaches to translation appears here:

while Borges reflects upon translation with an ironic detachment that takes its cue from Bertrand Russell's analytical philosophy, Benjamin's approach is neo-Hegelian, emphasizing as it does a vitalistic notion of language and art, and an idea of translation as a movement towards transcendence. Benjamin views translation as a process of historical, or to be more precise, philological, research about language which, through the study of "the central kinship of languages," arrives at a vision of "the predestined, hitherto inaccessible realm of reconciliation and fulfillment of languages." In such a transcendentalistic and messianic idea of translation, religious notions also have to come into play, and indeed Benjamin closes his essay with an evocation of Scripture, of sacred texts, as "unconditionally translatable," because in them the "text is identical with truth or dogma." Yet Benjamin is also aware in his essay that translation's promise of the ultimate reconciliation of languages and the discovery of "pure language" is simply that—a promise—and that, in practice, translation's linguistic transfer "can never be total. . . . Even when all surface content has been extracted and transmitted, the primary concern of the genuine translator remains elusive. . . . While content and language form a certain unity in the original, like a fruit and its skin, the language of the translation envelops its content like a royal robe with ample folds. For it signifies a more exalted language than its own and thus remains unsuited to its content, overpowering and alien. This disjunction prevents translation and at the same time makes it superfluous." Thus the "sacred text," with its total coherence between language and content, in which one is inseparable from the other, turns out to be, at the same time, translatable and untranslatable: because of its fixed meaning, the "sacred text" seems to offer its own "authorized translation" between the lines, a translation free from the disjunction between language and content that is produced in other texts by the uncontrolled play of meaning; yet, it is the very fixity of the "sacred text," its total coherence, which makes it impossible to translate, because it is not possible to "peel off"—following Benjamin's metaphor of the fruit—the skin of its language to get at its meaning. With its poetic and suggestive metaphors derived from philosophical vitalism and religion, Benjamin's meditation on translation gives a more poignant expression than Borges's to the essential double bind in which the act of translation is inscribed; as Jacques Derrida has pointed out in glossing this same essay by Benjamin, translation in general (not only that of "sacred texts") is caught in the paradox of its simultaneous possibility and impossibility: texts offer themselves up to be translated, to be transformed into other texts, while at the same time their essential propriety—the system of rules and conventions which governs the differences between languages—places insurmountable barriers to translation's total fulfillment. Harking back to the biblical myth of Babel, Derrida shows how translation is linked, in the Western cultural tradition, to the problematics of the proper noun: as in the mythical attempt by the tribe of Shem (whose name means, in fact, "Name") to impose their own name, their own language, on the whole universe through the erection of a tower that would carry them to the heavens, only to find themselves having to suffer the imposition by God of a new proper noun which enshrines difference and confusion (Babel), translation may be seen as a transgressive struggle between proper nouns, or, in more general terms, between two equally "proper" languages, one of which tries to deny the other's specificity. The name "Babel" (which was the Hebrew name for Babylon, meaning "Gate of God," according to most dictionaries) marks the limits imposed in the myth by a transcendental, sacred authority upon the dissemination of meaning which translation aims to bring about; yet Babel is the gate that translation, in its search for origins and originality, always aims to cross, even at the risk of bringing about confusion and the dispersion of meaning; in this sense, both Borges and Derrida are more radical in their thoughts about translation than Benjamin: for both, the notion of translation tends to deny the "sacredness" of any text, and raises the question of how it is that texts become "sacred." As Borges remarks in "The Homeric Versions": "To presuppose that every recombination of elements [of a text] is necessarily inferior to its original, is to presuppose that draft number nine is forcibly inferior to draft number H—since there can never be anything but drafts. The concept of the *definitive text* belongs only to religion or to exhaustion."

By now, it should not be difficult to see where these theoretical discourses about translation and *One Hundred Years of Solitude*'s implicit meditations on the same subject intersect. The plot of García Márquez's novel not only deals explicitly with the Buendías' task of translating Melquíades's manuscripts, but it also reinscribes that task, "translates" it, in a broader sense, into the language of kinship (with all that it implies in terms of the incest taboo and the importance of proper names) which configures the other half of the action in the novel, in a specular movement that is like a parody of Hegelian dialectics, and which leads not to synthesis, but to the novel's collapse into its linguistic origins. The text of the novel itself enacts the same process of genealogical research that the translators in the Buendía family have to perform in order to decode the manuscripts: research into the genealogy of language and into the genealogy of the Buendía family are both similar and complementary endeavors.

The associations of certain characters in the novel with specific languages already suggests this; as we have seen, in his insanity, José Arcadio Buendía, the founder of the line, reverts to the language that gave birth to Spanish, Latin, and he remains tied to a tree that is both a genealogical and a philological emblem; but there are also new additions, new branches, so to speak, added to the Buendías' linguistic/genealogical tree as the years go by: there are members of the family, as we have seen, who speak Indian languages, and others who learn English (like Aureliano Babilonia and Meme), plus Papiamento, French, Greek, Latin, and, of course, Sanskrit; Italian is also represented, not only in Pietro Crespi, but also in the last José Arcadio, who returns to Macondo from Italy; last, but not least, there is the contribution of José Arcadio the younger, who returns from his maritime adventures "speaking a Spanish that was larded with sailor's slang," but, perhaps more importantly, with his whole body (including his "unusual masculinity") covered with multilingual tattoos: José Arcadio's body-become-text is like an emblem of the family's linguistic cosmopolitanism, and it prefigures, of course, the "dry and bloated bag of skin" covered with ants of the last Buendía. Also, of course, kinship itself becomes another of those languages that must be mastered and decoded before the manuscripts themselves can be understood, and this is precisely what happens towards the end of the novel, when Aureliano Babilonia's relationship with Amaranta Ursula leads him to seek out his family origins.

We should now take a closer look at Aureliano Babilonia's task as a translator, at how he goes about translating the manuscripts. The first thing he does, of course, is to read and learn as much as he can about the world (Melquíades is, as always, present "like the materialization of a memory," to help); the manuscript is still, in Borges's terms, little more than "a complex equation which sets down precise relationships between unknown quantities"; José Arcadio Segundo had helped to define the equation—so to speak—by counting and classifying the letters of the alphabet in which the manuscripts were written, but it is Aureliano who discovers that the language of that alphabet is Sanskrit, and thus he begins to fill in the "unknowns" in the equation. Sanskrit, is, of course, the *Ursprache* of Spanish, and Aureliano's discovery has led him to the origins of the linguistic genealogy of Spanish; Aureliano's task of translation begins, as with every translation (as Benjamin reminds us), with a return to the origins, to the source: but if he now has the linguistic source of the text, the original language (in every sense) of the text, he still has no idea as to what its content might be; that is why Aureliano's readings are so wide-ranging, so encyclopedic, and at the same time so antiquarian: he obviously assumes that an ancient manuscript written in a dead language can only deal with past events. Later, when Aureliano manages to transliterate (not to translate, though) Melquíades's text into the Spanish alphabet, he discovers that there is another barrier to translation: the text is in code, that is to say, in still another language, and the full translation of the manuscripts depends on Aureliano being able to figure out the relationship, the "kinship," so to speak, between Spanish and Melquíades's secret code. This is where, finally, the apparently parallel lines of genealogy and translation in the novel converge: Melquíades's code, as we learn in the last pages of the novel and as the manuscripts' epigraph suggests, is the language of kinship itself: "*The first of the line is tied to a tree and the last is being eaten by the ants*." Yet, if we review certain portions of the novel, we shall see that the language of genealogy, of kinship, and the knowledge of languages that makes translation possible had been coinciding all along the text: there are a number of occasions in the text when translation, language learning, and sexual relations are linked; let us remember José Arcadio the younger's sexual encounter with the gypsy girl, in which translation figured so obviously; on the opposite extreme, we find Pietro Crespi's gentle courtship, which is also mediated in part by his translations of Petrarch; when Meme Buendía becomes involved with Mauricio Babilonia, it is because of her friendship with the Americans, which led her to learn English; let us also recall Aureliano Babilonia's relationship with Papiamento-speaking Nigromanta, in which "Aureliano would spend his mornings deciphering parchments and at siesta time he would go to the bedroom where Nigromanta was waiting for him, to teach him first how to do it like earthworms, then like snails, and finally like crabs"; but perhaps the emblem of this link between genealogy, writing, and translation in the text is, as I have said before, José Arcadio's tattooed male member: here the rather hackneyed Freudian symbolism of the writing implement as phallus becomes literalized, and the "words in several languages intertwined in blue and red" on José Arcadio's penis evoke the confusion of languages at Babel and the Shemites' phallic Tower. And the bond between genealogy and translation can be extended still further: in a broader sense of the word, isn't "translation" one of the consequences of the marriage of José Arcadio and Ursula, when they are forced to migrate from Riohacha after José Arcadio kills Prudencio Aguilar? Aren't Colonel Aureliano Buendía's seventeen sons engendered "on the march," so to speak? Doesn't Pilar Ternera substitute (translate?) Santa Sofía de la Piedad for herself in the shadows of Arcadio's room to avoid committing incest? And, leaving the Buendías' genealogy aside, aren't the gypsies themselves "translators" of a sort, moving about from here to there across the swamp and, indeed, across the world, bringing to Macondo their version of the outside world? Isn't Melquíades himself the translator of a foreign knowledge into Spanish, and of the future history of Macondo into Sanskrit? Clearly, when translation is understood in such a broad manner, the concepts of language, writing, genealogy, and translation all collapse into a single, chaotic vortex of dissemination that is reminiscent of the "biblical hurricane" that erases Macondo off the face of the earth.

The metaphoric equivalent of such a dissemination of the term "translation" in the novel's plot is, of course, Aureliano Babilonia's and Amaranta Ursula's violation of the incest prohibition. Translation and incest both share a transgressive nature; both are "improper" acts that imply breaching the barriers between members of the same family or between two languages. And just as incest serves to limit and thus define a kinship system, translation, as Benjamin puts it, "ultimately serves the purpose of expressing the central reciprocal relationship between languages. It cannot possibly reveal or establish this hidden relationship itself; but it can represent it by realizing it in embryonic or intensive form." As Benjamin notes, this idea that translation demonstrates the kinship of languages is a commonplace of traditional theories of translation; but Benjamin, as we will recall, goes a bit further: he proposes that translation in fact foretells or announces the existence of a "pure language," a kind of communicative essence freed from the contingent variations imposed upon it by the various tongues and by the author's intentions: "In this pure language—which no longer means or expresses anything but is, as expressionless and creative Word, that which is meant in all languages—all information, all sense, and all intention finally encounter a stratum in which they are destined to be extinguished." If we subtract the theological connotations from Benjamin's words, we arrive at Borges's and Derrida's understanding of translation as a critical, disseminating activity that arises from the questioning of the "property" or appropriateness of nouns. In this context, we can understand the anxiety with which Aureliano seeks out the origin of his name in the parish archives, not only to make sure he is not Amaranta Ursula's brother but also to ascertain the "propriety" of his name, of his origins; we can understand his confusion and his outrage when he becomes "lost in the labyrinths of kinship" and the priest, after hearing his name, tells him not to wear himself out searching, since "many years ago there used to be a street here with that name and in those days people had the custom of naming their children after streets." Yet Aureliano's name is even more "appropriate" than he could have ever imagined, since it is not, as he tells it to the priest, "Aureliano Buendía," but "Aureliano Babilonia." Aureliano Babel, Aureliano the Gate of God, Aureliano Confusion, Aureliano Translation.

However, we should recall here Derrida's observation about translation's contradictory, aporetic nature, its being at the same time possible and impossible: something always escapes the translator; in Aureliano's case, it is not only those eleven pages (or more) that he skips in order to anticipate the ending of the manuscript, but also, quite simply, the manuscript's end itself: translation is an endless activity, and appropriately, Aureliano, in his reading of the manuscript, is caught in a textual version of Zeno's paradox: he can approach the manuscript's end, but he can never reach or read it, because the text foretells his future and is always one step ahead of him; in order to reach the conclusion, he is forced, ineluctably, to cross a previous span of time (and of text), and no matter how much he skips, he will always have to read again and thus be chained to the text's tyrannical temporality. In much the same way, Aureliano's incestuous union with Amaranta Ursula has chained him irrevocably to his doomed genealogy, and, like José Arcadio Buendía, he too ends up tied to a (genealogical) tree, rooted to a spot that is like the eye of the "biblical hurricane" that razes Macondo. If the "biblical hurricane" is seen as a figure for interpretation, for criticism at its most extreme (as it is induced by translation), then it is significant that the "eye" of that vortex, the center which powers it, is Aureliano's tragic and impossible search for transcendence in the manuscripts, for a principle of perfect and coherent communication akin to Benjamin's "pure language." Translation, like incest, leads back to self-reflexiveness, to a cyclonic turning upon one's self which erases all illusions of solidity, all fantasies of a "pure language," all mirages of "propriety," and underscores instead language's dependence on the very notion of "otherness," of difference, in order to signify "something," as well as the novel's similar dependence on "other" discourses (those of science, law, and religion, for example) to constitute itself. The novel's proverbial generic indefinition may well be an indication that, of all the literary genres yet invented, it is the one which most closely mimics the rootlessness of language (and the complementary desire to find its roots that it engenders) as it was conceived after modern philology, at the end of the eighteenth and the beginning of the nineteenth centuries, finally debunked the myth of the divine origins of language. The myth of Babel may be one of the founding myths of translation, and indirectly, of the novel, but it is precisely in the novel where that myth is most visibly and consistently denied.

One Hundred Years of Solitude's foregrounding of translation as a vital constitutive element of the novel can thus be seen as a Cervantine gesture which tends to unmask the humble origins of the genre; like the *Quixote* and the popular romances of chivalry that the *Quixote* parodies, García Márquez's novel represents its own origins as translation, as that mildly illegal, somewhat treasonous act which violates the propriety of language and the laws of poetics and makes of the novel, metaphorically, a wandering orphan like the *pícaro*, cut off from or at odds with its mother (tongue), always seeking a new master, always seeking to master itself. But perhaps it is not necessary to return to Spain to seek out the origins of *One Hundred Years of Solitude*'s self-reflexive use of translation; isn't this, after all, already a part of the problematics of writing in America, a problematics that arose with the discovery and conquest of the New World, like a literalized version of the old Medieval topic of *traslatio imperii?* It may be enough to remember the founding example of the Colonial *mestizo* author Garcilaso Inca, who, by the way, translated Leone Hebreo's *Dialoghi di amore* into Spanish from the Italian, and whose monumental *Royal Commentaries* were, to a great extent, an attempt to translate the elements of Quechua culture into the sphere of European humanistic culture. From Garcilaso Inca to Sarmiento to Borges to García Márquez, the problematics of writing in America and the questions raised by translation have tended to become one and the same, and have generated a literature in which the topic of translation is ever-present, as a reminder of Latin American literature's "impure" and conflictive origins; Latin American literature, in turn, has called attention to *all* literature's origins in translation, in the transport—through violence or exchange—of meaning from other texts and other languages into the literary text.

Chronology

1928 Gabriel José García Márquez is born on March 6 in Aracataca, Colombia, a small town off the Caribbean coast, to Gabriel Eligio García and María Márquez Iguarán. Spends the first years of his childhood with his maternal grandparents.

1936 Wins a scholarship to the Colegio Nacional in Zipaquirá, a city near Bogotá.

1946 Receives his *bachillerato* from the Colegio Nacional.

1947 Enters the National University of Colombia in Bogotá to study law. Publishes his first short story "La tercera resignación" ("The Third Resignation") in a local newspaper, *El Espectador.*

1947–52 He publishes about fifteen short stories in *El Espectador.* He will later oppose their publication in book form.

1948 Presidential candidate Jorge Eliecer Gaitán is assassinated; civil war erupts in Colombia. García Márquez moves to Cartagena, a port city. Continues studies of law and works as a journalist at *El Universal.*

1950 Quits law school. Moves to Barranquilla and joins an important literary group, *el grupo de Barranquilla.* A first attempt at a novel, *La casa,* is rejected by the publisher.

1954 Returns to Bogotá. Writes stories and film reviews for *El Espectador.*

1955 Wins a national prize for a short story, and publishes his first novel, *La hojarasca* (*Leafstorm*). Writes account of Luis Alejandro Velasco's survival at sea for *El Espectador.* Travels to Geneva as a correspondent. The government closes down *El Espectador* because of the Velasco story.

1956 Lives in Paris, unemployed, and works on manuscripts for two novels, *La mala hora* (*In Evil Hour*) and *El coronel no tiene quien le escriba* (*No One Writes to the Colonel*).

1957 Finishes *No One Writes to the Colonel.* Travels to East Germany, Czechoslovakia, Poland, Russia and Hungary. Arrives in Caracas to work for the newspaper *Momento.*

1958 Marries Mercedes Barcha. Writes almost all of the stories in the collection *Los funerales de la Mamá Grande* (*Big Mama's Funeral*). Publishes *No One Writes to the Colonel.*

1959–61 Cuban Revolution. Works for Cuba's Prensa Latina in Bogotá, Cuba, and New York. His first child, Rodrigo, is born. Revises *In Evil Hour.*

1961 García Márquez is awarded the Colombian Esso Literary Prize for *In Evil Hour.* Resigns from Prensa Latina. Makes "Homage to Faulkner" bus trip across the Deep South to Mexico City.

1962 Publishes *Los funerales de la Mamá Grande.* A censored *In Evil Hour* is published in Spain (unauthorized by García Márquez). His second son, Gonzalo, is born.

1963 Cowrites his first film script with Carlos Fuentes.

1965 Goes into seclusion to write *Cien años de soledad* (*One Hundred Years of Solitude*).

1966 An authorized edition of *In Evil Hour* is published in Mexico.

1967 *One Hundred Years of Solitude* is published in Buenos Aires.

1969 *One Hundred Years of Solitude* wins the Chianchiano Prize in Italy and is named the Best Foreign Book in France.

1970 *One Hundred Years of Solitude* is published in English and chosen as one of twelve best books of the year by U.S. critics.

1971 Peruvian novelist and critic Mario Vargas Llosa publishes the first book-length study of García Márquez's life and work, *Gabriel García Márquez: Historia de un deicidio* (*Gabriel García Márquez: The Story of a Deicide*).

1972 Awarded Rómulo Gallegos Prize. Publishes *La increíble y triste historia de la cándida Eréndira y de su abuela desalmada* (*Innocent Eréndira and Other Stories*). Awarded *Books Abroad*/Neustadt Prize.

1973 Travels to France, Spain, and Mexico. Publishes *Cuando era feliz e indocumentado* [When I Was Happy and Uninformed], a compilation of journalism from the late 1950s.

1974 Founds *Alternativa,* a leftist magazine, in Bogotá.

1975 Publishes *El otoño del patriarca* (*The Autumn of the Patriarch*).

1977 Publishes *Operación Carlota* (Operation Carlota), essays on Cuba's role in Africa.

1981 Publishes *Crónica de una muerte anunciada* (Chronicle of a Death Foretold). Awarded the French Legion of Honor Medal.

1982 Awarded Nobel Prize for Literature. Publishes *El olor de la guayaba* (The Fragrance of Guava), conversations with Plinio Apuleyo Mendoza; completes *Viva Sandino*, a screenplay about the Nicaraguan revolution; and publishes "El rastro de tu sangre en la nieve" (The Trail of Your Blood on the Snow), a short story.

1986 Publishes *El amor en los tiempos del cólera* (Love in the Time of Cholera), a novel.

1989 Publishes *El general en su laberinto* (The General in His Labyrinth), a novel.

1992 Publishes *Doce cuentos peregrinos* (Strange Pilgrims), a collection of short stories.

1994 Publishes *Del amor y otros demonios* (Of Love and Other Demons), a novel.

1997 Publishes *Noticia de un secuestro* (News of a Kidnapping), a novel.

Contributors

HAROLD BLOOM, Sterling Professor of the Humanities at Yale University, is the author of *The Anxiety of Influence, Poetry and Repression,* and many other volumes of literary criticism. His forthcoming study, *Freud: Transference and Authority,* attempts a full-scale reading of all of Freud's major writings. A MacArthur Prize Fellow, he is general editor of five series of literary criticism published by Chelsea House. During 1987–88, he served as the Charles Eliot Norton Professor of Poetry at Harvard University.

MARIO VARGAS LLOSA, the internationally acclaimed novelist from Peru, is the author of *Time of the Hero, The Green House, Aunt Julia and the Scriptwriter,* and *The War of the End of the World,* as well as major critical studies of the work of García Márquez and Flaubert.

FLOYD MERRELL teaches in the Spanish Department at Purdue University. He is the author of *Pararealities* and *Semiotic Foundations.*

WILLIAM PLUMMER has written extensively on North and Latin American literature.

LOIS PARKINSON ZAMORA teaches in the English department at the University of Austin, Texas. She is the editor of *The Apocalyptic Vision in America.*

HARLEY D. OBERHELMAN teaches at Texas Tech University. He has published several articles on the relation between William Faulkner and García Márquez.

JOHN GERLACH teaches in the Department of English at Cleveland State University.

EDUARDO GONZÁLEZ is Professor of Romance Languages and Literature at the Johns Hopkins University. He is the author of *Alejo Carpentier: El tiempo del hombre* and of many articles on Latin American literature.

ROBERTO GONZÁLEZ ECHEVARRÍA is Professor of Spanish and Portuguese at Yale University. He is the author of *Alejo Carpentier: The Pilgrim at Home, Relecturas,* and *The Voice of the Masters.*

REGINA JANES teaches at Skidmore College. She is the author of *Gabriel García Márquez: Revolutions in Wonderland* and other articles on García Márquez.

RAYMOND WILLIAMS teaches at Washington University in St. Louis. He is the author of *Gabriel García Márquez.*

VERA M. KUTZINSKI is Assistant Professor of Afro-American Studies and English at Yale University. She has recently published *Against the American Grain: Myth and History in William Carlos Williams, Jay Wright, and Nicolás Guillén.*

HUMBERTO E. ROBLES teaches in the Department of Spanish and Portuguese at Northwestern University.

PATRICIA TOBIN teaches literary criticism at Rutgers University. She often writes about Latin American fiction and is the author of *Time and the Novel: The Genealogical Imperative.*

ISABEL ALVAREZ-BORLAND teaches in the Spanish Department at Holy Cross College.

MORTON P. LEVITT is Professor of Comparative Literature at Temple University.

MICHAEL PALENCIA-ROTH teaches at the University of Illinois, Urbana. He is the author of *Gabriel García Márquez: La metamorphosis del circulo.*

CARLOS J. ALONSO is Assistant Professor in the Department of Romance Languages and Literature at Wesleyan University and the author of numerous articles on Latin American literature.

ANIBAL GONZÁLEZ, who teaches in the Department of Spanish and Portuguese at the University of Texas, Austin, has written extensively on Latin American literature.

Bibliography

Arenas, Reinaldo. "In the Town of Mirages." *Review* 69 (1970): 101–8.

Barros-Lemez, Álvaro. "Beyond the Prismatic Mirror: *One Hundred Years of Solitude* and Serial Fiction." *Studies in Latin American Popular Culture* 3 (1984): 105–14.

Bell-Villada, Gene H. "García Márquez and the Novel." *Latin American Literary Review* no. 25 (1985): 15–23.

______. "Names and Narrative Pattern in *One Hundred Years of Solitude.*" *Latin American Literary Review* 9, no. 18 (1981): 37–46.

Bjorson, Richard. "Cognitive Mapping and the Understanding of Literature." *Sub-Stance,* no. 30 (1981): 51–52.

Borda, J. G. "'La hojarasca,' 1955." *Boletín cultural y bibliográfico* 12 (1969): 65.

Brotherson, Gordon. "An End to Secular Solitude." In *The Emergence of the Latin American Novel.* Cambridge: Cambridge University Press, 1977.

______. *Contemporary Latin American Fiction: Carpentier, Sabato, Onetti, Roa Bastos, Fuentes, García Márquez.* Edited by Salvador Vacarisse. Edinburg, Scotland: Scottish Academic Press, 1980.

Brushwood, John S. "Reality and Imagination in the Novels of García Márquez." *Latin American Literary Review* no. 25 (1985): 9–14.

______. *The Spanish-American Novel: A Twentieth Century Survey.* Austin: University of Texas Press, 1975.

Buchanan, Rhonda L. "The Cycle of Rage and Order in García Márquez's *El otoño del patriarca.*" *Perspectives on Contemporary Literature* 10 (1984): 75–85.

Carillo, G. D. "Los ciclico en *Cien años de soledad.*" *Razon y Fabula* 23 (1973): 18–34.

Christ, Ronald. "Review of *One Hundred Years of Solitude.*" *Review* 70 (1971).

Ciplijausjaite, Birute. "Foreshadowing as a Technique and Theme in *One Hundred Years of Solitude.*" *Books Abroad* 47 (1973): 479–84.

Coleman, A. "Bloomsbury in Aracataca: The Ghost of Virginia Woolf and Her

Influence on the Literary New-Novel in Spanish America." *World Literature Today* 59 (1985): 543–49.

Dauster, Frank. "Ambiguity and Indeterminacy in *La hojarasca.*" *Latin American Literary Review* no. 25 (1985): 15–23.

———. "The Short Stories of García Márquez." *Books Abroad* 47 (1973): 479–84.

Davis, Mary Eunice. "The Voyage Beyond the Map: *El ahogado más hermoso del mundo.*" *Kentucky Romance Quarterly* 26 (1979): 25–33.

Dixon, P. B. "Joke Formulas in *Cien años de soledad.*" *Chasqui* 15 (1986): 15–22.

Duran, Armando. "Conversation with Gabriel García Márquez." *Review* 70 (1971): 109–18.

Earle, Pete G., ed. *Gabriel García Márquez.* Madrid: Taurus, 1981.

Faris, Wendy. "Magic and Violence in Macondo and San Lorenzo." *Latin American Literary Review* no. 25 (1985): 24–28.

Fau, Margaret Eustella. *Gabriel García Márquez: An Annotated Bibliography, 1947–1979.* Westport, Conn.: Greenwood, 1980.

———, and Nelly Sefir de González. *Bibliographic Guide to Gabriel García Márquez, 1979–1985.* Westport, Conn.: Greenwood, 1986.

Foster, David William. "The Double Inscription of the Narrataire in *Los funerales de la Mamá Grande.*" In *Studies in the Contemporary Spanish American Short Story.* Columbia: University of Missouri Press, 1979.

———. "García Márquez and Solitude." *Americas* 21 (1969): 36–41.

Franco, Jean. "The Limits of Liberal Imagination: *One Hundred Years of Solitude* and *Nostromo.*" *Punto de Contacto/Point of Contact* 1 (1975): 4–16.

———. "Gabriel García Márquez." In *An Introduction to Spanish American Literature.* Cambridge: Cambridge University Press, 1969.

Fruchter, Barry G. "Miracles of Loss: García Márquez and History." *The Nassau Review* 4 (1983): 46–55.

Fuentes, Carlos. "Gabriel García Márquez: la segunda lectura." In *La nueva novela hispanoamericana.* Mexico City: Joaquín Mortiz, 1969.

———. "Macondo, Seat of Time." *Review* 70 (1971): 119–21.

Gallagher, D. P. "Gabriel García Márquez." In *Modern Latin American Literature.* London: Oxford University Press, 1973.

Garavito, Agustín Rodriguez. "*Los funerales de la Mamá Grande.*" *Boletín cultural y bibliográfico* 12 (1969): 108–9.

García, Samuel. *Tres mil años de literatura en* Cien años de soledad: *Intertextualidad en la obra de García Márquez.* Medellin: Editorial Lealon, 1977.

Goetzinger, Judith A. "The Emergence of a Folk Myth in *Los funerales de la Mamá Grande.*" *Revista de Estudios Hispánicos* 6 (1972): 237–48.

González-Echevarría, Roberto. "Big Mama's Wake." *Diacritics* 4, no. 2 (1974): 55–57.

———. "Polemic: With Borges in Macondo." *Diacritics* 2, no. 1 (1972): 57–60.

Gordon, Ambrose. "The Seaport beyond Macondo." *Latin American Literary Review* no. 25 (1985): 79–89.

Guibert, Rita. "Gabriel García Márquez." In *Seven Voices,* 305–37. New York: Knopf, 1973.

Halka, Chester S. *Melquíades, Alchemy and Narrative Theory: The Quest for*

Gold in Cien años de soledad. Lathrup, Mich.: International Book Publishers, 1981.

Hancock, Joel. "Gabriel García Márquez's 'Eréndira' and the Brothers Grimm." *Studies in Twentieth Century Literature* 3 (1978): 43–52.

Harss, Luis, and Barbara Dohmann. "Gabriel García Márquez, or the Lost Chord." In *Into the Mainstream,* 310–41. New York: Harper & Row, 1967.

Hart, Stephen. "Magical Realism in Gabriel García Márquez's *Cien años de soledad.*" *Inti* nos. 26–27 (1982–83): 37–52.

Hedeen, Paul M. "Gabriel García Márquez's Dialectic of Solitude." *Southwest Review* 68 (1983): 350–64.

Ivanovici, Victor. "The Colonel's Phantom: Aureliano Buendía and the 'Patchwork' of Fantasy." *Romanian Review* 37, nos. 2–3 (1983): 182–87.

Janes, Regina. *Gabriel García Márquez: Revolutions in Wonderland.* Columbia: University of Missouri Press, 1981.

Jelinski, Jack B. "Memory and the Remembered Structure of *Cien años de soledad.*" *Revista de Estudios Hispanicos* 18 (1984): 323–33.

Kadir, Djelal. "The Architectonic Principle of *Cien años de soledad* and the Vichian Theory of History." *Kentucky Romance Quarterly* 24 (1977): 251–61.

Kappeler, Susanne. "Voices of Patriarchy: Gabriel García Márquez's *One Hundred Years of Solitude.*" In *Teaching the Text,* edited by Susanne Kappeler and Norman Bryson, 148–63. London: Routledge & Kegan Paul, 1983.

Kazin, Alfred. "Leaf Storm and Other Stories." *New York Times Book Review,* 8 March 1970, 11–14.

Kennedy, William. "The Yellow Trolley Car in Barcelona and Other Visions." *Atlantic Monthly* 231, no. 1 (January 1973): 50–59.

______. *"The Autumn of the Patriarch." New York Times Book Review,* 31 October 1976, 1, 16.

Kercher, Dona M. "García Márquez's *Crónica de una muerte anunciada* (*Chronicle of a Death Foretold*): Notes on Parody and the Artist." *Latin American Literary Review* no. 25 (1985): 90–103.

Kiely, Robert. "*One Hundred Years of Solitude.*" *New York Times Book Review,* 8 March 1970, 5.

Kirsner, Robert. "Four Colombian Novels of Violence." *Hispania* 49 (1966): 70–74.

Levine, Susanne Jill. "A Second Glance at the Spoken Mirror: Gabriel García Márquez and Virginia Woolf." *Inti* nos. 16–17 (1982–83): 53–60.

Levy, Kurt. "Plane of Reality in *El otoño del patriarca.*" In *Studies in Honor of Gerald E. Wade,* edited by Sylvia Bowman et al., 133–41. Madrid: J. Porrua Turanzas, 1979.

______. *"One Hundred Years of Solitude* and *Pedro Páramo:* A Parallel." *Books Abroad* 47 (1973): 490–95.

Luchting, Wolfgang A. "Gabriel García Márquez: The Boom and the Whimper." *Books Abroad* 44 (1970): 26–30.

______. "Lampooning Literature: *La mala hora.*" *Books Abroad* 44 (1970): 26–30.

Luder, Josefine. Cien años de soledad: *una interpretación.* Buenos Aires: Tiempo Contemporáneo, 1972.

MacAdam, Alfred J. "Gabriel García Márquez." In *Modern Latin American Narrative.* Chicago: University of Chicago Press, 1977.

———. "Gabriel García Márquez: A Commodious View of Recirculation." In *Modern Latin American Narratives: The Dream of Reason,* 78–79. Chicago: University of Chicago Press, 1977.

McGowan, John P. "*A la recherche du temps perdu* in *One Hundred Years of Solitude.*" *Modern Fiction Studies* 97 (1982): 293–320.

McMurray, George R. "*The Aleph* and *One Hundred Years of Solitude:* Two Microscopic Worlds." *Latin American Literary Review* no. 25 (1985): 55–64.

———. *Gabriel García Márquez.* New York: Ungar, 1977.

McNerny, Kathleen, and John Martin. "Alchemy in *Cien años de soledad.*" *West Virginia University Philological Papers* 27 (1981): 106–12.

Meckled, S. "The Theme of the Double: An Essential Element Throughout García Márquez's Works." *Crane Bag* 6 (1982): 108–17.

Mena, Lucila. "La huelga de la companía bananera como expresión de lo 'Real maravilloso' americano en *Cien años de soledad.*" *Bulletin Hispanique* 74 (1972): 379–405.

Muller-Bergh, Klaus. "*Relato de un náufrago:* García Márquez's Tale of Shipwreck and Survival at Sea." *Books Abroad* 47 (1973): 460–66.

Oberhelman, Harley Dean. "García Márquez and the American South." *Chasqui* 5 (1975): 29–38.

Olsen, Lance. "Misfires in Eden: García Márquez and Narrative Frustration." *Kansas Quarterly* 16 (1984): 52–61.

Ortega, Julio. "Gabriel García Márquez: *Cien años de soledad.*" In *La Contemplación y la fiesta.* Lima: Editorial Universitaria, 1968.

———. "*The Autumn of the Patriarch:* Text and Culture." In *Poetics of Change: The New Spanish American Narrative,* 96–119. Austin: University of Texas Press, 1984.

Peel, Roger M. "The Short Stories of Gabriel García Márquez." *Studies in Short Fiction* 8 (1971): 159–68.

Penuel, Arnold M. "Death and the Maiden: Demythologization of Virginity in García Márquez's *Cien años de soledad.*" *Hispania* 66 (1983): 552-60.

Reid, Alastair. "Basilisks' eggs." *New Yorker,* 8 November 1976, 175–80.

Rabassa, Gregory. "García Márquez's New Book: Literature or Journalism?" *World Literature Today* 56 (1984): 48–51.

———. "Beyond Magical Realism: Thoughts on the Art of Gabriel García Márquez." *Books Abroad* 47 (1973): 485–89.

Rodriguez Monegal, Emir. "*One Hundred Years of Solitude:* The Last Three Pages." *Books Abroad* 47 (1973): 485–89.

———. "A Writer's Feat." *Review* 70 (1971): 122–28.

Shaw, Bradley A., and Nora G. Vera-Godwin, eds. *Critical Perspectives on Gabriel García Márquez.* Lincoln: Society of Spanish and Spanish-American Studies, 1986.

Shaw, Donald L. "Concerning the interpretation of *Cien años de soledad.*" *Ibero-Amerikanisches Archiv* 3 (1977): 318–29.

Shorris, Earl. "Gabriel García Márquez: The Alchemy of History." *Harper's* 242, no. 2 (February 1972): 98–102.

Silva-Caceres, Raul. "The Narrative Intensification in *One Hundred Years of Solitude.*" *Review* 70 (1971): 143–48.

Sims, Robert L. "The Banana Massacre in *Cien años de soledad:* A Micro-Structural Example of Myth, History and Bricolage." *Chasqui* 8, no. 3 (1979): 3–23.

______. "Theme, Narrative Bricolage and Myth in García Márquez." *Journal of Spanish Studies: Twentieth Century* 8 (1980): 145–59.

______. "García Márquez's *La hojarasca:* Paradigm of Time and Search for Myth." *Hispania* 59 (1976): 810–19.

______. *The Evolution of Myth in Gabriel García Márquez from* La Hojarasca *to* Cien años de soledad. Miami, Fla.: Ediciones Universal, 1981.

Sorensen, H. M. "A Critical Analysis of García Márquez's Magical Realism and the Film Version of His Novella *Eréndira.*" *Kosmorama* 32 (1976): 15–16.

Stevens, L. Robert, and G. Roland Vela. "Jungle Gothic: Science, Myth, and Reality in *One Hundred Years of Solitude.*" *Modern Fiction Studies* 8 (1980): 262–66.

Tobin, Patricia. "García Márquez and the Genealogical Imperative." *Diacritics* 4, no. 2 (1974): 52–55.

______. "García Márquez and the Subversion of the Line." *Latin American Literary Review* no. 4 (1974): 39–48.

Tyler, Joseph. "The Cinematic World of García Márquez." *Inti* nos. 16–17 (1982–83): 163–71.

Vargas Llosa, Mario. *Gabriel García Márquez: Historia de un deicidio.* Barcelona: Seix Barral, 1971.

______. "A Morbid Prehistory (The Early Stories)." *Books Abroad* 47 (1973): 451–60.

Wilkie, James W., Edna Monzon de Wilkie, and Maria Herrera-Sobek. "Elitelore and Folklore: Theory and a Test Case in *One Hundred Years of Solitude.*" *Journal of Latin American Lore* 4 (1978): 183–223.

Williams, Linda I. "Edenic Nostalgia and the Play of Mirrors in *Hopscotch* and *One Hundred Years of Solitude.*" *Latin American Literary Review* no. 11 (1977): 53–67.

Williams, Raymond L. "An Introduction to the Early Journalism of García Márquez: 1948–1958." *Latin American Literary Review* 13, no. 25 (1985): 117–32.

______. "The Dynamic Structure of García Márquez's *El otoño del patriarca.*" *Symposium* 32 (1978): 56–75.

______. *Gabriel García Márquez.* Boston: Twayne, 1984.

Woods, Richard D. "Time and Futility in the Novel *El coronel no tiene quien le escriba.*" *Kentucky Romance Quarterly* 17 (1970): 287–95.

Zamora, Lois Parkinson. "The End of Innocence: Myth and Narrative Structure in Faulkner's *Absalom, Absalom!* and García Márquez's *Cien años de soledad.*" *Hispanic Journal* 4 (1982): 23–40.

______. "Ends and Endings in García Márquez's *Cronica de una muerte anunciada (Chronicle of a Death Foretold).*" *Latin American Literary Review* no. 25 (1985): 104–16.

Acknowledgments

"García Márquez: From Aracataca to Macondo" by Mario Vargas Llosa from *Review* 70 (1971), © 1971 by the Center for Inter-American Relations, Inc. Reprinted by permission. This essay first appeared in *Editorial Universitaria*. Reprinted by permission.

"José Arcadio Buendía's Scientific Paradigms: Man in Search of Himself" by Floyd Merrell from *Latin American Literary Review* 2, no. 4 (Spring/Summer 1974), © 1973 by the Department of Modern Languages, Carnegie Mellon University. Reprinted by permission.

"The Faulkner Relation" by William Plummer from *Fiction International*, nos. 6/7 (1976), © 1976 by *Fiction International*, Joe David Bellamy, publisher. Reprinted by permission.

"The Myth of Apocalypse and Human Temporality in García Márquez's *Cien años de soledad* and *El otoño del patriarca*" by Lois Parkinson Zamora from *Symposium* 32, no. 1 (Spring 1978), © 1978 by Syracuse University Press. Reprinted by permission. Sections of this essay will appear in her forthcoming *Writing of the Apocalypse: Ends and Endings in Contemporary U.S. and Latin American Fiction* to be published by Cambridge University Press.

"The Development of Faulkner's Influence in the Work of García Márquez" (originally entitled "García Márquez's First Contacts with Faulkner") by Harley D. Oberhelman from *The Presence of Faulkner in the Writings of Garcá Márquez* by Harley D. Oberhelman, Graduate Studies—Texas Tech University, no. 22 (August 1980), © 1980 by Texas Tech Press. Reprinted by permission.

"The Logic of Wings: García Márquez, Todorov, and the Endless Resources of Fantasy" by John Gerlach from *Bridges to Fantasy,* edited by George E. Slusser, Eric S. Rabkin, and Robert Scholes, © 1982 by the Board of Trustees, Southern Illinois University. Reprinted by permission.

"Beware of Gift-Bearing Tales: Reading García Márquez According to Mauss" by Eduardo González from *MLN* 97, no. 2 (March 1982), © 1982 by the Johns Hopkins University Press, Baltimore/London. Reprinted by permission of the Johns Hopkins University Press.

"*Cien años de soledad*: The Novel as Myth and Archive" by Roberto González Echevarría from *MLN* 99, no. 2 (March 1984), © 1984 by the Johns Hopkins University Press, Baltimore/London. Reprinted by permission of the Johns Hopkins University Press.

"Liberals, Conservatives, and Bananas: Colombian Politics in the Fictions of Gabriel García Márquez" by Regina Janes from *Hispanofila*, no. 82 (September 1984), © 1984 by Regina Janes. Reprinted by permission of the editor of *Hispanofila* and the author.

"The Autumn of the Patriarch" by Raymond Williams from *Gabriel García Márquez,* by Raymond Williams, © 1984 by G. K. Hall & Co., Boston. Reprinted by permission of G. K. Hall & Co., Boston.

"The Logic of Wings: Gabriel García Márquez and Afro-American Literature" by Vera M. Kutzinski from *The Latin American Literary Review* no. 25 (January–June 1985), © 1985 by *The Latin American Literary Review.* Reprinted by permission.

"The First Voyage around the World: From Pigafetta to García Márquez" by Humberto E. Robles from *History of European Ideas* 6, no. 4 (1985), © 1985 by Pergamon Press Ltd. Reprinted by permission.

"The Autumn of the Signifier: The Deconstructionist Moment of García Márquez" by Patricia Tobin from *The Latin American Literary Review* no. 25 (January–June 1985), © 1985 by *The Latin American Literary Review.* Reprinted by permission.

"From Mystery to Parody: (Re) Readings of García Márquez's *Crónica de una muerte anunciada*" by Isabel Alvarez-Borland from *Symposium* 38, no. 4 (Winter 1984–85), © 1985 by the Helen Dwight Reid Educational Foundation. Reprinted by permission of the Helen Dwight Reid Educational Foundation.

"From Realism to Magic Realism: The Meticulous Modernist Fictions of García Márquez", by Morton P. Levitt from *Critical Perspectives on Gabriel García Márquez*, edited by Bradley A. Shaw and Nora G. Vera-Godwin, © 1986 by the Society of Spanish and Spanish-American Studies. Reprinted by permission.

"Prisms of Consciousness: The 'New Worlds' of Columbus and García Márquez" by Michael Palencia-Roth from *Critical Perspectives on Gabriel García Márquez,* edited by Bradley A. Shaw and Nora G. Vera-Godwin, © 1986 by the Society of Spanish and Spanish-American Studies. Reprinted by permission of the author and the Society of Spanish and Spanish-American Studies.

"Writing and Ritual in *Chronicle of a Death Foretold*" by Carlos J. Alonso from *Gabriel García Márquez: New Readings*, edited by Bernard McGuirk and Richard Cardwell, © 1987 by Cambridge University Press. Reprinted by permission of the author and Cambridge University Press.

"Translation and the Novel: *One Hundred Years of Solitude*" by Anibal González, © 1987 by Anibal González. Published for the first time in this volume. Printed by permission.

INDEX